A BULL OF A MAN

A BULL OF A MAN

Images of Masculinity, Sex, and the Body in Indian Buddhism

John Powers

HARVARD UNIVERSITY PRESS
Cambridge, Massachusetts
London, England
2009

Printed in the United States of America

Library of Congress Cataloging-in-Publication Data

Powers, John, 1957–
A bull of a man : images of masculinity, sex, and the body in
Indian Buddhism / John Powers.
p. cm.
Includes bibliographical references and index.
ISBN 978-0-674-03329-0 (alk. paper)
1. Masculinity—Religious aspects—Buddhism. 2. Sex role—Religious
aspects–Buddhism. 3. Buddhist literature—India—History and criticism.
4. Buddhism—Social aspects—India—History. I. Title.
BQ4570.M365P68 2009
294.3'37—dc22 2008038738

To my father,

my first and best teacher of manhood

Contents

Preface

In recent decades, scholars have begun to pay increasing attention to the socially constructed nature of gender identities. Social scientists have been at the forefront of studies of gender roles and of the psychological consequences for those who try to abide by them. At the same time, interest in discourses relating to the body and sexuality has increased among historians, and a number of excellent studies of varying attitudes toward such matters have been published. Most of these relate to Western societies, and exploration of gendered histories in Asia is still a relatively new field of inquiry.

I began studying Indian Buddhism in my early teens and was first attracted to the Pāli canon, which I read in translation. My interest later extended to commentaries and philosophical texts and then to Mahāyāna treatises. After finishing an undergraduate degree in philosophy, I enrolled in a graduate program with the intention of exploring Indian Buddhist philosophy in greater depth and took classes in Sanskrit and Pāli, along with Tibetan, Chinese, and Japanese. Along the way, I also developed an interest in theory because of encounters with a number of impressive studies that adopted a thematic and theory-driven approach to literatures and issues that had been well studied by earlier scholars but that in the new lens of a fresh approach appeared in a strikingly new light.

The great value of theory is that it enables one to recognize patterns that were previously invisible, to piece together what initially look to be unconnected bits of literature and historical artifacts, and to construct a story that highlights hidden connections and hegemonic social discourses. Many of these discourses are difficult to perceive because they were unconsciously appropriated as "truth" by people of the society in which they circulated, as an inviolable aspect of the world, or as nature. As a result, researchers often see these discourses and connections only when they begin specifically looking in new directions and interrogating them through theoretical approaches that have not been employed previously. When (predominantly female) scholars began producing studies of Buddhist discourses relating to women, many traditionalists initially dismissed them as insignificant explorations of justly marginalized figures, but as the new insights were absorbed these works began slowly to revolutionize the field, leading both male and female scholars to reexamine the tradition with new understanding.

Women were largely subverted in Buddhist texts and relegated to the periphery of concern of most traditional authors, sometimes situated as negative others to valorized male heroes or omitted altogether. When feminist scholars began highlighting these ellipses, it breathed new life into the study of Buddhism and opened new avenues of inquiry. There has been surprisingly little interest to date in discourses relating to masculinity, however, despite the fact that the vast majority of Buddhist texts were written by, for, and about men, and these texts contain a wealth of material on cultural notions of normative manhood, the body, sexuality, and male sociality.

While reading several books exploring masculinities in Western societies, it became apparent that this was a rich area for exploration in relation to Buddhism. The scope of Buddhism worldwide is far too vast for any book-length work that could adequately cover even a reasonable sampling of the permutations of masculinity discourses produced in Asian Buddhist countries (and in the modern period in the West), and so I have chosen to focus on a limited historical period, from the time of the Buddha (probably early fifth century BCE) until around the eighth century CE, with some discussion of later developments in India that are relevant to an understanding of the conceptual shifts that appeared in relation to historical events and the evolution of Buddhist doctrine and practice. This is a hybrid study, merging traditional Indology with contemporary studies of the body and sex, and is intended for specialists in the field, for readers with an interest in Buddhism, and for cultural historians.

Many Indological works are replete with untranslated terms in Sanskrit or other Indic languages or untranslated titles of texts, which render them inaccessible to all but a small coterie of initiates of this scholarly esoterica. In this book, I have endeavored to keep technical terms to a minimum and in most cases use English equivalents for titles. In the body of the text, most titles are translated, as are most technical terms. In endnotes that refer to passages in Sanskrit or Pāli texts, the titles appear in those languages, because only specialists will be able to access the original texts. Most names and places are given in Sanskrit if they appear in both Sanskrit and Pāli works, even if the text under discussion is in Pāli. This is intended to reduce confusion for nonspecialists, as providing equivalents in both Pāli and Sanskrit is unnecessary for specialists and irrelevant for nonspecialists. Some important terms have been given in both languages, but my intention has been to privilege readability over scholarly technicalities.

As the research and writing progressed, it became necessary to explore previously unknown areas of Indian culture and contemporary theoretical studies of gender and the body, and I had many guides along the way who provided key bits of advice and ideas for further reading. I wish particularly to thank Chris Forth, whose book *The Dreyfus Affair and the Crisis of French Manhood* (Baltimore: Johns Hopkins University Press, 2004) prompted me to begin thinking about a study of Indian Buddhist masculinities in the first place, and who appeared like the bodhisattva of Buddhist legends at key points in the process to suggest new books to read and clarify conceptual difficulties that had arisen. Sharmila Sen shared some key insights regarding Indian discourses relating to gender and suggested that I turn my still-developing ideas into a book. She also provided helpful comments at several stages. Bill Magee's comments on the social dimensions of Indian Buddhist masculinity were crucial in helping me to form the ideas behind Chapter 5. McComas Taylor also gave useful feedback and references to brahmanical texts that resonated with Buddhist notions I was exploring and provided additional ammunition for my arguments regarding their pervasiveness in Indian society. Charles Prebish generously read through the entire manuscript and made a number of corrections and provided encouragement in my confidence that my conclusions were supported by literary sources. My colleagues in the Australasian Association of Buddhist Studies came to the University of Sydney on a Friday afternoon at a crucial point of the research to consider my conclusions and to challenge them. In particular, Mark Allon, Peter Oldmeadow, Adrian Snodgrass, Judith

Snodgrass, Pankaj Mohan, and Jackie Menzies offered insights and critiques and helped me to conclude that I was on the right track regarding some of my still-tentative ideas. I also wish to acknowledge the vitally important contribution of the Australian Research Council in providing a grant that included teaching relief (and thus time) to work on this project. Finally, my wife, Cindy, was a rock of support and help during the difficult periods of this research and listened patiently while I rambled on about obscure details of Indian medicine and gender discourses.

A BULL OF A MAN

I

The Ultimate Man

Masculinities come into existence at particular times and places and are always subject to change. Masculinities are, in a word, historical.

—R. W. Connell, *Masculinities*

The Buddha's Body

In contemporary Western popular culture, the Buddha is commonly portrayed as an androgynous, asexual character, often in a seated meditation posture and wearing a beatific smile. Many (incorrectly) associate the Buddha with Hotei, a corpulent, jolly figure of Chinese Buddhism traditionally viewed as a manifestation of the future buddha Maitreya. Buddhist monks, such as the Dalai Lama, have also become images of normative Buddhism, which is assumed to valorize celibacy and is often portrayed as rejecting gender categories (at least in theory).[1] In Indian Buddhist literature, however, a very different version of the Buddha and his monastic followers appears: the Buddha is described as the paragon of masculinity, the "ultimate man" *(puruṣottama),* and is referred to by a range of epithets that extol his manly qualities, his extraordinarily beautiful body, his superhuman virility and physical strength, his skill in martial arts, and the effect he has on women who see him. Many Buddhist monks are depicted as young, handsome, and virile, and the greatest challenge to their religious devotion is lustful women propositioning them for sex.[2] This is even true of elderly monks, who also fend off unwanted advances.

The androgynous, asexual Buddha is not only found in contemporary popular culture, however. To date, most studies of the Buddha by both Western and Asian scholars have tended to emphasize the philosophical implications of those teachings attributed to him, events reported in various biographies, historical questions, or philological problems in Buddhist texts. There are many discussions of gender in relation to Buddhism, but most of these focus on Buddhist attitudes toward women or portrayals of women in Buddhist literature. While researching this project, I found two articles that examine Buddhist responses to homosexuality[3] and many studies of Buddhism from feminist perspectives, but as far as I am aware, no one has surveyed Indian Buddhist literature, art, or iconography in terms of how they present normative masculinity. This is a remarkable oversight, since Buddhist literature was overwhelmingly written by, for, and about men, and Buddhist canonical texts (as well as extra-canonical works, art, and other sources) abound with discourses and images of masculinity. Moreover, the pervasiveness of such discourses, the ways in which they are highlighted in many Indian Buddhist works, and the sheer inventiveness of Buddhist authors in developing the figure of the Buddha as the paradigm of masculinity indicate that they considered this paradigm to be of great importance.

Why, then, have contemporary interpreters of Buddhism generally overlooked these discourses?[4] Why has the supremely masculine Buddha depicted in the Pāli canon[5] and other Indic literature been eclipsed by the androgynous figure of modern imagination and the ascetic meditation master and philosopher of scholars? Part of the reason probably lies in the backgrounds of contemporary interpreters of Buddhism and the blind spots that every culture bequeaths to its inhabitants. The field of masculinity studies is a recent phenomenon, and many academic disciplines have only just begun to explore discourses relating to manhood. Feminist scholars who assert that religious traditions are overwhelmingly male-dominated and that most scholarship by definition focuses on men are no doubt correct, but studies of *masculinity discourses* are still relatively rare in religious studies.

In addition, most modern scholars of Buddhism were born and raised in societies in which Judeo-Christian traditions predominate, and even those who are not overtly religious have been influenced by them. The great founders of the Judeo-Christian-Islamic traditions—Abraham, Jesus, and Muhammad—are not, as far as I am aware, portrayed as paragons of masculinity, as exceptionally beautiful, as endowed with superhuman strength, or as masters of martial arts, and so people raised in cultures in which the Judeo-Christian-Islamic traditions predominate do not expect religious figures to be characterized in these ways.[6] Since undertaking this project, I have been struck by the pervasiveness of ultramasculine images in Indian Buddhist texts—texts that in some cases I had read many times without even noticing these tropes. Once I began looking, however, they seemed to leap from the pages and confront me with a completely new version of the Buddha, one who personified the ideals of the Indian warrior class *(kṣatriya),* who caused women to faint because of his physical beauty, and who converted people to his teachings through the perceptual impact of his extraordinary physique.

In the "Discourse to Cankī," for example, the Buddha is described as "handsome, good looking, graceful, possessing supreme beauty of complexion, with sublime beauty and sublime presence, remarkable to behold."[7] In the "Discourse to Soṇadaṇḍa," a group of brahmans comes to visit him. One of them, a young man named Angaka, is described as "handsome, good-looking, pleasant to look at, of supremely fair complexion, in form and complexion like the god Brahmā, of excellent appearance," but the brahman who gives this description hastens to add that the Buddha is even more handsome.[8] Similar passages abound in Indian Buddhist literature. The transcendent physical beauty of the Buddha is a core trope of every text I have seen that discusses his life and teaching career.

If one compares the way the Buddha is portrayed in Indian literature with descriptions of Abraham, Jesus, and Muhammad, a number of striking differences appear. Abraham and Muhammad were chosen as prophets by God, but their exalted status was not a recognition of their spiritual attainments over many lifetimes, as with the Buddha; rather, Abraham and Muhammad were chosen because they were chosen. God designates some as his messengers and then provides them with missions, but a buddha becomes a buddha by consciously pursuing a path leading to liberation and cultivating a multitude of good qualities over countless incarnations in a personal discovery of truth.

Jesus is believed by Christians to be both God and man, but as a man he is generally conceived of as physically ordinary. If he had superhuman strength or was better able to endure pain than other men, the religious import of the Passion would be seriously undermined. His unremarkable body and common physique are points of emphasis by most Christian churches, who have condemned as heresy various attempts to portray him as nonphysical or as possessing a body that is superior to that of other men. His very ordinariness allowed him to hide from the devil, who was unable to recognize him precisely because he did not stand out.[9] Thus Nicephorus the Patriarch asserts that

> Christ, having truly taken on a body like ours, is circumscribed by His humanity. Nor is it an illusion that this incorporeal being is circumscribed in space, He who, having no beginning but having subjected Himself to a

Bronze statue of Śākyamuni Buddha, Uttar Pradesh, India, Gupta period (ca. sixth century). Reproduced by permission of the Norton Simon Foundation, Pasadena, California.

> temporal one, is circumscribed in time. By condescending to become corporeally part of humanity, incomprehensible divinity also accepts enclosure within the boundaries of comprehension.[10]

Jesus's salvation mission required that he incarnate in a body like that of other men—that, like them, he would be sustained by food and water, would suffer when injured, and would die if crucified. In his study of representations of Christ in Renaissance art, Leo Steinberg refers to thousands of pictures that depict Jesus's genitals or highlight a bulge in his groin beneath diaphanous clothing to demonstrate that Jesus was truly a man like other men and connects this idea with sermons from the time that emphasized that Jesus was not different physically from the rest of male humanity. Referring to artistic works that highlight Jesus' anatomical masculinity, Steinberg remarks:

> So much of it proclaims over and over that godhood has vested itself in the infirmity of the flesh, so as to raise that flesh to the prerogatives of immortality. It celebrates the restoral which the divine power brought off by coming to share man's humanity. . . . Every right-thinking Christian, whether Latin or Greek, artist or otherwise, confessed that the pivotal moment in the history of the race was God's alliance with the human condition.[11]

The Buddha's mission, however, is aided by his extraordinary physical endowments. In the Indian context, most indigenous religious traditions (including Buddhism) assume that every being is reborn over and over again in a beginningless cycle *(saṃsāra)* and that every life situation is conditioned by volitional actions of past lives. Those who are well favored, wealthy, good-looking, and long-lived are experiencing the ripening of their past karma, while those who are ugly, misshapen, poor, and sickly similarly are reaping what they have sown. The *Legend of Miserly Nanda* asserts that "the form of a man, possessing the pleasant beauty of a bunch of flowers, which attracts . . . the eyes of men and women, unwavering in energy and strength and perfect in its proportions, is the reward of virtue."[12] And conversely, in the "Connected Discourses with the Kosalas," the Buddha describes various types of unfortunate humans and the endowments they have at birth: those of low social status, who are born in families of outcastes *(caṇḍāla),* bamboo workers, hunters, cartwrights, and flower scavengers, and those who are "ugly, unsightly, deformed, chronically ill, have deficient vision or maimed hands, are lame or paralyzed." Such people have trouble gaining food, drink, and clothing. Out of force of habit, they engage in misconduct of body, speech, and mind and so will be reborn in a bad destiny, even hell. This is characterized as "moving from darkness to darkness."[13]

During any given lifetime, it is always possible to reverse course, to make decisions and perform actions that will result in different future destinies, but habits of conditioning make this difficult, and most beings tend to follow established patterns. The great value of a buddha for others lies in the fact that he[14] has broken free from negative habituation and found a path to liberation. He then teaches others, and those who are wise and whose past training has made them receptive may follow his example and attain release from cyclic existence.

As a being seeking liberation engages in actions that produce positive karmas, one of the many rewards is improved physical condition. As a fruition of karma, the bodhisattva (a person working toward buddhahood) is born with a better body and greater resources, as well as improved intelligence, wealth, and beauty.[15] Moreover, in the Indian context, a great teacher must have such endowments; in the Buddha's time, a person who was ugly, poor, crippled, or stupid would have had great difficulty convincing people that he or she was a fully awakened master, because people claiming mastery of the religious path were expected to prove their bona fides with their physiques and other endowments. Thus Buddhaghosa (fl. early fifth century; the greatest commentator of the Theravāda tradition) asserts that the physical body of a buddha impresses worldly people, and because of this he is fit to be relied upon by laypeople.[16]

This notion is not confined to the canonical literature of elite monks; it is also found in non-Buddhist texts and in a range of other venues, such as an inscription from cave 22 in Ajaṇṭā: "This is the meritorious gift of the Śākyan monk . . . a follower of the Great Vehicle (Mahāyāna) made for the purpose of attaining supreme knowledge of all beings. Those who cause an image of the Conqueror (Jina, i.e., Buddha) to be made become endowed with good looks, good luck, and good qualities, acquire resplendent brightness in perfect aspects and insight, and become pleasing to the eye."[17] Nor is this notion of the association between physical beauty and morality confined to India. Roy Porter cites a range of discourses from the Enlightenment that link moral excellence with physical beauty and robustness and that depict blemishes or unattractive features as external proof of the sordidness of the inner beings of the people afflicted with them: "beauty of figure and countenance were expressive of goodness of soul, whereas an ugly face, or a deformed body, bespoke the knave. . . . [P]urity, nobility, virtue and health were all distinguished by beauty; ugliness was the mark of Cain."[18]

The Fictive Buddha

There is no way to know what the Buddha actually looked like or whether he was in fact a wealthy and handsome prince as reported in Indian sources, but the Buddha of Indian religious construction must be such a fortunate person.[19] It is important to note that we are not dealing with the historical Buddha, and this study is not concerned with questions of when he might have lived or what, if any, valid historical details might be gleaned from traditional accounts of his life. The only Buddha accessible to modern commentators is Buddha the literary character, who was created by his monastic followers.[20] This process probably began during his lifetime and continued for centuries after his passing. Various accounts of his life were constructed and embellished, a range of extraordinary qualities were attributed to him, and legends developed as a result. Even the teachings credited to him cannot with any confidence be assigned to the historical figure referred to as "Buddha." The discourses contained in Buddhist canons were redacted and edited by his followers over the course of centuries—according to tradition beginning with the "first council" at Rājagṛha in which five hundred *arhats* (monks who had eliminated mental afflictions and were assured of attaining nirvana at the end of their lives) gathered to recount from memory what they had heard the Buddha say during his forty-year ministry—and there is no good reason to believe that any of these texts represent his actual words. On the other hand, some parts of the canon may well hearken back to the Buddha's life and preaching, but in our present state of understanding of his times, any such attributions are most probably speculative.

Despite these qualifications, we do have a vast literature along with a wealth of art and iconography, epigraphic material, and some historical records that provide a great deal of information regarding prevailing attitudes during the centuries when Buddhism existed in India. Much of the literature concerned with the Buddha emphasizes his physique as well as his spiritual attainments. In Pāli texts, the Buddha is said to be distinguished by two types of power: wisdom power *(ñāna-bala)* and body power *(kāya-bala).* Most academic studies to date have focused on wisdom power, but it is abundantly clear from the tone of Indian canonical descriptions that the authors who created the Buddha character considered body power to be equally important.[21] In addition, there are numerous tropes intended to establish the manliness of the Buddha's male monastic followers and a substantial amount of information regarding monastic sexuality and how the monastic body was conceived, along with discussions of health, diet, and hygiene, which have also largely been overlooked by contemporary scholars. My goal in the following chapters will be to highlight discourses relating to masculinity, sex, the body, and male sociality as described in Buddhist literature and art, not in order to condemn or extol them or to recommend how they should be judged by contemporary readers, but rather to describe and analyze how they are presented in their cultural context, a context in which they apparently were generally considered to be normative and "true."

Masculinity and History

In recent decades, there has been a veritable explosion of studies of masculinity, most of which focus on contemporary Europe or North America. A recurrent theme in sociological examinations of masculinity is the concept of crisis: challenges or ruptures in traditional notions of what it means to be a man in a particular society have led to anxieties and confusion among males, rendering them unsure of how to behave or what attitudes and actions they ought to adopt.[22] As R. W. Connell has noted, the development of hegemonic notions of masculinity and femininity reflects particular places and times, and "their making and remaking is a political process affecting the balance of interests in society and the direction of social change."[23] Each culture constructs concepts of ideal body types and a performative repertoire for both men and women, and individuals are expected to conform to these norms. Moreover, they are judged by their peers on the basis of how well they manage to enact their society's expectations.

As Foucault has argued, from the point of view of those caught up in a particular discursive regime, such norms seem natural and given.[24] The body appears to most people as nature—as something outside of discourse and construction—but Connell contends that body image and normative masculinity vary considerably between cultures and are even adapted to specific situations: "Discursive studies suggest that men are not permanently committed to a particular pattern of masculinity. Rather, they make situationally specific choices from a cultural repertoire of masculine behaviour."[25]

This resonates with Judith Butler's notion that sex roles are performative, an enactment of socially constructed and prescribed attitudes and behaviors. Gender is not nature but, rather, something that people do, a repertoire of bodily actions repeated within a set of often unconsciously appropriated norms that appear natural but are actually learned and manifested for the benefit of both the individual and others. The male or female body serves as a symbol of society. The powers and prohibitions of a given culture are reproduced on the bodies of its members.[26] In Pierre Bourdieu's words, "The body believes in what it plays at. . . . It does not represent what it performs, it does not memorize the past, it *enacts* the past, bringing it back to life. What is 'learned by body' is not something that one has, like knowledge that can be brandished, but something that one is."[27]

In Indian Buddhist literature, there is a pervasive concern with bodies—particularly male bodies—and the Buddha's is held up as the highest development of the male physique. Some aspects of ancient Indian notions of ideal manhood resonate with contemporary discourses—such as depictions of the Buddha as being skilled in wrestling, archery, and various martial arts, and as extraordinarily strong, attractive to women, and admired by men—but others will strike most modern readers as strange, particularly descriptions of his unusual physiognomy. The Buddha's body is said to be adorned with thirty-two "physical characteristics of a great man" *(mahāpuruṣa-lakṣaṇa),* which are found only on buddhas and universal monarchs *(cakravartin)* and are signs of their extraordinary accomplishments during past lives. Lists of these traits vary among texts, but a standard grouping is found in the "Discourse on the Physical Characteristics," which contends that the Buddha had, among other things, flat feet; a thousand-spoked wheel pattern *(cakra)* on the soles of his feet and palms of his hands; hands that reached down to his knees without him bending over; webbed fingers and toes; soft and tender hands and feet; skin so smooth and delicate that no dust or dirt could settle on it; golden-colored skin; a prominent cranial lump on top of his head *(uṣṇīṣa);* a curl of white hair in the middle of his forehead that when unwound reached to his elbows *(ūrṇā)*; a straight torso; legs like an antelope's; a torso and jaw like a lion's; eyelashes like a cow's; hairs that grew one to each pore and curled to the right; a long and wide tongue; and a penis hidden by a sheath.[28] In later texts, he is also said to have eighty secondary physical characteristics *(anuvyañjana)*, including golden-colored fingernails; concealed and unknotted veins; the gait of a lion[29] or of a bull; a rounded body; a slender body; a male sexual organ that is perfect in every respect; a rounded belly; a slim abdomen; a mouth like a *bimba* fruit; sharp canine teeth; a voice like a roaring elephant or thundering clouds; and palms and soles marked with the *śrīvatsa, svastika, madyāvarta,* and *lalita* symbols (in addition to the thousand-spoked wheel pattern).[30]

These attributes are mentioned and emphasized throughout the Pāli canon, in scholastic treatises, and in Mahāyāna texts, and their pervasiveness and elaboration demonstrate that the authors considered them to be important. The thirty-two physical characteristics distinguished the Buddha from lesser men and were evidence of his superiority to all other beings. Men and women who saw his body were struck by his extraordinary beauty and mention the physical characteristics of a great man as a key factor in convincing them of the validity of his claims to authority. For most contemporary Westerners, however (both men and women), a person with such a body would appear as a freak. It is highly doubtful that any human has actually possessed all the attributes used to describe the Buddha's body, but the assertion that he did possess all these characteristics is a core feature of his persona in Indian Buddhist literature.

Many of the attributes generally associated with ideal manhood in contemporary Western society are absent in this list or are directly contradicted by it. For example, in the West, attractive male bodies are commonly presented as having a distinctive V-shape, with strongly delineated muscles, while Buddha images made in India generally have no muscle tone and appear effeminate to Western eyes. Buddha is often depicted with flaring hips, with no discernable muscles, and with a slight midriff bulge. He is said to be powerful and athletic in Buddhist texts, but these qualities are not displayed in images and are not associated with muscularity. Rather, male beauty requires smoothness of features, lack of protuberances and bulges, proportion between limbs, and dignified comportment.

In the ancient Indian cultural context, ideal male beauty is connected with proportionality; a rounded face and limbs; a physique that is symmetrically curved; and a decorous, restrained bearing. The Buddha's body is said to be like a banyan tree in that the reach of his arms equals his height from head to foot. His fingers are long and tapering and joined with webs up to the first joints. Buddhaghosa asserts: "His fingers are not like those of other humans, who have some long and some short [digits]. The great man's fingers are long, they are wide, and the roots gradually taper toward the tips, like those of a monkey."[31] The Buddha has seven convex surfaces, but these, too, are well rounded rather than bulging. Buddhaghosa describes these as having a "fullness of muscles," and he adds that "generally, in some human beings veins are seen on the surfaces of their hands and feet, bones jut out from the two shoulders and trunk, and they look hideous like human ghosts. Unlike such ill-shaped persons, the great man possesses seven convexities that give his body proper shape and beauty."[32]

Standing Buddha image from Ajaṇṭā (ca. fifth century). Photograph by John Powers.

Buddhaghosa also contends that there is no indentation between the Buddha's shoulders and that he has a smooth back. Nor does he have a depression in the middle, like most men who have ridges of muscle on either side of the spine. A buddha's body has a fleshy membrane extending from the hip upward and covering the whole back, which "appears like a straight golden slab."[33]

Buddha as a "Great Man"

The Buddha is commonly referred to in Indian Buddhist literature as a "great man" (Pāli: *mahāpurisa;* Sanskrit [Skt.]: *mahāpuruṣa*), and the notion that his body displayed the thirty-two characteristics typifying a great man forms a key aspect of this concept. The Buddha is also said to have perfected the qualities of moral behavior and to have cultivated wisdom surpassing that of other humans (and even of gods), but the Indian writers who constructed his mythos linked physical and mental accomplishments. In the "Connected Discourse on the Foundations of Mindfulness," the Buddha tells Śāriputra,

> It is on account of the liberation of the mind that I call a man "great man." Without that liberation there is no great man. And how is one thus liberated? With regard to his body, feelings, mind, and sensations, he is always master of them by way of insight that is keen, self-possessed, and mindful, and so he overcomes both the dejection and the craving that are commonly found in the world.[34]

In the *Gradual Discourses,* the Buddha defines such a person as one who has concern for the welfare of the great mass of people, who has mastered thought and can enter into the four trance states beyond thought, and who is free from lust and ignorance.[35] In these passages, mental and moral qualities are emphasized, but their attainment is also linked to physical perfection and ideal modes of comportment.

The lists of physical characteristics vary in detail and number, but there is a standard list of thirty-two that is found in a number of texts. Vasubandhu (ca. late fourth century CE) states that each characteristic is produced by cultivation of one hundred merits,[36] and Buddhaghosa similarly asserts that each characteristic "is born from its corresponding action."[37] The Everything Exists school (Sarvāstivāda) also taught that each of the characteristics relates to one hundred acts of merit, and that these acts of merit correspond to one hundred thoughts. A bodhisattva initially has fifty pure thoughts, which provide the basis for attainment of the state of a great man. Thus the first fifty thoughts initiate the process, and the second fifty complete the karmas needed to manifest a particular characteristic.[38] The Everything Exists school also believed that acquisition of the thirty-two traits occurs at the very end of a buddha's training period and represents the culmination of his eons of religious practice.[39]

Discussions of these attributes are found throughout Indian Buddhist literature, including a number of discourses in the Pāli canon, in scholastic works, and in Mahāyāna discourses *(sūtra)* and philosophical treatises *(śāstra)*. Some commentators appear to recognize the unusualness of the features ascribed to the Buddha's body and provide some interesting explanations of how these features should be conceived and why they are desirable and admirable. The *Extensive Sport,* for example, links the Buddha's sheathed penis with the practice of celibacy and his generosity in past lives and views this physical attribute as confirmation of his perfection of these disciplines.[40] The *Great Matter* portrays it as an essential feature of buddhas and states that hosts of buddhas have appeared in the past and that all possessed "penises enclosed in a sheath like a royal stallion."[41] Buddhaghosa explains that the penis retracts when not needed and so is not a dangling, disproportionate appendage like those of other men.[42] He compares the Buddha's penis to those of elephants or bulls and says that the sheath looks like the pericarp of a golden lotus.[43] Similarly, the *Flower Array Discourse* states that the Buddha's "testicles are well-hidden within a sheath, sunk deeply and fully covered, just like those of a thoroughbred elephant or a thoroughbred stallion."[44] Even though this is presented as the perfection of a man's private parts, the text claims that no one—woman, man, boy, girl, elderly person, middle-aged person, or even the lustful or potentially lustful—could possibly conceive thoughts of sexual desire when viewing the Buddha's genitalia because his past practice of celibacy has produced a body so transcendent that people cannot imagine having sexual intercourse with him (the "out of my league" syndrome). As we will see, however, in other texts women who see the Buddha are overcome with desire, while others swoon when in his presence.

Although in Pāli and Sanskrit texts composed prior to the tantras the Buddha is always represented as completely celibate following his attainment of buddhahood, he sometimes employs his penis for other purposes. In the *Discourse of the Ocean-Like Meditation of Buddha Remembrance,* for example, he uses it to convert heretics. His aid is requested in three instances: (1) to defeat the daughters of Māra; (2) to combat prostitutes in Śrāvastī who had become enormously wealthy and were corrupting the youth of the city; and (3) to convert a group of naked Jain ascetics. He and his disciples reportedly performed various miracles, including transforming Māra's daughters into hags and inflicting various torments on them, and the Buddha and his disciples also conquered the prostitutes and rescued the city. The culmination of their efforts is a scene in which the Buddha converts skeptical Jains: he creates a mountain like Mount Sumeru surrounded by water and lays on his back next to it. He begins to emit golden rays of light, and his penis emerges from its sheath, winds around the mountain seven times, and then extends upward to the heaven of Brahmā. Alexander Soper comments that the text declares that "the Buddha was not a eunuch and so naturally exempt from sexual temptation. He possessed, rather, a male member that was normally kept retracted, like a horse's; but that for purposes of demonstration, to quell disbelief, could be marvelously expanded."[45]

Like the retractable penis, the Buddha's enormous tongue is also linked with past practices. According to the *Extensive Sport,* he acquired this outsized tongue by abandoning wrong speech; by praising hearers *(śrāvaka),* solitary realizers *(pratyeka-buddha),* and buddhas; by requesting that they teach sūtras; and by reciting these sūtras himself.[46] Buddhaghosa asserts that "other tongues are either fat, thin, short, or hard. The great man's tongue is soft, long, and wide and also has a pleasing color. Because it is soft, he can extend the tongue and touch and stroke both ears with it. Because it is long, he can touch and stroke both nostrils; because it is wide, he can cover his own forehead."[47]

The *Discourse Resolving the Meaning* describes the Buddha's tongue as measuring a hand in length and breadth and states that it is tender like a lotus leaf. When it comes from his mouth, his tongue can cover his entire face.[48] The idea that a long, supple tongue is a desirable physical feature in men is also found in the classical medical text *Caraka's Medical Compendium,* which states that ideally the tongue should be long, wide, smooth, slender, and a healthy pink color.[49]

According to Buddhaghosa, because the Buddha's tongue is long, wide, and supple, he is able to deliver his words quickly. Unlike other men, he does not have to move his mouth very much when he speaks, and his soft and mobile tongue allowed him to teach the entire higher doctrine (*abhidharma;* a vast collection of scholastic discourses that is one of the "three baskets" of the Pāli canon) to his mother in only three months while he visited her in the Heaven of the Thirty-Three (*Trāyastriṃśa*).[50]

When the Buddha extends his tongue, his audiences conclude that he must be an awakened being. This feature is offered as proof of his attainments to the brahman Brahmāyu, "a master of the three Vedas" and an expert in the lore of the physical characteristics of a great man, who visits the Buddha in order to ascertain whether he is all his followers claim. Brahmāyu verifies thirty of the characteristics and asks, "Upon your body, Gotama, is what is normally concealed by a cloth hidden by a sheath, greatest of men? Though named by a word of the feminine gender, is your tongue really a manly *(narassika)* one?[51] Is your tongue also large? . . . Please stick it out a bit and cure our doubts." In response, the Buddha extends his tongue, inserts the tip into each ear hole, and covers his forehead with it. He then performs an act of supernatural power that enables the audience to view his sheathed penis. Brahmāyu and the other people in the assembly are reportedly highly impressed and conclude that he is indeed a great man, as his followers claim.[52]

Another of the oddities of the Buddha's physiognomy, the cranial lump or *uṣṇnīṣa,* has generated controversy among both Buddhist commentators and Western scholars.[53] It is commonly depicted icongraphically as a protuberance on top of his head, covered by tight curls of hair. According to the *Extensive Sport,* this lump is indistinct, and no one can clearly see its edges.[54] When Siddhārtha was taken to a schoolroom as a youth, the teacher exclaimed: "Although I can see his face, the crown of his head is so exalted it seems to disappear!"[55] Buddhaghosa describes the protuberance as a mass of flesh covering the forehead and extending to the base of the ears, resembling a royal turban that symbolizes sovereign power. Buddhaghosa also asserts that this feature can refer to the fact that the Buddha's head is perfectly rounded like a water bubble.[56]

Alex Wayman also notes that this feature is sometimes conceived of as turban shaped, while others consider it to be a mass of hair piled on top of the Buddha's head.[57] The Chinese pilgrims Faxian and Xuanzang claimed to have seen the bone relic of the Buddha's *uṣṇīṣa* in a monastery in Haḍḍa in modern-day Afghanistan. Faxian described it as a bone four inches in diameter and shaped like a wasp's nest or an arched hand. Xuanzang said it was twelve inches in diameter. In depictions of the Buddha in India, it is often a round lump on top of his skull covered with hair curls, and in Southeast Asia flames are often depicted coming out of this lump, representing stories in the Pāli canon in which rays of light emanate from the Buddha's head.

The Buddha's head is also distinguished by the *ūrṇā,* a coil of white hair in the middle of his forehead. According to Buddhaghosa, this coil is as long as half his arm when extended. It always remains twisted toward the right and pointed outward, and "it shines like a silver bubble on a golden slab and radiates light with brightness comparable to that of the Osadhī star."[58] The Buddha also issues light rays from the *ūrṇā,* particularly when he is about to preach a new sermon.

The *ūrṇā* and *uṣṇīṣa* are often found in images of the Buddha, along with a few of the other thirty-two physical characteristics.[59] Another common feature of Buddha statues, particularly ones that depict him in a reclining position, is perfectly flat feet marked with a spoked wheel design. According to Buddhaghosa, "The soles of the Buddha's feet are fully fleshed and perfectly flat like golden sandals. When he walks they do not move like the feet of ordinary men; rather, the whole underside of the foot touches the ground at the same time and leaves it at the same time. Nor does the end of the foot touch the ground before the other parts; rather, the entire sole touches the ground at the same time."[60] Caraka also considers this to be an attribute of the ideal masculine type, who has a stable gait in which the entire surface of the soles presses against the earth.[61]

This feature is often linked to the Buddha's dignified comportment and steady gait, which is compared to that of a mighty elephant. Like an elephant, the Buddha turns his entire body when he changes direction and does not swivel his hips or bend at the waist.[62] A related trope compares his straight torso to that of the god Brahmā. Buddhaghosa states that "the Buddha has a straight body like that of Brahmā. He does not stoop or lean backwards, as if catching at the stars, nor does he have a crooked spine, but towers up symmetrically like a golden tower gate in a city of the gods."[63] He is also depicted in some sources as taller than his contemporaries, and a number of texts assert that he had a six-foot halo that emanated from his entire body *(byāmappabhā)* and inspired faith in people.[64]

The Brahmanical Connection

In the Pāli canon, the lore of the physical characteristics of a great man is associated with brahmans and portrayed as an aspect of brahmanical learning,[65] but as T. W. Rhys Davids notes,

> The knowledge of these thirty-two marks of a Great Being . . . is one of the details in the often recurring paragraph giving points of Brāhmaṇa learning. No such list has been found, so far as I know, in those portions of the pre-Buddhistic priestly literature that have survived. And the inference from both our passages is that the knowledge is scattered through the Brāhmaṇa texts.[66]

He concludes that "many of the details of the Buddhist list are very obscure" and adds that further examination of ancient brahmanical literature would shed some light on "a curious chapter in mythological superstition."[67]

In a discussion of the thirty-two physical characteristics in his biography of the Buddha, Hajime Nakamura holds that these characteristics were taken from Hindu sources and adapted by Buddhist authors. He concludes that Buddhists were the first to formulate the list found in the Pāli canon but provides no evidence of non-Buddhist sources.[68] Sten Konow expresses the opinion that the concept of the great man "is, in its origins, influenced by notions connected with Viṣṇu/Nārāyaṇa."[69] Eugene Burnouf traces the attributes of the great man to the idea of the cosmic man in the "Hymn of the Man" *(Puruṣa Sūkta)* of the *Ṛg Veda,* but the description of Puruṣa in this text bears no resemblance to the physical attributes of the Buddha as described in the Pāli canon.

Some Vedic hymns, such as the *Śathapatha Brāhmaṇa* and the *Atharva Veda,* associate auspicious physical signs with greatness. In the *Atharva Veda,* physical marks are used as predictors,[70] and the *Śathapatha Brāhmaṇa* describes auspicious bodily signs.[71] The *Atharva Veda* also contains a charm to remove undesirable marks from a woman's body and another to remove them from one's own body,[72] but neither of these texts contains any listing comparable to that of the Pāli canon.

The notion that great beings are marked by special physical characteristics is found in a number of brahmanical texts, some of which contain mentions of a few of the major and minor physical characteristics ascribed to the Buddha. In the *Ancient Lore of Viṣṇu,* for example, a description of Kṛṣṇa states that he has dark blue eyes; that his breast is marked with a *rīvatsa;* that he has long arms and a broad chest, a lovely complexion, flat feet, and copper-colored nails; and that like the Buddha he has markings on his palms.[73] Rāma, another great icon of Indian manhood, is also said to possess some of these characteristics, but his description in the *Adventures of Rāma (Rāmāyaṇa)* is of a huge and muscular figure with a "collarbone set deep in muscle," whose arms reach down to his knees (a feature associated with physical strength in India). Like the Buddha, Rāma is extraordinarily handsome and has a graceful gait and a beautiful (but dark) complexion, and his body is "marked with all auspicious signs."[74] As in a number of descriptions of the Buddha, Rāma's kingly demeanor is emphasized, and he is presented as the paradigm of Indian royalty,

> the very image of the king of *gandharvas*, and renowned throughout the world for his manliness as well. His arms were long, his strength immense, and he carried himself like a bull elephant in rut. He was extremely handsome and his face had the lovely glow of moonlight. With his beauty and nobility he ravished both the sight and the hearts of men.[75]

The *Ancient Lore of the Lord* contains a description of Śuka, a son of Vyāsa, whose exceptional spiritual accomplishments are manifest on his physique. He has "tender feet, hands, thighs, arms, shoulders, cheeks, and body; his face has wide and beautiful eyes, a prominent nose, symmetrical ears, and beautiful eye-brows; his neck is shaped like a conch, his collar bones are concealed, his chest is broad and rounded; his navel is withdrawn and turned to the right, and his belly is beautified by folds of flesh." His hands reach down to his knees, he has curled hair, and he captivates women with his beautiful body.[76] Many of these attributes are also found among the two lists of physical characteristics of the great man, but most of the features in the Buddhist lists are omitted in the description of Śuka.

A number of Buddhist texts in which the thirty-two major physical characteristics and eighty minor ones are mentioned attribute them to the lore of brahmans, but I have not been able to identify any Vedic, Purāṇa, or Epic text or passage that contains a similar list (although some elements appear in a number of brahmanical works).[77] Buddhaghosa appears to acknowledge that his research led to a similar conclusion:

> When the time comes for the birth of a buddha, the Suddhāvāsa Brahmā gods visit the earth in the guise of brahmans and teach humans about their bodily signs as constituting a part of the Vedic learning, so that by this means humans may recognize the Buddha. After his death, this knowledge generally vanishes. That is why it does not exist in the Vedas.[78]

Thus, according to Buddhaghosa, the gods responsible for maintaining and dispersing Vedic lore give this knowledge to brahmans in order that they will recognize a buddha when he is born; but following a buddha's passing there is no longer any need for humans to have this knowledge because the only being who possesses the characteristics of a great man is no longer available for physical inspection.[79]

Bodies and Culture

Whatever their sources or provenance, the repetition of these lists and references to them indicate that the notion of the physical characteristics of a great man was widely accepted by Buddhist authors and that this notion formed a core part of the mythology of the Buddha. This body image apparently appealed to people of the Buddha's time and to later authors of Buddhist texts as the most sublime development of the male physique, one to which other men aspired and which women viewed as supremely attractive. The Buddha's good qualities and spiritual development were displayed on his body, and others read it as a canvas that proved his claims of having attained the ultimate state, that of a buddha.

As Margaret Lock and Nancy Scheper-Hughes note, the body functions "as simultaneously a physical and symbolic artifact, as both naturally and culturally produced, and as securely anchored in a particular historical moment."[80] In a study of Śāntideva's *Compendium of Training,* Suzanne Mrozik has also noted a "close relationship between physical and moral transformation."[81] The ideal body of Indian Buddhism was a public terrain on which social truths were inscribed and also a place on which, as we will see, social contradictions were played out. Judging from the available textual evidence, the presentation of normative bodies and discourses of masculinity seem to be entirely hegemonic; there is no hint of crisis or of serious doubts regarding how men should act and look. The situation resembles Gramsci's notion of hegemony, in which the ideology appears to members of a society as natural and right, and so there is no need for overt coercion or political repression to ensure acceptance. Connell, referring to Gramsci, asserts that hegemony

> refers to the natural dynamic by which a group claims a leading position in social life. At any given time, one form of masculinity rather than others is culturally exalted. Hegemonic masculinity can be defined as the configuration of gender practice which embodies the currently accepted answer to the problem of the legitimacy of patriarchy, which guarantees . . . the dominant position of men and the subordination of women. . . . It is the

> successful claim to authority, more than direct violence, that is the mark of hegemony.[82]

Connell further remarks that when violence is used to perpetuate gender hierarchies this is a sign of their imperfection. If a gender regime is widely viewed as legitimate, members of both sexes, even those who are oppressed or marginalized, will propagate it. No indication of coercion appears in Indian Buddhist discussions of gender, and texts from the wider society also demonstrate a general acceptance of normative male and female physicality and gender roles. There is widespread agreement—evidenced in Indian literature and art as well as in a range of other artifacts from the period—about the characteristics embodied by the ideal male. Not only is there no suggestion of coercion in the advancement of these notions, they appear to be tacitly assumed, and there is no argumentation for them or hints of alternative discourses.

When such roles function as normative and are generally accepted within a society, they serve to confer power and authority on certain elites, but as Foucault has noted, there is no central bureau that organizes such discourses (although there are some who benefit from them and whose continued dominance requires their perpetuation). Even those who are marginalized or disempowered by these discourses play a role in their continuation, and as long as these notions are hegemonic, their operations and contingent nature will be mostly invisible to people within a particular society.

> The logic is perfectly clear, the aims decipherable, and yet it is often the case that no one is there to have invented them, and few who can be said to have formulated them: an implicit characteristic of the great anonymous, almost unspoken strategies which coordinate the loquacious tactics whose "inventors" or decision makers are often without hypocrisy. Where there is power, there is resistance, and yet . . . this resistance is never in a position of exteriority in relation to power.[83]

Bodies serve as symbolic terrains on which a society's values and preferences are inscribed, and those who most closely exhibit these norms acquire what Bourdieu calls "symbolic capital," accumulated attributions of prestige, celebrity, power, knowledge, and honor that are redeemable in certain social situations and that serve to legitimate elites, who by claiming to possess attributes regarded as desirable or admirable are able to establish and defend their social status. This process is "neither conscious nor calculated, nor mechanically determined," and the norms can change over time.[84] While in place and functioning without question, however, these preferences have a powerful normalizing effect on members of a particular culture.

The Buddha on Display

In Indian biographies of the Buddha, he is depicted as constantly aware of being observed by humans, gods, and various other types of beings. Every important event of his life—for example, his birth, the decision to leave his home and pursue the life of a wandering ascetic, his attainment of awakening,[85] the delivery of his first sermon, and his final entry into nirvana—follows a pattern that is said to have been enacted by all other buddhas of the past and that will be followed by future awakened beings.[86] The Buddha is aware of being the focus of attention and views his life as a performance of normative actions, attitudes, and qualities.

This awareness is particularly evident in the *Extensive Sport,* in which every action the Buddha performs is preceded by reflection on what is expected of him. He is portrayed as consciously following a paradigm and enacting deeds that conform to the expectations of his human and divine audiences and that will serve a didactic purpose for those who witness these deeds. Every major exploit is witnessed by countless legions of gods, who know in advance the sequence of events and eagerly anticipate the Buddha's display of the stages of awakening. Similarly, humans expect certain bodily signs of accomplishment and conformity to religious norms and judge the Buddha's physical enactment accordingly. His oral teachings are important, and they also accord with those of past buddhas—but the physical displays of his awakening are probably more decisive in convincing skeptical observers of his status.

Indian Buddhist literature abounds with stories of people who are overwhelmed by the Buddha's physical presence and become his followers after beholding his body. The commentary on the *Verses of the Elder Monks,* for example, contains the story of Vakkali, a brahman "wise and learned in the Vedas" who upon seeing "the perfection of the Master's physical form" joined the monastic order. Vakkali was so obsessed with the Buddha's beauty, however, that he constantly followed the Buddha around and stared at him incessantly, which eventually annoyed the object of his fascination to the point where he requested Vakkali to stop. The Buddha asked him, "What do you see in this foul body of mine? One who sees the doctrine [dharma] sees me." After this gentle rebuke, Vakkali stopped his constant staring but was unable to leave the Buddha's presence. He asked, "What is life to me if I cannot see him?" and was about to kill himself from grief. Reading Vakkali's mind, the Buddha recognized that if Vakkali went ahead with his planned suicide, he would undo all the progress he had made since joining the order, and so the Buddha "revealed his radiant glory" (which appears to imply that he showed Vakkali his naked body). Following this display, Vakkali gained insight and became an arhat (and presumably overcame his former fixation).[87]

Performing Hierarchies

Status is a prevalent concern in Indian Buddhist literature. It relates to possession of a perfect body that proclaims Śākyamuni's spiritual attainments and substantiates his claim to buddhahood as well as his social position. Indian biographies of the Buddha all agree that he was born into a wealthy royal family, and several sources assert that all buddhas take birth in either brahman or *kṣatriya* lineages, depending on which is most socially respected at a particular time. *Kṣatriyas* were better regarded in the Buddha's society, and so he chose to be incarnated in a particularly prominent royal family that was admired by all classes of people.[88] According to the *Extensive Sport,* the men of his father's capital city of Kapilavastu "all had powerful bodies, each with the strength of several elephants. They excelled at archery and all the arts of war, but none would harm another even to save his own life."[89] The Buddha's mother and father are also presented as paragons of humanity. His mother, Māyā, is described as having thirty-two good qualities—which may be an intentional correspondence with the Buddha's thirty-two physical characteristics—and she had wisdom, intelligence, and morality; was respected by all; had a perfect body that had never given birth; was not a gossip; and "was free from all typical faults of the female gender."[90] The members of his clan are similarly extolled for their physical beauty, their strength and warrior abilities, and their wisdom. An extraordinary person is expected to issue from the best human stock.

The Buddha's perfect body is particularly important in these tropes, and it serves to persuade skeptics of his claims to ultimate authority. In a number of such stories, unconvinced brahmans listen to the Buddha's sermons and are favorably impressed, but they note that people of mediocre attainments can repeat words of wisdom. In order to assuage lingering doubts, they examine his body to determine whether he has the marks of a great man. All of these brahmans are said to be well versed in the Vedas and to be experts in the lore of the great man, and they are impressed by the fact that they can verify all but two of the physical characteristics: the enormous tongue and sheathed penis. The Buddha, reading their minds and understanding their doubts, extends his tongue and covers his forehead with it. He then inserts the tip into each of his ears. He also enables them to view his sheathed penis.[91]

In every case the brahmans become convinced that he is in fact the embodiment of the great man described in their scriptures. The Buddha's actions resonate with Harold Garfinkel's notion that life is performance and that social constructions of gender are not simply a matter of anatomical endowment but also require the adoption of certain attitudes and the enactment of expected qualities.[92] The Buddha's life is depicted as a daily performance in which he presented to people (as well as to gods and various other types of beings) a series of images that conformed to ideal norms of masculinity and of the persona of an awakened being. These images differ according to individuals and situations, and when his audience includes learned brahmans, the thirty-two physical characteristics are repeatedly portrayed as an expected part of his repertoire.

In these accounts of his life, the Buddha's perfect body holds out a promise to his followers that they also can transcend the harsh realities of the flesh: through his austerities and accumulation of good karma over many lifetimes, he progressively developed a body that was ideally suited to the religious life, and the perfection of his body was obvious to all who viewed it. People who follow his path are assured by viewing his physical perfection (or reading about it in Buddhist literature) that their practice can lead to future acquisition of just such a body or that they might follow his example and attain release from birth and death in this life.

In the following chapter I will examine some of the popular hagiographies of the Buddha. The details of his life are widely known and have been studied by a number of scholars, and so my aim will not be a comprehensive consideration of every event or discrepancies between accounts; rather, I will highlight important tropes relating to masculinity and some of the discourses that develop the notion of the Buddha as the ultimate man.

2

A Manly Monk

> A highest thing . . . would have to be one which has all reality. . . . Fundamentally we can only think of God by ascribing to him without any limitation everything real which we meet with in ourselves. . . . [W]e ascribe it to God and admit the inability of our reason to think it in a wholly pure way.
>
> —Immanuel Kant, *Lectures on Philosophical Theology*

The Buddha in History and Legend

According to Buddhist tradition, the boy who would grow up to become the Buddha was born in the royal family of a small kingdom in the southern part of modern-day Nepal. The dates given for his lifespan have been a topic of debate among scholars, but in recent decades a consensus appears to have developed that places his death at around twenty years on either side of 400 B.C.E.[1] There is no good reason to doubt the traditional notion that he lived for eighty years, which would place his birth at around 480 BCE.

There are a number of accounts of the Buddha's life, but all abound with mythological motifs and are unreliable as historical records. These texts do, however, contain a wealth of information regarding how the Buddha was perceived by his followers and how his legend developed, along with discourses relating to norms of masculinity that prevailed in India during the centuries when Buddhism remained on the subcontinent.

The sermons (*sutta;* Skt.: sūtra) and monastic code *(vinaya)* of the Pāli canon have many biographical stories and anecdotes, and there are several Indic works that purport to tell his life story, including Aśvaghoṣa's *Deeds of the Buddha (Buddha-carita),* the *Extensive Sport,* and the *Great Matter.* In the Theravāda tradition, the standard account is found in the *Discussion of the Links* [*of Dependent Arising*] (*Nidāna-kathā*) of the *Discussion of the Meaning of the Birth Stories* (*Jātaka-aṭṭha-kathā*) and the *Buddha Chronicle* (*Buddha-vaṃsa*). These and other biographical sources differ in many details and in how they conceive of the Buddha's abilities. There are also comparatively late hagiographies composed in various Buddhist countries, but this chapter is mainly confined to Indic materials and some commentaries on them composed in Southeast Asia.

One of the recurring tropes of Buddhist modernism, particularly in Theravāda countries, is the notion that in the Pāli canon the Buddha is "only a man,"[2] but even a cursory examination of those texts that describe him indicates that this is not the way in which the tradition viewed him. The most modest descriptions of the Buddha credit him with superhuman strength and wisdom; physical skills surpassing those of all other people; a perfect physique; and the ability to perform a range of magical feats, including levitation, walking on water, passing through solid objects, wading through earth as though he were in water, mentally creating bodies that can travel anywhere in the universe, telepathy, clairaudience, and clairvoyance.[3] His wisdom and power transcend those of gods, and the Indian deities Indra (generally referred to in Buddhist texts as Śakra; Pāli: Sakka) and Brahmā appear at various junctures in his life, proclaim his complete superiority to them, beg him for instructions, and declare themselves his disciples.

In the texts of the Transcendentist (Lokottaravāda) school, the Buddha is credited with even greater capacities: in athletic contests he easily bests the strongest men; his greatest rival, Māra, is utterly humiliated by the Buddha with almost no effort on the latter's part; and the Buddha's body is said to be supramundane and immutable. Moreover, his entire life story is recast: this new and improved Buddha, we are told, actually became awakened in the distant past, and his existence on earth was a magical display for the benefit of human and divine audiences.

This notion is extended still further in Mahāyāna texts, in which the Buddha becomes a godlike figure who is omnipotent and omniscient and who can easily abrogate the laws of physics. Among other new abilities, the Buddha of Mahāyāna imagination can place an entire galaxy into a pore in his skin without either expanding the pore or shrinking the galaxy, and its residents are mostly unaware that anything has happened. This chapter will primarily examine non-Mahāyāna depictions of his life and will highlight some of the most important and interesting tropes relating to his personification of ideal masculine traits as conceived by the followers who constructed these legends.

The Buddha's Manly Qualities

In all Indian accounts of the Buddha's life there is a pervasive concern with establishing his masculinity. He is referred to by a range of epithets that highlight his manly qualities, including "ultimate man," "great man," "manly," "leader of men," "best of men," "god among men," and "possessing manly strength." Other epithets emphasize his royal heritage and sovereign power: "lord of bipeds," "king of kings," "king of the dharma," "best in the world," "victor in battle," "decisive leader in battle," "crusher of enemies," "god above all gods," and "unsurpassed tamer of men." Another recurring trope links the Buddha with various powerful or ferocious animals: "bull of a man," "fearless lion," "lion-hearted man," "savage elephant," and "stallion."[4] As Wendy Doniger has noted, bulls and stallions are recurring symbols of strength and virility in India: "The Indo-Aryans were a nation of warriors whose conquest of much of Europe and Asia was made possible by the fact that they had tamed the horse and harnessed him to the chariot. Men rather than women are the creatures of Vedic life—aggressive, sexually potent men, symbolized by the stallion."[5]

The notion that the Buddha is like a lion also recurs throughout Indian Buddhist literature; the "Connected Discourse on the Aggregates," for example, compares him to a mighty lion emerging from his lair and stretching himself. He lets out a roar, and all the animals who hear it are terrified: "they urinate and defecate and flee here and there."[6] Similarly, when a buddha arises in the world, many gods are filled with fear because he is more "majestic and mighty" than any of them.

The *Extensive Sport* elaborates on this theme and links the Buddha's leonine qualities with various aspects of his ministry. He is referred to as a "man-lion," and the four noble truths are his teeth and claws; his canines are the four Brahmā abodes.[7] His noble head is composed of the four means he uses to convert disciples,[8] and his powerful body is perfected by his comprehension of the twelvefold cycle of dependent arising *(pratītya-samutpāda)*.[9] His majestic mane is formed of knowledge and wisdom and is braided into the thirty-seven limbs of awakening, which are perfectly complete.[10] The three doors of deliverance are his roaring mouth;[11] his clear eyes result from his profound insight and deep calm. Like a lion, he dwells in deep grottoes and the mountain caves of meditation, complete deliverance, contemplation, and equanimity. Striding forth from the forest of discipline, he treads the four paths of pure action. He bears himself with the power of the four fearlessnesses and the ten strengths.[12] His mighty roar of egolessness tames heretics, "those herds of deer and donkeys."[13]

Preamble to Perfection

Traditional accounts assume that the Buddha's final birth was the result of countless lifetimes of training, during which he progressively accumulated the matrix of exalted qualities that accompany the attainment of awakening. Near the end of his previous existence, while residing in Tuṣita heaven, he decided that the time was ripe for his last incarnation. *So It Has Been Said* reports that he reflected on his past lives: he had been a god many times, including several lifetimes as a Brahmā, the world-creator and keeper of Vedic lore, "a conqueror, unconquered one, all-seeing, all-controlling." Thirty-six times he had been Śakra, king of the gods in the Vedas, and in hundreds of lifetimes he had been the greatest of monarchs, a *cakravartin,* endowed with "mighty power and majesty."[14]

The state of universal monarch is often presented as the epitome of human perfection short of buddhahood. The "Discourse on Mahāsudassana" describes one such fortunate being, King Mahāsudassana, who was "handsome, good to look at, with a complexion like the finest lotus, surpassing other men." As a result of his long practice of virtue and generosity, he was long-lived and free from illness, had good digestion, was not bothered by cold or heat like other men, and was loved by brahmans and householders as a father is loved by his children. When he died, his passing was painless, like a man falling asleep after a good meal, following which he was reborn as a god.[15]

The purport of such descriptions is clear: the authors wished to establish that the Buddha experienced every possible exalted situation and spent many lifetimes at the very apogee of power and divine embodiment within cyclic existence. Thus when he decided to renounce the world, he did so with full knowledge of exactly what he was leaving behind. Also related is the notion that birth as a buddha transcends all mortal conditions, even those of the highest gods. Gods are described as having transcendent bodies, but the Buddha's is even better. It is important that the Buddha experienced the best situations in past lives because buddhahood is the highest possible state. He is fully aware of his final existence as the epitome of all forms of life because he personally incarnated in the full range of destinies in the past. As a buddha, he will surpass even the gods in wisdom, power, and splendor, and his body will be more beautiful than those of beings in the highest realms.

This trope appears in a number of biographies, including the *Extensive Sport,* which describes the effect of the Buddha's physique on the residents of Rājagṛha when he goes there begging for alms. It reports that all who see him are filled with wonder and think he is Brahmā, Śakra, or another god:

> Crowds of men and women gaze at the man who is like pure gold. His self-mastery is complete; he is marked with the thirty-two physical characteristics. And no one tires of looking at him. . . . [They ask,] "Who is this being? Never before have we seen one like him; he makes the city radiant with his splendor." Thousands of women, wishing to see the most outstanding of men, leave their houses empty; they stand on the rooftops, in doorways, at windows, and in the streets to gaze at him. The merchants stop doing business; in the houses and in the streets all drinking and revelry cease, so intent are the people on watching the most remarkable of men.[16]

The Perfect Man's Perfect Birth

After making his decision to be reborn in our world, the buddha-to-be surveyed the earth for a woman of unblemished moral qualities who only had nine months and seven days left to live. All mothers of buddhas die shortly after giving birth, according to some texts, because this act is the culmination of their own spiritual progress up to that point. Other sources indicate that they have to die because it would be inappropriate for a buddha's mother to be subjected to the leering gazes of lustful men.[17] All Buddhist sources stress the notion that his conception and birth were unnatural. According to the *Great Matter,* "bodhisattvas are not born of the intercourse of a father and a mother, but by their own merit independently of parents."[18]

Most mainstream Christian churches assert that Christ's mother remained a virgin and that his conception was not the product of sexual intercourse, but some theologians feared that this notion would undermine Christ's claims to share a common humanity with those he came to save. Gregory of Nazianzus, for example, insisted on the naturalness of Mary's pregnancy and Christ's residence in the womb. For the Buddhists who composed the legends of the life of the founder of their religion, a different imperative operated: they needed to separate the Buddha from the common mass of humanity and to develop tropes that portrayed him as different from—and better than—other men in every conceivable way.

In some accounts, his mother, Māyā, reports a dream in which a white elephant enters her womb, and she realizes that she is pregnant. The *Great Matter* asserts that from the moment the Bodhisattva entered her womb, she lived a completely pure and chaste life, and she is depicted as a virgin. Similarly, the *Middle Length Collection* avers that she never had sensual thoughts regarding any man and that no man with a lustful mind could approach her. Both the *Great Matter* and *Extensive Sport* emphasize the notion that she chose strict celibacy from the moment of conception. Underscoring the unusual nature of both the Buddha's parents, when Māyā told her husband, Śuddhodana, of her intention to remain celibate, he enthusiastically agreed.[19]

During her pregnancy, Māyā experienced constant physical pleasure and no discomfort or fatigue of any kind. The Bodhisattva entered a transparent crystal casket in her womb, and all of his limbs were fully formed from the first moment.[20] He resided in his mother's right side with his legs crossed.[21] During his sojourn in her womb, he was untouched by uterine fluids, and gods appeared regularly and washed him with pure water.

According to some accounts, the Buddha was able to communicate with his divine visitors while residing in Māyā's womb. In the *Extensive Sport,* some gods express amazement that the most exalted of beings could endure the foulness of a stinking human womb and that even deities would find such a situation repulsive. At this point in the narrative of the *Extensive Sport,* Ānanda exclaims, "It is astonishing, O Blessed One, how base is the body of a woman, as the Thus Gone One (Thatāgata) has said, and how subject to passion!" He adds that the Bodhisattva "surpassed all the worlds" but descended from Tuṣita "into a human body with its disagreeable odor and dwelt within on the right side of his mother. I cannot explain it!"[22]

Vasubandhu considers this problem and states that the Buddha decided to be born from a womb for three main reasons: (1) because he knew that the mighty Śākya clan (to which his father and mother belonged) would embrace the dharma because of its relationship with him; (2) because he was born from a womb like them, humans can relate to him, and they will wish to emulate his example because he is a man who has reached perfection; and (3) because he was a physical being, after death his remains could be cremated, and thus relics would be produced that could be worshipped by succeeding generations, allowing them to make merit.[23]

When the time arrived for the Bodhisattva's birth, hosts of deities gathered. Unlike ordinary babies, he emerged from his mother's right side, and she delivered him standing up, leaning against a tree.[24] In keeping with the Indian distaste for bodily fluids and their polluting capacities, the Buddha never came in contact with any part of his mother's body and was completely clean.[25] His emergence happened quickly, and Māyā experienced no pain, only pleasure. The newly born Bodhisattva is depicted as fully mindful and as able to speak.[26] The *Extensive Sport* describes him as an infant "endowed with tremendous power and strength."[27] He declares that this is his final birth and that he will attain awakening after defeating Māra: "I will destroy Māra and his army. I will extinguish the fires of hell with rain from the great cloud of dharma, filling beings in the hell realms with joy."[28]

The *Discourse Sections* states that when the child emerged from the womb celebrations ensued among the gods. The brahman sage Asita was visiting Tuṣita, and when he asked what had caused this commotion, he was told that a bodhisattva had been born, "a superlative being without comparison, a precious pearl of the health and goodness of the human world. . . . [O]f all beings this one is perfect, this man is the pinnacle, the ultimate, the hero of creatures." Upon hearing this description, Asita traveled to see the Buddha; he saw an infant who was "shining, glowing, and beautiful. It was like seeing molten gold in the hands of a master craftsman as he takes it out of the furnace." Asita inspected the Buddha's body, saw that the child had all the signs of a great man, and declared, "This is the ultimate, this is the perfect man!"[29]

The *Deeds of the Buddha* (ca. second century CE) also reports this event and indicates that Asita's wonderment was connected with his observation of the physical characteristics of a great man: "The great seer wonderingly gazed at the prince, the soles of his feet marked with a wheel, the fingers and toes joined by a web, the circle of hair growing between his eyebrows and testicles withdrawn like an elephant's."[30]

Michael Radich argues that a body endowed with the physical characteristics of a great man is not specific to buddhas because other beings possess some or all of these features and because bodhisattvas are born with them prior to their full attainment of buddhahood.[31] This first part of his argument is flawed, however, because although it is true that Buddhist sources mention some beings who possessed some of the physical characteristics, only universal monarchs and buddhas have all of them. Moreover, only buddhas have perfect physical characteristics, and so this constitutes a distinguishing feature that is unique to them. Although it is technically correct that (at least in Pāli sources) a bodhisattva in his final lifetime is born with these attributes prior to full actualization of buddhahood, the characteristics are unique to beings who will soon become buddhas and whose attainment of the ultimate state is portrayed as inevitable in Indian Buddhist literature. The physical perfection of a buddha is the somatic culmination of a process of moral development and spiritual attainment that results in a final birth in which he is endowed with the best of all bodies and during which he will attain supreme awakening. At this point the buddha's cognitive attainments and physical endowments are perfected to the highest degree. Moreover, as we will see, in descriptions of the period immediately following the Bodhisattva's attainment of full buddhahood, the perceptual impact of his physical form is enhanced. People who knew him previously remark that he is even more beautiful than before, and skeptics are converted and become his disciples (often after seeing the newly perfected physical characteristics of a great man). Thus it appears that his body reaches its full excellence only with the attainment of awakening and that both the cognitive and somatic aspects of buddhahood are jointly attained.

Contested Destinies

In accordance with custom, shortly before his son was born, Śuddhodana enlisted seven astrologers to prognosticate on the child's future. The first six astrologers declared that the boy would become a universal monarch and would rule with righteousness, but the seventh demurred and stated that the prince would pursue this path only if he were sheltered from the harsh realities of cyclic existence. If he were to see four things—an old man, a sick man, a corpse, and a world renouncer, referred to by Buddhists as the "four sights"—he would understand the futility of worldly entanglements and would leave home to seek liberation from rebirth. Alarmed at the prospect of his son rejecting his royal heritage, Śuddhodana ordered that henceforth no sick or old people or ascetics would be allowed in the palace and that dead bodies should be quickly removed before he could see them.

In keeping with his auspicious birth and remarkable physiognomy, the infant was named Siddhārtha (He Whose Aims Are Accomplished). His clan name was Gautama, and because he belonged to the lineage of the Śākyas, he is often referred to as Śākyamuni, "Sage of the Śākyas."

Soon after he was named, Siddhārtha's family brought him to a local temple for a traditional introduction to the gods, but he protested, saying "Mother, what god is so distinguished by his superiority over me that you take me to see him today? I am the god above the gods, greater than all the gods; no god is like me. I am without equal!"[32] Despite this, he agreed to participate in the ritual, but when he entered the temple all the statues of the gods—Śiva, Skanda, Nārāyaṇa, Kubera, Candra, Sūrya, Vaiśravaṇa, Śakra, Brahmā—rose to greet him and bowed down, touching their heads to his feet.[33] All the gods and humans agreed that he was a "god of gods" *(deva-deva).*

Sex and the Future Buddha

Hoping to lure his son to embrace the world and its pleasures, Śuddhodana created a cocoon of sensual pleasures for young Siddhārtha. As the prince grew up, he was surrounded by the best a wealthy royal family could offer, including a bevy of beautiful women whose sole aim was to entice him with their feminine wiles, provide him with sexual pleasure, and ensure that his thoughts would never stray from his artificial environment to the problems inherent in the world at large.

During his teens and twenties, he "resided in the women's quarters" and was surrounded by thousands of courtesans who were skilled in the erotic arts. The *Deeds of the Buddha* describes his harem: "There the women delighted him with their soft voices, enticements, playful intoxications, sweet laughter, curvings of eyebrows and sidelong glances. Then a captive to the women, who were skilled in the arts of love and tireless in sexual pleasure, he did not descend from the palace to the ground, just as one who has won paradise by his merit does not descend to earth from the heavenly abodes."[34]

The *Extensive Sport* indicates that enjoyment of women is one of the activities of a bodhisattva and that all past buddhas had huge harems.[35] Siddhārtha lived this sensual life because it was expected of him, and the *Extensive Sport* also states that it provided him an opportunity to convert the harem women to the dharma.[36] The aim of these accounts appears to be to counteract suspicions that when he later decided to leave the palace he might have done so because he was not a real man. It is important that when a future buddha rejects sensuality he does so after fully experiencing all its purported pleasures. His renunciation is undertaken with the full knowledge of what he has given up. Moreover, he should not leave home life as a result of a painful relationship breakup or a personal trauma or because his sexuality is in any way impaired; rather, the bodhisattva must be a "stallion," a supremely virile superman able to pleasure huge numbers of women.

The extraordinary virility attributed to Siddhārtha had its costs, however. David Halperin notes in his discussion of notions of masculinity in Europe that excessive sexual indulgence was associated with effeminacy, and the same was true in India during the Buddha's time. Manly men, particularly *kṣatriyas*, ought to prefer the rough company of other males and to eschew the soft realm of womenfolk, and they viewed with suspicion those who

> deviated from masculine gender norms insofar as they preferred the soft option of love to the hard option of war. In the culture of the military elites . . . normative masculinity entailed austerity, resistance to appetite, and mastery of the impulse to pleasure. . . . A man displayed his true mettle in war . . . and more generally in struggles with other men for honor—in politics, business, and other competitive enterprises. Those men who refused to rise to the challenge, who abandoned the competitive society of men for the amorous society of women, who pursued a life of pleasure, who made love instead of war—they incarnated the classical stereotype of effeminacy.[37]

Siddhārtha reportedly excelled in all martial arts, but some people who knew of his opulent, hedonistic lifestyle entertained doubts about his manly bona fides. When the time came for Śuddhodana to arrange a marriage for his son, one prospective father-in-law worried that Siddhārtha might not be man enough to shoulder his responsibilities. The marriage was an important part of Śuddhodana's plan to keep his son involved in worldly affairs: he hoped that it would lead to the birth of male heirs and that family entanglements would keep Siddhārtha preoccupied with his wife, children, and royal responsibilities. In traditional India, a man has a sacred duty to produce at least one male heir, who would continue the lineage and perform ceremonies for him after his death. Men who died without sons were objects of pity, and those who produced no progeny or who had only daughters were believed to have deficient sperm.

Śuddhodana's plan to marry off his son hit a snag when Daṇḍapāṇi, father of the beautiful Yaśodharā, questioned whether a pampered prince raised in the women's quarters could be a true *kṣatriya:* "It is the custom of our family to give our daughters in marriage only to men skilled in the worldly arts *(śilpa),* and your son has grown up in luxury in the palace. If he does not excel in the arts, does not know the rules of fencing or archery or boxing or wrestling, how could I give my daughter to him?"[38]

When he heard of these concerns, Siddhārtha assured his father that his martial skills would prove his manly qualifications. He asserted that no one in the kingdom could rival him in the warrior arts, and so his father arranged a tournament in which five hundred young Śākya men participated. The best representatives of local manhood assembled to demonstrate their skills at fencing, archery, elephant riding, swordsmanship, boxing, and wrestling. In the *Great Matter,* the events listed are "archery, fighting, boxing, cutting, stabbing, speed, and feats of strength, use of elephants, horses, chariots, bows, and spears, and argument."[39]

In all accounts of this episode, Siddhārtha is clearly the best in every event and wins easily. The *Extensive Sport*'s version opens with a contest of strength; first his half brother Nanda and cousin Ānanda come forward to wrestle him, but he tosses them to the ground by merely touching them. Then his cousin Devadatta (who will become his nemesis when he founds the monastic order) parades around the ground displaying his strength, but Siddhārtha picks him up with one hand, tosses him around in the air, and then sets him down on the ground. The prince then declares that no one man can begin to match him and calls on all of the contestants to come at him at once, but again he easily defeats them. In the *Extensive Sport,* he is presented as a god toying with mortals who have no hope of providing any sort of contest for his superhuman strength, speed, and skill. The *Great Matter* is not as grandiose in its attributions, but still he overcomes all rivals with no real difficulty, and the narrative concludes: "Then an exhibition was given by prince Siddhārtha in which he displayed his feats in all the arts. There was no one to equal him in either wrestling or boxing."[40]

The final competition pitted the young men against each other in an archery contest. The *Extensive Sport* states that Siddhārtha picks up a bow that no one else could draw and that few could even lift. He grasps it while sitting down, lifts it easily, and shoots an arrow through every target, which utterly eclipses the performances of all the others.[41] The arrow plunges into the ground and disappears after piercing the final target. All accounts of the contest conclude that Siddhārtha has proved himself the superior to all gods and men in the worldly arts and that he has won the hearts of all the women in the audience, including Yaśodharā.

His doubts assuaged, Daṇḍapāṇi happily gives his daughter to the prince. According to some accounts, Siddhārtha also had two other wives (the others are generally named Gopā and Mṛgajā, but they seldom play any significant roles in these narratives). The *Great Matter* also assigns Siddhārtha thousands of beautiful courtesans,[42] and the *Monastic Discipline of the Fundamental Everything Exists School* says he had three wives: Yaśodharā, Gopā, and Mṛgajā, each of whom was accompanied by twenty thousand courtesans.[43] Siddhārtha is credited with the ability to fully satisfy every one of his women, and each imagined that he spent time only with her.

Every account of his harem emphasizes the idea that the women represent the pinnacle of female attractiveness; they are "beautiful, faultless, loving women, with eyes bright as jewels, with large breasts, resplendent white limbs, sparkling gems, firm and fine waists, soft, lovely, and black-colored hair, wearing bright red mantles and cloaks, bracelets of gems and necklaces of pearls, ornaments and rings on their toes, and anklets, and playing music."[44]

Despite their beguiling physical charms, when his father first presented these women to him, Siddhārtha had no interest. The king grew concerned that his son might be deficient in manhood and asked, "are you not then as a man excited by a woman's beauty?"[45] To Śuddhodana's consternation, his son informed him that he did not find them attractive, but still the king persisted in his efforts to focus Siddhārtha's attention on carnal pursuits. This section of the *Deeds of the Buddha* contains an elaborate and flowery depiction of the women his father chooses to entice the prince. They are beautiful enough to "make lust-free sages waver, and captivate even gods who are accustomed to celestial nymphs *(apsarasa),*" but they are so overwhelmed by the prince's beauty, "like that of Kāma (the god of physical love) in human form," that they become shy and unable even to approach him. Eventually, urged on by a priest's son named Udāyin, they enact the full repertoire of feminine blandishments of Indian courtesans.[46]

> Then some of the young women pretended to be intoxicated and touched him with their firm, rounded, close-set, alluring breasts. One made a false stumble and clasped him strongly with her tender arm-creepers, which hung down loosely from her drooping shoulders. . . . Another repeatedly let her blue garments slip down under the pretext of intoxication, and with her girdle partly seen it seemed like a lightning flash at night. Some walked

> around in order to make their golden zones tinkle and displayed to him their hips veiled by diaphanous robes. . . . Thus these young women, to whose minds love had given free rein, assailed the prince with their wiles of every kind.[47]

Despite this impressive display—which we are told would reduce any ordinary man to a quivering mass of helpless lust—Siddhārtha is unmoved, and he "firmly guarded his senses, and in his distress at the inevitability of death was neither cheered nor disturbed."[48] Udāyin, described as an expert in the sacred treatises *(śāstra),* rebukes Siddhārtha for his indifference and advises him to stop whining about the futility of worldly existence, to shoulder his responsibilities, and to perform "the duty of a man." Udāyin claims to be acting solely out of friendship and genuine concern for the prince's best interests, and the priest's son makes a point that is repeated throughout Buddhist literature in regard to the wider culture's view of celibate monasticism: that it should be practiced only by those men who are advanced in years, who have fulfilled their duties as fathers and husbands, and who have produced male heirs after productive lives as fully contributing members of society.[49] In a sentiment often expressed in contemporary singles bars, Udāyin adds that "such lack of courtesy to women is not suitable for one as young in years and beautiful in form as you are. The gratification of women, even by the use of falsity, is right, for the sake both of countering their bashfulness and for one's own enjoyment."[50]

Despite his marriage and his retinue of seductive women, Siddhārtha remained dissatisfied with his life. He felt that something wrong lay beneath the surface of his happiness but was unable to articulate clearly what was troubling him. His father, perceiving his son's discontent, redoubled his efforts to convince Siddhārtha of the value of the princely life and his future royal duties.

Confronting Suffering

At a crucial juncture in the story, Siddhārtha decides that he should venture forth from the palace to tour the city he is destined to rule one day. In order to prevent Siddhārtha from seeing any of the "four sights," Śuddhodana orders that the streets be cleared of all sick or old people, that no funeral processions be allowed anywhere near the prince's route, and that all world renouncers be similarly banned. At the appointed time, the royal chariot sweeps through Kapilavastu's streets, accompanied by the cheers of the populace. As in many other parts of its narrative, the *Deeds of the Buddha* is particularly concerned with Siddhārtha's effect on the women who see him. He is said to be "loved by the women," who are described as having large breasts and wide hips, which numerous statues attest are core attributes of classical India's conception of ideal feminine beauty.

> Some of these magnificent women, though longing made them try to rush, were delayed in their movements by the weight of their chariot-like hips and full breasts. . . . The palaces were full of young women, who threw open the windows in their excitement; the city appeared as magnificent on all sides as paradise with heavenly mansions full of celestial nymphs. . . . Beholding the king's son in the full glory of his beauty and majesty, the women murmured softly, "Blessed is his wife," with pure minds and from no ulterior motive. They viewed him with reverence and considered that this man with long, strong arms, with a form like the visible presence of the god symbolized by flowers [Kāmadeva] was reportedly preparing to renounce his royal heritage and pursue the dharma.[51]

During Siddhārtha's first trip into the city, an old and decrepit man passes in front of the royal chariot. Channa, the driver, stops, and the feeble figure painfully makes his way across the street. Siddhārtha asks how this man came to be in such a deplorable situation and is told that age is the inevitable fate of all beings. Never having witnessed the debilitating effects of senescence before, Siddhārtha becomes deeply distressed and orders Channa to take him back to the palace so that he can contemplate the ramifications of his newfound understanding of time's ravages.

On subsequent trips, the chariot is stopped by a sick man in severe distress and by a weeping funeral procession that carries a foul-smelling corpse. Upon being informed that such fates are common to all and that none can escape the scourges of disease or the inevitability of death, Siddhārtha realizes with a shock that his young, healthy body will one day begin to degenerate, that he will become sick from time to time, that he will grow old and feeble, and that he will inevitably die and decompose like the corpse he has seen in the city.

His fourth journey, however, provides him with hope; this time he sees in the distance a wandering ascetic, a man who has renounced all worldly possessions and attachments and lives on alms, seeking liberation from cyclic existence. His calm demeanor and aura of peace so impresses the young prince that he decides on the spot to emulate his example and to pursue the religious life.

On his return to the palace, Siddhārtha is buoyed by a new sense of purpose and the promise of a resolution for his existential crisis. He eagerly tells his father that he has finally made a career choice, but when Śuddhodana hears his son's plans he feels a dread that reaches to the marrow of his bones. His only son, his pride and joy and the heir to the throne, has resolved to give up his royal heritage and to join the ranks of ascetics who wander from place to place without fixed abode, subsisting on alms gained by begging. As it would most parents, this prospect alarms him beyond words, and he tries through various means to dissuade Siddhārtha. Śuddhodana promises his son everything he could ever desire, including vast amounts of money and land, even more women, and upon the father's abdication a wealthy kingdom, but his son replies that he will remain in the palace only if his father can promise him one thing: that he will never age, never experience illness, and never die. Powerless to grant such boons, Śuddhodana hangs his head and agrees that these fates are unavoidable for all who remain enmeshed in mundane concerns.

The *Monastic Code of the Fundamental Everything Exists School* reports that Siddhārtha then reflected on things that remained undone. He feared that if he were to leave home without first producing a male heir, other *kṣatriya*s might think that he was not a manly man, and so he resolved to impregnate Yaśodharā before abandoning her to pursue his religious quest.[52] In contemporary idiom, he had decided not only to walk out on his faithful and loving wife, but also to saddle her with the burdens of a single mother so that other nobles and warriors would not call him a girly man. His actions are defended by his biographers, who assume that his public reputation is a crucial aspect of his mission and that his attainment of buddhahood benefits all living beings and provides them with a paradigm to follow in their pursuit of the ultimate good. In both ancient and contemporary India, a man who is unable to produce a male heir is suspect, and such an inability negatively reflects on his masculinity.[53]

The *Great Matter* asserts that at midnight on his final night in the palace Siddhārtha touched Yaśodharā, after which his future son Rāhula descended from Tuṣita into her womb, but that no intercourse was involved.[54] Understandably upset at what appeared to Yaśodharā as the selfish and callous treatment of a devoted and loving spouse, she asks her husband how he can leave her despite her exemplary wifely behavior.

In the opening section of the *Birth Story of Canda the Kiṃnara,* Siddhārtha gives Yaśodharā instructions to remain faithful to him and to obey his commands, even though he is about to leave her to pursue his own religious path. He will never again share her bed, but she is ordered to have no relations with other men. Moreover, she should continue to love him and to preserve her chastity, because her actions reflect on him, even though he is no longer a part of her life.[55] A man's honor is closely linked with the behavior of women under his control; Siddhārtha intends to renounce the duties expected of a husband, but he still assumes that he can rightfully exert control over her actions and orders that she continue to be a dutiful and faithful wife. The text adds that Yaśodharā would live as a widow while Siddhārtha pursued the path to liberation.

In one account of this episode, in which the Buddha later tells his followers about his decision to leave the palace, he refers to a tale of one of his past lives, the *Śyāmā Birth Story,* in which he was a caravan leader named Vajrasena who was wrongly accused of committing a crime and was sentenced to death. As he was being led to his execution, the beautiful courtesan Śyāmā saw him and fell in love. She then tricked another man who was her lover into confessing to the crime, which led to his death. Vajrasena then became Śyāmā's lover, but he worried that she might someday betray him like she did her former partner. He soon left her and moved to another city, but she still loved him and pursued him there. The Buddha when recounting this story tells his audience that Śyāmā was a previous incarnation of Yaśodharā and that she had been his wife in numerous other former lives. Moreover, he always leaves her to pursue his own interests. The upshot is that he has no compunction about abandoning his wife because he has done so countless times in the past: this is the pattern of their relationship.[56]

The Long Road to Awakening

Siddhārtha announced that he would leave the palace as soon as possible, but the king ordered his guards to shut the gates and prevent his son's escape. He threw lavish parties, hoping vainly that such entertainments might dissuade Siddhārtha from leaving. One night, after a particularly wild revel, all the court women lay drunk or asleep on the floor. Siddhārtha alone remained conscious and fully awake. Surveying the partygoers sprawled on the floor in unflattering poses, he thought he was viewing a charnel ground. The women—previously so alluring with their fine clothing and skillful use of makeup to hide physical imperfections—lay disheveled, many drooling or muttering, and their makeup ran, revealing what they had attempted to conceal about the superficial nature of their beauty:

> When the prince saw the young women lying in these various poses and looking so repulsive with their uncontrolled movements, although ordinarily their forms were beautiful and their speech pleasant, he was moved to disgust: "Such is the real nature of women in the world of the living, impure and repulsive; but men, deceived by clothing and ornaments, succumb to passion for women."[57]

Profoundly disgusted by the scene, Siddhārtha decided that the time had finally come to leave his opulent life behind and pursue the career of a world-renouncing ascetic. He ordered Channa to make ready the royal chariot one last time and to drive him to the edge of the wilderness, where he would set forth in pursuit of final liberation. Unable to refuse, Channa saddled the faithful stallion Kanthaka and drove Siddhārtha out of the city. In a last effort to dissuade him, Channa questioned whether the prince, accustomed as he was to a life of leisure, was tough enough to endure the rigors of the ascetic life, "because this delicacy of limb, suited only for lounging in a palace, is not compatible with the ground of the grove of asceticism, covered with sharp blades of *darbha* grass."[58] Siddhārtha assured him that his body was hard and firm despite his opulent surroundings and that he could endure any privations required of him.

When he reached the limits of civilization, Siddhārtha dismounted; stroked the horse with his webbed hands, marked with a *cakra* and *svastika* on the palms;[59] and bade Channa farewell, declaring that he would not pause in his efforts until he had found the path of release from the pains of cyclic existence.

The prince then walked into the forest toward an uncertain future. The *Deeds of the Buddha* reports that he soon encountered a circle of ascetics, who saw him approaching from a distance and were struck by his physical perfection: "The majesty of his person captured the eyes of the monks. Like a second form of the king of the gods, like the magnificence of the world of moving and stationary things, he illuminated the entire grove, as if the sun had come down by itself."[60] They invited him to join them and were happy to hear that such an obviously well-favored individual had decided to pursue the religious life. His physique indicated to them that he had unusual mental endowments as well, and they expected great things of this newly arrived ascetic.

In keeping with Aśvaghoṣa's concern with the effect of the Bodhisattva's actions on women, the *Deeds of the Buddha* reports that whenever they saw him in an ascetic's robes,

> women looked up at him with restless eyes, like young deer, as their earrings, swinging back and forth, touched their faces, and their breasts heaved with uninterrupted sighs. [The Bodhisattva], bright as a golden mountain, captured the hearts of the best of women and captivated their ears, limbs, eyes and beings with his voice, touch, beauty and qualities respectively.[61]

In a later section, Aśvaghoṣa returns to this theme and paints a picture of utter emotional devastation upon Channa's return to Kapilavastu with Siddhārtha's riderless horse in tow:

> The women's eyes flooded with tears . . . with downcast eyes they wept, like cows lowing in the middle of the jungle when deserted by the herd-bull. . . . And as they hurt their breasts with their hands, so they hurt their hands with their breasts. The women, all feelings of restraint diminished, made their hands and breasts inflict mutual pain on each other.[62]

Siddhārtha's stepmother, Prajāpatī—who raised him after his mother died—was so upset that she went blind from crying. The *Deeds of the Buddha* describes her distress at the thought that the handsome prince—with curls of long, black, and glossy hair; long arms and a gait "like the king of beasts"; eyes "like a mighty bull"; a broad chest; a voice like the drum of the gods; and perfect skin that shone with the brilliance of gold—could leave his family and kingdom behind and reside in a hermitage. Like Channa, she feared that Siddhārtha was too delicate for such a harsh existence:

> His feet are soft with a beautiful webbing spread between the toes, tender as the fiber of a lotus or a flower, with his ankle bones concealed and wheels in the middle of the soles. How can they walk on the hard ground of the jungle? His powerful body is accustomed to sitting or lying on the palace roof and has been adorned with priceless clothes, aloes, and sandalwood. How will it fare in the forest in the heat, the cold, and the rains?[63]

Fearing for his son's safety and still hoping to dissuade him from his decision, Śuddhodana sent messengers to beg Siddhārtha to return, but they were all unsuccessful; to the king's frustration, most decided to follow his example. As Siddhārtha wandered from place to place, all who saw him marveled at his magnificent body and the dignity of his comportment: "perceiving his gravity and might and his glorious form surpassing that of all mankind, like [the god] who has taken the pillar vow and has the bull for his sign [Śiva], they were lost in amazement."[64] People who passed him on the road stopped and stared at this perfect specimen of manhood, and many followed after him. Women were particularly entranced by his appearance: "The gaze of the women . . . on the royal road—even though they were occupied with other affairs—was not satisfied with looking reverently on this human god."[65] The goddess of fortune of Rājagṛha was upset that a man whose physique proclaimed the destiny of a universal monarch, "with the circle of hair between his brows, with the long eyes, radiant body and hands beautifully webbed," was wearing a monk's robes and begging for alms.

This theme is repeated in all of the accounts of this part of Siddhārtha's life. Numerous people lecture him on the inappropriateness of a man so beautiful, well endowed, and physically gifted tossing away his royal inheritance for the life of a religious mendicant. Śreṇya, the lord of Magadha, exhorted him: "You should not let these two strong arms, suited for drawing a bow, lie useless. . . . [T]hey are capable of conquering the three realms, how much more this earth?"[66] The *Extensive Sport* recounts a similar incident in which the king of Magadha tries to tempt Siddhārtha with an offer to share the king's lands, by citing the notion that that religious pursuits are best postponed until later in life: "You are in the flower of your youth! Your complexion is brilliant; you are clearly robust. Accept from me abundant riches and women. Stay here in my kingdom and enjoy yourself!"[67]

Despite such entreaties, the young ascetic persisted in his new career path. He informed the king that he regarded the body as unstable and without essence, a mass of suffering that is constantly oozing foul substances, and he concluded: "O king, I no longer have any impulse of desire. I abandoned all that is desirable and gave up thousands of beautiful women. Finding no joy in the things of the world, I renounced them all to gain supreme awakening, the greatest happiness."[68]

Sampling Training Options

Siddhārtha decided that the path to liberation requires meditation training, and so he began to search for a teacher. Other religious seekers told him about a great master named Ārāḍa Kālama, whom Siddhārtha then traveled to see. As he approached Ārāḍa's hermitage, the old sage exclaimed, "look at the man who approaches! How beautiful he is!" His disciples replied, "we see him; he is indeed wonderful to behold!"[69]

Siddhārtha followed Ārāḍa's instructions and soon attained an advanced meditative state, which is now referred to in Buddhist texts as the third "formless absorption" *(ārūpya-samāpatti).* When he emerged from this blissful concentration, however, Siddhārtha asked Ārāḍa whether it could lead to final liberation from cyclic existence, but the sage admitted that it could not. Deeply impressed that this young man had quickly mastered a practice that had taken the master years to attain, Ārāḍa offered to share leadership of his order with Siddhārtha, but the Bodhisattva declined because he wished to find the solution to the problem of suffering.

He next studied with Udraka Rāmaputra, who had attained an even more advanced meditative state, which later came to be referred to in Buddhist soteriology as the fourth formless absorption. Although it was superior to the previous level, it was still transitory and so could not fulfill Siddhārtha's quest.

At this point, he joined a group of ascetics who believed that the path to true happiness lies in severe asceticism and self-abnegation. By starving their bodies and subjecting themselves to harsh penances, these ascetics hoped to transcend all physicality and to attain a deathless state of bliss. In order to test their claim that austerities can lead to the ultimate state, Siddhārtha threw himself into this discipline: "In a variety of ways I persisted in the practice of tormenting and mortifying the body. Such was my asceticism."[70] According to the "Greater Lion's Roar Discourse," their practice involved a range of painful techniques, including sleeping on spikes and extended fasting. Siddhārtha stopped bathing, and dirt became caked on his body. He did not bother to brush it off, and due to his fasts—during which he lowered his food intake until he was eating one grain of rice per day—his body reached a state of extreme emaciation. His formerly lustrous hair fell out, his skin became discolored, and his ribs and spine stuck out prominently, with desiccated skin covering his bony frame.[71] The *Extensive Sport* provides a graphic description of his heroic attempts at self-mortification:

> For eight winter nights I oppressed and tortured my body. Sweat ran from my armpits and from my forehead and fell to the ground in shining drops so hot they evaporated like smoke. Like a strong man who grasps a weak man by the neck and overpowers him, so, monks, did I subdue my body with my mind.[72]

Despite his best efforts on this path, "by such conduct, by such practice, by such performance of austerities, I did not attain any superhuman states, any distinction in knowledge and vision worthy of the wise."[73] One day Siddhārtha fainted from weakness due to lack of food, and when he recovered he recognized the utter futility of severe asceticism. A young woman carrying a dish of sweet rice happened to be passing by at the time, and he accepted her offer of food. Eating heartily, his strength and vitality were restored, but his fellow ascetics were shocked by his apparent indulgence and concluded that he had fallen prey to weakness. They decided to leave him behind and travel elsewhere, but he cared nothing for their negative judgment, since he knew that their path led nowhere but pain, weakness, and premature death.

From Bodhisattva to Buddha

After this Siddhārtha traveled to the Seat of Awakening (Bodhimaṇḍa), located at modern-day Bodh Gaya in northern India, a place where, according to Buddhist tradition, countless buddhas had attained awakening in the past. The majesty of his approach to this sacred spot is described in the *Extensive Sport:* he walked "with the stride of a great man . . . with the gait of a lion, the gait of the king of geese, the gait of the king of elephants, the gait of Nārāyaṇa, the gait which does not touch the earth. . . . He moved with the stride that dominates Śakra, Brahmā, Maheśvara, and the Guardians of the World."[74]

Siddhārtha was given some grass by a passing grasscutter, which the Bodhisattva made into a cushion and placed under the branches of a tree that is referred to by Buddhists as the "Tree of Awakening" (Bodhi-vṛkṣa). Tradition holds that past buddhas also sat in the same spot on the eve of their final awakenings. According to some accounts, Siddhārtha then proceeded immediately to the meditation practices that would lead to his final attainment of buddhahood, conquest of suffering, elimination of the final vestiges of mental affliction, and the beginning of his career as the expositor of the eternal dharma that is realized by all awakened beings.

In several texts, however, an interesting subsidiary narrative is inserted: his conquest of Māra. Māra serves a function roughly equivalent to Satan in Christianity: his purpose in life is to lead beings to commit actions that will have negative consequences and result in continued suffering and repeated rebirths. Unlike Satan, who works to beguile humans to sin, Māra's tool is ignorance. For Buddhism, sin is a second-order problem and is the consequence of ignorance, and so if mental affliction is removed, one no longer engages in sinful activities.

Māra appears throughout Indian canons as the nemesis of the Buddhist monastic order, and monks and nuns who lapse commonly credit their actions to his malign influence. He constantly works his wiles—particularly on those who seek liberation—and the appearance of a buddha is an unmitigated disaster for him because buddhas teach the dharma to others, many of whom then follow the path, escape from cyclic existence, and thus are forever freed from Māra's snares. Unlike Satan, however, Māra is regarded as a high-ranking god who attained his position as a result of past cultivation of positive karma. As a result, he was reborn as a deity in the Desire Realm, and his attempts to lure beings into actions motivated by ignorance are the result of a misguided desire to prevent his constituency from being depleted.[75]

Māra first tried a direct approach on Siddhārtha: the tempter's hordes of terrifying demons emitted a roar that shook the world and converged on the lone ascetic sitting unprotected beneath the Tree of Awakening, but the Bodhisattva exerted his supernatural power to prevent them from reaching him. The demons then hurled rocks and spears at him, but he calmly turned them into flowers that fell harmlessly at his feet. Frustrated and enraged, Māra created a mighty storm with torrential rain and large hailstones, but the king of the *nāgas* (beings with the bodies of snakes and human heads) rose up behind Siddhārtha, spread his hood, and created a shelter. The *Deeds of the Buddha* reports that during the assault the Bodhisattva, "like a lion seated among cows, was not frightened, nor was he at all perturbed."[76]

Siddhārtha then informed Māra that he had no chance of prevailing because during the course of countless past lives the Bodhisattva had accumulated vast stores of merit, which gave him unconquerable power. He asserted that he gave his life for others more times than could be recounted and had willingly cut off his hands, feet and head for those who wished him to do so, that he had gouged out his eyes and had freely donated all his possessions. Because of his mighty deeds, he had become "like a lion, without concern or fear, terror or weakness, without uncertainty, without confusion, without agitation, without the dread that makes the hair stand on end."[77] The passage also links his beautiful body to the accumulated merit of his practice.

Opting for another tactic, Māra asserted that Siddhārtha had no right to inhabit the piece of earth under the tree. As a homeless world renouncer, Siddhārtha owned nothing, and so Māra ordered him to leave. As a high-ranking deity of the Desire Realm, Māra has a certain claim to dominion. In response, the Bodhisattva extended his right hand toward the earth, which bore witness to the appropriateness of his residence there by generating a tremor.

Māra then played a stronger card. In the Desire Realm, the predominant mental affliction is desire, and in Indian Buddhist texts sexual lust is the essence of the afflictive emotions that motivate beings to wallow in actions that lead to negative karma and repeated rebirths. Māra hoped to halt the Bodhisattva's progress toward buddhahood by enticing him with the sensual attractions of his daughters, who are said to surpass all other females in beauty and seductiveness. Their names are given as Craving (Tṛṣṇā), Discontent (Aratī), and Passion (Rāgā), indicating their respective specialties, and they are credited with possessing thirty-two feminine wiles that drive men to blazing passion.[78]

Observing correctly that "men's tastes are diverse," Māra's daughters then proceeded to create beautiful women of various types. Some were young, others middle-aged, still others old. Some were virgins, and others had given birth once, twice, or more. They also danced seductively in front of the serene ascetic, hoping to appeal to the natural desires of human males. All these women's blandishments fell on lustless eyes, however, causing the seductresses to lament:

> if we had assailed any ascetic or brahman who was not devoid of lust with such tactics, either his heart would have burst or he would have vomited hot blood from his mouth, or he would have gone insane or become mentally deranged; or else he would have dried up and withered away and become shriveled.[79]

The Buddha described himself as "tranquil in body, in mind well liberated, not generating [desires], mindful, homeless, knowing dharma, meditating free from thoughts, not agitated, or wavering, or tense."[80] He calmly told Māra's daughters that he had completely rid his thoughts of even the slightest hint of desire, that nothing in the world held any interest for him, and that he perceived their superficially enticing bodies as bags of filth, containing foul substances and covered with a membrane of skin.[81] He added that their actions were as futile as attempting to dig through a mountain with one's fingernails or chewing iron with one's teeth. On hearing this, they acknowledged defeat and remarked that any normal man "would, on seeing us in all our beauty, be overcome and fall down in a faint. The warm blood would be drained from his face, and he might die from his affliction or lose his mind. But [Siddhārtha], being an arhat and rid of passion, aversion, and delusion, has proved superior."[82]

Talking Trash and Defeating Demons

The *Extensive Sport* presents an interesting variant on the Māra story. In this account, the incipient Buddha's power is so great that the Evil One (Pāpīyān) is completely unaware that the Bodhisattva is in Bodh Gaya preparing for his final assault on the summit of buddhahood. The story even indicates that Siddhārtha really became awakened in the distant past and that his activities were merely a display for the benefit of human and divine audiences, who by observing his performance would be provided a salutary example of the path to liberation.

Māra, sitting in his palace and plotting his evil designs to ensnare hapless sentient beings, had no idea that his greatest fears were about to be realized and that a buddha would soon emerge in northern India and subsequently proclaim the dharma. Siddhārtha reflected: "when he is conquered, all the gods of the Desire Realm and all others will be subdued as well. Moreover, among Māra's entourage there are deities of his realm who have previously generated virtuous roots. When these deities have seen how the lion sports, they will then turn their thoughts toward perfect and complete awakening."[83] He then dragged Māra against his will to Bodh Gaya, where Siddhārtha proceeded to talk trash to him in a scene that reads much like a playground bully threatening a physically weaker opponent:

> The Bodhisattva will overcome you, in the same way as a conqueror defeats an enemy army. Today, evil one, the Bodhisattva will seize you, in the same way as a powerful wrestler grips a weakling. . . . Today, evil one, the Bodhisattva will frighten you, in the same way that a lion terrifies a jackal. . . . Today, evil one, the Bodhisattva will bring you to ruin, in the same way a great king destroys a hostile city.[84]

The conclusion of all these accounts is a complete rout of Māra and his minions. Utterly humiliated, the hapless demon fled the scene with his fearsome hordes and seductive daughters. He returned to his palace to lick his wounds and plot future stratagems to undermine the Buddha and the members of the order the latter would soon found.

Inception of the Buddha's Mission

After Māra and his hosts were overcome, Siddhārtha entered into progressively more sublime meditative states, gradually removing the final vestiges of ignorance and comprehending the true nature of reality. At dawn of the following morning, he attained buddhahood. For the next several days, he remained in a profound, blissful state of meditative equipoise, basking in the serene joy of his accomplishment. He reflected that what he had realized was sublime, subtle, and difficult to comprehend and at first thought to pass into nirvana without teaching his wisdom to others. Fearing that he might do so and that the world would thus lose the rare opportunity to learn from a buddha, Śakra and Brahmā approached the Buddha and begged him to share his insight with others. Śakra pointed out that while the vast majority of people are ignorant and blinded by passion, some had only a small amount of obscuration and would quickly break through their cognitive barriers if only they could see and hear him. Brahmā then declared that those who are fortunate enough to encounter a buddha should exhort him to teach others with the following words: "Rise up O hero, victor in battle! O caravan leader, free from debts, wander in the world! Teach the dharma, O Blessed One; there will be some who will understand!"[85]

The Buddha acknowledged the validity of these words and surveyed the world for suitable students. He first considered his former teachers Ārāḍa and Udraka, but his supernatural insight revealed that they had both recently died. He then saw that his five former ascetic companions were currently residing in Sarnath, a small town near Varanasi, and he decided that they would be the beneficiaries of his first sermon. This is referred to in Buddhist tradition as the "Discourse Turning the Wheel of Doctrine" because with it the Buddha initiated his teaching career, which would span more than forty years: "Then the sage, whose eye was like a bull's, whose gait was like a rutting elephant's, desired to go to the land of Kāśi in order to convert the world and, turning his entire body like an elephant, he fixed his unblinking eyes on the Tree of Awakening."[86]

The Buddha then proceeded toward Sarnath, but as he approached the five ascetics they agreed not to rise and greet him because he had fallen from the true way and become "lax" and a "glutton."[87] As he came nearer, however, they were overwhelmed by his physical beauty and the aura of wisdom he radiated. They became increasingly ill at ease and felt like caged birds because "there is no person anywhere who, on seeing the Thus Gone One, would not arise from his seat. The closer the Thus Gone One came, the less the five were able to endure his splendor and majesty; they became agitated on their seats and, breaking their agreement, each stood up to honor him."[88]

They inquired about the change in his demeanor and remarked, "Venerable Gautama, your features are perfectly clear. Your complexion is perfectly pure."[89] They then proceeded to describe to him the effect of his physical presence on them and various features of his perfect physique, following which he delivered his first discourse. He taught them about the "middle way" *(madhyama-pratipad),* which avoids the extremes of hedonism and severe asceticism, and the four noble truths, which focus on the causes of suffering and the path to its eradication.

The "Greater Discourse to Assapura" describes the Buddha's teachings regarding moderation with regard to food: monks should not eat for amusement

The Buddha delivering his first sermon to the five ascetics in the Deer Park in Sarnath. Photograph by John Powers.

or for the sake of physical beauty but only for sustenance and continuation of the body, in order to alleviate discomfort, and to have enough energy to pursue religious goals.[90] Thus he tacitly acknowledged that restraint with respect to food consumption is a valid aspect of the path but his five former companions clearly carried this restraint to counterproductive extremes. One member of the group named Kauṇḍinya immediately grasped the purport of the Buddha's words and became an arhat. All of the others similarly experienced profound insights, and the Buddha initiated them as the first members of his monastic community.

For the next forty years, the Buddha traveled around northern India, teaching all who cared to listen. As his reputation spread, the curious, the envious, and seekers of truth all came to see him in order to ascertain the validity of his claims to buddhahood. His beautiful body played a key role in assuaging the doubts of skeptics. Fools may parrot words of wisdom, but only a great man can back them up with the proof of his attainments provided by his unique physiognomy.

The Short Journey Home

According to most accounts, the Buddha never strayed very far from his place of birth, and his father regularly sent spies to check on him. A number of interesting stories recount the Buddha's triumphant return to Kapilavastu after attaining awakening; these stories also note the responses of his relatives and the townspeople.

One day Śuddhodana, unaware that his son was coming, looked out from his palace and saw some of the Buddha's monastic followers and became distressed at their unkempt and famished appearance. He lamented that his beautiful son had forsaken his royal heritage and the comforts it afforded to join the company of such mendicants. Reading his mind from afar, the Buddha sent one of his monks ahead and ordered him to perform a magical display for the king. Witnessing the monk's miraculous powers, Śuddhodana experienced a change of heart and decided to travel from the city to visit his son.

As he approached, the Buddha reflected that the Śākyas were a proud and arrogant clan and would be offended if he were to remain sitting rather than rising to greet their king, but such a display would undermine his claim to be superior to all human monarchs and even the gods. As a solution, he rose up into the air and strode toward his astonished father, following which he too put on a magic show. Remaining at the height of a tree, he caused the lower part of his body to erupt in flames, while jets of water poured from the upper half. He then transformed into a bull "with a quivering hump"; the bull's form next disappeared, and he manifested in various places. All who saw this performance were overwhelmed by the Buddha's beautiful physique and supernatural abilities. He then caused one of the water jets to spray Prajāpatī's eyes, and she thus regained her sight.[91]

The *Deeds of the Buddha* again dwells on how he affected women. It reports that they were overcome by his beauty and lamented his career choice: "His beautiful body is transformed by the shaving of his head and wearing cast-off garments, but he is still covered in the color of gold [radiating] from his body." They concluded that he "should be humbling enemy princes" and "be gazed at by hordes of women."[92]

The Buddha's presence also physically affected his son, Rāhula, whom he had never seen. Yaśodharā, understandably upset at having been abandoned, ordered that no one tell the prince that the Buddha was his father, but as the Buddha strode into the town his shadow fell across Rāhula, causing "the hairs to stand on end on his whole body, his limbs to perspire, and his whole frame to rejoice."[93] He inquired about the identity of this extraordinary man and asked whether the Buddha might be his long-lost father. Rāhula felt a deep physical connection and thought that they must be related in some way, his physical reaction being blood responding to blood. Reluctantly, Yaśodharā—who had previously told her son that his father was in the north and had been unable to return due to political strife—replied:

> My son, the one whom you see there in golden beauty, rising among his noble company like a golden elephant, is your father. He, my son, whom you see there in golden beauty, like a fanged and powerful lion surveying all around him, is your father. He, my son, whom you see there in golden beauty, surrounded by his noble company, like a bull among the herd, is your father.[94]

To his mother's profound chagrin, Rāhula then grabbed a corner of the Buddha's robe and declared that he too wished to become a monk. In one version of this story, Yaśodharā, still seething over her abandonment, sends Rāhula to see the Buddha and instructs their son to ask his father for his royal inheritance, intending to shame the Buddha. In response, the unperturbed

Buddha complies by inducting him into the monastic order, causing Yaśodharā to become even angrier at him.

In another account Yaśodharā confronts her wayward husband and lists her grievances:

> "[You ask], Why do I cry? I am angry because my husband has not even greeted me. We were married for only seven years and he abandoned me. I was still young. It was not as though my Lord was leaving me in his old age. I felt very lonely." . . . [Then,] unfastening her hair, she dusted off his feet and fanned [them] back and forth, moving tenderly like the fronds of a banana tree. . . . Sobbing, she spoke to the [Buddha]. . . . "O my Lord, I pay my respects to you. I am unlucky and ashamed before you. . . . You abandoned me and your child without any compassion. In the old days I never considered myself unlucky. You never gave any indication that you would leave me alone for such a long time. Prince Rāhula was just born, but you left without any concern for me. You made your departure at midnight . . . [and] I was left deserted."[95]

In the *Great Matter* account, the announcement that the young prince has become a monk and will emulate his father in abandoning his kingdom causes the citizens to utter a loud wail of lamentation. Śuddhodana begins to weep, and Yaśodharā tries to dissuade her son, but he remains committed to his new path. As she had when her husband declared his intention to renounce the world, she questions Rāhula's toughness and points out that his entire life has been spent as a pampered prince living within the confines of an opulent palace, with servants attending to his every need. In the wilderness, he would be subjected to various terrifying things, such as the roars of lions, tigers, and jackals. He would be unable to sleep on the hard ground after lying on the softest pillows since he was an infant.

Rāhula replies that his father also lived in comfort in the palace and that he is confident that he too will become an exemplary ascetic. Śuddhodana then berates his son for taking his last hope for maintaining the royal lineage, and in an apparent recognition of the validity of familial sentiment, the Buddha promises that initiates would henceforth be required to obtain parental permission before being admitted to the order. He did not, however, relent in his decision to ordain Rāhula, because once a person has taken monastic vows before the Buddha these vows are binding for the remainder of his or her life. The Pāli canon reports that many of the Buddha's monastic followers were young men in the prime of life, much as Siddhārtha was, and one of the common complaints from the general public was that the Buddha's order took away their children, made wives into widows, and destroyed families.[96]

Can a Buddha Have Bad Karma?

In a number of places in the Pāli canon, there are reports that the Buddha, despite his exalted status, occasionally experienced pain or discomfort. These episodes are sometimes taken as proof of the notion that the Pāli Buddha was "only a man," but their significance has been debated by a number of commentators. Some assert that any apparent travails were merely for show and that the Buddha had completely transcended all pain. Others, however, accept the literal import of these passages and explain that even though he was the most exalted of beings, the Buddha still retained some residual negative karma from past lives or from his excessive indulgence in austerities.

He sometimes reported headaches, for example, and several commentaries contend that these were caused by his fasting. Fasting also led to digestive problems; the Buddha often complained of stomach pains, and he is said to have died of a disease that sounds similar to dysentery. Because of his physical ailments, he consulted Jīvaka, the physician of king Bimbisāra, who is said to have treated members of the Buddhist order for free.[97]

The "Thread of Past Actions" of the *Instructions* discusses ten incidents of vexation experienced by the Buddha and attributes them to past bad karma. Among these incidents are the following episodes from his previous lives and their subsequent effects in his current incarnation: (1) the Buddha murdered his brother in order to gain access to his brother's wealth, which leads in this life to his malicious cousin Devadatta throwing a boulder at him and slightly injuring the Buddha's foot (this is significant because in a number of places powerful beings threaten to harm him, but he assures them that no one, not even a god, can cause physical harm to a buddha); (2) he was happy to see a fish killed, and so in this incarnation he suffers a headache when Vidudabha kills his kinsmen; (3) he killed a rival wrestler by breaking his spine, and so he now often experiences backaches; and (4) he once as a doctor knowingly gave the wrong medicine to the son of a good man, which leads to his subsequent stomach troubles.[98]

For the Transcendentists and the Mahāyānists, however, the notion that the most exalted of beings could possibly suffer in any way was simply absurd. Even gods enjoy long lifespans free from the slightest discomfort as a result of their practice of past virtue, which is utterly inferior to that of a buddha. Thus any reports of physical ailments must be viewed as a display on the Buddha's part intended to impart a salutary lesson to his followers, who should conclude that if even the Buddha's perfect body can experience pain there is no place within cyclic existence that is entirely free from suffering.

The *Great Matter* asserts that every aspect of his life was a display and that every action was transcendental, including walking, standing, sitting, and lying down. His body was also supramundane, and the way a buddha wears his robes, eats, and even defecates provides lessons for his followers. Reports that Śākyamuni washed his feet and performed other conventional daily functions are true, but he only did so in conformity with accepted custom, even though no dirt ever settled on the Buddha's body and he never required any sort of maintenance. He also ate food even though he had no need of sustenance in order that others could make merit. Even wearing clothes was a concession to worldly attitudes; if he were naked, he would appear fully clothed to others. He did not really age, but he did alter his appearance in accordance with expectations in order to demonstrate the debilitating effects of time. A buddha's body is never created through vulgar sexual intercourse, but he can point to his parents and produce a son in order to meet the world's expectations for a fully functioning virile man.[99] According to the *Extensive Sport,* "that most exalted of beings is immutable. His body is as solid as diamond and unshakeable. He has the power of Nārāyaṇa. Strength, energy, and gravity are his."[100]

The Final Days of the Ultimate Man

The Buddha's youth and vitality eventually faded, as they do with all people. In his later years, the Buddha complained of being "vexed" by constant pain in his back.[101] He told Ānanda that this discomfort was relieved only when he entered advanced meditative states but that it returned when he left them. He said that his body was like an old cart that is held together only by cords and hinted that the time of his final departure was near.[102] He indicated that if he wished he could prolong his life for a century or more, but Ānanda failed to pick up on the nuances of this statement. Had Ānanda requested that the Buddha remain, he would have done so, but because Ānanda did not understand the subtext, the Buddha then declared that he would pass into nirvana in three months' time.[103]

Despite his growing infirmity, the Buddha endured his pains with complete equanimity: at one point his foot was cut by a stone splinter, and "severe pains assailed the Blessed One—bodily feelings that were painful, racking, sharp, piercing, harrowing, disagreeable. But the Blessed One endured them, mindful and clearly comprehending, without becoming distressed."[104] He then lay down on his right side in the "lion posture,"[105] and several deities praised his composure in the face of physical torment: "the ascetic Gotama is indeed a *nāga,* sir! . . . [T]he ascetic Gotama is indeed a lion, sir! . . . [T]he ascetic Gotama is indeed a thoroughbred stallion *(ājānīya),* sir! . . . a bull of a man," who endured pain heroically.[106]

In a scene reminiscent of his first journey from the palace as a youth, when the sad condition of the feeble old man had first prompted prince Siddhārtha to recognize the sufferings endemic to the worldly life, on one occasion during this period his faithful attendant Ānanda saw the Buddha sitting in the sun warming himself. He massaged his teacher's limbs in order to assuage his pain and compared him with the transcendently beautiful youth he had been. The Buddha's complexion was "no longer clear and bright, his limbs were all flaccid and wrinkled, his body stooped, and some change was seen in his faculties—in the eye faculty, the ear faculty, the nose faculty, the tongue faculty, the body faculty."[107] The Buddha ruefully agreed with this assessment and commented that in youth one is always subject to aging, in health to illness, and in life to death.

Following his last meal with the layman Cunda, the Buddha experienced intense abdominal distress, but then Ānanda noted a recovery and remarked that his body appeared especially radiant. In response, the Buddha informed him that there are two momentous occasions when this occurs: on the night of a buddha's awakening and when he is about to attain final nirvana. He then informed Cunda that the layman had prepared an excellent meal and that because of the merit Cunda would receive from this offering in future lives he would be blessed with physical beauty.

In the Sanskrit version of the story, the Buddha also bared his body for the benefit of his followers so that they could witness his perfect form one more time:

> Then the Blessed One took off his upper robe and baring his body said: "Monks, gaze now upon the body of the Thus Gone One! Examine the body of the Thus Gone One! For the sight of a completely awakened

buddha is as rare an event as the blossoming of the *udumbara* tree."[108] The Buddha then provided instructions regarding disposition of his remains: his corpse should be handled like that of a universal monarch and wrapped in linen, placed in an iron vat filled with oil, and then cremated. The relics left over should be placed in a reliquary mound *(stūpa)* at a crossroads so that in the future people might venerate them and gain merit.[109]

Imaging Perfection

After the Buddha's passing, his followers faced the problems common to all religious movements with charismatic founders. The Buddha had been the driving force of the community, and although there were a number of prominent monks renowned for their wisdom, meditative attainments, and magical powers (as well as their beautiful bodies and masculine virility), none could approach the Buddha's impact on others. He refused to nominate a successor, instead urging his followers to adopt a roughly democratic system in which issues would be decided by meetings of an entire monastic community.

As we have seen, Buddhist writers emphasized the beauty of the Buddha's physique and its perceptual impact on those who saw him. Simply viewing the Buddha was often enough to trigger a conversion experience and instill lifelong devotion, but none of the surviving monks possessed his beauty or the physical characteristics of a great man.[110] Following his passing, the dharma thus had to be spread by the force of persuasion rather than through charisma and the Buddha's physical impact. The visual aspects of conversion remained important for Indian Buddhists in later times, however, and artists soon began to create images to represent Buddhist themes, to inspire the faithful, and to express truths that once had been displayed on the body of the founder but now required creative minds that could suggest the inexpressible through art.

For several centuries after his death, artists avoided depicting the body of the Buddha. He was commonly alluded to in early monuments—for example, Sāñchī—by such symbols as a *stūpa,* an empty throne, the Tree of Awakening, or footprints containing a wheel pattern. Albert Foucher coined the term "aniconism" to characterize this apparent reticence to represent physical perfection in plastic art, but Susan Huntington has challenged this notion, claiming that the images in which the Buddha is represented by a symbol indicate a cultic context, that because the Buddha was no longer physically present in public ceremonies his absence was depicted by an empty space marked by a sign of his previous residence there.[111] Both theories are still debated among art historians, but in either case several centuries had elapsed since the Buddha's passing before artists ventured to represent his resplendent body.

The Chinese pilgrim Faxian recorded a story he heard during his travels in India of a sandalwood statue of the Buddha that was fashioned during his lifetime for King Prasenajit of Kosala. Upon hearing that the Buddha planned to spend several months visiting his mother in the Heaven of the Thirty-Three, Prasenajit lamented that the Blessed One's followers would be deprived of his physical presence. In response, the Buddha ordered that a statue be carved, and it turned out to be a perfect image of his glorious body, inspiring wonder

Frieze from Sāñcī representing the Buddha with the Tree of Awakening. Photograph by John Powers.

in all who viewed it. When he returned from his heavenly sojourn, the statue rose to greet him, but the Buddha ordered it to sit down (because it is inappropriate even for an image of a buddha to enact physical attitudes of humility). Faxian states that this was the first physical representation of the Buddha and that all subsequent ones were copies of it.[112]

The earliest images of the Buddha probably appeared around the first century CE during the reign of King Kaniṣka of the Kuṣaṇa empire. The Kuṣaṇas came from central Asia and conquered a substantial territory in northern areas of the subcontinent. Their two capitals of Mathurā in north-central India and Gandhāra in modern-day Afghanistan became major centers for the development of Buddhist art. The first images of buddhas and bodhisattvas were created there around the first century CE. One of the earliest datable representations of the Buddha as a human figure is on a gold coin dating from Kaniṣka's reign. The figure's features are indistinct, but the coin depicts him with unusually long arms and a proportionate physique, in accordance with scriptural descriptions.

These early artists obviously faced significant difficulties in fashioning the Buddha as represented in Buddhist texts.[113] He was portrayed as the epitome of male beauty, but any attempt to create a figure endowed with the physical characteristics of a great man would probably end up looking like a freak rather than an inspiring representation of human perfection.

As noted previously, most artists chose to include only a small sampling of the physical characteristics and adopted styles of masculinity that reflected cultural norms. Images produced in Gandhāra are notable for their incorporation of motifs from Greek sculpture. A number of small Bactrian kingdoms had been established in the Gandhāra region following the invasions of Alexander's armies from 327 to 325 BCE, and these kingdoms became conduits for the importation of European culture. Many of the Gandhāran buddhas and bodhisattvas have European features; are adorned with the kind of wavy hair, moustaches, and ornamentations that are typical of Greek and Roman art; and are often depicted clothed in the same togas that were used in Greco-Roman sculptures of the period.

Mathurān artists, however, adopted a more Indian style and eschewed the sharp features and foreign clothing of the Gandhāran figures. Like the Gandhāran sculptures, Mathurān buddhas often have muscular frames and powerful-looking V-shaped torsos, but they wear Indian dress and have rounded facial features.

As Buddhist art developed during the reign of the Guptas (between the fourth and fifth centuries CE), the muscular figures of the Central Asian Kuṣaṇa artists were abandoned in favor of physiques that resonated with Indian notions of male beauty. Many art historians consider the Gupta period to be the golden age of Indian Buddhist art, and a number of images from this time have survived intact. The preferred style in these images is a graceful, gently curved figure, with no sharp features; a rounded face and limbs, with no bulging muscles; a straight or almost straight torso; long arms; a lump on the cranium

Seated Buddha from Mathurā (ca. second century), which depicts several of the physical characteristics of a great man, including *cakras* on the feet, the *uṣṇīṣa,* and the *ūrṇā.* Red sandstone, 129.5 (h) × 101.5 (w) × 30.5 (d) cm. National Gallery of Australia, Canberra. Purchased with the generous assistance of Roslyn Packer, Order of Australia, 2007. Reproduced by permission.

surmounted by short curls;[114] and often a slight midriff bulge (see Figure on page 4 in the first chapter of this book). These characteristics reflect societal notions of the ideal physique of a warrior, who is slender and lithe, strong but not muscle-bound. The warrior also develops his archery skills rather than bludgeoning his opponents with his fists; archery requires both skill and strength and allows men to dispatch their opponents from a distance rather than in the messy confrontations of hand-to-hand combat.

In keeping with these notions, the Buddha was generally shown as slender, and a heavy lower lip and half-closed eyes were also common. His slight smile and relaxed posture indicate the ease with which he bears his immense physical strength without needing to flex his muscles in order to impress others, as well as his cultivation of inner peace and equanimity. This style was also imported to other countries in the region after they adopted Buddhism and can still be seen in images produced today in Southeast Asia.

During the Pāla period (760–1142 CE), the Buddha image continued to develop, and new motifs were explored. Pāla Buddhas are commonly depicted in monks' robes and, as befits a world renouncer, generally do not wear adornments (except in representations of his early life as a prince). The Buddha often has a slightly accentuated posture, with his hip thrust to the right. Susan and John Huntington note an "overall simplicity of composition" and grace in these depictions.[115] One of the most popular motifs of this time is the "Defeat of Māra" (Māra-vijaya), in which the Buddha is shown sitting beneath the Tree of Awakening in the lotus position *(padmāsana),* often making the "earth-touching gesture" *(bhūmi-sparśa mudrā).*[116] The motif of kingship that pervades the Buddha's biography is often suggested by figures of Śākyamuni wearing crowns, diadems, or ornaments associated with Indian royalty. The "Headdress Bearer" (Mukuṭadhārin) motif, for example, represents his association with royalty, and the conceptual connections that his biographies make between buddhas and universal monarchs also appear to suggest a linkage between his attainment of awakening and a royal coronation. This is also adumbrated by his common depiction sitting atop a throne that has an elephant and two roaring lions at the sides.[117]

These motifs continued in later Indian Buddhist art, but other permutations were added, some reflecting Jean-Luc Marion's distinction between an image and an icon. Marion defines an icon as the visible form of the divine, as found in statues, paintings, and names. An idol is visible, and what makes it function as an idol is the act of gazing: "the idol thus acts as a mirror, not as a portrait: a mirror that reflects the gaze's image, or more exactly, the image of its aim and of the scope of that aim."[118] Like a mirror, it reflects back the gazer's ability to conceive the divine, but it also necessarily limits the unlimited godhead:

> In the idol, the divine actually comes into the visibility for which human gazes watch; but this advent is measured by what the scope of particular human eyes can support, by what each aim can require of visibility in order to admit itself fulfilled . . . that god whose space of manifestation is measured by what portion of it a gaze can bear.[119]

Like the absent Buddha of post-parinirvāṇa India, God is invisible, and so the idol limits the divine to what the gazer can imagine. The image reflects the worshipper's ability to visualize divinity; the deity "is figured in the idol only indirectly, reflected according to the experience of it that is fixed by the human authority."[120]

Icons, however, represent a different approach. Marion contends that an icon and an idol may be contained in the same object, but they serve different functions; they are "two modes of apprehension of the divine in visibility. Of apprehension, or also, no doubt, of reception."[121] An idol restrains the gaze, while an icon liberates it and opens the mind to imagination. An idol is created for worship of an external figure, while an icon represents potentialities in the gazer, which the act of gazing, followed by internalization, seeks to actualize: "the icon does not result from a vision but provokes one. The icon is not seen, but appears." The icon attempts to provide a visible focus for the divine reality, not in order to render the invisible visible, but so that the qualities of the invisible godhead might be reproduced in some fashion in the beholder:

> Thus the icon shows, strictly speaking, nothing, not even in the mode of the productive *Einbildung*. . . . The gaze can never rest or settle if it looks at an icon; it always must rebound upon the visible, in order to go back in it up the infinite stream of the invisible. In this sense, the icon makes visible only by giving rise to an infinite gaze.[122]

The icon leads the viewer beyond his or her ordinary ability to conceptualize. In the case of a Buddha image, it aids in contemplation of the supreme person, endowed with an infinity of good qualities (both physical and mental). More important, the gazer engages in this activity as part of a program of religious training designed to result in actualization of these qualities, either in the present life or in a future incarnation. The supernatural body of a buddha cannot adequately be represented visually, nor can his supreme meditative attainments. His cultivation of morality or sovereign power may be suggested by stylized hand gestures *(mudrā)* that represent some of the attributes assigned to him by Buddhist tradition, but because the perfection in the mind and body of a buddha transcends any possibility of comprehension by ordinary beings, each devotee necessarily approaches an image from a particular place on the continuum of the Buddhist path and relates to the Buddha from the perspective of the devotee's age, gender, class, historical situation, language, and imaginative capacities.

The Buddha's good qualities are infinite, and infinity cannot be represented visually. An image can only suggest his transcendence as a means of facilitating contemplation beyond the visual. It adumbrates his buddhahood, along with the person of the Buddha. For some worshippers, the cognitive attitude toward an image will be one of faith; they will view the Buddha as the ultimate man and generate merit through their veneration. Such people will generally conceive of the Buddha as a transcendent figure and will not imagine themselves one day occupying his position, but gazers engaged in active meditative practice will appropriate the Buddha image as a template for their own progress, and this template will serve as an aid for their spiritual development.

This approach became prominent with the development of Mahāyāna, which denigrated the arhat who only pursued individual liberation and did not integrate compassionate activity for the benefit of others into the religious path. Mahāyāna valorized the bodhisattva, who pursues buddhahood in order to benefit others, and many Mahāyāna texts portrayed this as the only valid path. Tantric Buddhism further developed this trend and created a plethora of images, symbols, and rituals designed to facilitate the internalization of buddhahood and to aid practitioners in imagining themselves as fully awakened beings. This approach was thought to facilitate rapid progress on the path because it allowed trainees to work at the goal of the path—the actualization of the body, speech, and mind of a buddha in one's own person—rather than merely subsidiary trainings such as morality, patience, and effort.

The Greatest Thing

In the quote that opens this chapter, Kant describes the theological imperative behind the creation of a concept of God who is perfect in all respects, who embodies the best of all imaginable qualities, and who deserves the most superlative epithets. A similar dynamic applied in the development of the Buddha's narrative. For a Buddhist believer, the Buddha by definition is a being who has reached the highest level of spiritual attainment, who has the best possible body and the greatest mind, whose abilities transcend those of all other beings, even the highest gods.

Because the Buddha has the form of a human man, he is constructed as the greatest of men, endowed with physical and mental capacities far beyond the comprehension of ordinary beings. As Kant implied in a phrase that was omitted in this opening quotation, however, attempts to assign maximal greatness face the problem that by conceiving the ultimate being as "completely determined with respect to all possible opposed predicates," the theologian (or buddhalogian) must contend with the issue of reconciling such conceptually opposed attributes as justice and mercy. If God is completely just, how can his justice ever be tempered by mercy? Similarly, if the Buddha has the best of all masculine qualities valued by the society of his time, how can he be both a contemplative, wise ascetic and a virile, fearsome warrior endowed with superhuman strength? And if the main point of his religious career is his attainment of awakening and subsequent mission to share it with other beings so that they might attain liberation themselves, why should martial skills and a likeness to bulls, stallions, and lions contribute to this?

The Buddha implicitly hints at this contrast in qualities in several places in both Pāli texts and Mahāyāna sūtras. He indicates that two very different concepts of manhood were valorized by his society and accepts both as admirable. One is the scholarly, religiously inclined brahman who memorizes and recites the Vedas and performs sacrifices for the benefit of the world,[123] and the other is the warrior and ruler *kṣatriya,* whose martial skills and leadership protect his country from enemies. He indicates in a number of places that he does not accept that all of those who inherit the title "brahman" through birth deserve it, but he does accept that men who fulfill the ideals of the priestly class are deserving of alms and respect and are sources of merit. Much of the popular image of the Buddha resonates with the notion of the ideal brahman, and when he defines normative brahmanhood, it appears that the authors are attempting to appropriate aspects of this image and imply that the Buddha possessed these characteristics (and as we have seen in a number of passages. sages represented as exemplary brahmans declare that the Buddha is the fulfillment of the notion of the ultimate man described in their sacred scriptures).

But the authors of these texts were clearly unwilling to leave the Buddha open to the charge that he was a physically weak, bloodless scholar-mystic whose life represented a flight from the virile pursuits of warriors. The authors also wanted a Buddha who had proven himself a stallion with a sexual appetite beyond the wildest dreams of ordinary men (as when he sexually satisfied his harem of tens of thousands of women) and who outshone the greatest warriors of his day in strength, speed, and fighting prowess. When he went into the forest to pursue the path to awakening, he did not abandon one ideal in favor of another; rather, he continued to embody both, and the numerous stories in which audiences remark on his strength, beauty, and overpowering physical presence attest to this.

This tension is reflected in the symbolism of the two Indian gods most often associated with the Buddha: Indra and Brahmā. They are prominent deities in the Vedas, and their depiction as often fawning devotees of the Buddha serves a polemical purpose. The writers who constructed the Buddha narrative wished to portray the gods of the mainstream religious tradition of their society as subordinate to their founder, and they also attempted to co-opt the lore of the brahmans by depicting the Buddha as the fulfillment of their sacred texts. According to several accounts of the Buddha's life, when he returned from the Heaven of the Thirty-Three the gods created three jeweled staircases. The Buddha in the middle was flanked by these two divine devotees as he descended to earth.

Brahmā is an obvious choice for narrative linkage because he is the father of brahmans and the guardian of the sacred Vedic lore. The figure of Indra associates the Buddha with the king of the gods and the paradigm of the Āryan warrior, who is always victorious in battle, mightiest of the gods, and slayer of their enemies.[124] The *Ṛg Veda* praises Indra's masculinity *(pauṃsya)* and relates it to ideal kingship: "As far as we know, no one surpasses Indra in terms of martial power. The gods together conferred manhood and resolve on him, as well as authority after authority. They cheer on your sovereignty."[125] Indra is impetuous and violent and revels in war and conquest, but he is also generous, particularly to his friends and associates.

Indra's propensity toward violence is an important part of his nature, and although it sometimes causes him to act rashly, if properly channeled, aggression can be a positive attribute of a warrior. It is also linked with masculinity: "O lord of men with an excellent mace, [come here] for great manhood, for great dominion, for masculinity, O warlord!"[126] "What act of masculinity is there that has not been performed by this one, by Indra?"[127] He is closely associated with bulls, which are common symbols of masculinity, virility, and violent strength, and his greatest deed is the slaying of the demon Vṛtra, an episode portrayed as an epic battle, with graphic descriptions of its intensity. For this and other reasons, Indra is "manly due to his resolve and acts of masculinity."[128]

Every society produces and socializes the kinds of bodies it values. Ancient Āryan society conceived warrior bodies as the ideal—bodies developed by courageous, even foolhardy men who willingly rushed into battle against great odds, who slew their enemies without compunction and stole their cattle, and who then distributed the spoils among members of the warriors' own clans. By the Buddha's time, the emphasis had shifted: there was still a need for brave, strong warriors and rulers, but the society appears to have been more stable and less violent than in Vedic times. The two dominant paradigms that appear in literature of the time are the brahman—who is scholarly, gentle, and learned—and the *ksatriya,* adept in the martial arts and trained for battle but who tempers this with learning and self-control. Unlike Indra, the paradigmatic Āryan warrior, who is impetuous and always engaged in warfare, the ideal *ksatriyas* of the Buddha's time were well suited to violence when needed, but they could also employ diplomacy and strategy, and they avoided unnecessary conflict.

Masculinity studies have highlighted a range of ideals from various societies, and sometimes very different norms can operate at the same time. Thus Jewish communities often view the ideal man as a scholar, who deeply penetrates the nuances of the Torah and Talmud, but this archetype is often criticized from the perspective of those who valorize more vigorous notions of manhood—the soldier, athlete, and others characterized by strength and physical prowess. For ordinary men, it is difficult to apply oneself successfully to such contrasting ideals, but as a literary figure, Buddha was constructed as a man who was able to do so successfully and whose entire life demonstrated his complete and effortless mastery of all possible desirable masculine traits. However, as with the problems that arise by crediting God with perfect justice and infinite mercy, the writers of the Buddha story faced conceptual slippage when creating a character who pursued a religious career involving long periods of time sitting in one spot while immersed in meditation, whose life was a largely sedentary one of teaching, with no mention of any physical exercise or regimens to maintain his strength, but who also had to be the embodiment of a mighty warrior with a perfect body.

This chapter has highlighted portions of the narrative in which such qualities appear, and some readers might well accuse me of neglecting the scholarly Buddha, the religious teacher renowned for wisdom, patience, compassion, and communication skills. The reason for this is straightforward: that Buddha is already well known and is the subject of virtually every study to date of his life and message. What has been overlooked is the manly Buddha, who wins converts with his beautiful body, who defeats warriors in martial contests, and who excites lust in women. I have followed the general chronology of the standard biographies of the Buddha produced in India, highlighting tropes of masculinity. Every one of the texts that recount the Buddha story incorporates discourses of masculinity. The tropes highlighted in this chapter could be multiplied many times over, and the reason for drawing them from a variety of texts is not to disguise their scarcity but rather to demonstrate how widespread and pervasive they are in literature relating to the figure of the Buddha and his life story. Every account of the Buddha's biography produced in India of which I am aware devotes significant attention to establishing his paradigmatic masculinity.

The story recounted in this chapter is a cultural artifact of a particular time and place. No doubt many contemporary readers will find some aspects of the portrayal of women offensive, and the Buddha's callous treatment of his loving wife also sounds cruel and selfish in parts, but before condemning the Buddha as a misogynist and a cad, it should be remembered that there is no reason to conclude that the historical figure referred to as Buddha by his followers actually did any of these things. No details of his life story have anything resembling the surety of historical events attested by contemporaneous court records, histories, or inscriptions. Rather, this narrative is the creation of authors who lived long after his decease, who created a character that reflected cultural values and whose actions accorded with accepted norms. Even so, some of these narratives required often tortured rationalization or explanation. We cannot legitimately condemn the historical Buddha for the moral lapses (from an early twenty-first century perspective) of the literary character Buddha.

3

Sex and the Single Monk

A man without children is like a solitary tree that produces no shade, which has no branches, which bears no fruit. . . . He has led a purposeless life. . . . The man with numerous children . . . is praised as being auspicious, worthy of praise, blessed, virile, and the source of many genealogical branches.

—Caraka the Physician, *The Caraka Saṃhitā*

Seductions of Homeless Men

Once upon a time in India, a homeless man dressed in garments made from cast-off rags took an afternoon nap beneath a tree. As he dreamed, he developed an erection. A group of six women passing by noticed his condition and, naturally, decided to have sex with him. One by one, they mounted him and took their pleasure, and when the last was finished they continued on their way, praising him as "a bull of a man."[1]

The homeless man was a Buddhist monk, forbidden by his religious vows from engaging in any sexual act. Some of his monastic companions noticed a stain on his robe and reported him to the Buddha. Through his supernatural powers of perception, the Buddha ascertained what had happened and absolved the monk of any wrongdoing because he had not initiated the intercourse, had not actively participated, had somehow remained asleep while six women vigorously violated him, and did not enjoy it. Although he decided that the monk was blameless, the Buddha cautioned his monastic followers to take their naps indoors whenever possible and to bar the door in order to prevent lustful women from breaking in and taking advantage of them in their sleep.

If we examine this scenario, a number of anomalies appear, and the description of the episode sounds implausible in several aspects. First, the monks of the early Buddhist order were wandering mendicants *(bhikṣu)* who dressed in robes made from cast-off material (ideally found in cemeteries and cremation grounds), lived outdoors, bathed infrequently, and only owned meager possessions. Several of those who were sexually accosted by women are described as being elderly or middle-aged, and they engaged in meditative practices designed to eliminate sensual desire. The monk in this story would have been long out of practice, an unwilling sex partner if he were awake, and because he had remained inert during the encounter would have contributed little to the experience of the women who had violated him. The women are depicted as young, vigorous, and attractive and so could presumably have found enthusiastic partners to fulfill their sexual desires—men who would have been younger and fitter, who had bathed and anointed themselves with pleasing scents and oils.

If the discussions of monastic sexuality in the *Discourses (Sutta)* and *Monastic Discipline (Vinaya)* of the Pāli canon are to be believed, however, the Buddha's followers were regularly beset by unwanted sexual advances from young, attractive, and lustful women. The opening sections of the *Monastic Discipline* contain numerous episodes of such advances, many of which were successfully resisted by the monks, while other men of weak resolve succumbed. The monks are generally depicted as manly and as having beautiful bodies. Everywhere they go, women are attracted to them, and the monks must remain constantly on guard lest they commit an infraction of their discipline.

In one variation on this story, an elderly monk sleeps in the Jātiyā Grove at Bhaddiya, and his limbs are stiff with pain. A woman mounts him and departs after taking her pleasure,[2] but like the monk above he managed to remain asleep throughout the encounter. When the incident was reported to the Buddha, he said, "Monks, this is a perfected man; there is no offense for this monk."[3] Another monk who was sleeping in a forest near Sāvatthī, however, consented after waking up to find that a cowherdess was actively violating him. The Buddha declared this an expulsionary offense.[4]

Similar stories depict monks being sexually accosted by a female goatherd, a woman gathering firewood, and a woman gathering cow dung.[5] All come upon sleeping monks and decide to have sex with them. In one variation, a monk is violated by a young woman in a forest near Vaiśalī. He wakes up to see her standing over him and laughing. When he realizes that she has raped him, he feels remorse, but the Buddha absolves him because he did not consent. Another monk wakes up in the middle of such an encounter and throws the woman off him; he too is absolved.[6] The *Monastic Discipline* recounts the story of an unfortunate monk who resists his former wife's sexual advances, but she forces herself on him anyway. His demeanor makes her realize that he will never consent to sex, but because he is old and feeble she is able to push him to the ground and rape him: "she immediately fell on him and performed a sexual act as much as she desired." The monk was a nonreturner *(anāgamin)* who had eliminated all passion and was destined for nirvana, and so he did not enjoy the experience (the text does not explain how he managed to develop the erection that made the rape possible).[7]

A recurring element in these stories and the judgments attached to them is volition. Those who initiate a sexual action, or who first resist but later agree, are considered guilty. Only those monks who resist at all junctures of the encounter are blameless, as are those who are insane or otherwise mentally impaired at the time. Similarly, sexual thoughts while sleeping may indicate a lustful mind, but they are not subject to censure. The *Monastic Discipline* reports several stories of monks who experienced erotic dreams, such as one unnamed man who dreamed he had sex with his former wife. When he reports it to Upāli, the master of the monastic code, the monk is absolved.[8] Another monk, described as "thoughtless and careless," had a wet dream and became remorseful when he awoke. The Buddha declared that seminal emissions while asleep do not constitute an offense. Only conscious and deliberate violations of the rule of chastity merit censure.[9]

Monks Behaving Badly: The Story of Sudinna

According to the *Monastic Discipline,* when the monastic community was first founded, all the monks were advanced practitioners, and so no rules and regulations were needed. When Śāriputra approached the Buddha to promulgate a code of conduct, the latter responded that such a code was unnecessary and that as long as the order consisted of exemplary monks, their comportment would remain blameless. Any imposition of rules would only confuse them and the lay community.[10] Buddhaghosa explains that if the Buddha were to dictate regulations when there were no depravities in the community, people would think that the Blessed One had not properly discriminated the capacities of his followers. Buddhaghosa compares the Buddha to a skillful physician who waits until the correct time to lance an ulcer. If he cuts too soon, it will cause great pain and spread the infection. Moreover, the Buddha's disciples might have thought him dim-witted if he began setting down laws when no one was even close to violating monastic norms.[11]

As more people took ordination, however, this balance within the monastic community began to change, and as transgressions of the still-uncodified expectations of monastic conduct occurred, offenders were reported to the Buddha, who promulgated appropriate regulations, often including possible permutations of a particular misdeed that might occur in the future. The first serious violation of the basic rule enjoining sexual abstinence is credited to Sudinna, depicted as an earnest and committed monk who left his wife and wealthy family to join the *saṃgha.*

Sudinna had failed to impregnate his wife before renouncing the world, and his parents feared that unless an heir were produced the government would take the family fortune when they passed away and their lineage would disappear. They conceived a plan in which his former wife would seduce him and become pregnant. They hoped that the experience would convince their son to leave the monastic life and return to them, but they were prepared to be satisfied with just a grandson. One day Sudinna approached his former home seeking alms, and his parents instructed his wife to put on her best ornaments, "adorned with which you were dear to our son and beloved by him." When Sudinna arrived, his father showed him the vast stores of wealth that could be his if he turned his back on the order, but he replied that he had no interest in money and was fully content with the practice of celibacy *(brahma-carya).*

Sudinna's mother then told his wife that when she began to menstruate she should tell her, and when the time of maximum fertility arrived Sudinna's wife was decked out in the finest jewelry. The two women went to see Sudinna, who was meditating in the forest. His mother remonstrated with him, reminding him of the duties of a son to his parents, the most important of which is to ensure that the lineage continues. Sudinna reportedly had overcome any feelings of sexual desire, but he realized that unless he complied his parents and former spouse would continue to pester him, and this might disturb his practice. So he agreed, reckoning that he had had intercourse with his wife in the past, and so he would only be engaging in the same actions. His motivation was, he thought, unimpeachable, since he only wished to honor his parents' wishes. He then "took his former wife by the arm and walked into the Great Wood. Seeing no danger, since the path of training had not then been explicitly formulated, three times he induced his former wife to indulge in sexual intercourse with him. As a result she conceived." He was alone with her, and no other monks were aware of his deed, but earth deities of the area witnessed the scene and declared that the Buddhist order was shameless and immoral.[12]

Sudinna's wife subsequently gave birth to a son, and he returned to the community without telling anyone what had happened. As time passed and he reflected on the Buddha's numerous admonitions against sexual indulgence, he became "haggard, miserable, of a bad color, yellowish, the veins showing all over his body, melancholy, of sluggish mind, heartbroken, depressed, repentant, weighed down with guilt." His friends were concerned and inquired about the reason for his physical condition. He replied, "I have done an evil deed; I indulged in sexual intercourse with my former wife." They were shocked and replied that he should feel remorse for this violation of the discipline; they stated that the Buddha taught the dharma "for the sake of passionlessness, not for the sake of passion." After rebuking him, they reported his misdeed to the Buddha, who convened an assembly of monks and publicly castigated him:

> You stupid man! You have done what should not have been done! The impure act you have done is not in conformity with the doctrine. It is not proper for an ascetic. . . . Stupid man, it would be better for you if your penis had entered the mouth of a poisonous, terrifying snake than a woman. Stupid man, it would be better for you for your penis to enter a charcoal pit, burning, ablaze, afire, than a woman. . . . For that reason, stupid man, you should go to death, or suffering similar to death, and following the breakup of the body after death pass into a bad state, into hell![13]

The Buddha concluded his rebuke by promulgating a rule: "any monk who indulges in sexual intercourse is one who is defeated; he is no longer in communion." The general practice was to spare punishment of the first offender because there was no formal rule when the violation occurred, but because Sudinna's offense was so grave he was expelled from the monastic community, with no possibility of reinstatement.[14] This penalty is referred to as "defeat" *(pārājika),* because one who perpetrates such a transgression forever removes him- or herself from communion with the order and commits such a fundamental breach of conduct that no expiation is possible. The karma generated by this sort of action also influences future existences.

Buddhaghosa comments that Sudinna engaged in sexual intercourse only in the hope that his former wife and parents would be satisfied and would leave him alone to pursue his religious practice. He adds that Sudinna's transgression was manifested in his physical condition and elaborates on how Sudinna degenerated after the tryst.[15] Returning to the subject of monastic sex, Buddhaghosa states that when the Buddha told the assembly that it would be better for a monk to insert his penis into the mouth of a poisonous snake than into a vagina, the reason is that a snake might inflict a bite and inject venom, which would lead to death, but when a monk has sexual intercourse he will go to hell after he dies and will suffer excruciating torment for a long period of time.[16]

The Width of a Sesame Seed

After deciding to promulgate a rule following Sudinna's offense, the Buddha proceeded to define exactly what constitutes sexual intercourse, stating that it "is truly not dharma; it is village dharma, low-caste dharma, lewdness, unclean,[17] secrecy after having come together as a couple. . . . Whenever the male organ is made to enter the female, the male member to enter the female, even for the width of the seed of the sesame plant, this is called sexual indulgence."[18]

Buddhaghosa provides a detailed description of what sort of behavior constitutes a complete act of sexual intercourse: it is something polluting that requires that one bathe afterward, that is practiced by two people "in a secret place," when the external part of the male sexual organ is inserted into the female organ, "the humid region where even wind does not reach, even as far as the width of a sesame seed." He distinguishes four phases: (1) initial entry, (2) the period inside the vagina, (3) the time during which the penis is withdrawn, and (4) the subsequent period. If a monk feels pleasure during any of these times, he is guilty of an offense.[19]

In an apparent move to forestall creative members of the order from thinking that other types of partners might be acceptable, the Buddha forbade intercourse with three types of beings: (1) human females, nonhuman females, and female animals; (2) human hermaphrodites, nonhuman hermaphrodites, and animal hermaphrodites; and (3) human sexual deviants *(paṇḍaka),* nonhuman sexual deviants, and animal sexual deviants. He also forbade sexual intercourse with any of the three types of males and stated that anyone who violates these norms should be expelled from the order.[20]

Other passages specify that penetration of any of the three possible orifices is forbidden[21] and that even if a monk at first resists but subsequently enjoys the experience, this constitutes an expulsionary offense: "If opponents of a monk bring a human female to his presence and insert his male organ into her rectum [or vagina or mouth] and he agrees to enter, if he agrees to having entered, if he agrees to remain, or if he agrees to withdraw [his penis], there is an offense involving defeat."[22] If he does not assent to entry but later decides to remain inside the woman or if he withdraws his penis in a way that causes stimulation, he is also guilty. Even if he takes no interest but later reflects that it was pleasurable, he violates the rules. Only if he resists every aspect of the ordeal can he be absolved of any wrongdoing. The Buddha adds that it is an expulsionary offense if the woman is drunk, asleep, insane, or dead (but not decomposed). For reasons not explained, if the monk has intercourse with a decomposed corpse, a less serious "grave offense" occurs.

The *Monastic Discipline* contains a number of permutations that appear to be intended to pre-empt possible exceptions. In one such story, a woman approaches a monk and says, "come honored sir, indulge in sexual intercourse!"[23] When he replies that sex is not proper for a monk, she offers to do all the work, while he remains motionless. He assents to this offer (apparently reasoning that his lack of participation constitutes resistance), and this is declared to be an expulsionary offense,[24] as is the case of a monk who allows a woman stroke him until he ejaculates.[25] Another monk inserts his penis into a (nondecomposed) corpse and is expelled, as is another who uses a severed head for sexual stimulation.[26]

Once the process of prohibition and definition began, it led to the creation of hundreds of rules (generally with accompanying stories of the first offense) and the compilation of the *Monastic Discipline,* a huge compendium of tales and anecdotes relating to the spectrum of monastic conduct. Sexuality is particularly important in this collection, which constitutes one of the "three baskets" of the Pāli canon. The monastic community was to police the regulations and mete out punishment to offenders. The Buddha instituted a system of fortnightly gatherings, in which all monastics residing in a particular area convened and recited the rules. Anyone who had violated one was required to make a public confession, and monks who said nothing asserted their purity with their silence. The detailed and frequent recitation served the purpose of fostering solidarity and prevented the possibility of a monk claiming ignorance of the regulations.

This system accords with Foucault's description of confessional regimes in which "sex was not something one simply judged; it was a thing one administered. It was the nature of a public potential; it called for management procedures; it had to be taken charge of by analytical discourses."[27] In the Buddhist monastic order, confession of misdeeds became routinized, and offenders were forced to publicly admit their transgressions and be judged by the assembly of their peers. All were expected to be familiar with the code regulating monastic conduct, and all were subject to its rules. The community determined the relative severity of a particular act and collectively decided on punishment. The most severe violations required expulsion, but minor ones might be punished only by a verbal confession, restitution, or a period of suspension.

Manly Monks versus Lustful Ladies

Indian Buddhist literature depicts the male members of the *saṃgha* as sexually irresistible to women. They are portrayed as physically attractive, virile, athletic men, often young and in their sexual prime, whose comportment and dignity stimulate women to thoughts of lust. The most powerful factor undermining their resolve to live the holy life (*brahma-carya,* which connotes celibacy) is the unwanted advances of women, some of whom are former lovers or wives, while in other stories women fall in love at first sight and sexually proposition them. As Serinity Young states, "women try to impede their progress; women are the opposition. Women are not participants in the same human journey, but are obstacles to it. The Buddha's biographies identify women with materiality *(saṃsāra)* and sexuality, in contrast to men who are identified with spirituality *(dharma).*"[28]

Women are generally given negative characterizations in the Pāli canon. *So It Has Been Said,* for example, equates them with monsters and demons intent on dragging down virtuous monks.[29] In the "Ones Section" of the *Gradual Discourse Collection,* the Buddha warns his followers:

> Monks, I know of no physical appearance that reduces a man's mind to slavery as does that of women. The minds of men are completely obsessed with women's physical appearance. Monks, I know of no sound that reduces a man's mind to slavery as does the voice of women. The minds of men are completely obsessed with women's voices. Monks, I know of no scent that reduces a man's mind to slavery as does the scent of women. The

minds of men are completely obsessed with women's scent. Monks, I know of no taste that reduces a man's mind to slavery as does the taste of women. The minds of men are completely obsessed with women's taste. Monks, I know of no caress that reduces a man's mind to slavery as does the caress of women. The minds of men are completely obsessed with women's caresses.[30]

The trope of woman as seductress will be well known to anyone familiar with classical Indian literature. From the time of the Greeks, expert consensus in Western medicine held that men were the hotter sex, while women were thought to be cooler and less driven by passion.[31] This is presented as an aspect of their inferiority, but in classical India the assumptions are exactly opposite: women embody lust and men are inclined toward the higher and nobler pursuits of celibacy and religious practice. Women are men's adversaries and creatures of passion who seek to satisfy their own cravings and as a result drag down men who would otherwise remain in undisturbed engagement with the path to liberation. It is commonly assumed in India that women are inherently lustful and that they derive perverse satisfaction in seducing unwilling ascetics. The *Kāmasūtra,* for example, asserts that a woman's desire is eight times greater than that of a man.[32] Buddhaghosa exclaims, "women, you live saturated with passion!"[33] The *Renunciant Nārada's Spiritual Teaching (Nāradaparivrājaka Upaniṣad)* describes the effect women have on men seeking to pursue the religious life:

> A man becomes intoxicated by seeing a young woman just as much as by drinking liquor. Therefore, a man should avoid from afar a woman, the mere sight of whom is poison. He shall avoid speaking or chatting with women, looking at them, dancing, singing, or laughing with them, and reproaching them.[34]

The Buddha as depicted in the Pāli canon shared this view of women. In the "Discourse at Cātamā," he compares women to sharks and states that when a man enters the order he does so because he realizes the problems inherent in cyclic existence, but when later he sees a woman "lightly clothed, lightly dressed . . . lust infects his mind," and he abandons his quest for nirvana and returns to the "low life."[35]

In some stories, young, attractive women travel great distances into the wilderness and face dangers from wild animals and bandits in order to seduce unwilling ascetics. Many of these men are old and have been celibate for decades. All initially resist the temptresses' advances, and there is no indication that the intercourse is particularly pleasurable for the women. Their satisfaction appears to derive mainly from seducing a celibate man with no interest in sex. In a story from the *Ṛg Veda,* Lopāmudrā tries to entice her ascetic husband, Agastya, who initially resists but eventually succumbs to her charms. As Wendy Doniger notes, her motivations are purely sexual, but what finally wins him over is the realization that it is his duty to beget sons.[36] He

Wall carving from Ajaṇṭā of Yaśodharā remonstrating with the Buddha during his return to Kapilavastu. Photograph by John Powers.

has spent decades in celibate meditative retreat, and she "desires the bull who is held back." A recurring notion in these stories is that the sage becomes more potent and more desirable as a result of avoiding sex. In the end, Lopāmudrā wins, and the text reports that "the foolish woman sucks dry the panting wise man."[37]

The Buddhist monk Ramaṇīyakuṭika was more successful in fending off unwanted female advances. His story in *Verses of the Elder Monks* reports that he lived in a comfortable hut deep in the wilderness. One day a group of wanton women ventured into the woods to seduce him. They are described as young and attractive, and they danced provocatively in front of the ascetic and flashed parts of their bodies in order to entice him, but he told them that his hut was the only thing he needed and ordered them to leave.[38] Other stories depict monks being accosted by women in the street who force their unwanted attentions on them. An example is Sundara, who was approached by a woman who said that she wanted to pay homage to him. When he assented, she reached inside his robes and grabbed his penis.[39]

In the classical Indian imagination, women are inherently lustful, incapable of the sort of restraint practiced by male ascetics, but fully capable of using their wiles to seduce the men. *The Birth Story of Ṛṣipañcaka* describes the lengths to which women—who are conceived of as naturally timid but whose lust is so great that it overcomes their trepidation—will go in order to have sex:

> [Women] who have fear and trembling even when they hear the sound of familiar music inside their houses will venture out during the night when the light fades, motivated by passion, and go to places wrapped in thick darkness, with the frightening howls of jackals because these women are going to meet their lovers. Those young women, with hands like lotuses that are held by their lovers, who become tired from just walking gently and playfully on the upper terraces of their mansions which are festooned with flowers, lose control of themselves due to their overwhelming passion and go out during the night, even in the rainy season, with impetuous quick steps, walk past highways which are difficult to reach because they have deep, rutted mud from being trampled by the hooves of many buffaloes. Those young women, who live in beautiful mansions, who tremble when touched by scented breezes . . . travel on roads at night like excited deer, and their garlands of flowers are torn apart by showers of rain, and the sound of their mud-caked anklets is dulled.[40]

How should monks intent on higher things protect themselves from women who throw themselves at them, begging for sex? In one famous passage, Ānanda asks the Buddha how to relate to women. The Buddha answers, "do not look at them Ānanda!" But, Ānanda continues, what if he cannot help but see a woman, to which the Buddha responds, "do not speak with her, Ānanda!" But what, Ānanda asks, if a woman should talk to him first? The Buddha advises him to "maintain constant mindfulness and self-control."[41]

Ānanda reportedly experienced a number of problems with women. His pale white skin and friendly demeanor made him a favorite of nuns and laywomen, and there are several instances in which when the Buddha agreed to send a monk to preach the dharma to groups of women, they always asked for Ānanda.

His fellow monks also had difficulties with women on numerous occasions. In some cases, the monks initiated interactions with women, but in most stories they are unwilling recipients of female advances. A number of tales contain cautionary notes regarding the pitfalls of any sort of entanglement with women, however well intentioned. The *Monastic Discipline* recounts an incident in which a woman fought with her husband and decided to leave him. As she walked out of her village, she encountered a Buddhist monk and asked him to accompany her for protection. He agreed, fearing that she might be attacked if she were in a remote area by herself. Her husband went after her and was told that she had been seen in the company of a Buddhist monk, and when he found the two walking on the road he attacked the monk and injured him. She told her husband that it was her decision to leave and that the monk had merely agreed to protect her, but the monk's fellow ascetics criticized him for agreeing to accompany her in the first place. The Buddha agreed with their assessment and issued a rule prohibiting monks from traveling alone with women.[42]

The Buddha advised his followers to be constantly on guard against the blandishments of women. In the "Connected Discourse on the Foundations of Mindfulness," he described the proper mindset: if word circulated that the most beautiful woman in the land would be dancing at a particular time and place, every man would be interested, and a large crowd would gather. But if a man in the crowd were to learn that an enemy with a drawn sword had come to kill him, he would forget all about the woman and focus on the danger to his life. If his enemy forced him to carry a bowl filled to the brim with oil and told him that if a drop spilled he would immediately be killed, his concentration on his task would drive all other thoughts from his mind. Monks should develop this sort of commitment in their quest for nirvana.[43]

What's Wrong with a Little Sex?

Contemporary readers may wonder why absolute sexual continence is considered necessary for Buddhist monks and nuns. Today's conventional wisdom holds that sexual intercourse is beneficial to physical and mental health if it is done in moderation, but the literature of ascetic movements in India presents a very different assessment. In ancient India, semen was associated with the energy of life, and men who recklessly shed their seed were said to become physically diminished. Excessive ejaculation leads to various morbidities and premature death. By contrast, the heroic ascetic who retains his seed is the most manly and virile of men and enjoys robust health, tremendous physical energy, and mental alertness, and he also develops supernatural powers *(siddhi)*. Those who practice celibacy and other acts of austerity accumulate an energy called *tapas,* which literally means "heat." Sages who remain chaste for long periods and who combine this with advanced levels of meditation can even challenge the gods in terms of power and wisdom. Unfortunately, a single ejaculation can undo the accumulated *tapas* of decades, or even centuries, and so men must be constantly vigilant in guarding their senses against the seductive blandishments of women.

This notion is exemplified in the myth of Candra, the moon god, who is married to the twenty-seven (or twenty-eight) daughters of Dakṣa. They are manifested as the stars that make up the *nakṣatras*, lunar mansions through which the moon passes on its journey through the sky during the waxing and waning phases. On each night, Candra has sex with one of his wives, but he passes most of his time with Rohiṇī, his favorite. At this point, he is close to the sun and expends his vital energies in embrace with his celestial wife to such an extent that he almost disappears. His vital essence *(rasa)* is depleted, and so he has to perform a *soma* sacrifice in order to replenish himself. *Soma* is the ritual beverage of the Vedic sacrifices and is linked with semen.[44] It is also the substance of the moon, which is associated with semen because of its silver-white color. Candra's dalliances progressively diminish his seminal stores, and by the time he finishes his circuit through the heavens he is just a tiny sliver. He is in danger of disappearing altogether unless he restores his vital essence.[45]

According to classical Indian medical theory, semen is the by-product of a process of gradual refinement of food, which occurs in six stages. When food is ingested, it is first turned into blood, then flesh, then fat, then bone, then marrow, and finally semen.[46] One portion of semen requires sixty portions of blood to produce, and so it is considered precious. It is also thought to permeate the tissues of the entire body and to be the source of physical vitality. During coitus, the rubbing of the two partners generates energy, which causes semen to flow from the tissues in which it is stored into the testes, from where it is ejaculated. As Caraka describes the process, "During sexual intercourse, semen is ejaculated due to excitement. It is the sign of masculinity. It is called seed *(bīja).*"[47] The *Mahābhārata* contains a similar image: "as butter is churned out from milk by the churning sticks, so seed is churned out [of a man] by the churning sticks born of bodily desires."[48]

Because of its association with life and energy, semen is linked to longevity, and sages who successfully resist the urge to copulate can live for centuries.[49] Thus Caraka cautions men:

> If due to excessive mental excitement a man indulges in sexual intercourse in excess, his semen will soon diminish and he will become emaciated. He will succumb to various diseases, and even death. Therefore, a man who wishes to have good health should definitely preserve his semen.[50]

Caraka adds that semen becomes polluted due to sexual indulgence, and he praises yogis who retain their seed.[51] Caraka warns against seminal retention by men who do not engage in yogic training, because this can also lead to seminal morbidity, but if one remains chaste while pursuing the physical and mental disciplines of yoga, one's semen is converted into a buttery consistency that is thick and rich and promotes health and vitality.

Yogic literature asserts that such adepts store refined semen in their cranial vaults and also develop breasts in which semen accumulates. Some even appear pregnant because their stomachs swell as a result of the stored semen.[52] Peter Brown indicates that the link between semen and vitality is not confined to India but is also found in Western contexts: according to some Christian monastic theorists, "the most virile man was the man who kept most of his vital spirit—the one, that is, who lost little or no seed." He cites Galen's belief that if Olympic athletes could be castrated in such a way that their reserves of heat would not be disrupted by the operation, they would become stronger and faster. Soranus agreed that "men who remain chaste are stronger and better than others and pass their lives in better health."[53] Such ideas are still a part of popular medical lore and physical culture in India today. In a study of wrestling societies, Joseph Alter states:

> It is a common belief among Hindus that the essence of life is contained in semen. Consequently, there is a good deal of anxiety concerning the need to prevent semen from being discharged either voluntarily or involuntarily. . . . It is the source of all strength, all energy, all knowledge, all skill. Semen fuels the fires of self-realization just as *ghi* fuels the lamps of devotional worship. . . . [Ātreya says:] "a man should guard his semen just as a jeweler guards his most valuable diamonds."[54]

Alter also notes that the Buddha is revered by contemporary wrestlers as an outstanding example of chastity and its beneficial effects on health, strength, and longevity, and he quotes one wrestler who points to the serene expressions on Buddha statues as evidence of the positive effects of his renunciation of sex.[55] One paradox of this process is that a man who refrains from seminal emission becomes more and more attractive to women, who use their wiles to seduce him, but as soon as he succumbs he loses all his hard-won energy and descends to the level of other men. Thus the *Truth of Yoga* cautions, "the yogi becomes as strong and beautiful as a god, and women desire him, but he must persevere in his chastity; on account of the retention of semen an agreeable smell will be generated in the body of the yogi."[56] Celibate men are even said to be better lovers than their more passionate counterparts, because those who are not overly lustful can sustain lovemaking for long periods of time and are not subject to premature ejaculation.

There is substantial agreement between classical Indian medical literature and Buddhist notions of sexuality and the body, and throughout this book I use examples from Caraka and Suśruta, the two most influential exponents of traditional Indian medical lore, to illustrate how these notions were conceived. Kenneth Zysk has persuasively argued that the concordances between Buddhist sources and the great physicians of Indian antiquity are probably not coincidental; he provides evidence to support his opinion that empirical medicine in India probably began in Buddhist monasteries and was later brahmanized, correlated with Vedic texts, and attributed to brahmanical authorities.[57]

Sexual Deviants

The term *paṇḍaka,* which I translate as "sexual deviant," is commonly rendered as "eunuch," but the extensive discussions in Buddhist literature of these unfortunate beings indicate that eunuchs are only one class of *paṇḍaka.* The term is probably derived from *apa* plus *aṇḍa* plus *ka,* "without testicles." Monier-Williams states that the derivation of the term is obscure but thinks that the root is *paṇḍ,* "to destroy, annihilate." He contends that a *paṇḍaka* is a "eunuch, weakling, or impotent man."[58]

Buddhaghosa, Asaṅga, and Yaśomitra enumerate five types of sexual deviant: (1) nonmanly sexual deviant *(napuṃsaka-paṇḍaka),* (2) envious sexual deviant *(usūya-paṇḍaka),* (3) sexual deviant for a fortnight *(pakkha-paṇḍaka),* (4) voyeur sexual deviant *(āssita-paṇḍaka* or *āsakta-prādurbhāvi-paṇḍaka),* and (5) artifice-employing sexual deviant *(oppakkamika-paṇḍaka).*[59] The first type is a hermaphrodite *(ubhatobyañjanā),* who is born impotent and has no obvious sexual organ, or a man whose testicles do not perform properly.[60] Buddhaghosa states that such people are congenitally impotent.[61] Envious sexual deviants become aroused by watching others having sex and are jealous of them. The sexual deviant for a fortnight is able to perform normally during the fourteen light days of the lunar month *(juṇha-pakkha)* but is impotent during the fourteen dark days *(kāla-pakkha),* from the day of the full moon until the new moon. Monier-Williams quotes Suśruta to the effect that the voyeur (Skt. *īrṣyāsaṇḍa-paṇḍaka*) is a "semi-impotent man whose power is stimulated through jealous feelings caused by seeing others in the act of sexual union."[62] Such a person experiences sexual satisfaction when another man ejaculates into his mouth during fellatio. The final type of sexual deviant is able to ejaculate only by using a device or artifice.[63]

A common theme in commentarial discussions of sexual deviants is the notion that they are unsuitable for the monastic life because they have greater lust than other people. Vasubandhu, for example, states that sexual deviants, along with eunuchs *(saṇḍa)* and hermaphrodites, "possess, to an extreme degree, the defilements of the senses." They lack the ability to engage in introspection and thus cannot eliminate mental afflictions.[64] Buddhaghosa asserts that they are controlled by unquenchable lust and are slaves to their libidos. He compares them to prostitutes or wanton young girls, who have no self-control.[65] Vasubandhu concurs with this assessment and states that because of their mental makeup sexual deviants cannot engage in religious practice. They have the defiling passions of both sexes and lack any sense of modesty or shame. A similar notion was propounded by Saint Basil, who denounced eunuchs as

> neither feminine nor masculine, woman-mad, envious, of evil wage, quick to anger, effeminate . . . disgusting, crazed, jealous—and yet why say more?—at their very birth doomed to the knife! How can their minds be right when their very feet are twisted? They are chaste (thanks to the knife), and it is no credit to them; and they are lecherous without fruition (thanks to their own natural vileness).[66]

Vasubandhu blames the parents of sexual deviants for their sorry state. He asserts that their parents gave them incomplete bodies and so were poor benefactors. As a result, sexual deviants do not generate strong reverence for their parents as normal people do and cannot be blamed for their lack of respect.[67] This accords with Caraka's assertion that deviants are born as they are because of a deficiency in the father's seed. If a man's sperm is stronger than the female contribution to conception (often said to be menstrual blood, but in some sources it is an unspecified female semen equivalent), a male will be produced.[68] If the female portion is stronger, a girl will be conceived, but if the sperm is very weak, the result may be a eunuch or hermaphrodite.[69]

In one *Monastic Discipline* account, a sexual deviant who had been ordained approaches some young monks and says, "come, venerable ones, defile me!"[70] They drive him away, and he then propositions some mahouts and animal keepers, who agree to sodomize him.[71] After they do so, they criticize the Buddhist monastic order: "these monks . . . are sexual deviants, and those who are not sexual deviants commit offenses with sexual deviants. Thus they are all unchaste."[72]

Sexual deviants and hermaphrodites are portrayed in Indian Buddhist literature as the lowest human types. Rebirth as such an unfortunate person is the result of very negative karma.[73] The *Meritorious Virtue of Making Images* enumerates four causes for being born in the state of a sexual deviant: if one in a past life had (1) castrated another man; (2) laughingly scorned and slandered a recluse who maintains the precepts; (3) transgressed the precepts oneself because of lustful desires; and (4) not only transgressed the precepts but also encouraged others to do so.[74]

The types of *paṇḍaka* enumerated in the list above and the commentaries of various authorities indicate that translating this term as "eunuch" is inadequate. As Leonard Zwilling notes, except for impotent men, all the others are capable of having erections, of ejaculating, and of experiencing sexual pleasure.[75] Only the "nonmanly sexual deviant" is actually a eunuch, and discussions of this term in commentarial literature indicate that this type can also include effeminate men or others who do not correspond to the masculine ideal common to Indian society. A range of sexual dysfunctions are included within the rubric of the five types of sexual deviant, and all indicate a failure to perform normally. This is significant in the Buddhist monastic context because while monks and nuns are required to maintain total sexual abstinence they must also have no sexual impairments.

The *Monastic Discipline* prohibits a wide range of sexual activities and attempts to forestall any sort of behavior that might lead to coitus, but monks must be capable of intercourse. There are no shortcuts to abstinence and self-control. Some monks who were meditating in the forest found that they were unable to control their lust and decided to smash their penises between two rocks, and the Buddha told them that they smashed the wrong thing: what was needed was to crush desire.[76] Self-mutilation in pursuit of celibacy was declared a grave offense.[77]

The same dynamic operated in medieval Christian monasticism. In Matthew 19:12, Jesus tells his disciples, "There are some eunuchs, who were so born from their mothers' wombs; and there are some eunuchs who were made eunuchs of men: and there are eunuchs who have made themselves eunuchs for the kingdom of heaven's sake." The third type was seen as the ideal, but some monastics who found celibacy difficult considered it an injunction to self-mutilation. One such example was Origen, who castrated himself but later regretted his "rash deed," realizing that true celibacy requires an ongoing battle against one's passions.[78]

As Taylor notes in his discussion of celibacy in medieval Christian monasticism, what is demanded

> is not the mere absence of sexual activity, but the presence of willpower. A man who is physically incapable of sex does not need self-control; therefore, by rendering himself incapable of sex, a man who castrates himself robs himself of any need or opportunity to suppress his immoral physical urges by a moral act of will. By this logic, castration becomes a shortcut to continence, a cheap evasion of temptation, an attempt to cheat God.[79]

A similar imperative operated for the Buddhist monastic community. From the time they entered the order, monks were taught meditative techniques designed to eradicate sexual desire. Those who were successful no longer had to struggle against their passions, because they had none. This was the ideal state: a man fully capable of sexual functioning, who had absolutely no inclination to engage in any sort of sexual activity. In the "Discourse on All the Defilements," the Buddha admonishes his followers: "a monk should not tolerate an arisen thought of sensual desire. He should abandon it, remove it, do away with it, annihilate it."[80]

This training made monks exceptional among humans and conferred on them a superior status, derived from their extraordinary self-control. As Brown notes with respect to Christianity, celibates gave themselves a separate and higher status, access to power, and separation from the laity; they sacrificed their sexuality "for the kingdom of heaven"[81] (or for nirvana in the case of Buddhist monks).

The Buddha indicated on several occasions that he only wished to admit exceptionally gifted men and women to his order. He explicitly forbade ordination of sexual deviants and hermaphrodites,[82] and the *Monastic Discipline* contains a long list of other prohibited types, including people whose hands or feet had been cut off (a common punishment for theft) or whose ears, nose, fingers, nails, or tendons had been severed (other common legal punishments); dwarves; hunchbacks; people with goiters; people with brands on their skin (indicating that they were slaves); people who had been whipped; those who had crooked limbs; and those who were very ill, deformed, lame, paralyzed on one side, blind, mute, or deaf.[83]

These prohibitions are not unique to the Buddhist community but reflect societal norms for world renouncers. The *Renunciant Nārada's Spiritual Teaching* contains a similar list, forbidding the conferral of renunciant status on blind persons; eunuchs; outcastes; cripples; effeminate or childish men; and people who are deaf, dumb, or heretics.[84]

The *Monastic Discipline* provides no reasons for these discriminatory prohibitions, but reading between the lines in the Pāli canon these exclusions are clearly based on cultural assumptions prevalent at the time. Religious mendicants were highly regarded, and sincere aspirants to liberation were viewed as exceptional individuals whose moral behavior and generation of merit in past births had placed them in a life situation in which they could pursue the religious path. Such people should also be marked with the physical signs of past karma, including a beautiful body and excellent health. If the *saṃgha* were to admit the crippled and lame—or, like sexual deviants, people with moral deficiencies—laypeople would regard them as a group of social outcasts, rather than as an admirable order of monks deserving of support.

For these reasons, the Buddha mandated that if a hermaphrodite, for example, were to be inadvertently ordained, he should be expelled from the order as soon as his physical condition was discovered. During the ordination ceremony, males are asked, "Are you a man?," because Vinaya rules stipulate that only physically normative human males can become monks.[85] This question is asked because of a story in the *Monastic Discipline* in which a *nāga,* disgusted with his condition, adopted the form of a human man and was ordained. One day when he slept he reverted to his true shape, and the monk who shared a cell with him arrived home to find a giant snake whose coils slithered out through the windows. When the frightened monk reported the incident to the Buddha, he ordered the *nāga* expelled and declared that no nonhumans could be ordained.

Auto-Eroticism

A number of Vinaya accounts report permutations of self-stimulation by both monks and nuns, along with rules prohibiting such behavior. One monk with a supple back was able to perform auto-sodomy, and another well-endowed man could engage in auto-fellatio.[86] The Buddha forbade these activities. Buddhaghosa explains that the first monk had been a dancer before entering the order and so had developed the ability to twist his body in unusual ways.[87]

One *Monastic Discipline* story recounts how a monk named Seyyasaka became dissatisfied with the practice of celibacy, and his mental condition affected him physically; he grew "thin, wretched, his color bad, yellowish, the veins showing all over his body."[88] In contrast to Western lore that claims that masturbation leads to physical degeneration, his preceptor suggested auto-eroticism as the solution to his difficulties.[89] He added that Seyyasaka should also bathe as much as he liked and sleep late. Seyyasaka was unsure that this was permissible for Buddhist monks, but was assured that no infractions of conduct would occur.

Taking his preceptor's advice, Seyyasaka frequently "emitted semen using his hand," slept as long as he wished, and indulged in long baths. As a result, "in a short time he became good-looking, with rounded features, bright complexion and clear skin." Other monks remarked on the change in his physical condition, and when he described the remedy he had employed they were shocked and asked him whether he used the same hand for masturbation and accepting alms. When Seyyasaka stated that he did, they became angry and rebuked him: "Stupid man, it is not right, it is not proper, it is not suitable, it is not worthy for an ascetic, it is not correct, it should not be done!" They added that the dharma is taught in order to help people remove passions, not for indulging in them, for freedom and not for bondage. The Buddha subsequently declared such auto-eroticism an offense requiring a formal meeting of the *saṃgha.*[90]

The code of monastic conduct forbade not only sexual intercourse but any sort of sensual pleasures, which are described by the Buddha as "low, vulgar, worldly, ignoble, and leading to no good."[91] Acts of auto-eroticism were viewed as less serious than actions performed with another person but were prohibited because masturbation still involves lust and sexual stimulation. The Buddha also criticized other self-styled ascetics who renounced sexual intercourse but who enjoyed being bathed, massaged, and rubbed by women. He declared that although these men were technically celibate, "their chastity is torn, distorted, stained, and blemished," and their actions tied them to cyclic existence.[92] Such people cannot attain liberation, and the same is true, the Buddha declared, of men who bathe with women, look at them with desire, think fondly of past sexual pleasures, or are envious of the pleasures of householders. These men practice celibacy only in order to be reborn in heaven, but remain trapped within cyclic existence. Any cognitive attachment to the pleasures of the world ensures that one will continue to be reborn in it, and so the Buddha's code of monastic conduct aimed at helping his followers develop complete disinterest in anything the world has to offer, because as long as worldly concerns excite a positive mental response, this will create the causal conditions for continued rebirth. Thus the *Verses on Doctrine* states: "Self-control with the body is good. Self-control with speech is good. Self-control with the mind is good. Self-control in every aspect is good. A monk who is self-controlled in every aspect is free from suffering."[93]

Creative Eroticism: The Case of Udāyin

Many of the men whose sexual peccadilloes led to the establishment of rules for the monastic order are not named, but the monk who most often appears as the first transgressor is Udāyin, who has the distinction of having more sex-related regulations linked to his actions than any other person mentioned in the *Monastic Discipline.*[94] He is often censured, but because he is the first person to attempt a particular variation on a sexual theme, he escapes expulsion.

In one story, Udāyin is said to have built an attractive dwelling, and one day a brahman man and his wife come to have a look at it. At one point the man leaves his wife alone with Udāyin to inspect another part of the residence, and Udāyin rubs himself against her. When the husband returns, he comments on the quality of Udāyin's lodgings and observes that Udāyin must be an exemplary monk, but when the wife describes Udāyin's conduct the husband is scandalized and denounces the monastic community. He declares that Buddhist monks are outwardly virtuous but really reprobates. Other monks hear the brahman's comments and report them to the Buddha, who rebukes Udāyin and declares that "whatever monk, affected by desire, with perverted heart, comes into physical contact with a woman, holding her hand, or holding a braid of her hair, or rubbing against any one of her limbs" commits an offense requiring a formal meeting of the monastic community.[95]

Another Vinaya account indicates that Udāyin was guilty of speaking lewdly to women, and again the Buddha chastises him, adding that such speech is motivated by desire and perverted thoughts and so is inappropriate for monks. This conduct also requires a formal meeting of the *saṃgha.*[96] The commentary helpfully adds that lewd speech is "talk connected with private parts and unchastity."[97]

In one instance of Udāyin's misdeeds, a woman offers him alms, but he answers that food and other necessities are easily obtained. "That which is difficult to find" is sex. The woman replies, "would that be of use to you?," and he eagerly agrees that it would. The woman—who is depicted as acting with sincere religious motives—then accompanies Udāyin into an inner room, takes off her clothes, and lies on a couch. At that point, Udāyin has a change of heart and says, "who would touch this foul-smelling wretch?" He spits on the floor and departs from the room.

The spurned woman is understandably upset and tells the Buddha about the incident; he declares that any monk who propositions a woman for sex is guilty of an offense requiring a formal meeting, regardless of the outcome of the encounter.[98] Udāyin's conduct also led to regulations regarding contacts between monks and women. He often met women in secluded places, and when the Buddha heard of this he forbade monks to meet privately with women.

One time Udāyin sat with a woman "in a secret place on a secluded and comfortable couch,"[99] and the Buddha declared that this incident was "undetermined," because it was not clear that anything untoward had occurred. Nonetheless, private meetings between monks and women were prohibited, and the Buddha declared that, depending on the outcome, such behavior could result in expulsion, a formal meeting of the community, or expiation.[100]

The *Monastic Discipline* reports that Udāyin had been married before entering the order and that he had regular contact with his former wife and enjoyed a close relationship with her. They frequently had meals together, and on one such occasion she displayed her private parts to him. He became impassioned and inadvertently ejaculated. She offered to wash his stained robe and for an unexplained reason inserted one part in her mouth and another in her vagina. As a result she became pregnant, and other nuns reported her to the Buddha. When she explained the origin of her condition, the Buddha forbade monks and nuns from meeting alone in a private place and also ordered that women who are not relatives should not wash a monk's robes.[101] Interestingly, she was apparently not chastised for exposing herself to him.

Udāyin's actions frequently led to difficulties for other monks, and in some cases the Buddha had to emend rules promulgated in response to Udāyin's conduct. One such story reports that Udāyin once taught the dharma to several women in a secluded place, upon which the Buddha declared, "if any monk teaches dharma to women, this is an offense." As a result, some monks refused to instruct women in any circumstances, which led the Buddha to change the wording of his regulation: it is permissible for monks briefly to teach the dharma to women, as long as they restrict themselves to statements of five or six sentences.[102]

Udāyin's actions and the Buddha's responses display a dynamic of resistance to authority and imposition of norms that reflects Foucault's notion that wherever there is sexual repression there will also be attempts to undermine it, "a plurality of resistances, each of them a special case: resistances that are possible, necessary, improbable; others that are spontaneous, savage, solitary, concerted, rampant, or violent."[103] As Foucault notes, sometimes this resistance is organized, but the stories in the *Monastic Discipline* mainly present individual permutations of sexuality that attempt to allow experience of sensual pleasures while still remaining within the framework of the rules. Human sexuality has a disruptive potential that threatens to fracture the harmony that is the ideal of the monastic code; these "mobile and transitory points of resistance"[104] constitute challenges to the integrity of the system and require new and more exacting regulations to prevent their recurrence and to avert future attempts to remain within the order while still engaging in "village dharma."

In his study of medieval Christian monasticism, Brown notes a similar imperative. Monastic groups received public admiration for their dignified comportment, and in a society that valued order (which is also true of ancient India), such self-control was highly regarded.[105] As Connell notes, such disciplinary regimes are connected with gender ideals, and the imposition of normative regulations is designed to produce a particular sort of public physical persona: "Part of the struggle for hegemony in the gender order is the use of culture for such disciplinary purposes: setting standards, claiming popular assent and discrediting those who fall short. The production of exemplary masculinities is thus integral to the politics of hegemonic masculinity."[106]

The Buddha's responses to Udāyin's explorations of the limits of permissible actions show that he wanted to ban not only fully consummated sexual intercourse but any sexually motivated actions. In some cases, his concern appears to have been that sexually explicit talk or use of innuendo could reflect badly on the monastic community, but the general thrust of the regulations indicates that the Buddha saw sex as a cascading series of progressively more intimate and passion-driven acts that culminate in coitus. Confession of minor transgressions could interrupt this process and help monks to cultivate mental protections that would prevent them from going any further. This resonates with Foucault's notion that regimes of sexual repression emphasize the beneficial effects of confession: "Tell everything, the directors would say time and again: not only consummated acts, but sensual touchings, all impure gazes, all obscene remarks . . . all consenting thoughts."[107] The regular recitation of the monastic rules in the individual liberation *(prātimokṣa)* provided monks with an opportunity to reflect on their conduct, admit their transgressions, and resolve to avoid wrongdoing in the future.

Public Relations

The condemnation of Udāyin's behavior is primarily based on its effect on the lay population. As an order of mendicants whose very survival depended on positive public relations, Buddhist monks needed to demonstrate the comportment expected of religious ascetics. A group with a negative reputation would experience difficulty in obtaining alms and would probably disappear. Thus it is not surprising that a large number of *Vinaya* stories report that a negative public perception of a particular action led the Buddha to condemn that action and to promulgate a rule prohibiting it in the future. The Buddha stresses the reliance of the monastic community on laypeople in his definition of a monk:

> He is a monk because he is a beggar for alms, a monk because he submits to wandering for alms, a monk because he is one who wears the patchwork cloth, a monk by designation [of others]. . . . A monk is endowed with going to the three refuges, a monk is auspicious, a monk is essential, a monk is a learner, a monk is an adept, a monk means one who is endowed with harmony for the order . . . with actions in accordance with doctrine and monastic discipline, with steadfastness, with the attributes of a perfected man.[108]

In some cases, rules were made in order to prevent the possibility that people might think badly of Buddhist monks. In one *Monastic Discipline* passage, the Buddha admonishes monks not to enter the quarters of a king's harem because a woman might smile at them and provoke the king's jealousy. Or the king might forget that he dallied with one of his harem women and think that a monk is responsible when she becomes pregnant. Moreover, harems are dens of temptation, with many wonderful and sensuous things, which might beguile the mind.[109]

As we saw with the Buddha, the bodies of Buddhist monks are viewed as public spaces on which their virtues are displayed. Physical beauty, good health, an athletic frame, and sexual virility are all associated with good conduct, practice of morality, and attainment of advanced meditative states. Spiritual perfection is also linked with physical dignity and a calm demeanor. Monks are enjoined to avoid looking around or making jerky bodily gestures, and they should adopt a demeanor that proclaims their restraint and freedom from worldly entanglements. One *Monastic Discipline* passage criticizes a group of young monks who walked into a village swaying their hips and swinging their arms. The Buddha declared that monks' limbs should be controlled and that their bodies should be kept straight. While walking into a town, they should fix their eyes on the ground several feet in front of them in order to avoid looking at women.

The *Monastic Discipline* portrays the Buddhist community as living in close proximity with a lay population that sustains it with alms and that judges its behavior. Everything monks do is scrutinized, and any lapses are criticized by laypeople, who are depicted as taking a personal interest in the purity of the *saṃgha.* One probable reason for this is the notion that monks are "fields of merit" *(puṇya-kṣetra),* meaning that when one donates something to a monk it yields greater rewards than if one were to give to another needy person, such as a beggar. The moral behavior of monks and their meditative attainments lead to greater merit for donors, but only those monks who are truly pure are suitable to function as fields of merit. If one unknowingly provides food for a lapsed monk, one's donation is wasted, and so lay donors had a personal stake in the purity of the community.

Because they had a vested interest in the community's conduct, laypeople had a right to criticize *saṃgha* members for perceived laxness. In addition, the monks had a duty to accept alms, and refusal to do so constitutes an offense according to the *Monastic Discipline* because it deprives devout donors of a chance to make merit. The only exception was if a layperson had been excommunicated due to bad behavior. Several incidences of this punishment are recorded in Indic sources, but it was also possible for the offender to make a confession to the *saṃgha* and be reinstated. As long as a layperson was under suspension as a donor, monks would turn their bowls upside down when he or she approached, indicating that they would not accept any alms.

Laypeople looked for signs of integrity in monks' physical demeanor and even in their personal grooming. In one *Monastic Discipline* account, some nuns reportedly let their body hair grow and bathed naked in a river. A group of prostitutes saw them enjoying themselves in the water and accused them of behaving like laywomen who enjoy the pleasures of the senses. Modest nuns criticized their fellow monastics' behavior, and the Buddha declared it an offense for nuns to let their hair grow or to be naked in a public place.[110]

A number of other religious orders operating in the Buddha's time prescribed nudity for their monastics, declaring it a sign of complete renunciation of worldly entanglements. The Buddha, however, rejected nudity on the grounds that it offends many people, even in a country like India in which naked ascetics are a common sight. He connected the dignity of his order with their clean, neat robes, all dyed the same saffron color. In one passage in the *Great Division,* a monk expresses his admiration for naked ascetics who display their disregard for possessions through their nudity, and he asks for permission to follow their example:

> Blessed One, nakedness is an efficient method, in various ways, to become moderate and contented with little, to eliminate defilements, to tame the

> passions, to become pure, devoted and sincere. Blessed One, it would be good to mandate this practice for the whole order.[111]

The Buddha refuses the request and chastises the monk, saying, "that is not true, stupid man; nudity is not suitable for monks, but rather is unworthy for them. It is not the proper thing to do. Stupid man, why would you want to adopt nakedness as practiced by other ascetics?"[112]

In another story illustrating the *Monastic Discipline*'s emphasis on public decorum, a group of monks from Āḷavī went to a public shrine to hear a dharma discourse. Afterward, the elders went to their dwelling, but some young monks lay down in a public sleeping place with laypeople, some of whom were naked, snoring, or mumbling. People who saw the monks consorting with such common folk disparaged them and thought their conduct improper. The Buddha agreed and forbade monks to lie down with the public or to associate with naked people.[113]

Even minor aspects of decorum were thought to reflect on the dignity of the *saṃgha.* The monastic community seems to have been in close proximity to a surrounding lay population, which observed and judged both public and private affairs. Monastics who lived in communities shared latrines, and one *Vinaya* rule states that monks should not groan when relieving themselves because passing laypeople might consider this undignified.[114] Other regulations stipulate that bodily wastes should not be thrown over the walls (because they might fall on someone outside); rather, they should be taken away from the monastic precincts and buried in a remote place.

A number of regulations are concerned with ensuring that monks do not give physical offense to other monks or the lay community. In order to prevent monks from having stained teeth or bad breath, the Buddha ordered that they should chew tooth wood.[115] The *Monastic Discipline* reports on a monk who loved the taste of garlic, which resulted in foul breath and body odor. He sat apart from other monks during assemblies, and when the Buddha asked the reason the monk replied that his breath was offensive. As a result, the Buddha forbade monks from eating garlic except for medicinal purposes.[116]

Men Who Prefer Other Men

The *Monastic Discipline* contains numerous passages on various permutations of sexual deviance—including incidents of bestiality and necrophilia, as well as an extensive catalogue of heterosexual practices—but it has surprisingly little to say about homosexuality. There are several stories of monks having sexual encounters with other men, but they are not depicted as homosexuals; rather, their orientation is clearly heterosexual, and the underlying assumption is that they are motivated by lust and would prefer to satisfy it with women, if such were available. Heterosexuality is the default position, and there is no inkling in these accounts that the monks have a particular sexual orientation that favors other men or that their behavior constitutes a lifestyle. This is similar to David Halperin's observation that prior to the modern "discovery" of the homosexual as a type, a man who played the dominant role by penetrating another man "might not be sick but immoral, not perverted but merely perverse. His penetration of a subordinate male, reprehensible and abominable as it might be, could be deemed a manifestation of his excessive but otherwise normal male sexual appetite."[117]

Men theoretically entered the Buddhist order in order to pursue its goals, one of which is sublimation of passion, but many fell short of this ideal and succumbed to lust-inspired deeds. All of the various permutations of desire attributed to Buddhist monks are conceived of as essentially the acts of heterosexual males who are unable to maintain their discipline due to excessive desire and thus satisfy themselves through various forms of genital stimulation. As José Cabezón notes, "the principal question for Buddhism has not been one of heterosexuality vs. homosexuality but one of sexuality vs. celibacy. In this sense homosexuality, when condemned, is condemned more for being an instance of sexuality than for being homosexuality."[118]

Buddhaghosa forbids any penetration of the "passage of cereals" or "passage of feces," even to the width of a sesame seed, and he indicates that this area is an erogenous zone with flesh that is easily stimulated.[119] But such activity is just as reprehensible for a monk as vaginal coitus or fellatio. In *Monastic Discipline* descriptions of homoeroticism, friction, not gender preference, is the key factor. One such passage describes two monks named Kaṇḍaka and Mahaka who committed sodomy with each other, but after they were separated they discontinued such behavior.[120] Homosexual love is a temporary aberration, and Indian Buddhist literature assumes that men do not form strong, lasting commitments in the way heterosexual couples do, and so this sort of activity is not seen as having the destabilizing effects on the order attributed to affairs between men and women. Men and women who fall in love marry, procreate, establish families, and develop long-term emotional bonds;

men who fornicate do so in order to scratch a temporary itch, but any partner will do.

The attitude toward sexual activity between male members of the *saṃgha* parallels Foucault's observation that prior to the "discovery" of homosexuals as a "species" in the nineteenth century, the sodomite was viewed as a man who engaged in temporary acts that were aberrations.[121] The acts were condemned, but there was no notion that some men might be naturally inclined to prefer sex with other men. In Indian Buddhist literature, heterosexuality is also assumed, and men and women are assumed to be naturally attracted to each other. There are mentions of a "third gender," which includes people with deficient bodies—for instance, sexual deviants, eunuchs, and hermaphrodites—but men and women with normal equipment are viewed as heterosexual.[122] Even those of deviant sexuality are not seen as having an inclination toward members of their own sex, but rather are thoroughly promiscuous, deriving pleasure from a range of (condemned) practices. For such people, sexuality and preference are fluid, connected with the pursuit of physical pleasure in various forms, but "normal" men and women are naturally attracted toward the opposite sex.

Some Buddhist texts recognize the existence of desire between men, but it is viewed as a result of negative karma that creates psychological abnormalities. The *Meritorious Virtue of Making Images,* for example, lists four actions that can cause a man to "be born with the lusts and desires of a woman, to enjoy being treated as a woman by other men": (1) despising other men or defaming them, even as a joke; (2) enjoying dressing as a woman or wearing women's jewelry; (3) engaging in prohibited actions with female relatives; and (4) accepting reverence that one does not deserve. Such deeds can lead to a psychological state in a future life in which normal sexual desires become perverted and cause someone with a man's body to experience emotions associated with women.[123]

Monks Who Love Animals

The Vinaya contains some interesting examples of the Buddha's followers' creative attempts to adhere to the letter of the law while still indulging in sexual activities. One of these concerns a monk who lived in a hut in the forest and kept a female monkey as a pet. One day when he was away in Vaiśālī seeking alms, some other monks came to visit him, and when they approached, the monkey bent over and assumed a sexually submissive posture. The monks surmised that she did so because she was conditioned to being violated by a man in monk's robes. Buddhaghosa notes that some monks fed forest animals and that a few had taught the animals to provide sex in exchange for food. When the visiting monks saw the monkey thrust her vagina at them, they realized that she was accustomed to having sex with the monk, and so they hid themselves and later witnessed an act of bestiality.[124]

They confronted the errant monk, who protested that the Buddha had only forbidden intercourse with human females, but they rebuked him for his failure to practice proper celibacy and reported him. The Buddha convened the monastic community and promulgated a rule prohibiting sexual indulgence with any sort of animal, adding that offenders should be expelled from the order.

Another monk figured that if he were to take off his robes and don laymen's clothing he could indulge in sex, but the Buddha declared that once one has taken monastic vows these apply for the rest of one's life, regardless of what one wears. There are no holidays or time-outs. The *Monastic Discipline* reports that one monk dressed as a layman and had sexual intercourse, while another told a woman that if he took off his robes he could behave as a layman, but the Buddha declared that these monks should be expelled. The same was true of a monk who had sex after donning a grass skirt and another who wore a garment of bark in the manner of other ascetic orders of the time.[125]

A surprising number of *Monastic Discipline* passages describe incidents of bestiality. In one, a group of monks drive a herd of cows across a river. They mistreat the cows, grab their horns, pull their ears and dewlaps, touch their genitals, and develop lustful thoughts.[126] The Buddha declared that such actions constitute an offense. Buddhaghosa lists various animals, including snakes and millipedes, that were apparently used by some monks for sexual gratification. He repeats the rule that any penetration of any orifice (of any species) beyond the width of a sesame seed constitutes an expulsionary offense.[127] He then asserts that some monks inserted their penises into the mouths of fish, iguanas, and turtles. He adds that some also attempted to do this with frogs, but because a frog's mouth is too wide to provide sexual pleasure, this activity, while reprehensible, is not an offense according to the monastic code. With remarkable thoroughness, he catalogues a variety of species—including hens, crows, pigeons, jackals, dogs, otters, buffaloes, elephants, horses, cows, mules, and camels—and forbids monks from inserting their penises into any of the previously mentioned three orifices, nor into the animals' noses or ears.[128]

In a discussion of Buddhist notions about sex that focuses on the Pāli *Monastic Discipline,* Janet Gyatso discusses some of the bizarre permutations of sexuality and the meticulous detail with which the compilers of the collection treat sexual offenses. She speculates that this may be an instance of "monastic humor" that nonetheless "drives home" a "serious message" and that these stories were intended to elicit a "monastic giggle,"[129] but given the context this is highly unlikely. Legal codes like the *Monastic Discipline* that attempt to spell out rules in detail and that describe proscribed behavior and the mechanisms for punishment are seldom consciously funny. They may appear so to people from other societies who encounter them as foreign artifacts, but the rules in this collection were clearly viewed with great seriousness by their compilers. The prescriptions regarding sex were accompanied with dire warnings regarding punishments that could involve very serious consequences, including expulsion from the order. Moreover, the negative karmas attached to forbidden actions were said to lead to rebirths in hell realms in which pain beyond human imagining would be inflicted. Even lesser offenses required the public embarrassment of having one's failings meticulously recounted before one's fellow monks and could lead to periods of prolonged banishment or a humiliating public rebuke. A "defeated" monk lost all chance of attaining any significant religious goals in the present life and any possibility of reestablishing communion with the *saṃgha.* The mental anguish of such punishment was equaled or surpassed by promised physical torments in future existences.

Contemporary Western (and particularly American) society is saturated with images of sex, arguably to a degree unsurpassed by any previous cultures. Sexual peccadilloes and permutations on erotic acts are both core elements of much popular humor and focal points for moralizers who condemn acts they consider sinful along with those who engage in them, and so it is perhaps not surprising that the detailed descriptions of prohibited deeds in the *Monastic Discipline* might strike modern readers as either scandalous (as with Horner; see note 21) or funny (as with Gyatso), but the overall tone of this collection is very serious indeed. In addition to its sections on sexuality, the *Monastic Discipline* contains minutely detailed rules for all aspects of dress, comportment, eating, communal living, and so forth, and one would have to have a generous view of humor to find any in these passages. Given the extreme seriousness with which sexual activity was viewed by the compilers of this collection,

I strongly suspect that any apparent giggles are unintentional. Rather, the lengthy descriptions of possible acts and the extensive lists of variations on potential exceptions to the rules are probably designed to forestall any attempts at circumventing them, rather than an attempt at ribaldry. The collection as a whole appears to have been written by serious monks of a legalistic bent with a serious purpose. Their concern with the reputation of the order is evident in every aspect of the *Monastic Discipline,* and their descriptions of sex-related offenses are designed to elicit repugnance in monks who read them and a resolve to avoid actions that could result in punishment or besmirch the reputation of the community of Buddhist monastics.

The sheer number of often graphic descriptions of sexual activities have caused some commentators to doubt the veracity of the accounts. Dutt, for example, is of the opinion that many accounts in the *Monastic Discipline* are "farfetched."[130] It is true that at first glance some stories appear formulaic, and others are variations on a theme. Some of the actions attributed to monks also sound unlikely on the surface, but anyone who has endured an afternoon of American daytime talk shows has heard vivid descriptions of far more bizarre permutations of sexuality than anything contained in the Buddhist canon. Guests on the *Jerry Springer Show*, for example, commonly recount in great detail sexual deeds and convoluted relationships well beyond the creative vision of the early Buddhist monastic community as described in the *Monastic Discipline.*

But the point may not be that monks actually performed such actions. Rather, the goal of the authors of these discourses seems to be an exhaustive catalogue of possible deeds motivated by desire. By deriving variations on a particular theme, the compilers of this literature probably hoped that a reasonable person reading it would conclude that any action motivated by sensual lust is inadmissible for Buddhist monastics. The approach is similar to what Foucault attributed to chroniclers of sexual acts during the Victorian period, which aimed at an intensification of description and confession of such deeds:

> This carefully analytical discourse was meant to yield multiple effects of displacement, intensification, reorientation, and modification of desire itself. Not only were the boundaries of what one could say about sex enlarged, and men compelled to hear it said; but more important, discourse was connected to sex by a complex organization with varying effects, by a deployment that cannot be adequately explained merely by referring it to a

> law of prohibition. A censorship of sex? There was installed rather an apparatus for producing an ever greater quantity of discourse about sex, capable of functioning and taking effect in its very economy.[131]

In the case of the *Monastic Discipline,* the goal was clearly to undermine the sexual drive by cataloguing various sorts of prohibited actions and attitudes and providing the underlying principle that any physical deed motivated by sexual desire is improper for monastics. Unlike the population of Victorian Europe whose lives the sexual discourses described by Foucault sought to control, membership in the Buddhist *saṃgha* was voluntary, and men requesting monastic vows had to prove themselves suitable candidates before they could be admitted. The main normative reason for seeking ordination and voluntarily renouncing sensuality was the promise of even greater pleasure in advanced meditative states, rebirth in a heaven, or liberation from the sufferings of cyclic existence. Those who failed to attain nirvana but practiced diligently could still look forward to future lifetimes with progressively better bodies, greater wealth and other resources, blissful sojourns in heavens, and, as the Buddha's life shows, more and better sex. In *The Use of Pleasure* and *The Care of the Self,* Foucault refers to voluntarily adopted regimes of discipline as "technologies of the self." This term encompasses a range of regimens in which subjects choose to engage in practices that restrict their possible actions in order to bring about a desired transformation. The regulations of Buddhist monastics are of this type: they are specific to an elite of religious virtuosi who choose to adopt a rigorous lifestyle constrained by a detailed set of rules in the hope of attaining moral perfection, equanimity, and advanced mental states.

An example of a monk pursuing the path with such a motivation is the story of the Buddha's half brother Nanda, who is described as extremely handsome. He was betrothed to the most beautiful woman in the land, but the Buddha coerced him into joining the monastic community. Nanda, however, continued to pine for his fiancée, who waited faithfully for him, renouncing all other men. Nanda began to lose interest in the religious life, and the Buddha noticed his distress. Hoping to cure Nanda's malaise, the Buddha took him to the Heaven of the Thirty-Three and showed him five hundred beautiful celestial nymphs in Śakra's retinue. He asked Nanda whether his fiancée could match them in beauty, and his brother responded that compared to the nymphs his betrothed was like a deformed and mutilated monkey he had seen on his journey. The Buddha then promised Nanda that if he dedicated himself to religious practice he would be reborn in the Heaven of the Thirty-Three and cavort with nymphs for the duration of a long and blissful lifetime as a god. Spurred on by thoughts of sexual dalliances with nymphs, Nanda threw himself enthusiastically into his training and attained progressively higher trance states. As the Buddha had intended all along, however, when Nanda reached the highest realization he transcended any interest in sex and thoughts of nymphs faded from his mind.[132]

The many and varied prohibitions against sexually motivated actions were designed to aid in the process of overcoming desire, the primary factor that keeps beings enmeshed in cyclic existence. Sexual activity requires passion, which is antithetical to attainment of advanced meditative states and nirvana, and it leads to ongoing involvement in the world and its travails. In the *Verses of the Elder Monks,* Gotama sums up this idea: "sages who are not bound to women sleep at ease."[133]

People whose actions are motivated by passions are subject to the cycle of birth, old age, and death, and married life symbolizes all the attachments and worries that monks seek to avoid. Married people are beset with concerns about housing, children, medical problems, family incomes, and interactions with other families and the larger society. If monks were to immerse themselves in such concerns, there would be no possibility of establishing a monastic order.

Sexuality also breaks down the bonds of the community of male ascetics that the Buddha founded. It leads to emotional attachments between couples, who commonly live together, raise children, and form families. The *saṃgha* was designed as a family of renunciants whose primary attachment is to the group, which was conceived as a society whose members cooperate in the pursuit of shared religious ideals, following a path to liberation that is enhanced by the support of one's companions.

Exemplary Masculinity

According to the texts of the Pāli canon, many of the Buddha's monastic followers were young men in the prime of life who, like him, left behind wives and families. A number of tales recount attempts by the abandoned wives to win back their husbands using their most important asset: their sexuality. In one such story, the former wife of Sangāmaji comes to him with their young son, demanding that Sangāmaji support them as a father should. He remains silent while she verbally abuses him. Hoping to awaken his fatherly instincts, she leaves the boy with him and walks away, but when she looks back she sees that Sangāmaji neither looks at his son nor speaks to him. Realizing that Sangāmaji has become free from any attachments, she retrieves her son and goes away defeated. The Buddha praises Sangāmaji, saying, "He takes no pleasure in her visit, does not care when she leaves. Sangāmaji is free from bondage; this is what I call a brahman!"[134]

A similarly heroic response is credited to Vīra, who is described as an outstanding athlete and mighty warrior. He too left his wife and attained arhathood. His former wife attempted to seduce him, but he spurned her, saying, "this woman trying to tempt me is like a person trying to shake Mt. Sumeru with the wing of a gnat."[135] She was reportedly so impressed by his indifference to her charms that she then entered the order of nuns.

The Pāli canon abounds with descriptions of Buddhist monks as handsome, virile, and manly, in the prime of their lives. Women are attracted to them, and the men are commonly chided for opting for the religious life while still young. In one such account, a deity says to the monk Samiddhi, "You have gone forth while young, monk, a lad with black hair, endowed with the blessing of youth, in the prime of life, without having dallied with sensual pleasures. Enjoy human sensual pleasures, monk! Do not abandon what is directly visible in order to pursue what takes time."[136] Samiddhi replies that in fact he undertook the discipline precisely in order to pursue that which is obviously valuable. He adds that the Buddha pointed out that indulgence in sensual pleasures is "time-consuming, full of suffering, full of despair, and the danger in them is much greater."[137]

As we saw in the previous chapter with regard to the Buddha, the compilers of the Pāli canon constructed depictions of his monastic followers as paragons of masculinity and used a range of epithets to establish this. Buddhaghosa states that a well-trained monk is like a "mighty king of panthers" *(mahādīpirāja),* who hides in tall grass or trees and watches his prey, such as a buffalo. In the same way, a student devotes himself to meditation in the forest.[138]

In a number of places Śāriputra is singled out as an example of monastic manhood. In the *Verses of the Elder Monks,* ten thousand gods in Brahmā's retinue come to pay him reverence and proclaim him "a general, a hero, a great meditator," and praise him, saying, "homage to you, stallion of a man, homage to you, best of men! We cannot even understand that on which you meditate!"[139]

On another occasion, while Śāriputra was engrossed in meditation, a passing demon *(yakṣa)* decided to attack him. The demon delivered a mighty blow to Śāriputra's head, but the great monk did not even notice it. Other demons declared that Śāriputra was "a mighty man, of great power and majesty." His friend Maudgalyāyana—renowned as the most advanced disciple in the development of psychic powers—saw what occurred and asked about Śāriputra's health. When Śāriputra replied that he felt fine but had a slight headache, Maudgalyāyana marveled that the blow Śāriputra had sustained would have "felled an elephant or split a mountain peak" but only caused him minor discomfort. As a result of this attack on such a holy personage, the demon experienced immediate karmic retribution, and screaming "I burn! I burn!," he plunged into hell.[140]

Even monks of lowly birth can become objects of admiration by gods. The *Verses of the Elder Monks* report that Sunīta was born into a family of flower scavengers and was "despised and abused" prior to taking ordination. Through diligent practice he attained advanced levels of insight, and Indra and Brahmā came to do homage to him: "Hail to you, nobly born man! Hail to you, mightiest of men!"[141] The prospect of a rise in status from the despised levels of Indian society to an object of admiration by the greatest of the Vedic gods must have seemed very attractive to people from the lower classes, and there are a number of such stories reported in various sources.

Tough Monks

A trope that is repeated throughout Indian Buddhist literature concerns the notion that Buddhist monks exhibit exemplary manly toughness. They endure hardships of the ascetic lifestyle that would defeat ordinary men, live in the wilderness among fearsome beasts in complete equanimity, and subsist on meager alms food and the bare necessities of life. In the "Connected Discourse with Similes," the Buddha praises monastic toughness and links it to success in religious practice. He further predicts that in the future the order will degenerate, that monks will no longer have the rugged self-control of his followers, and that the standard of attainment will thus suffer. He extols the Licchavis, who sleep on wooden pillows, and predicts that because of their rough discipline King Ajātaśatru will be unable to conquer them. He describes monks who sleep on wooden blocks as "diligent and ardent in striving" and adds that Māra will never defeat such men. He contrasts them with future monks, who will be too weak-willed to maintain this standard, who "will become delicate, with soft and tender hands and feet; they will sleep until sunrise on soft beds with pillows of cotton wool. Then Māra the evil one will gain access to them; he will gain a hold on them."[142]

Some exemplary monks are extolled for their strength, virility, and even martial qualities, all of which help them in their religious pursuits. An example is Piyañjaha, who had been a king and fond of battle prior to ordination and whose warrior courage enabled him to live in the forest without fear.[143] He reportedly attained arhathood. Another arhat named Abhibhūta is said to have "shaken off the armies of Māra as easily as an elephant does a straw hut."[144] In a later passage from this collection, Bhāradvāja applauds awakened monks as "lions roaring in the hill ravines, heroes who have won the holy war and conquered evil, Māra and his host." A number of other monks are credited with triumphing over Māra and his minions, including Kāśyapa, a "supreme man" who has "defeated Māra and his elephant."[145] He and other monks are also acclaimed for their wisdom, and the passage adds that even the most learned brahman is nothing compared with Kāśyapa and urges brahmans to pay homage to Buddhist monks.[146]

A number of men who desired ordination faced opposition based on their perceived softness and had to prove themselves tough enough to endure the privations of monasticism. Many of them are described as having fine hairs on the soles of their feet, an attribute that is linked to their sumptuous lifestyles. They never trod on hard ground and wore soft sandals and thus had no calluses. One such man was Lomasakangiya, whose whole body was covered with fine hair and who was described as being very delicate. When he requested ordination, senior monks were worried about his health, but despite concerns that he lacked the requisite toughness he persevered with painful sores on his feet and eventually became an arhat.[147]

In a similar story, a young man named Gahvaratīriya announced to his family that he intended to enter the Buddhist order, but his parents tried to dissuade him by describing the rigors of the ascetic lifestyle. He would be constantly attacked by mosquitoes and gnats in the forest, they told him, but he replied, "I wish to roam, like a warrior elephant, in the front of the battle, mindful and vigilant!"[148]

Such martial tropes abound in the descriptions of Buddhist monks. A common notion is that by taking their vows monks enter into a life-or-death conflict with Māra. *So It Has Been Said* declares that when a monk shaves his hair and puts on robes the gods declare that he is a noble disciple who intends to battle Māra. After the monk attains release, they say: "Here is a noble disciple who has conquered in battle! He now resides victoriously at the front of the battle . . . we worship you, O stallion of a man!"[149]

The dangers and terrors of the wilderness are described in great detail. They include extremes of cold and heat, rain, thunder, and other weather phenomena; bandits and other dangerous people; wild animals; and various nonhuman demonic figures capable of causing harm. The notion that ordinary people find these phenomena terrifying is highlighted in Indian Buddhist literature, and a number of monks are praised for their ability to maintain perfect equanimity in situations that would reduce most humans to abject fear. In verses ascribed to the arhat Saṃkicca, for example, he states that other men are afraid of wildernesses, but such places "delight" him. He adds that he is untroubled by beasts of prey and other dangers.[150]

The verses of Revata link this attitude with removal of mental afflictions and diligent attention to cultivation of morality: "just as a rocky mountain is unmoving, well-founded, so a monk, like a mountain, does not tremble after the annihilation of the obscurations."[151] In the same vein, the *Discourse Sections* equates the life of a solitary monk living in the wilderness with the way "a lion, the king of beasts, with strong teeth, roams overcoming other beasts, living in solitary surroundings."[152] The arhat Nigrodha sums up the ideal attitude of the forest-dwelling monk thus: "I have no fear of fearsome things."[153] In the "Connected Discourse to Deities," the Buddha tells a group of monks that forest dwellers attain great serenity because "they do not sorrow over the past, nor do they concern themselves with the future. They maintain themselves with what is present. Hence their complexions are so serene."[154]

The mental ease and peace of advanced monks is often contrasted to the anxieties of worldly life. A former king named Bhaddiya joined the order and left behind a mighty and wealthy kingdom for a life as a forest-dwelling ascetic. He was often heard to exclaim, "What bliss! What bliss!" Other monks thought that he might be reminiscing about his former lifestyle and longing for its pleasures, but when they mentioned this to him he declared that as a king he enjoyed all the perquisites of royalty but lived in constant fear of being robbed or assassinated. Other kings coveted his rich lands and treasury, and he was surrounded by armed guards day and night. He was always "fearful, anxious, trembling, and afraid." As a monk, however, he owned nothing, and so no one wished to steal his possessions. He dwelt in the forest "fearless, assured, confident, and unafraid." He added that he lived "at ease, unstartled, buoyant, with a heart like a wild creature."[155] His exclamations of delight related to his former life, but in a way that exalted the joys of monasticism.

Such equanimity in the face of danger is attributed to meditative training. Buddhist monks familiarize themselves with the doctrine of karma, which holds that every person has been reborn countless times in the past and that each existence has ended in death. Moreover, painful experiences are the result of one's own actions and so are inevitable for those who remain within cyclic existence. The arhat Adhimutta sums up the benefits of meditation:

> There is no mental pain for one who is without longing, a chieftain. Truly all fears have been overcome by one who has annihilated the fetters. When that which leads to renewed existence is annihilated and the physical world is seen as it really is, there is no fear at death, just as there is none when one puts down a burden. . . . I am dissatisfied with the physical frame; I am not concerned with existence. This body will be broken and there will not be another. Do whatever you wish with my physical frame. There will not be hatred or love there from me on that account.[156]

The ideal state of mind for a monk is described in a story in the "Bakkula Discourse," which recounts a meeting between the elder Bakkula and his friend Kassapa, a naked ascetic. Kassapa asked Bakkula how long he had been a member of the Buddha's order, to which the monk replied that it had been eighty years since his ordination. Kassapa then asked how many times during that period he had engaged in sexual intercourse. Bakkula informed him that he had asked the wrong question: the real issue was "during those eighty years, how many times did perceptions of sexual pleasures arise in my mind?" Bakkula informed his friend that from the time of his ordination no thought with the slightest hint of desire had entered his consciousness. He then added, "In the eighty years since I went forth I do not recall ever having grasped at the signs and features of a woman . . . ever having taught the dharma to a woman . . . ever having gone to a nun's quarters . . . ever having taught the dharma to a nun . . . or a female practitioner." His complete indifference is described as a "wonderful and marvelous quality of the venerable Bakkula."[157]

Another example of the proper monastic mindset was Mahātissa, who once encountered a beautiful woman on the road after she left her abusive husband. She laughed and displayed her physical charms in order to incite lust in the ascetic, but he had no interest and gave no response. When her husband later asked him whether he had seen a beautiful woman, Mahātissa replied that he had only seen a heap of bones passing the other way.[158]

Sometimes these attempted seductions resulted in spiritual growth, as when a courtesan propositioned Sundarasamudda (Handsome Samudda) by speaking "softly, sweetly, with a smile." She told him that he was too young and handsome to be a monk and that he should enjoy sensual pleasures with her until they both grew old, at which point they would become world renouncers. In this way, they could enjoy the best the world had to offer when they were young, and in their later years could pursue liberation. Sundarasamudda, however, remained steadfast and viewed her "like a snare of death spread out, and he realized the danger she represented and developed disgust with the world." As a result of his resoluteness, he became an arhat.[159]

The rigors of the monastic lifestyle created a common bond among men who considered themselves to be distinguished by their toughness and their fortitude in the face of attempted seductions. Some had come from privileged backgrounds, but all had to endure the privations of living in the open, sleeping on the ground, begging for food, and wandering from place to place with no fixed abode. They formed a community of men who willingly submitted themselves to the discipline of monasticism in pursuit of the supreme goal of nirvana, and they viewed this lifestyle as utterly superior to that of the lay community that supported their religious endeavors. Despite the constant assertions of the benefits of monasticism, the need to proclaim it over and over again indicates that many were uncertain about the wisdom of their choice, and some monks succumbed to temptation and returned to lay life. Such men are castigated as fools and weaklings, but their stories contain at least a tacit admission that life in society and raising a family, with their attendant rewards and travails, have some appeal.

Other Ascetic Orders

The Buddha and his community were in competition with other groups for disciples and lay support. Buddhist literature contains a number of descriptions of their rivals, none of which are particularly flattering. These rivals are portrayed as engaging in counterproductive activities that they believe will result in rebirth in heaven or liberation from cyclic existence, but which in reality lead only to negative karma and lower rebirths.

One such account of a "dog ascetic" states that a man who came to see the

Buddha described a practice that emulated the actions of dogs in the belief that this would result in a future life in heaven. The man walked around on all fours, howled and barked, and ate food from the ground, convinced that this difficult regimen would win him religious merit. To the ascetic's horror, the Buddha revealed that what this practice was really doing was cultivating the conditions for a future existence as a dog. He realized the futility of his training and joined the Buddhist order.[160] A similar story describes an ascetic who imitated the behavior of an ox: Vasubandhu states that various groups of non-Buddhists "adopt the habits of bulls, deer, or dogs" in order to "obtain purity, deliverance, liberation."[161]

The dignity and comportment of Buddhist monastics are regularly contrasted to the physical conditions of other religious communities. Buddhist monks are required to shave their heads and wear robes that are clean and neat. Robes should not be stained or frayed at the edges, and the outward appearance of monks is regularly cited as a reason why members of the monastic order are viewed positively by laypeople. In the "Monuments to the Doctrine Discourse," for example, King Pasenadi of Kosala visits the Buddha and exclaims that he is highly impressed by the Buddha's followers. The king states that he has seen men in other orders spend ten, twenty, thirty, or forty years leading a "limited holy life," but the next time he encounters them they are "well-groomed and well-anointed, with trimmed hair and beards, enjoying themselves with . . . sensual pleasures." Buddhist monks, in contrast, "lead the perfect and pure holy life for as long as life and breath last," and he adds that he has not seen any holy life anywhere as perfect as that of the *saṃgha.* Other orders are rife with internal discord, but the Buddhists live together in communal harmony, "in concord, with mutual appreciations, without disputing, blending like milk and water, viewing each other with kindly eyes."[162]

Rival groups fail to meet these standards. Moreover, their moral and spiritual accomplishments are displayed on their bodies: members of other ascetic movements are "lean, wretched, unsightly, jaundiced, with veins standing out on their limbs, such that people would not want to look at them again." The king concludes that they must be miserable in their misspent quest for liberation and that perhaps they committed evil deeds in the past that led them to such misfortune. This physical evidence leads him to proclaim: "that is why I infer that . . . the *saṃgha* of the Blessed One's disciples is practicing the correct way."[163]

Other ascetics are described as dirty and emaciated, and one such group is said to have "hairy armpits, long fingernails, and long body hairs."[164] This accords with descriptions in contemporaneous texts; the *Kuṇḍikā Upaniṣad,* for example, forbids world renouncers from shaving their armpits or crotches.[165] Walter Kaelber notes that this was a common practice for ascetics, because body hair and nails were thought to be saturated with *tapas,* and that by not cutting their hair and nails ascetics thought that they were maximizing their psychic power. A similar notion applied to bathing, and some yoga theories held that the dirt and sweat of unwashed skin help one to retain *tapas.*[166]

A number of texts indicate that although some people might regard the *saṃgha* as one among many ascetic orders, there is really no comparison. The "Brahmā Net Discourse" states that the Buddha was not, like other religious teachers of the day, a mere propounder of a speculative system but a sage who discovered a dharma of great antiquity that had been realized by other awakened beings before him. Buddhism is eternal truth, not merely one sect in the religious marketplace.[167] Buddhaghosa sums up the difference between Buddhist monastics and adherents of other systems:

> The thus gone ones [buddhas] behave like lions: by causing suffering to cease and showing the cessation of suffering, they concern themselves with the cause, not the effect. But heretics behave like dogs: by causing suffering to cease and showing the cessation of suffering, they concern themselves not with the cause, but with the effect by teaching such things as mortification of the body.[168]

Buddhaghosa notes that a lion pierced by an arrow will turn toward the person who shot it and prepare an attack, but dogs will foolishly assault the arrow that has caused them pain. He also indicates that Buddhist monastics are noble and wise and that they avoid petty speculative wrangling, while their opponents revel in useless quibbling. In the same vein, the *Discourse Sections* says of the Buddha: "None of those disputing heretics, whether fallacious reasoners (Ājīvaka) or bondless ascetics (Nigaṇṭha), can overcome you by wisdom, as one who is stationary cannot overtake one who walks swiftly."[169]

Prompted by jealousy of the obvious superiority of their Buddhist rivals, some other ascetic groups attempted to slander them. One such group became so incensed at the excellent public reputation of the *saṃgha* that members killed a woman who often went to the Jeta Grove to hear sermons and blamed it on Buddhist monks. They went so far as to publicly display her body and loudly proclaim that members of the Buddhist community were responsible for her death and that these Buddhists were false monks. They accused the monks of having sex with her and then committing murder to cover up their shameful deed and asked, "how can a man, after playing a man's part [i.e., having sex with her], then take the life of a woman?" Their deception was soon uncovered, however, and the public reputation of the Buddhist order remained unblemished.[170]

Performance and Observation

Accounts of monks and nuns in Indian Buddhist texts demonstrate a pervasive concern with public opinion and portray the community as one among a number of rival groups that is constantly scrutinized by a wary public that regards some self-styled ascetics as charlatans seeking a free meal. The laity police the conduct of those who seek alms from them to ensure that their gifts go to worthy recipients and thus yield maximum merit. They look to the bodies of world renouncers for signs of spiritual attainment; physical health, beauty, an athletic frame, a calm demeanor, and pleasing features are evidence of inner virtues, particularly of control of normal urges. As Margaret Lock and Nancy Scheper-Hughes state, "the individual body should be seen as the most immediate, the proximate terrain where social truths and social contradictions are played out, as well as the locus of personal and social resistances, creativity, and struggle."[171] Thus the Buddha proclaims that if monks dress in the morning, put on their robes and beg, and then teach the dharma, laypeople will have confidence in them, and thus monks "will increase in beauty and strength."[172]

It is important, however, that this comportment be natural and not contrived. Buddhaghosa criticizes monks who imitate the physical attitudes of realized beings in order to impress others, who adopt "an affected style of walking or lying down, who walk, stand, or sit with the intention of keeping up appearances . . . as though they possess concentration and pretend to be rapt in trance."[173] For the ideal monk, the performance is uncontrived. Foucault's description of the goal of hygienic regimens is similar to that of Buddhist monastics, for whom

> the practice of regimen as an art of living was something more than a set of precautions. . . . It was a whole manner of forming oneself as a subject who had the proper, necessary, and sufficient concern for his body. Entailing a reflexive approach to the body that made matters of health, cleanliness and morality the personal responsibility of the individual, hygiene reinforced bodily boundaries and separated bodies from one another.[174]

The discipline of Buddhist monks was designed to allow them to perform their social role flawlessly, to display an outward calm and dignified demeanor that required years of intensive cultivation, but which should appear as the unforced manifestation of their true nature. Their bodily comportment provided the public with a window into their inner beings, one that revealed their virtues to the world. In ancient India the body was considered a natural symbol that proclaims and substantiates cultural and religious values and norms. The culture valorized those who could make thoroughly cultivated attitudes and physical states appear artless, innate components of the individual and social identities of those who possessed them.

Repression of their desires was a key component of the process, one that required that monastics overcome the normal sexual urges with which all humans are born; Buddhist meditative training promised that those who were successful could attain a level of consciousness in which struggle would be transcended and a state of perfect passionlessness attained. Monks or nuns who succeeded in this are described as leading lives of undisturbed peace and happiness, experiencing sublime joys beyond the comprehension of worldly beings whose greatest pleasures are those of the senses—which are denounced as low and vulgar in Buddhist texts. Humans share the ability to enjoy transitory sexual release with animals, but only advanced monastics can attain the higher trance states and the perfect peace of nirvana. This accords with Foucault's notion that repression promises greater benefits: "indefinite extension of vigor, health, and life,"[175] and for this reason Buddhist monastics willingly gave up mundane pleasures for others that were considered more sublime.

As we have seen, the *Monastic Discipline* is profoundly concerned with the physical comportment and public conduct of monks, who are the standard bearers of discipline. Buddhists, like other religious groups of the time, viewed the male body as naturally more conducive to self-control than the female body was. Females are depicted as constantly oozing fluids and as prone to emotional instability, while men are physically stronger, more controlled, and less subject to the vagaries of emotion. The pervasive use of warrior epithets directed toward the Buddha and his male monastic followers emphasizes the differences between men and women: the male members of the order arrive at ordination with bodies that are stronger, tougher, and more suited to the religious path, and their natural masculine qualities of courage, determination, resoluteness, self-restraint, and physical strength appear to give them an edge.

There are numerous stories of women who successfully engage in meditation and attain arhathood, but the overwhelming emphasis is on men.

As Connell notes, "masculinity and femininity are inherently relational concepts, which have meaning in relation to each other, as a social demarcation and a cultural opposition."[176] This applies in the characterizations of Buddhist monks in Indian Buddhist texts: those who fall short of the ideal are commonly referred to as effeminate and are often assigned womanly qualities, while those represented as successful exemplars of monastic ideals are equated with fierce and powerful animals, such as lions, bulls, and stallions, which are associated with masculinity.

Monks' heroic renunciation of the joys of household life and sexuality heightened their sense of difference from the surrounding society and their moral superiority to those involved in the "low life." Their sexual continence distinguished them from nonmonastics, who are often portrayed as living loose and immoral lives. Buddhist monastic lore acknowledged the universal force of sexual desire, but it promised a training program that could completely eradicate it and presented those who exemplified its ideals as heroes who had given up lesser pleasures in pursuit of the highest good. The perfect body of the Buddha held out a promise to his followers that they too could transcend the harsh realities of the flesh and overcome death. Through his austerities and accumulation of good karma, the Buddha developed a physique that was ideally suited to the religious life, whose perfection was obvious to all who viewed it. By following his path, his followers could either acquire such bodies in future lives or emulate his example and attain release from birth and death in their present existences.

The next chapter will examine in more detail how the body was conceived by the authors of Buddhist canonical texts and the wider society. As we will see, ancient Indian understandings of human physiology differ in significant ways from those of contemporary Western medicine and anatomy. It is also important to understand these discourses because there is no notion of a mind-body division in Indian Buddhist texts: meditative training involves both, and physical discipline is closely linked to meditation. A disciplined body and a serene mind are part of a package in the system attributed to the Buddha.

4

The Problem with Bodies

Man is formed of dust, mud, and, what is even viler, of foul sperm. . . . Who can ignore the fact that conjugal union never occurs without the itching of the flesh, the fermentation of desire and the stench of lust?

—Pope Innocent III, "De Contemptu Mundi"

A curse upon bodies, evil-smelling, on Māra's side, oozing. There are nine streams in your body that flow all the time. Do not think much of bodies.

—Nandaka, *Theragāthā-aṭṭhakathā,* II.116–117

Oozing

Indian Buddhist literature abounds with admonitions against attachment to the body and with vivid descriptions of the foulness of the body's contents. At the same time, there is a pervasive concern with maintaining health, with physical cleanliness, and with certain bodies like the Buddha's that reflect the spiritual attainments of adepts. In addition, even though the human body is described as vile and repulsive, it is also the best physical situation within cyclic existence for those who seek liberation.[1] The lower destinies of hell beings *(nāraka),* hungry ghosts *(preta),* and animals *(tiryak)* are subject to continual suffering, and the minds of these beings are clouded by passions, while the higher rebirths are also antithetical to recognition of the negative realities of cyclic existence. Demigods *(aśura)* are consumed by jealousy and engage in constant warfare, while gods *(deva)* live long and blissful lives and are unable to grasp the fact that their tenure in the divine realms will eventually come to an end and they will be plunged into lower rebirths. Humans are ideally situated: they have enough intelligence to recognize patterns of rebirth and suffering, they experience sufficient unpleasantness themselves that they wish to eliminate it, and those whose past actions have brought them to favorable life situations have the time and resources needed to abandon household life and devote themselves to full-time religious practice. Thus for all its faults, the human body is the ideal vehicle for liberation.

In Indian Buddhism, the final goal of nirvana is conceived as a state beyond embodiment and future birth and is also said to be perfect bliss. One who attains it passes beyond all categories, even existence and nonexistence. Those who enter nirvana have no further need of bodies, but people on the path do.

This ambivalence is reflected in Buddhist discussions of the body. On the one hand, it is important for trainees to overcome attachment to and excessive concern with their physical forms, but monastics are also urged to maintain a neat and clean appearance, which is part of their appeal to the lay community that supports them. Thus Buddhaghosa instructs monks to be observant of the cleanliness of the physical basis of existence, which involves cleansing both external and internal bases. One should regularly wash the hair and keep it short, because if the hair of the head or body or the nails of the hands and feet are long, this is a sign that the "internal physical basis is not clean, not pure." Similarly, robes should be washed regularly, and one should not wear stained or smelly garments in public: "when the robe is old, dirty, foul-smelling, or one's dwelling is full of rubbish, then the external physical basis is not clean, not pure." A monk with such a soiled physical basis will attract condemnation from fellow monastics and the lay community; and his body and environment will negatively affect meditation. Buddhaghosa states that insight developed in such situations is tainted, like a flame produced by a dirty wick, lamp, or oil.[2]

Buddhist monastics are admonished to engage in practices that discipline, restrain, and control their bodies, but at the same time the body is conceived as a source of uncontrolled functions, such as oozing, digestion, excretion, and menstruation, all of which undermine attempts at subduing it. Vivid descriptions of the body's unstable nature are commonplace in Indic literature, and in the "Discourse to Māgandiya," the Buddha refers to it as "a disease, a tumor, a calamity, an affliction,"[3] adding that people who do not understand this reality cannot attain nirvana. In the *Discourse Sections,* he notes that the body leaks various liquid substances and describes it as dirty: "in [the body] nine streams of impurity constantly ooze: from the eye conjunctivitis, from the ear otitis, from the nose mucus; sometimes the body emits vomit from the mouth and ejects bile and phlegm. From the body come sweat and filth."[4]

In the *Verses of the Elder Monks,* writers often denounce their bodies; this is connected with their meditative practice, which involves close analysis and observation of the body's functions and a resultant sense of disgust. In one such passage, Kappa declares:

> Full of stains of different sorts, a great producer of excrement, like a stagnant pool, a great tumor, a great wound, full of pus and blood, immersed in a toilet, trickling with water, the body always oozes foully. Bound by sixty tendons, plastered with fleshy plaster, covered with a jacket of skin, the foul body is worthless. Held together with a skeleton of bones, with bonds of sinews, it produces its various postures by the union of many things. Set out with certainty for death, the vicinity of the king of death, a man who has abandoned it in this very place goes where he wishes. The body is covered with ignorance, tied with the fourfold tie; the body is sinking with the flood, caught in the web of latencies. . . . [T]he blind ordinary beings who cherish this body fill up the terrible cemetery; they take on renewed existence. Those who avoid this body like a drug-smeared snake, having spurned the root of existence, will be quenched without defilements.[5]

The body is open to the environment and permeable, but it can be closed off through meditative practice, which has both mental and physical dimensions. Meditators learn to observe the functions and changes of the body, and they discipline its movements. Control over bodily functions increases, and the practice of restraint helps the meditator to develop resistance to negative influences. The *Verses on Doctrine* compares the process to the way poison can enter one's hand if it has an open wound, but not if the skin is intact. In the same way, one who guards the doors of the senses and the body against evil influences will leave no place for evil to enter either the mind or body.[6]

Many Indian ascetic orders engaged in yoga practices that involved bending the body into various positions as part of a program of physical discipline, but Buddhism generally rejected such techniques as pointless, a waste of time and energy, and as counterproductive. The "Greater Discourse to Saccaka" reports a debate between the Buddha and Aggivessana, a proponent of the value of yoga for physical discipline, in which the Buddha rejects the ascetic's contention that yoga is a worthwhile religious practice. Aggivessana accuses Buddhist monks of "pursuing development of mind, but not development of body." He views the body as one's most important possession and believes that it should be trained and developed through exercise. The Buddha responds that he teaches techniques like mindfulness of the body that contribute to physical development but that difficult exercises are ultimately exhausting and useless. The goal of religious practice should be to dissociate oneself completely from sensual pleasures and to acquire knowledge, vision, and finally awakening. Exercise is superfluous and wastes time that could better be spent in productive meditation.

The Buddha describes various yogic regimens but concludes that in the final analysis these only tire the body and do not contribute to any of the core aims of the religious path. He points out that during his ascetic period he performed a wide range of such practices, but "my body was overwrought and not calm because I was exhausted by the painful striving."[7] Instead the Buddha prescribes meditative procedures that involve sitting or walking slowly, cultivating calming attitudes of body and mind that foster awareness and insight, and he sees no value in physical performances that only seek to manipulate the body.

In an ironic literary twist, after the Buddha has refuted Aggivessana's points, his opponent's body manifests his abject defeat. The Buddha boasts to the assembled monks that Aggivessana has become terrified, that large beads of sweat have formed all over his body. The ascetic "shakes, trembles, and sweat appears under his armpits." The Buddha emphasizes Aggivessana's physical discomfort, highlighting the irony of a self-proclaimed master of yogic discipline whose uncontrolled body manifests his internal turmoil: "now there are drops of sweat on your forehead, and they have soaked through your upper robe and fallen to the ground. But there is no sweat on my body now."[8] The Buddha then "uncovered his golden body before the assembly" to prove that his skin was dry and that he was completely calm, while Aggivessana had been reduced to a sweating mess of anxiety and humiliation. Aggivessana then "sat down silently, dismayed, with shoulders drooping and head down, glum, and without response," and admitted that the Buddha was correct in his statement that the body is "not mine," but rather an impermanent collection of aggregates that are constantly changing and unworthy of confidence.

Meditation on the Foul

As part of the meditative regimen designed to eradicate lust and attachment to the body, the Buddha taught a technique referred to as "meditation on the foul," which involved contemplating the stages of decomposition of corpses. These are classified into various types: the newly dead, the slightly decomposed, the bloated and discolored, those that are torn apart by wild animals, skeletons with bits of flesh clinging to them, and bare skeletons.[9] In the "Greater Discourse of Advice to Rāhula," the Buddha describes the benefits of such contemplation to his son: "develop meditation on foulness, for when you develop meditation on foulness any lust will be abandoned."[10] Vasubandhu states that this technique eliminates four types of cravings *(rāga):* for colors, shapes, contact or tangibles, and honors.[11] He adds that meditation on a corpse that is turning blue eradicates the first craving, while contemplating a corpse that is wasted and torn to pieces banishes the second. Taking as one's meditative object a skeleton held together by tendons removes the third, and an immobile cadaver is the antidote to the fourth. He advises meditators who engage in this practice to mentally visualize a part of the body, such as a toe or the forehead, and then to "purify" the bone, which means removing flesh from it. One then enlarges the visualization to view the whole body as a skeleton and extends the image to include another individual. Continuing the process, one imagines that the area is covered by skeletons and then increases the scope to larger and larger regions, finally encompassing the entire earth. One then reduces the visualization in order to strengthen its power and the recognition of one's own mortality by viewing only one's own body as a skeleton.[12]

Buddhaghosa provides a detailed description of this practice in the *Path of Purification.* He states that a meditator who wishes to engage in meditation on the foul should first approach his teacher and receive instruction. This is important because such meditation is a powerful technique that has many attendant dangers. A trainee should be thoroughly familiar with what is to be done, with the aims of the meditation, and with potential pitfalls. Once the student has been given advice, he should not eagerly rush out into wild places when he hears that a corpse has been spotted, because dead things attract fierce animals and nonhuman beings that can cause harm. Buddhaghosa also cautions that when a monk is alone in a remote place he might encounter a woman who will attempt to seduce him.[13] Another danger is that the corpse might be of the wrong gender: males should meditate only on male corpses, because counterproductive lust might arise if he should view a dead female, particularly one without clothing: "A body very recently dead has a pleasant appearance, and so there may be danger to his religious practice."[14] Several examples of this problem are presented in Indian Buddhist literature, including the story of Rājadatta, who saw a female corpse in a cemetery and experienced unwelcome feelings of desire: "truly I was blind to the oozing body." Fortunately he soon recovered his sense of meditative purpose and fled from the decomposing but still attractive form. He recalled the Buddha's instructions on the foulness of the body, and as a result of his experience and subsequent contemplation became an arhat.[15]

Buddhaghosa advises trainees to travel with companions when venturing into remote areas. The latter can provide protection as well as emotional bolstering if one should falter. While walking to the place where the corpse (referred to as "the foul thing") lies, one should remain upwind if at all possible in order to avoid becoming overwhelmed by odors of decomposition. One should also approach with caution, because dangerous people such as thieves commonly inhabit charnel grounds, and a gang might stash its loot near a dead body. An innocent monk in the vicinity could be accused of stealing it. His companions can vouch for him and can also help in scaring off dangerous animals.

Buddhaghosa promises that a monk who takes the proper precautions and enlists such aid from his fellows will "derive joy and gladness from a desire to see the sign of the foul." Buddhaghosa describes an analytical procedure in which the meditator dispassionately observes the location of the corpse, its surroundings, color, gender, shape, boundaries, joints, curves, and parts. He advises against standing either too near or too far from the object of observation: if one is too far away, details will be indistinct, but if one is too close, there is danger of being overwhelmed by the smell of decomposition. After thorough observation and analysis, the meditator is said to have acquired the corpse as an internal object of observation and can bring it to mind anywhere.

In both the *Path of Purification* and the *Explanation,* Buddhaghosa adds that one should remain aware that a living body is as foul as a corpse and is composed of the same disgusting substances.[16] Living bodies are covered by clothing and ornaments and their odors are disguised by washing and scents, but these are only temporary and superficial. Living bodies also attract flies and parasites, and they are constantly oozing various substances.

The *Monastic Discipline* mentions a potential danger of this practice: it can cause meditators to be so overwhelmed by the foulness of their own bodies that they can no longer stand to be associated with them. A story that illustrates this states that once the Buddha was living in Vaiśalī, and he "spoke in many ways on meditation on the foul," following which he went into solitary retreat for two weeks. The monks he had instructed applied themselves diligently to the technique and became "troubled by their own bodies, ashamed of them, loathing them," and felt as if they had a carcass of a dog or a snake hanging from their necks. As a result, they decided to commit suicide and asked a "false ascetic" to kill them. After dispatching a few monks, the false ascetic began to feel remorse as he washed off his bloody knife, but a minion of Māra came to him and praised his actions, stating that he had helped them to fulfill the goal of the religious path. After this he went from monastery to monastery seeking monks who desired to be similarly liberated and sent a total of sixty to their deaths in one day.

When the Buddha emerged from his retreat, he asked Ānanda: "How is it that the company of monks is so diminished?" Ānanda replied: "It is because the Blessed One talked to the monks in many ways on the subject of the foul." Ānanda added: "It would be good, Blessed One, if you were to give another instruction so that the company of monks might be established in profound knowledge." Recognizing the pragmatic value of Ānanda's advice, the Buddha then ordered the surviving monks in the area to gather, and he instructed them to stop meditating on the foul and instead to cultivate mindfulness of breathing.[17]

Recollecting the Buddha

Not all bodies are conducive to meditation on the foul. As we saw, monks are advised to avoid taking a female corpse as the object of this practice because of the danger of becoming sexually aroused.[18] Several Buddhist texts also assert that the Buddha's body cannot generate revulsion either when it is alive or dead because it is perfect. According to the Everything Exists School, the physical form of the Buddha was sublime in every respect, and because it was pure, clear, bright, and subtle, it is impossible to find any fault with it. Even minor injuries, as when Devadatta attempted to kill the Buddha by rolling a rock down a hill and only slightly cut the Buddha's foot, healed immediately and left no scar. There were no blemishes or faults of any kind on the Buddha's physique.

Because of its perfection, the Buddha's body can serve as the basis for another meditation: recollection of the Buddha *(buddhānusmṛti)*. As Buddhaghosa describes it, a meditator should first develop complete confidence in the Blessed One and should catalogue the Buddha's many good qualities. He or she then finds a solitary retreat place and reflects: "the Blessed One is such since he is accomplished, fully awakened, endowed with vision and good conduct, sublime, the knower of worlds, the incomparable leader of men to be disciplined, the teacher of gods and humans, awakened and blessed."[19] This meditation serves as a basis for attaining advanced trance states.

Buddhaghosa avers that when one contemplates the Buddha's body and his exalted qualities, spontaneous happiness is produced. This leads to tranquility and bliss: "when one is blissful, one's mind, with the Awakened One's special qualities for its object, becomes concentrated, and so the factors of concentration eventually arise in a single moment."[20] On this basis, one begins to emulate the Buddha's attainments, and Buddhaghosa states that this also helps one develop respect for the Buddha, aids in development of mindfulness, and produces understanding and merit. One who succeeds in bringing to mind a vivid image of the Buddha experiences gladness and joy and conquers fear and dread. Buddhaghosa also promises increased resistance to pain and states that "one comes to feel as if one were living in the Master's presence."[21] In describing this practice, Buddhaghosa advises meditators to use Buddha images as a way of forming a mental image of him.

As we saw in previous chapters, Buddhist writers held up the Buddha's body as the epitome of physical perfection, and there are numerous stories of people (and nonhumans) being spontaneously converted by the mere sight of him.

Reclining Buddha, Wat Pho, Bangkok, Thailand, which depicts several of the physical characteristics of a great man, including flat feet, *cakras*, and various other symbols. Photograph by John Powers.

This quality is also thought to inhere in well-constructed images, which reflect the good qualities of their subject and produce feelings of devotion in those who view them. An interesting permutation on this idea is a story in which Upagupta (a renowned Buddhist monk who lived after the Buddha's death and who is said by tradition to have been the preceptor of King Aśoka) was engaged in a struggle with Māra that eventually resulted in the latter's conversion (a feat that not even the Buddha was able to accomplish). At one point Upagupta realized that Māra had seen the Blessed One in the flesh and that he had the ability to assume any shape he wished. He asked Māra whether he could manifest the form of the Buddha, and the demon agreed that he could easily do so but made Upagupta promise that he would not show any devotion to the Buddha's form, which he said would be embarrassing for both of them. Upagupta replied that there was absolutely no chance that he would ever pay reverence to Māra, but when he saw the Buddha's glorious body before him, endowed with the major and minor physical characteristics and shining like smelted gold, he was so overcome with piety that he threw himself on the ground and began prostrating. Māra reminded him of his promise, and Upagupta was able to regain his composure and recognize that despite the beauty of the form in front of him, it was only Māra in disguise.[22]

Mindfulness of the Body

Discussions of Buddhist ethics commonly emphasize the central role of volition. Inadvertent actions are generally regarded as less morally significant than those involving conscious choice. Harmful deeds based on inattention are also condemned, and Buddhism makes people responsible for their actions and the effects they have on other beings. Indian Buddhist discourses on ethics focus both on mind and body, and there is no clear separation between the two. The ideal state is one of mindful awareness, in which meditators develop an attitude of alertness toward the body and its changes as well as toward their emotional states, consciousness, and environment. The Buddha regularly exhorts his followers to be aware of their physical conduct and its impact on others and their surroundings and to cultivate proper bodily comportment. In the "Discourse on What Should and Should Not Be Cultivated," for example, he provides a set of guidelines for Śāriputra regarding what should and should not be done with the body, which is divided into what should be cultivated and what should not be cultivated. The latter includes any attitudes or actions that "cause unwholesome states to increase and wholesome states to diminish"—for example, the murder of living beings; violence; stealing; indulgence in sensual pleasures; and intercourse with women who are protected by their mothers, fathers, brothers, sisters, or relatives or who are married, protected by law, or engaged. Wholesome states result from the abandonment of such activities and the cultivation of kindness and compassion as well as the avoidance of theft and sensual indulgence.[23]

Buddhist monks are expected to develop a calm demeanor and to walk slowly and thoughtfully and in full understanding of their actions, looking at the ground about three feet ahead. Their dignified bearing proclaims their inner virtues. One of the most important techniques for attaining this state is mindfulness of the body *(kāya)*, which is one of the four "foundations of mindfulness" (Skt.: *smṛtyupasthāna;* Pāli: *satipaṭṭhāna*).The other foundations of mindfulness are of feelings *(vedanā)*, mind *(citta)*, and phenomena *(dharma)*. Mindfulness involves observing and calmly categorizing physical states, developing awareness of bodily changes, and abandoning the inattentive attitude of most people, who move through life largely unaware of what is happening with their bodies. The Buddha promises that such concentration will lead to diminution of desire and aversion with regard to the world, as well as an attitude of equanimity toward the body:

> A monk exercises clear comprehension when moving forward and returning; when looking ahead and looking to the side, when drawing in and extending the limbs; when wearing his robes and carrying his outer robe and bowl; when eating, drinking, chewing his food, and tasting; when defecating and urinating; when walking and standing, sitting, falling asleep, waking up, speaking, and keeping silent.[24]

This practice provides a basis for observing one's feelings and categorizing them. When a pleasant feeling arises, one recognizes it as pleasant and concentrates on it with calm dispassion, rather than fixating on the agreeable experience. One then considers whether the feeling is dependent or independent and understands that it is dependent on the body. The next stage of the contemplation analyzes the body itself: it too is impermanent, dependent on causes and conditions external to itself for its birth and maintenance. When a pleasurable feeling dependent on the body arises, it must also be impermanent and so is unworthy of confidence because it will inevitably fade, often resulting in a sense of loss and longing. The meditator then considers the transitory nature of pleasant feelings, reflecting on how they arise from nowhere, abide for awhile, and then vanish: "as he dwells thus, the underlying tendency to lust in regard to the body and in regard to pleasant feeling is abandoned by him."[25] The same analysis is then applied to painful and neutral feelings, and through this one develops an attitude of equanimity toward physical phenomena and the feelings prompted by them.

In the "Discourse on Mindfulness of the Body," the Buddha provides detailed instructions for this practice. The meditator should go into a forest and sit under a tree or in an empty hut, fold his legs, keep the body erect, and breathe in and out while maintaining awareness that he is doing so. He should be mindful of long breaths, mindful of short breaths, and should breathe in while experiencing the whole body. This makes the body tranquil, and the meditator becomes "diligent, focused, and resolute."[26] He then expands the practice to include mindfulness of the body while moving: he should walk slowly in a circumscribed area, maintaining a close focus on the body and its states. Similarly, mindfulness should be applied to every physical activity, including sitting, lying down, moving, extending the limbs, washing, and defecating. Every action, no matter how trivial, is a basis for the development of mindfulness.

> In this way one abides contemplating the body as body internally; or one abides contemplating the body as body externally, or one abides contemplating the body as body both internally and externally. Or else one abides contemplating in the body its arising factors, or one abides contemplating in the body its vanishing factors, or one abides contemplating in the body both its arising and vanishing factors . . . and one abides independent, not clinging to anything in the world. . . . [W]hen walking, a monk understands "I am walking"; when standing, he understands "I am standing"; when sitting, he understands "I am sitting"; when lying down, he understands "I am lying down"; or he understands accordingly however his body is disposed.[27]

The next stage involves an analysis of the constituents of the body, which is composed of the four great elements—earth, air, water, and fire—and has various components, such as skin, bones, hair, and limbs.[28] Beginning at the soles of the feet, the meditator mentally catalogues all the parts of the body, meticulously focusing on each in turn and drawing attention to it. This is often followed by meditation on corpses, which is accompanied by the realization that the meditator will share the same fate.[29] The "Larger Discourse on the Foundations of Mindfulness" contains a version of this practice in which one mentally dissects the body like a butcher cutting up a cow and displaying various parts for inspection by potential customers. One first observes the arising and cessation of phenomena in the body and develops sustained awareness of every physical activity, including urination and defecation, and then proceeds to an analysis of the body's component parts.[30]

Training in mindfulness of the body has many benefits, including enhanced powers of observation and development of equanimity. In the "Discourse on Mindfulness of the Body," this practice is said to conquer discontent and delight, fear and dread, as well as physical discomfort caused by cold or heat, hunger or thirst, stinging insects, wind, sun, and creeping things. One is no longer bothered by verbal abuse, and one can easily enter the four concentrations and develop various supernatural powers, including "wielding bodily mastery as far as the Brahmā world."[31] Successful meditators also acquire the divine ear, which allows them to hear sounds at vast distances. They can read others' minds, perceive events of their past lives, and eliminate mental afflictions.

Vasubandhu states that one who is absorbed in mindfulness of the body can perceive the atoms that compose the body and the successive moments of its states. He recommends a number of focal points for observation, including ingestion of food, origin of food, origins of the body, disappearance of food, disappearance of the body, origin of physical contact, origin of cessation, origin of name and form *(nāma-rūpa),* and origin of mental activity *(manasikāra).*[32] Buddhaghosa indicates that the equanimity generated by this contemplation leads to elimination of anger and of other negative mental states. He advises meditators who find themselves becoming angry with another person to perform a similar analysis: When I get angry, am I annoyed by the elements that compose the other's body? Or am I irritated by the aggregates of the psychophysical personality (form, feelings, discriminations, compositional factors, and consciousness), the sense organs, or other parts of the body?[33] When one realizes that there is no true focal point for anger, its force diminishes.

The Buddha indicates that those who successfully cultivate mindfulness of the body develop an attitude of detachment toward the phenomena of experience. Bodily sensations are no longer personal; rather, one learns to observe them from a cognitive distance. Both pleasant and painful feelings are viewed objectively and are no longer conceived as "mine." Even life and death become matters for observation:

> If one feels a pleasant feeling, one feels it in a detached manner; if one feels a painful feeling, one feels it in a detached manner; if one feels a neither painful nor pleasant feeling, one feels it in a detached manner. When one feels a feeling terminating with the body, one understands, "I feel a feeling terminating with the body." . . . One understands: "With the dissolution of the body, following the end of life, everything I feel—because I do not take pleasure in it—will become cool right here; mere bodily remains will be left."[34]

Meditators who become adept in this practice are no longer bothered by anything, even extremes of pain or pleasure. By viewing the body in terms of the four great elements and its various constituents, one becomes indifferent to its vicissitudes. In the "Greater Discourse on the Simile of the Elephant's Footprint," the Buddha indicates that for such an adept, even if bandits "sever you savagely limb by limb with a two-handled saw," no animosity arises if one has the proper mental orientation.[35] No matter what physical harms are inflicted, one considers the body as a collection of gross elements, and the suffering no longer is experienced as one's own. When viewing the various physical constituents, monks should constantly reflect: "this is not my self."[36]

The Buddha adds that the elements have no concern with how they are treated; if water is used to wash away disgusting substances, for example, it does not complain or even notice. The body is composed of water and the other elements, and none of them are affected by our emotional responses to physical occurrences.[37] Moreover, the elements that currently constitute the body are only temporarily a part of it; new matter is ingested, waste is excreted, various substances ooze out from orifices, and skin peels off and is discarded; and so the body should be understood as a process, not as a fixed possession that one can hold onto and maintain indefinitely.

Impermanence

Mindfulness of the body is connected with recognition of its impermanence. Ordinary beings move through life as though they will live forever, but everyone who has ever lived has died, and there is no reason to suppose that any currently living individual will be spared that fate. When he saw the first three of the "four sights," the Buddha was reportedly shocked by the fact that most people encounter the signs of impermanence—age, sickness, and death—every day but fail to draw the obvious conclusion that they ought to live in a way that takes these realities into account. Instead, they pursue short-term ends and fleeting pleasures, all the while moving closer to their inevitable demise. Buddhist meditators, by contrast, are urged to spend time every day contemplating the impermanence of their bodies and the inevitability of death. In the "Discourse on the Fruits of the Homeless Life," the Buddha describes the proper attitude toward physical transitoriness: "This body of mine is material, composed of the four great elements, born of mother and father, fed on rice and gruel, impermanent, liable to be injured and cut, broken and destroyed, and my consciousness is bound to it and dependent on it."[38] The *Verses on Doctrine* urges practitioners to maintain diligence in this practice, because the time of death is uncertain and every moment is precious: "Knowing that this body is [fragile] like a jar, making this thought [firm] like a city one should fight Māra with the weapon of wisdom, and one should guard what has been conquered; one should not rest. Before long this body will lie on the earth, rejected, without consciousness, like a useless bag of wood."[39]

Making Bodies

In keeping with the importance Buddhist meditation literature places on awareness of the body and its processes, significant attention is devoted to describing how bodies are produced and develop and the processes that contribute to their degeneration and death. Discussions of medical topics in Buddhist texts generally agree with those of Āyurvedic treatises. In Indian medical texts, the male body is normative; females are born as they are because of deficient karma and due to the dominant influence of the mother. Except for depictions of gynecological problems and pregnancy, most of the images in Indian medical texts are male. The same is true of the orientation of medical discussions in Buddhist texts. Most of the compilers of these works were men, and thus they focus on the male body almost exclusively, except when they specifically discuss women. There is a clear bias in favor of male bodies, which are assumed to be stronger and more conducive to development of self-control. Thus Buddhaghosa asserts, "of these two, the masculine sex is superior, the feminine is inferior. Therefore the latter may be brought about by weak morality." He adds that a man who commits many grave offenses may be changed into a woman in this very life as retribution. Conversely, a woman who performs good deeds may be rewarded by a spontaneous sex change: "thus [the marks of] both sexes change—[those of males] disappear on account of many offenses, while with many good actions [a female] becomes a male."[40]

In both Buddhist and non-Buddhist medical lore, a similar picture of conception, gestation, birth, physical development and pathologies, and old age and death appears. As noted in chapter 3, there is compelling evidence that empirical medical science first emerged in India in Buddhist circles, and thus this convergence is not surprising. Kenneth Zysk contends that the Buddhist origins of this lore were disguised by the creation of a brahmanical pedigree, according to which Brahmā is said to be the originator of medicine. He taught it to Prajāpati, who gave it to the Aśvins, the physicians of the gods, and they instructed Indra. He passed it on to Dhanvantari, who manifested in the form of Divodāsa, king of Kāśī, and thus it appeared among humans. Divodāsa was Suśruta's teacher, and he wrote down the lore he received in *Suśruta's Medical Compendium.* Indra also transmitted medical knowledge to the sage Bharadvāja, who gave it to other sages, including Ātreya, who trained six disciples, among them Agniveśa and Bhela. In order to benefit humanity, Agniveśa composed a treatise that was codified by his student Caraka and later redacted by Dṛḍhabala, entitled *Caraka's Medical Compendium.* Zysk dismisses this lineage as "merely the result of a later Hinduization process applied to a fundamentally heterodox body of knowledge in order to render it orthodox," an attempt to disguise the fact that medicine's real origins lie in techniques developed in Buddhist monasteries.[41] Dominik Wujastyk states that the earliest version of *Caraka's Medical Compendium* probably was compiled around the third or second centuries BCE but that it was not widely quoted until the period of the Gupta dynasty (320–480 CE).[42] Wujastyk accepts the idea that the system of Āyurvedic medicine represented in the treatises of Caraka and Suśruta probably originated around the time of the Buddha.[43]

In Āyurveda and Buddhist texts, conception is said to result from a mingling of sperm and the female equivalent (sometimes said to be menstrual blood), and their relative concentrations and strengths were believed to have a significant impact on the gender and physical endowments of progeny. According to Caraka, if the sperm is more powerful, a male child will be produced, and if the mother's contribution to the zygote is more potent, a female will be conceived.[44] A woman is most fertile immediately after menstruation, and this is the ideal time for intercourse: "When a woman after her menstruation cohabits with a man of a different clan in a secluded place, the man ejaculates something composed of the four great elements and having six tastes, which results in conception by a woman."[45] The commentary adds that for healthy conception the man and woman must be of different clans; coitus among members of the same clan is a "sinful act that does not have the sanction of scripture."[46]

Privacy is necessary for undisturbed ejaculation, and both partners must be in the appropriate (missionary) position. Any intercourse performed in alternate positions will result in physical abnormalities in the fetus. Caraka cautions that use of such positions can result in hypospadia,[47] and he describes a range of defects that are caused by sexual experimentation. A male child conceived by a father with weak sperm *(āsekhya)* will have a tendency to develop an erection from swallowing other men's semen. If the father uses a "polluted genital tract," the child will become aroused by the smell of female and male genital tracts *(saugandika).* If the sperm is weak or absent, the offspring will be an impotent man or woman.[48] The child may also be a non-man with some masculine characteristics *(trinaputrika).*[49] Another permutation is for a man to find satisfaction in being sodomized by another man *(kumbhika).*[50]

Physical cleanliness and ritual purity are also important factors. Caraka advises women who desire healthy children to have a purificatory bath immediately after their menstrual periods and following the influx of fresh menstrual blood. Buddhaghosa describes the process of conception:

> Every month a watery bloom is produced. This is the blood known as the specialty of the woman. At the time when the woman entertains a desire for sex-pleasure, at the place where the child rests a clot of blood is produced. On the seventh day, it breaks by itself. On account of this, blood oozes out. When the flow of blood has not yet stopped, a man's semen cannot settle. It immediately flows out. If the flow has completely ceased, then the man's semen rotates all over that place and then conception takes place, just like a field which a family tills and makes fit by burning. But if there is excessive water and grain put into it, the grain floats over the surface of the water and flows out in all the four directions. Why? Because water is excessive. The grain does not get in touch with the mud and does not get rooted. The same is the case with a woman. If the flow of blood has completely stopped, a man's semen gets settled and then there is conception.[51]

In addition to such physical factors, the mother's state of mind is crucial in determining both the gender of her child and its physical endowments. Caraka advises women who desire sons to continuously and intently observe a large white bull or a stallion every morning and evening.[52] Such large, powerful animals symbolize masculinity, and her practice will create a propensity for maleness in the embryo, as will concentration on white things in general (as this is symbolic of semen).[53] Caraka notes that "a woman will give birth to a child resembling that person of whom she thinks at the time of conception."[54] He adds that ideally a woman should desire a son, an assumption generally made throughout Indian literature.[55] Caraka recommends that the woman focus her mind on the goal of producing male progeny and that she regularly recite these verses: "May I obtain a son, large of limb, white, with eyes like those of a lion, full of vigor, pure and endowed with intelligence!"[56]

After conception has occurred, various physiological signs indicate the probable gender of the fetus: according to Indian medical lore, female fetuses naturally gravitate toward the left side of the uterus, and males reside in the right.[57] Caraka states that if a pregnant woman has a propensity to use her left hand, if she desires the company of men, if she craves food and drink associated with women, and if milk appears first in her left breast, the fetus is a female. The opposite is true for males.[58]

The quality of the father's semen plays a determinative role in the process of conception and development. Indian medical lore holds that semen is produced by a process of refinement of the elements comprising food and that semen pervades the tissues of the entire body.[59] Caraka states that just as sugar is found in the whole cane, so semen is present throughout the body. It is also "a formative principle in all bodies in the universe."[60] According to Wendy Doniger, in the Vedas, semen is conceived of as both a substance and a process, and it is connected to rain, which links heaven and earth and makes things fruitful.[61] The energy contained in rain seeps into plants and other types of food and is then ingested and refined into semen, which becomes the vital force that provides energy and sustains life.

Semen is the source of physical vitality (in some sources menstrual blood is the female equivalent).[62] Buddhaghosa differentiates among various types of semen and rates their relative quality. He states that if a man's semen smells like honey he will be wealthy, and if it smells like fish he will beget many children. If it is thin he will produce daughters, and if it smells like flesh he will live comfortably. A man who ejaculates quickly will live a long time because he does not waste his vital energies in lengthy love play, and if he prolongs the experience of coitus he will die early.[63]

Indian medical literature contains many examples of medicines and foods that can increase seminal potency and the chance of conceiving a son. Caraka mentions several such potions and promises that "these preparations make one highly virile, robust, and strong. One who ingests them develops the vigor of a stallion; such a man enjoys sexual intercourse."[64] The ideal is an abundance of semen; the more one produces, the greater the chance that a son will be conceived. In describing the benefits of one such potion, Caraka promises, "he who wishes to have an inexhaustible store of semen and great phallic strength should take four portions before meals."[65] Another potion results in the "virility of a stallion," allowing a man to "copulate with a woman for as long as he wishes."[66] Caraka promises that men who "eat as much as they can of rooster's meat fried in the semen of a crocodile will not be able to sleep at night due to maintaining a continuous erection of the penis."[67]

Medical authorities link copious amounts of semen to female satisfaction. In describing the benefits of a potion to increase seminal volume, Caraka states that a man who ingests it will fully satisfy a woman with a seminal discharge like that of an elephant.[68] Both Buddhist and non-Buddhist sources assume that women crave semen, because it allows them to produce male progeny, and relative volume is commonly linked with female sexual pleasure. The more they get, the happier they are. Women also play a central role in producing sexual desire in men. Summing up a discussion of various potions and foods that can increase semen production, improve the quality and duration of erections, and enhance sexual performance, Caraka concludes that ultimately an attractive partner is the best aphrodisiac:

> The best means of stimulating one's penis is having an exciting sexual partner for a wife. When the desired sense objects bring great pleasure, even if experienced by one of the senses, then there is no need to speak of a woman in whom all the desirable objects of the senses are found together. Such combinations of enticing objects of all the senses are found only in women and nowhere else. . . . A woman who is beautiful, young, endowed with auspicious physical attributes, pleasant, and skilled in the erotic arts is the best sexual stimulant.[69]

The same is true of men. Those who are young, athletic, and physically attractive and whose bodies excite their partners are more likely to impregnate these women, and such men will provide greater pleasure during coitus. Interestingly, a number of Indian sources agree that a long penis is not a desirable attribute for a man, and length is not connected with female stimulation in any text I have seen. The *Bṛhat-saṃhitā* asserts that a small penis is best and that men fortunate enough to be endowed with such members will be wealthy, while those who have large ones will be unable to produce sons.[70] The *Kāma Sūtra* classifies penises into three types: hare *(śaśa),* bull *(vṛṣa),* and stallion *(aśva);* the first type is the smallest and the most desirable.[71] The hare type man has greater penis dexterity and a nature that is calm and gentle, while the other two are linked with large, powerful bodies and violent, willful personalities. The hare type has an agreeable and well-proportioned body and a pleasant personality.

As Thomas Laqueur has noted with respect to Western conceptions of sexuality, traditional Indian medical literature conceived of the bodies of men as normative and viewed women's bodies as inferior copies.[72] The female equivalent of semen is either menstrual blood or an undefined substance, which is also produced through a process of refinement of food and contained in bodily tissues. One reason for considering women to be weaker and more prone to loss of vitality is the belief that the process of menstruation robs them of their vital essence.

Wujastyk states that in Āyurvedic literature there is no obvious equivalent to semen for women, though women are assumed to possess some sort of generative substance that is involved in conception. He cites Suśruta to the effect that two women engaged in sexual intercourse might "somehow" produce semen and thus conceive, and he adds that in this system ordinary conception is understood as a mingling of semen and menstrual blood.[73] The blood that is discharged during menstruation mixes with sperm and is subsequently retained during pregnancy, constituting the mother's contribution to the development of a fetus.[74] As Walter Kaelber notes, semen was regarded as fertile by itself and as capable of producing offspring without female blood, but women require semen to conceive.[75] Semen is also productive of other things, such as rain and good crops, and there are numerous stories in Indian literature of the semen of gods and human sages contributing to the fructification of the natural world.

Buddhaghosa asserts that conception can occur in six ways: (1) through "mutual contact of bodies," that is, sexual intercourse; (2) when a woman holds a piece of cloth that has semen on it; (3) from drinking semen; (4) by touching a man's penis; (5) by looking at a man's penis; or (6) by smelling it. In addition, a woman can conceive if a man touches her erogenous zones while aroused by desire. Coitus is not necessary if she is in her fertile period, and the potency of semen can also cross the divisions of species. According to a story cited by Buddhaghosa, a female deer once ate grass on which an ascetic had inadvertently shed his seed, and she became pregnant.[76] Buddhaghosa notes that a fertile woman need only look at a man in order to conceive, and pregnancy can result from hearing the sound of a rooster or from smelling a bull's breath.[77]

The potency of semen is linked to the energy it contains as a result of the process of refinement of food into the essence of the matter that comprises the semen.[78] One of the key reasons monks retain their seed is the belief that loss of semen results in weakness and premature death. Some Indic sources assert that it is possible to reclaim lost seed, however; according to the *Bṛhadāraṇyaka Upaniṣad,* if a man wishes to engage in sexual intercourse with a woman but does not want her to conceive, during the encounter he should place his mouth over hers, exhale, and say, "With power, with semen, I reclaim the semen from you."[79] Through this the potency of the semen returns to him, and she is deprived of it. The text also states that it is possible to recover the virile essence of semen that has been inadvertently shed on the ground by pronouncing a mantra: "Whether asleep or awake, if one should spill his semen, he should touch it and say, 'That semen of mine which was today spilled on the earth, or has flowed to plants or to water, I reclaim that semen. Let virility return to me, and energy and strength. Let the fire be put in its right place, on the fire altar.'"[80]

I have not seen any Buddhist texts that contain similar techniques for reclaiming shed semen or the vital energy lost through ejaculation. The Buddhist literature generally appears to regard semen as gone forever once it emerges from the penis, and so monks are urged to guard the doors of the senses and cultivate meditations designed to eliminate lust. Nocturnal emissions are not considered offenses against the monastic code, but several discussions in Buddhist literature link them to residual feelings of sensual desire, and monks who attain a state of complete dispassion are generally thought to eliminate the possibility of inadvertent ejaculation, even in dreams.

Developing Bodies

A being's physical endowment is closely linked with karma. Suzanne Mrozik, citing Elizabeth Grosz, states that Indian Buddhism conceives of bodies as inherently "pliable"—"that is, subject to transformation, because bodies are largely the products of our own actions. . . . Karma dictates the kind of body we get in any given lifetime—whether male or female, healthy or sick, beautiful or ugly, and so forth."[81]

When a child is born, it is endowed with a controlling faculty, either a "factor of masculinity" (Skt.: *puruṣendriya;* Pāli: *purisindriya*) or a "factor of femininity" (Skt.: *strīndriya;* Pāli: *itthindriya*). Buddhaghosa points out that female bodies are different from those of males and relates this to the effects of the female controlling faculty, which is the cause of a woman's features, body form, shape of hands, feet, neck, breasts, and so forth, all of which differentiate women from men: "The female lower body is broad, the upper body is small . . . the female breast is prominent. The face is without beard or moustache. The way they fix their hair and the way they wear clothes are also unlike those of a man."[82]

Buddhaghosa also states that the female controlling faculty produces the secondary sexual characteristics along with certain predilections that he regards as natural, such as a tendency to play with dolls, baskets, or household dishes. Moreover, there are innate physical mannerisms, such as "a lack of assertion in women's walking, standing, lying down, sitting, eating, or swallowing. Indeed when a man of that description is seen, people say, 'he walks, stands, etc., like a woman.' " A woman is born a woman as a result of past karma, and gender can be changed only in exceptional circumstances. The outward signs of femininity, such as body shape and facial features, are not the feminine controlling faculty, but only its manifestations. The faculty itself cannot be perceived with the eyes, but its effects can. Buddhaghosa adds that "by natural law the controlling faculty of a woman is of the woman only."[83]

The male controlling faculty leads to manifestation of "masculine sex, attributes, behavior, and features":[84]

> Masculine features should be understood as the opposite of the feminine. The shape of the hands, feet, neck, breast, etc. of a man is unlike the shape of those of a woman. A man's upper body is broad, the lower body is less broad; his hands and feet are large, the face is large, the breast flesh is less full; beards and moustaches grow. The way they wear their hair and their clothes are not like those of women. In youth they play with chariots and ploughs, etc., make sandbanks and dig ponds. There is assertion in their walking, etc. When a woman is seen taking long strides, etc., people say, "she walks like a man."[85]

Thus, according to Buddhaghosa, the respective gender controlling faculties predispose people toward certain physical mannerisms and preferences for particular actions and occupations. This is considered entirely natural, and Buddhaghosa assumes that culturally produced gender roles and preference for certain body types are also the result of nature. Even clothing, choice of adornments, and other transient aspects of fashion are linked to the respective controlling faculties.

Changing Bodies

In the modern West it is generally assumed that bodies can be made; through the proper physical regimen, we can turn ordinary bodies into physiques that elicit admiration from others. Exercise, diet, and lifestyle all contribute to this process, and people who fail to properly address themselves to practices of bodily improvement are regarded as blameworthy. Those who are disinclined or too busy for regular exercise or who enjoy eating fattening foods often feel the need to apologize for their lack of attention to physical enhancement. The popular media abound with images both of people who conform to society's physical ideals and of those who fall short, and the latter are often subjected to an overt judgment of their actions that implies a certain moral deficiency.[86]

In ancient Indian conceptions of the body, however, one is born with a particular physical endowment as a result of past actions, and there is little that can be done to improve it. During any given lifetime, one has the body one received at birth. Exceptional bodies like that of the Buddha are the result of nature in the sense that they are produced at conception. As children grow, some physiques quickly attain perfection with little effort, while other people are born with sickly or weak bodies, and they too are predetermined to remain that way. Those who are not strong or who suffer from chronic physical ailments, who are too tall or too short, or who are deficient in some way are not to blame (except in the sense that they are as they are because of past karma), and there is little point in devoting oneself to physical culture, lifting heavy weights, running, jumping, and so forth because those with superior physical endowments will always surpass their less-favored fellow citizens as a result of their karmic legacy. The Buddha makes this point when he asks Aggivessana if one can change one's body by merely wishing, "May my form be thus; let my form not be thus." Aggivessana, a proponent of the value of exercise and physical training, reluctantly admits that the body is what it is, and only minor changes can be achieved through physical regimens.[87]

Alongside this fatalistic conclusion, however, there is a widespread belief in both Buddhist and non-Buddhist sources that some bodies are able to change form and that in certain circumstances it is possible to shift genders. And as Wendy Doniger states, transgender change is regarded in Indian culture as a fairly common occurrence: "The Hindu myths assume that a man can be a woman; there is no problem about it at all."[88] In one such story, the sage Āsaṅga was cursed by the gods and changed into a woman, but he was able to use his psychic power *(tapas)* to reverse the transformation, and the process also stiffened his formerly "boneless" male organ, to the delight of his wife.[89] The *Ancient Lore of Viṣṇu* contains a story of multiple gender transformation, which began when Manu offered a sacrifice intended to produce sons. The ritual was corrupted, however, and as a result a daughter named Ilā was born. The gods Mitra and Varuṇa took pity on Manu's misfortune and changed her into a man, who was given the name Sudyumna. Subsequently he attracted Śiva's ire and was again turned into a woman. Later the sage Budha fell in love with her and they married. Together they had four sons, but out of compassion for her condition Viṣṇu caused her to regain her male form.[90]

In another non-Buddhist myth, a brahman named Bhaṅgāśvana had acquired great power by performing many horse sacrifices *(aśva-medha)*. Indra resented the fact that Bhaṅgāśvana had conducted more of these rituals than him, and one day when the sage bathed in a lake Indra changed him into a woman. As a man he had produced one hundred sons, and in his female form s/he married a male ascetic and gave birth to one hundred more. The two hundred men shared his/her kingdom in harmony until Indra incited them to war against each other. All of them perished in the conflict, but Indra later repented his actions and restored them to life. He gave Bhaṅgāśvana a choice between remaining a woman or being changed back into male form, but s/he chose to remain female because s/he claimed that women derive greater pleasure from sex.[91] This conclusion would appear obvious to most Indian authors. In classical Greek myth, Tiresias was blinded by Hera for agreeing with Zeus that women enjoy sex more than men, but few if any commentators of Indian antiquity or the classical period would demur.

In Buddhist texts, the ability to shift shape is credited to several of the Buddha's disciples, particularly Maudgalyāyana, whose powers of transformation were surpassed only by those of the Buddha himself. The *Path of*

Discrimination states that this is a common ability among advanced meditators, who can

> abandon their normal appearance and manifest the appearance of a boy or the appearance of a *nāga,* the appearance of a *supaṇṇa* (winged demon), the appearance of a demigod, the appearance of the ruler of the gods (Indra), the appearance of some deities, the appearance of a Brahmā, the appearance of the sea, the appearance of a rock, the appearance of a lion, the appearance of a tiger, the appearance of a leopard. They can manifest as elephants, as horses, as chariots, as foot soldiers, or as a manifold military array.[92]

In the *Path of Purification,* Buddhaghosa describes how adepts with great supernatural power *(siddhi)* can create various forms, can appear in a mind-made body, or can make a physical image of a boy, a snake, or an army merely by wishing it.[93] This ability can be used to impress non-Buddhists and to cause them to convert, or it can serve various pragmatic purposes, such as protection from danger. In one story of physical transformation, Sumana went to a lake to get water, but a giant *nāga* rose up from it and threatened to attack him. The monk assumed the form of a *garuḍa,* a fierce winged creature with sharp claws, and defeated the *nāga.*[94]

A number of Buddhist stories of physical transformation involve sex change, and this appears to have been a significant concern for the men who composed and redacted Indian Buddhist texts. In one famous example reported in the *Discourse Spoken by Vimalakīrti,* the lay bodhisattva Vimalakīrti pretends to be sick in order to induce the Buddha to send his disciples to inquire about his health, which will initiate a discussion of dharma.[95] When they arrive at his house, a dialogue between Mañjuśrī and Vimalakīrti ensues, and following a particularly noteworthy speech a young goddess who lives in the house causes heavenly flowers to rain down on the assembly. When the flowers touch the bodhisattvas, the flowers fall from their bodies onto the ground, but Hīnayānists like Śāriputra find that the flowers cling to their robes, and they frantically strive to brush them off. The reason is that monks are forbidden to wear any adornments, and flowers are mentioned in the *Monastic Discipline* as a prohibited decoration. Thus the monks, who are portrayed as attached to the letter of the law, consider them to be a violation of their vows.

The goddess addresses Śāriputra and asks him why the monks want to remove the flowers, and he replies, "Goddess, flowers are not fitting for monks; that is why we reject them." The goddess rebukes the great elder and states that the flowers present no obstacle to the religious vows of monks: "The flowers are flowers and are free from conceptuality; it is only yourselves, the elders, who conceptualize them and create conceptuality toward them. Venerable Śāriputra, among those who have renounced the world to take up monastic discipline, such conceptualizations and conceptuality are not fitting."[96] She points out that because the bodhisattvas have eliminated the false conceptuality imprisoning the thoughts of the Hīnayāna monks, the flowers fall off them: "Flowers stick to those who have not yet abandoned the latent predispositions; they do not stick to those who have abandoned them."[97]

Śāriputra appears to become embarrassed by the situation: the greatest of the Buddha's followers in cultivation of wisdom, an elder male monk admired by all his fellows, is completely upstaged in his specialty area by a young woman in front of the entire assembly. In what appears to be an attempt to bring her down a peg by pointing out her gender, he asks, "Goddess, why do you not change your womanhood?"[98] She responds by stating that concepts of gender are merely conceptual creations with no real basis, and to illustrate her point she changes her body into that of a man, while Śāriputra is transformed into a woman.

The elder monk is profoundly uncomfortable in his new form: monastic vows prevent him from any physical contact with women, but now he is unable to avoid his own body and so is in intimate physical association with a woman. The goddess asks him why he does not change his womanhood, and he replies, "I cannot see either how I lost my male form nor can I comprehend how I acquired a female body." The goddess replies that if he could change his female body, then all females could do the same, and she adds, "just as you appear to be a woman, so also all women appear in the form of women, but they appear in the form of women without being women. It is with this hidden thought that the Blessed One said: 'Phenomena are neither male nor female.' "[99] She then changes Śāriputra back into his original form, much to his relief, and she returns to her female body.[100]

This passage is remarkable on several accounts. First, it was probably written around the second century CE and anticipates contemporary analyses deconstructing gender categories by centuries. Second, it was composed in a highly patriarchal society in which male superiority was commonly assumed. The unnamed goddess is not only female but also young, which challenges Indian associations of wisdom with elder males, and the fact that Śāriputra, the epitome of wisdom in the Pāli canon, is depicted as utterly unable to match her insight and eloquence is also significant.

In some Indian Buddhist stories, gender changes occur voluntarily, and advanced meditators can temporarily assume a form for a particular purpose and then shift back. Two such incidents are credited to Upagupta. In one of these, a monk who is a student of Upagupta is unable to stop thinking of his former wife, and his attachment is a barrier to progress. Upagupta takes on the form of the student's wife, and the sight of the guru in a woman's body—particularly one for which the younger man felt lust—shocks the student into recognition of his failure to leave his former life behind. Upagupta then returns to his normal form and delivers a sermon that helps his student commit himself fully to the monastic regimen.

In another story, a second student of Upagupta rescues a drowning woman from a raging river, but when he brings her safely to shore he becomes inflamed by desire and begins to force himself on her. To his horror, the young and attractive woman suddenly transforms into his teacher Upagupta, and the student immediately tries to disengage. Upagupta, however, wraps his arms and legs around the monk more tightly and asks why he no longer appears to desire him. The experience of finding himself atop the elder monk in a sexual position was reportedly so traumatic that the young man is completely cured of his lustful tendencies.

Most gender transformations in Indian Buddhist literature are involuntary, and when men change to women it is commonly portrayed as a tragedy for them and as a result of extraordinarily negative conduct. Vasubandhu mentions a hypothetical case of how this might occur: a monk unthinkingly insults other members of the *saṃgha* by saying, "You are nothing but women!," and because they are faultless monks the offhand slight has serious consequences. In immediate retribution, the offending man is changed into a woman himself. Vasubandhu cites this as an example of an action with a weak intention directed toward an excellent field.[101] He also mentions a case of a eunuch who rescues bulls about to be castrated, and as a result regains his own sexuality. In both cases, the results are concordant with the actions performed and also relate to the recipients of those actions.

A similar story concerns a young brahman man named Soreyya who was riding in a carriage with some friends and happened to see the arhat Mahākaccāna putting on his upper robe before going out on his alms round. When

Soreyya saw the beautiful, golden-skinned body of the elder, he inadvertently thought, "I wish that elder would become my wife! Or may the color of my wife's body be like the color of his body!" As a result of this impure thought in regard to such a pure object, Soreyya was instantly transformed into a woman. He was so startled by the change that he bolted from the carriage before his friends could see what had happened to him. S/he ran away and eventually settled in the city of Takkasilā, met the son of the city's treasurer, and married. During the next four years, Soreyyā lived with her husband and gave birth to two sons. One day a former companion visited the city and saw her, and Soreyyā invited him to her house. When she recounted the story of her transformation, the friend advised her to find Mahākaccāna and ask his forgiveness for thinking lustfully about him. Soreyyā took the advice and went to the elder's hut the next day. After explaining what had happened, Soreyyā asked the monk to absolve her. As soon as Mahākaccāna spoke the words "I pardon you," she regained her male form. The experience led Soreyya to enter the Buddhist order and renounce the household life. He eventually became an arhat, and his experience with gender bending was a significant aspect of the process.[102]

In some cases, gender reversal can apparently occur without any noticeable precipitating event. Buddhaghosa provides advice for monks who find that their cell mates have suddenly changed into women during the night. Monastic rules forbid monks from cohabiting with women, and so if one's companion becomes a woman one must immediately leave the residence, even if it is dark and there is nowhere else to stay. If the change occurs during the day, Buddhaghosa advises the monk who remains male to console his cell mate and help him recover emotionally from the tragedy that has befallen him. He cannot continue to share a residence with him, of course, and so the still-male monk should lead his former companion to the nuns' quarters and tell him that all is not lost because it is possible for a woman to pursue the holy life.[103]

For most women, there is little chance of being transformed into a man in the present life, no matter how diligently they engage in religious practice and accumulate good karma. Most stories of women changing into men happen across lifetimes; the positive actions of one birth are rewarded by a male body in subsequent lives. In one such account, Gaṅgādevī pays devotion to the Buddha, and he promises her that the merit she receives from this will lead to her rebirth as a man in her next life and that she will remain in the male gender until she attains buddhahood.[104] Several Indian Buddhist sources indicate that mental attitude is important, and if a woman develops distaste for the female form she improves her chances of moving up to manhood. An example is Gopikā, who "observed the precepts scrupulously. She rejected the status of a woman and thought of becoming a man. After her death she was reborn as a male deity in the Heaven of the Thirty-Three.[105] According to the Chinese *Middle Length Collection,*

> Gopī, a daughter of the Śākyas, was a disciple of the Blessed One. She followed the Blessed One and practiced celibacy. She abhorred the female body and loved the male form; she changed her female body and took a masculine form. She renounced desires and abandoned desires. On the dissolution of her body after her death, she was reborn in a good place, among the gods of the Heaven of the Thirty-Three.[106]

In the *Heroic Meditation Career Discourse,* the deity Gopaka refers to this story and recounts his past life as a woman of the Śākya clan. Dṛḍhamati asks him, "through what good-rooted action did you change your female body?" Gopaka replies, "those who are pledged to the Mahāyāna do not see any difference between man and woman. Why? Because the omniscient thought is not found in the three worlds and because [notions] of man and woman are caused by conceptuality. You ask me, O friend, through what good actions I changed my female body: well, it is because in the past I served the Bodhisattva with a mind free from hypocrisy."[107] This is an interesting interpretation, because the accounts of this story in the *Middle Length Collection* and *Long Discourse Collection* clearly link the successful gender change to Gopikā's revulsion toward the female body and to desire for a male physique.

Vasubandhu promises that a woman who attains the meditative state of supreme mundane qualities *(laukikāgra-dharma)* will receive a male body in her next life.[108] One who reaches this plane will be reborn as a man in all future existences. He adds that an adept at this level completely destroys any propensities to femaleness.[109] For most beings, however, the future is more uncertain. It is assumed in Indian Buddhist literature that rebirth as a human male is the result of cultivation of past merit, often over many lives. Such a state is high in status and provides a precious opportunity for religious practice. A man has a clearer mind and a stronger body and is less susceptible to emotions, and male bodies are more controlled and less prone to oozing than are those of women.

Texts in which gender change is discussed evince an underlying concern with the fragility of the male state and the threat of losing what one has gained from past good deeds. An inadvertent thought can reverse one's positive karma and result in immediate gender shift. In addition, inattention in the present life or failure to recognize the tenuousness of one's current endowment can lead one to squander a male birth on sensual pleasures or to engage in acts of arrogance or violence that will result in future retribution, perhaps as a female or a lower form of life. For every story of a woman who successfully escapes the female condition and is predicted to be blessed with male physiques in subsequent existences, there are many cautionary tales of men who are changed into women or cursed to spend future lives in female forms.

This chapter has mainly focused on discourses relating to physicality produced by Indian Buddhists. The body is the proximate locale of individual practice and exhibits the relative level of spiritual development of an individual practitioner. The next chapter will examine the collective aspect of Buddhist monastic life, particularly how those who chose full-time religious vocations were supposed to relate to each other and forge a cohesive community of seekers with shared orientations and goals.

5

The Company of Men

In poverty and other misfortunes of life, true friends are a sure refuge. The young they keep out of mischief; to the old they are a comfort and aid in their weakness, and those in the prime of life they incite to noble deeds.

—Aristotle, *Nicomachean Ethics*

Friendship

The "Connected Discourses on the Path" reports that Ānanda once told the Buddha his view of the value of friendship for men pursuing the religious life: "It seems to me, Blessed One, that good friendship is half of the holy life." The Buddha admonished him for this notion and exclaimed: "Do not speak thus, Ānanda! Noble friendship is more than half the holy life; it is the entire holy life!"[1] He added that without the Buddha, their best friend, there would be no way for monks to receive instruction.

Monastic friendship is regarded as essential for men pursuing the goals of the Buddhist path, which include serenity, equanimity, attainment of trance states, wisdom, the major stages of accomplishment (stream enterer, once returner, nonreturner, and arhat), and the final bliss of nirvana. Fellow monks provide guidance and serve as role models of successful practitioners, and they also help their compatriots in maintaining vows of celibacy and in their adherence to monastic discipline.

A number of anecdotes indicate the importance the Buddha placed on having a support group who are committed to the same goals, who are one's companions on the path and helpers in times of distress. In one such account, a monk became gravely ill with a digestive disorder. His condition worsened, and as he became weaker he could no longer clean himself and became covered with his own filth. His fellow monks who were concerned with maintaining their purity abandoned him and moved to other quarters, leaving him to fend for himself. Instead of simply admonishing them, the Buddha provided a personal example of how monks should support each other: together with Ānanda he went to the ailing monk's quarters and personally bathed him, provided him with sustenance, and then removed the detritus from his residence.

The Buddha later convened an assembly of the community and chastised them for abandoning their brother monk. He pointed out that renunciants leave behind family, friends, and other social networks in pursuit of a difficult path aiming at the ultimate goal of nirvana. There are many pitfalls along the way, and one's companions constitute an essential support group that can help in difficult times and that is committed to the same goals. Monks should view each other as brothers—even as closer than their biological brothers because of their fellow monks' central importance to the religious life—and they should commit themselves to helping each other.[2] As Mohan Wijayaratna points out, "Buddhist monks were essentially social beings, for two reasons. First they were members of a society . . . in which they had responsibilities. Second . . . they depended on lay people for clothing, medicine, and food, and they also had responsibilities, duties, and rights in relation to lay society. So they were not isolated, without social relations or friendly contact with their neighbors."[3]

Male friends, particularly those who are also monks, are the only dependable companions. Women are presented in Indian Buddhist texts as oppositional figures who try to impede progress. Former wives importune their estranged spouses to return to them and their children; mothers lament their sons' career choices and try to induce them to renounce their vows and reenter lay society. Women are driven by lusts, fears, and passions and with few exceptions (such as some exemplary nuns and female lay supporters) are only able to comprehend short-term benefits, while men appear to have a greater capacity for religious pursuits and enter the order in greater numbers than women.

Even those women who choose the religious life cannot become members of one's support group because of the dangers of potential sexual attraction. Monks and nuns were expected to live in separate communities, and contact between them was fraught with danger and circumscribed. There is no indication in Indic sources that a man might fall in love with another man and consequently leave the order in order to pursue a romantic relationship. Men are ideal friends because their bonds are nonsexual, and they can develop relationships that are close and lasting without the destabilizing factor of sexual attraction. Laypeople, who are essential to the survival of the order because they provide necessary alms, can also present difficulties for monks because the pleasures and luxuries of their lifestyles may tempt those of weak resolve. Male members of the *saṃgha,* however, are the best companions for men on the religious path because they are similarly committed to lives of celibacy and meditative practice, they can bolster those whose enthusiasm wanes, and they provide the sort of encouragement and aid that laypeople derive from their spouses and extended families.

Joining the Order

The standard procedure for entering the order has two stages. The first is novice ordination, which can be conferred on any boy who is old enough to scare away a crow (generally around six years of age). A period of at least ten years is then required before one can request the full ordination, which has a minimum age of twenty. Each aspirant must have a preceptor (Pāli: *upajjhāya;* Skt.: *upādhyāya*) who is willing to commit himself to providing religious instruction. The right to confer ordination ultimately rests with the community, which must approve both the preceptor and the ordinand's request. The preceptor must have spent at least ten years as a fully ordained monk and be recognized as an elder *(thera).*

The relation between novice and preceptor is conceived as an intimate one. The older monk provides instruction and guidance and acts as a role model for how to live the religious life. According to the *Monastic Discipline,* preceptor and novice should be like a father and son: the student should respect and care for his mentor, and the preceptor should make sure that the pupil's needs are met. These include spiritual, physical, and financial matters. The senior monk is expected to ensure that his pupil has enough to eat and that he owns two sets of proper robes, and if he is sick the preceptor should beg for food and medicine to help him recover. The elder monk should also teach his student the doctrine and monastic discipline, both through oral instructions and personal example.

The student commits himself to an attitude of respect and promises to follow his teacher's instructions diligently. A preceptor has the right to dismiss a pupil who is disrespectful, lazy, or fails to make progress. If this occurs, the novice should be assigned to another preceptor, and if the problems persist he might be required to leave the order. The harshest penalty for monastic offenders in the early community was "highest punishment" *(brahma-daṇḍa),* which was imposed on monks who persisted in arrogance or other bad behavior. This involved being frozen out of the society of the order: other monks were not to speak to such wrongdoers or have any personal dealings with them. One person who received this penalty was Channa, the former charioteer of the Buddha who later joined the *saṃgha* but was reportedly guilty of repeated acts of arrogance and refused to repent.[4]

The student may also help to ensure that his teacher is correct in the details of his comportment, as is illustrated by a story in which Śāriputra was told by his novice that his robe was not properly arranged. The great monk thanked him for his observation and commented that his trainee aided him in his practice.[5] Ideally the relationship between master and disciple should be a partnership, although the senior monk is clearly in the dominant position: "Both must establish deference, respect, and commitment to communal life between them, in order to grow prosperous and strong in the doctrine and monastic discipline."[6]

The *Monastic Discipline* indicates that this relationship is crucial to the survival of the order, and several instances of incompetent preceptors are recorded. In some cases the students became so disenchanted that they left the order.[7]

Rambling Men

As originally conceived by the Buddha, the *saṃgha* was supposed to be a loosely organized community of wandering ascetics, who would travel from place to place with no fixed abode, begging for alms and other necessities of life. The sole exception to the wandering lifestyle was the rainy season retreat (Pāli: *vassa;* Skt.: *varṣa*), when monks were enjoined to spend their time in a temporary residence, ideally in the company of others. The Indian monsoon often brings torrential rains that turn roads to mud, and travel becomes difficult. It is also a time of increased danger from disease and waterborne parasites, and so the injunction to remain in one place had a pragmatic basis. It also served to create an enhanced sense of community.

During the Buddha's lifetime, he and his band of disciples traveled from place to place. They owned some donated pieces of land where they could reside when they wished, and they often returned to these places, but part of their lifestyle involved moving into new areas and spreading their teachings. This imperative was initiated by the Buddha eight months after his awakening as he traveled toward the village of Senāni: "Monks, take to the road; travel for the good of the many; travel for the happiness of the many, out of compassion for the world. Travel for the good, benefit, and happiness of humans and gods. Preach the doctrine!"[8]

Wijayaratna contends that in the early days of the religion the imperative to disseminate the doctrine and attract new followers (and financial support) made travel necessary.[9] Some monks wandered all the time, proselytizing widely and working to expand membership in the new community, while others stayed for varying lengths of time in one place. Charles Prebish believes that this eremitical lifestyle lasted only for a short time following the death of the founder and that the *saṃgha* largely switched to a cenobitical system within a hundred years or so of the Buddha's passing.[10]

The rainy season retreat, which may initially have been a concession to the practicalities of the local environment, proved to be an important aspect of the development of a sense of community among the early Buddhist monks. It generally lasted between three and four months, from June to October. There were a number of restrictions on where monks could settle: the Buddha forbade them from spending the period outdoors, in hollow trees, in graveyards, under umbrellas, or in earthenware pots. Texts from the period indicate that such shelters were used by some other ascetic orders.[11] The *Āruṇi Upaniṣad* states that it was common practice for world renouncers to remain in one place during the rainy season, and it advises them to abide in a fixed residence for two or three months.[12] According to Buddhist texts, monks often constructed small huts or had residences built for them by laypeople seeking to make merit. These were generally temporary structures, often erected near a forest, a river, a valley, or at the foot of a mountain. They were always situated close to a town so that the monks would have easy access to alms. At the end of the retreat, these shelters would be dismantled, and the monks would resume their eremitic wandering.

For other ascetic orders, the rainy season retreat was often a solitary affair, but for Buddhist monastics it became a time to live together. When the Buddha finished his first preaching tour in Vaiśalī, he instructed his followers to spend the monsoon period in the village of Beluva, "each according to the place where his friends, acquaintances, and companions might live." As he conceived this period, it was not a time of solitary contemplation, as in other sects, but rather should be spent among others with whom one was close, among friends and esteemed companions.

In addition to providing an opportunity for study and contemplation, the retreat was a time for discussion of the dharma with fellow monks. Some ascetic orders required that members observe vows of silence during this period, but the Buddha forbade such practices. The Vinaya reports one incident in which he asked some monks from Kosala how they had spent their retreat, and they replied that they had enjoyed perfect harmony by not speaking a word: "We maintained the virtue of silence and remained without speaking for three months, and so we were very happy." The Buddha later held them up as an example of misguided conduct:

> Monks, these stupid men spent their time uncomfortably, but they pretended to be very happy. Monks, these stupid men spent their time like a flock of sheep, like a bunch of slackers, but they pretended to have a very successful time. How could these stupid men embrace the practice of silence, in imitation of other religious sects?[13]

The Buddha forbade monks from taking vows of silence during the rainy season retreat and stated that open communication was an essential aspect of his order. It is a monk's duty to help fellow monks, and in another passage the Buddha notes that if a monk receives a message that one of his brother monks is losing heart, it is a monk's duty to help his brother, even if it means breaking his retreat and traveling during the rainy season. This is significant because the Buddha reportedly placed a great emphasis on the importance of this period for the religious lives of his followers and permitted them to abandon the retreat only in instances of exigency. In one such exception, the *Monastic Discipline* states that if a monk is approached by a woman desperate for sex—who offers him gold, cows, slave women, her daughter, or another woman—and he fears that her overtures might lead him to compromise his celibacy, then he can flee the threat she poses and move to another place.[14] Except in the most dire emergencies, however, monks were instructed to remain in their huts for the duration of the season and to enjoy the company of their companions.

The Buddha recognized that when people live together in close quarters for extended periods of time with little opportunity to move outside, frictions often develop, and so he instituted a practice of asking forgiveness (Pāli: *pavāraṇā;* Skt.: *pravāraṇā*) for any smoldering resentments that might have developed during the retreat. This ritual was intended to promote harmony by overcoming lingering animosities caused by inadvertent acts.

The ideal communal atmosphere of a retreat is described in a discussion between the Buddha and Anuruddha, Ānanda's half brother. Characterized as a monk who preferred solitude to communal living, Anuruddha spent the rainy season in the Gosiṅga forest with two like-minded monks, Nandiya and Kimbila. When the Buddha came to visit them, they paid their respects and he asked how they were getting along. Anuruddha replied: "We are living in concord, in mutual appreciation, without disputing, blending like milk and water, viewing each other with kindly eyes." The Buddha inquired how they managed to maintain such good rapport in close quarters for several months, and Anuruddha explained:

> I do so by thinking, "How blessed and fortunate I am to be living with such companions in the holy life!" I maintain loving kindness in bodily action, speech, and thought toward my companions, and I think, "Let me set aside what I wish to do and do what these venerable ones want to do." In this way, although we are different in body, we are of one mind.[15]

The Buddha approved of this attitude and asked them about their meditative practice. Anuruddha stated that all had attained the four concentrations (Pāli: *jhāna;* Skt.: *dhyāna*), the four formless absorptions (Pāli: *ārūpa-samāpatti;* Skt.: *ārūpya-samāpatti*), as well as cessation of perception and feeling, and that all three were now arhats. Because they had eliminated all mental afflictions and were free from anger, desire, and obscuration, they were able to live together in perfect concord. After the Buddha left, Anuruddha's two companions asked him how he could be so certain about their attainments, as they had never described them to him. He replied that his mind and theirs were in harmony, which allowed him to recognize that they had all reached the culmination of the path.

Settling Down

As the order grew and developed, it also attracted some wealthy lay patrons, some of whom donated land to the *saṃgha.* Many monks spent most of their time traveling between these places. The first such land grant was made by King Bimbisāra a few weeks after the Buddha's awakening. Another important donor was Anāthapiṇḍika, a wealthy banker from Sāvatthi, who bought a park for the order and commissioned the building of dwelling places for Buddhist monastics, as well as store rooms, meeting halls, enclosed areas with fireplaces, toilets, walkways, rooms for hot baths, and lotus ponds. Another monastery was financed by Visākhā Migāra-Māta. It is described as a seven-story building that took years to complete.[16] Another major monastery called Kukkuṭa's Park (Kukkuṭārāma) was financed by a banker named Kukkuṭa, who also provided funds for the construction of several other monastic residences.

The development of settled monasticism probably occurred in stages. Originally the monks remained in one place for any length of time only during the rainy season, which they spent in generally temporary retreat huts. These were referred to as residences *(āvāsa)* or parks *(ārāma)*. Residences were generally built in the countryside, often by the monks themselves, and the term "park" designated an area reserved for monks in a town or city; these were often donated and maintained by a lay patron. The first monasteries were called hermitages *(leṇa)* and were generally owned by a particular fraternity. Residences or parks could be used by any monks who needed them, while hermitages were commonly restricted to one group. As monasticism grew, new forms developed, the two most important of which were the monastery *(vihāra)* and shelter *(guhā)*, both of which were types of hermitages.[17]

Acquisition of land and buildings also led to promulgation of regulations regarding ownership. These rules stipulated that all donations—whether of land, money, or other goods—were the property of the entire order and not personal gifts. Monks were forbidden from accepting donations intended solely for one person and could not reserve dwelling places for themselves. When traveling monks arrived at a monastery, the general rule was first come, first served, and new arrivals were admonished not to disturb other residents. Nor was it permissible for one monk to expel another: any such decisions had to be arrived at through a communal process.

As the order developed, a number of collective activities were instituted. The rainy season retreat was an important example of this tendency, as was the practice of fortnightly gatherings to recite the "individual liberation" (Pāli: *pātimokkha;* Skt.: *prātimokṣa*), the condensed set of rules that applied to monastics. The *Monastic Discipline* indicates that one purpose of this ceremony is promotion of group solidarity and harmony: "Members of the community who live united, in friendship and without disputes, are happy, recite [the disciplinary code] together and live in comfort."[18] Other communal gatherings included the robe conferral *(kaṭhina)* ceremony, which marked the conclusion of the rains retreat, when lay donors would present the community with new robes; and the confession of faults, in which monks would ask their companions' forgiveness for transgressions of etiquette.

According to Buddhaghosa, the individual liberation is so named because it promotes self-restraint and discipline. It leads to nontransgression of monastic rules in body, speech, and mind.[19] Muller states that etymologically the term *pātimokkha* means "bond."[20] The formula contained in the *Great Division* appears to derive from a stage of development of the *saṃgha* following the death of the Buddha when the order had split up into various congregations, each of which held its own fortnightly recitation service, which was attended only by those who lived in a particular area with defined boundaries. The regular repetition of the rules that applied equally to all helped to forge a bond between them and promoted unity within the community. According to Dutt, the earliest formulation was a brief statement of faith that was only rarely recited, but the developed individual liberation was a listing of over two hundred regulations conjoined with a rite of confession that was enacted every two weeks.[21]

This practice is extolled in the Pāli canon as a key factor in the continuation of the dharma after the passing of the Buddha. In the "Discourse to Moggallāna the Guardian," Ānanda is asked by a man working on some monastic buildings how the *saṃgha* has fared without its founder and whether the Buddha named a successor. Ānanda replies that he did not, nor did the order see a need to appoint one on its own because the regular confession of the individual liberation provided the basis for ongoing concord.[22]

The Buddha emphasized the value of communal meetings for group harmony and in the "Discourse of the Great Final Nirvana" told Ānanda that the Vajjians would prosper because they held frequent assemblies, debated harmoniously, did not repeal their old laws, followed the advice of elders, did not rape women, honored their temples and shrines, did not revoke gifts to religious places, and gave hospitality and protection to all true priests and ascetics.[23] The Buddha exhorted his followers to emulate their example:

> Monks should assemble frequently and should conduct their affairs amicably; they should not make new rules but should obey the old ones. They

should honor the elders of the *saṃgha* and heed their advice. They should resist craving, enjoy solitude, and practice mindfulness at all times, so that people of similar disposition will be attracted to the order.[24]

Rules and Regulations

With the development of permanent monastic structures, some monks spent more of their time in such places, with the result that in a short time the wandering ideal had become a thing of the past. Communal living required the development of codes and regulations, and the *Monastic Discipline* has an extensive listing of norms of etiquette designed to facilitate harmony within the group. The focus of *Vinaya* descriptions of monastic life and regulations for smooth operation within the community relate to an ideal vision of homosociality in which groups of men reside together as a fraternity dedicated to the pursuit of shared religious ideals. From the time of the Buddha, these strictures were intended to promote a simple life dedicated to meditative practice, study, and productive conversation between monks, as well as their health and comfort. Thus the *Verses on Doctrine* declares: "The unity of the community is happiness, and the life of united monks is happy."[25] Several *Monastic Discipline* passages indicate that the purpose of these rules was to protect the order, ensure its comfort, keep away people who might be a negative influence, facilitate the practice of well-behaved monastics, destroy their mental afflictions and prevent the arising of future afflictions, benefit outsiders, increase the numbers of adherents (both monastic and lay), establish the discipline, and ensure adherence to it.[26]

The Buddha apparently saw no need to name someone to take his place as leader of the order and instead instituted a system of collective decision making. Matters that concerned the integrity of the order, such as transgressions of the monastic code, were to be adjudicated in meetings of all the monks in a particular congregation. Their collective decision was referred to as a "transaction of the monastic community" (Pāli: *saṅgha-kamma;* Skt: *saṃgha-karma*). This became the basis for the functioning of the order as a corporate body with land holdings, far-flung groups of monks and nuns, and lay supporters who expected all of the order's members to conform to the rules of the *Monastic Discipline* and to display the comportment of alms-worthy ascetics.

By the time this tradition was codified, Buddhist monastics were no longer wanderers, and the order developed a system with features of democracy:

monks or nuns deliberated as a body, and no one had more power than any other in these matters. All were equal participants, and the outcome was decided by a majority of votes. A transaction of the monastic community is an act of the entire corporate body against one or more of its members, an act that is performed according to a set of prescribed rules that derive their authority from their association with the Buddha. A full assembly of monks from a congregation was required in order for a decision to be valid, and all relevant rules and regulations had to be followed. Once a decision was reached, the matter was settled, and any attempt to reopen the case constituted an infraction, except in cases where the procedures had not been properly observed.

Group harmony is a pervasive concern in the *Monastic Discipline* and, as we saw in Chapter 3, was cited by King Bimbisāra as a key reason why he considered the *saṃgha* superior to rival groups. When monks visited the Buddha, he often asked them how they were getting along with their companions, and the ideal was a community that blended together "like milk and water," in which monks had different duties and practices but were "of one mind" as a group.[27]

When asked by Ānanda how one should live happily in the order, the Buddha replied that one should look after one's own conduct and not waste time criticizing others. One should be personally virtuous and not worry about faults in other members of the community. The Buddha warned against being overly judgmental and overlooking one's own transgressions and also stated that monks should not be concerned about lack of recognition. They should work at their own practice, the benefits of which might not be apparent to others.[28]

Sometimes, however, personality conflicts arose, particularly when feuding monks held to entrenched opinions. In one such case, two monks from Kauśāmbī had a protracted quarrel that began when one monk, described as a dharma preacher, left some waste water in a communal area. Another monk, described as a student of the monastic discipline, informed the preacher that this was an offense against the monastic code and demanded that he publicly confess his transgression. The other monk declared that he was unaware of the rule and so had not committed any infraction.

Despite the trivial nature of the disagreement, both monks held firmly to their positions. Generally when a monk inadvertently violates a minor rule there is no transgression, but in this case the other monk initiated a formal meeting of the community and a penalty of probation was imposed. The offending monk, however, refused to accept the judgment and lodged an appeal. This led to the formation of two opposed factions. The Buddha attempted to mediate the conflict and ordered the two parties to settle their differences and establish harmony, but by this point they were so adamant in their respective factions that they refused to comply. He asked them two more times to resolve their differences, but still they resisted, and he became so disgusted with their pettiness that he left town without telling anyone where he was going.

He went into retreat in a solitary part of a nearby forest for the duration of the rainy season, attended by a wild elephant. He mused about the bitter but trivial quarrel, referring to the monks as "makers of strife, makers of quarrels, makers of disputes, makers of brawls, makers of legal quibbles for the monastic order," and added that when he endured their company he "did not live in comfort; but now that I am alone by myself, I am living in comfort, removed from those monks."[29]

The monks apparently were not perturbed by the Buddha's disgust toward them, but the laypeople who supported them were. Upon learning that the Buddha had left the area because of the petty quarrels of the local monks, the lay community stopped providing them with alms. As a result, the monks became both hungry and ashamed, and they sought out the Buddha, begged him to return, and asked his forgiveness and help in reestablishing group harmony. Satisfied by their change of heart, the Buddha agreed to leave his retreat, and the matter was soon resolved.

Monastic Couples

The Buddha conceived the *saṃgha* as a group of men joined by bonds of friendship and shared goals. There are a number of stories in the Pāli canon that indicate the importance of friendship, including some in which one man decides to join the order and his action prompts other friends to follow his example. In one such case, a young man named Yasa became a monk, and because he was well regarded by other men, several emulated him. Similarly, Upāli, who had been a barber for the Śākya clan, decided to become a monk at the urging of his friends Ānanda and Anuruddha.[30]

Many men joined the order in groups and remained close to their companions throughout their monastic careers. Indian Buddhist literature describes some particularly intimate bonds between pairs of men who appear as couples, who spend most of their time together, travel together, spend rainy season retreats together, and are perceived as couples by other monks. Their associations are nonsexual, but they often remain in committed and close relationships for decades. Sometimes they have strong friendships with other monks but are particularly devoted to one monastic partner.

The most prominent example of such a monastic couple is Śāriputra and Maudgalyāyana, who are often pictured on either side of the Buddha in images from India and Sri Lanka and are referred to by the Buddha as "the chief pair of disciples, the excellent pair."[31] According to biographical sketches in the Pāli canon, both were born brahmans, which seems to have given them a natural affinity, as did the shared *kṣatriya* birth of the Buddha and Ānanda. Several *Birth Story* accounts report that Śāriputra and Maudgalyāyana spent many past lives together and that they were always close companions.[32] The *Great Matter* asserts that they were also connected with the Buddha and Ānanda in many lives and that Śāriputra and Maudgalyāyana aspired to be the chief disciples of a buddha.[33]

Śāriputra and Maudgalyāyana were reportedly conceived on the same day and also born on the same day. Śāriputra's parents named him Upatiṣya (Pāli: Upatissa), and Maudgalyāyana's parents named him Kolita, and both families lived in Rājagṛha and had close ties. The young men became friends at an early age, and this is attributed to their past karmic connections. They spent most of their time together and reportedly had little interest in women.[34] One day they attended a public festival, but they sat apart from the crowd and were unmoved by the entertainments. At the same time, both realized that all the revelers would be dead within a few short decades, and so the festivities appeared pointless and counterproductive to them. Upatiṣya told his friend about his misgivings, and Kolita stated, "My thoughts are exactly the same as yours." At that point, they decided to enter the homeless life and pursue a path to liberation from cyclic existence; they made a pact that if one should "discover the deathless" he would find the other and tell him. Both joined an ascetic order at the same time and studied with the same teacher for several years.[35]

They continued to remain close friends but occasionally traveled to different teachers to seek instruction. One day Śāriputra was walking along a road and encountered a Buddhist monk named Upasena, who immediately impressed him with his outward appearance and calm comportment.[36] The *Great Matter* reports that he was "like a *nāga,*" and "he had finished his task. His faculties were turned inwards; his mind was not turned outwards. He was unwavering as one who had achieved harmony with the dharma. He did not look before him farther than a plough's length."[37] Śāriputra was struck by his surpassing beauty and calm demeanor. He approached the monk and said, "Your reverence, your faculties are very pure, your complexion is very bright, very clear," and asked him about his teacher and the dharma he followed.[38] Upasena responded that the Buddha was his teacher, and he spoke briefly about the dharma to Śāriputra: "The Thus Gone One has explained the cause of those elements of reality that arise from a cause, and he . . . has spoken about their cessation." On hearing this short summary, Śāriputra experienced a spontaneous and profound flash of realization and immediately set out to find Maudgalyāyana and share it with him. When Maudgalyāyana saw his friend approaching, he noticed a change in his appearance, commented that his faculties were pure and his countenance shining, and eagerly asked, "Have you attained the deathless?"

Śāriputra replied in the affirmative and repeated the verse of dharma to his friend, and Maudgalyāyana also experienced deep realization. They then decided to travel to where the Buddha was residing and become his disciples. They first gathered all their own followers and told them that the Buddha's dharma was superior to theirs and that all should join the *saṃgha.* According to the account in the *Great Matter,* the Buddha knew of their approach due to his supernatural insight and instructed his disciples to prepare places for them. He added that Śāriputra and Maudgalyāyana would become his foremost disciples and that Śāriputra would be the greatest in wisdom and Maudgalyāyana would surpass all others in magical powers. As the new disciples drew near, the Buddha exclaimed to the assembled monks that they were "an excellent pair."[39]

After the two joined the community, they fulfilled the Buddha's predictions and soon were regarded as the most advanced of all his disciples. The Buddha reportedly advised his followers that all should aspire thus: "May I become like Śāriputra and Maudgalyāyana" because they "are the model and standard for my monk disciples."[40] On another occasion, he told some monks, "associate, O monks, with Śāriputra and Maudgalyāyana, and keep company with them! Śāriputra is like a mother who brings forth [offspring], and Maudgalyāyana is like a nurse to a newborn child. Śāriputra trains [his students] in the fruition of stream-entry, and Maudgalyāyana trains them for the highest goal."[41]

Śāriputra is regularly praised for his great humility and friendliness, and several anecdotes recount the various ways in which he helped younger monks and promoted harmony in the monastic community. One such story tells of a monk who resented Śāriputra's standing and wished to be recognized as the most advanced of the Buddha's disciples in wisdom. One time when Śāriputra was lecturing, he referred to several monks by their personal names, but he did not know the disgruntled monk's name, which caused the latter to feel slighted. On another occasion, Śāriputra's robe brushed the monk as he passed during an assembly, and the man became even angrier at the great monk and told the Buddha that Śāriputra had purposely struck him and injured his ear. The Buddha called Śāriputra to his presence, but instead of angrily protesting his innocence, Śāriputra humbly stated that he had not wished to inflict any harm and regretted any injury that he had caused. The Buddha knew that Śāriputra was blameless and that the accusation was motivated by petty spite, but when the great elder humbly asked forgiveness, the disaffected monk felt remorse and confessed that he had falsely accused him. The other monks were highly impressed by this example of humility by the greatest of the Buddha's disciples, and the Buddha later praised Śāriputra's actions as a lesson for how the community should overcome personal animosities and promote harmony.

On another occasion, a monk named Kokālika was reportedly jealous of the standing of Śāriputra and Maudgalyāyana and accused them of secretly harboring evil thoughts, but the Buddha rejected the notion and advised Kokālika to repent or suffer negative karmic consequences for slandering blameless fellow monks: "they have good and loveable behavior." Ignoring his teacher's admonition, Kokālika persisted in his calumny, and as a result his body soon became covered with boils, which continued to grow and ooze pus until he died. He was reborn in a hell, and his story was used as an example of the consequences of promoting division within the order.[42]

Pāli sources report that Śāriputra and Maudgalyāyana generally spent the rainy season retreat together in the same cell and that they used the occasion to hold dialogues on matters of doctrine and discipline for the benefit of other monks. One such example is described in the "Discourse on Absence of Blemishes," in which Maudgalyāyana poses a number of questions to Śāriputra to prompt him to discuss ways to remove evil tendencies.[43]

Although the pair spent most of their lives together, traveled from place to place in each other's company, lived in close proximity in a tiny cell during rainy season retreats in perfect harmony, and worked together to instruct and uplift their fellow monks, they died separately. According to accounts of

Śāriputra's death, when he knew his entry into final nirvana was imminent, he went to pay his last respects to the Buddha. The Buddha stated that Śāriputra's death would be the final culmination of a process that began countless eons ago, when he prostrated in front of the Bodhisattva and made the aspiration to be reborn with him in his final lifetime as a buddha and to become his chief disciple.

Before he died, Śāriputra decided to convert his mother, a proud brahman woman who had disapproved of his decision to renounce his heritage and enter the Buddhist order. He returned home and moved into the room he had occupied as a child, and various Indian gods came to visit him, including Śakra, the four divine kings, and finally Brahmā, the god his mother worshipped. She was astounded to learn that the great divinity, holder of Vedic lore, paid obeisance to her son, and this convinced her to become a Buddhist. Just before he passed away, Śāriputra asked the monks who attended him to forgive him for anything he might have done to offend them, but they replied that he had never done anything that might cause the slightest hard feelings. He then entered into progressively more subtle trance states, culminating in blissful nirvana, and he passed away with no pain and in perfect equanimity.

Śāriputra's demise is described in the commentary on the "Discourse to Cunda," which reports that when his robe and bowl were brought to the Buddha following his passing, Ānanda exclaimed: "Then, Blessed One, my own body felt as though it had been drugged. I feel disoriented, and the teachings are no longer clear to me since I heard of the final passing away of the venerable Śāriputra."[44] In the account of the *Verses of the Elder Monks,* Ānanda laments: "When my noble friend had gone, the world was plunged into darkness for me."[45]

The Buddha admonished Ānanda for his response and reminded him of Śāriputra's many good deeds and contributions to the community. From the Buddha's perspective, Śāriputra's life and legacy should be celebrated, and monks should consider themselves fortunate to have known him and to have benefited from his example. He asked Ānanda, "did he take from you your portion of virtue, or your portion of concentration, or your portion of wisdom, or your portion of deliverance?" Ānanda replied in the negative but added, "he has been a mentor to me, a teacher, an instructor, one who rouses, inspires and gladdens, untiring in preaching the dharma, a helper of his fellow monks. And we remember how inspiring, enjoyable, and helpful his dharma instruction was."[46]

While Śāriputra's death was peaceful, Maudgalyāyana's was violent and painful. This was said to be recompense for past negative actions. During a retreat in the forest, Maudgalyāyana became the object of hatred of a group of naked ascetics who were jealous of the good reputation of the Buddha and his order, which they blamed on Maudgalyāyana's mastery of supernatural powers. They hired assassins to kill him, but with his insight he could tell when they were approaching and either render himself invisible or levitate to another location. He did this not out of fear of death but from compassion, wishing to spare the assassins the karma of killing an arhat. For two consecutive months they came to his hut, but every time he foiled their attempts on his life. At the beginning of the third month, however, his powers failed him, and the assassins were able to seize him and deliver a beating that left his bones broken and his whole body shattered. In a past life he had caused his parents' deaths, and his failure of power in his present one was the consequence of this.

The thugs left him for dead after they had "pounded his bones until they were as small as grains of rice." His magical abilities returned at this point and allowed him to survive until he could visit the Buddha one last time. He flew through the air to where the Buddha was staying and informed him that he was about to enter nirvana. The Buddha asked him to deliver one last sermon to the monks, and Maudgalyāyana complied with his teacher's request. He then paid homage to the Buddha and entered into final nirvana.[47] According to Pāli sources, Śāriputra died on the full moon day of the month of Kattika, which begins in October and ends in November. Maudgalyāyana died two weeks later on the day of the new moon.[48] Despite his admonitions to Ānanda regarding overcoming attachment to people, the Buddha himself reportedly found that he also missed his two greatest disciples. According to the *Discourse Sections,* while delivering the "Discourse to Ukkacelā" shortly after their deaths, the Buddha said, "This assembly, O monks, indeed appears empty to me, now that Śāriputra and Maudgalyāyana have passed away." He eulogized them as an "excellent pair of disciples" and stated that all past buddhas had a similar pair of followers and that all future buddhas would also be blessed with disciples of the stature of Śāriputra and Maudgalyāyana.[49]

These two great examples of monastic camaraderie reportedly formed close bonds in many past lives, which continued in a committed relationship in their last lifetimes. They died separately but were later posthumously reunited. When the great *stūpa* at Sāñcī was opened in the middle of the twentieth century, the relic chamber was found to contain two stone receptacles: one in the north end of the chapel held Maudgalyāyana's remains, and one in the south end held those of Śāriputra.

Buddha with Śāriputra and Maudgalyāyana on either side of him, Rumtek Monastery, Sikkim. Photograph by John Powers.

The Buddha and Ānanda

Another prominent monastic couple was the Buddha himself and his cousin and personal attendant Ānanda. Just as Śāriputra and Maudgalyāyana are said to have shared a bond due to their birth as brahmans, the Buddha and Ānanda had similar dispositions because they were *kṣatriyas*. A number of stories of the Buddha's past births report that the two shared intimate connections in many lives and that Ānanda had been a brother, father, son, assistant, colleague, and friend to the future Buddha. These stories stress Ānanda's exemplary qualities in past existences and his efforts to perfect himself, along with his devotion to the Bodhisattva. Like the Bodhisattva, Ānanda reportedly came to earth from Tuṣita. His father, Amitodana, was Śuddhodana's brother, and the two cousins grew up together and were close friends. Ānanda joined the monastic community at the age of thirty-seven and attained the level of a stream enterer during his first rainy season retreat. He was recognized as an outstanding monk and praised for his friendliness and diligence.

Because of the many demands on his time as the leader of a growing order, the Buddha required a personal attendant, and he asked his longtime friend Ānanda to take on the position. Ānanda agreed to do so only if eight conditions were met: (1) the Buddha should never pass on a gift of robes to Ānanda; (2) alms food given to the Buddha should never be passed on to Ānanda; (3) the Buddha should never give Ānanda a dwelling place that had been donated to him; (4) he should never include Ānanda in any personal invitation; (5) if Ānanda were invited to a meal, he could pass the invitation to the Buddha; (6) if people came from outlying areas, Ānanda should have the privilege of leading them to the Buddha; (7) if Ānanda had any personal doubts regarding the dharma, he had the right to have them answered at any time; and (8) if the Buddha gave a discourse in his absence, he would later repeat it to Ānanda.[50] The first four conditions were intended to ensure that other monks would not think Ānanda took the position for personal gain, and the last four ensured that he could do his job well. Among other duties, as the person who spent the most time with the Buddha, Ānanda was expected to remember the master's teachings, and according to tradition, during the "first council" at Rājagṛha Ānanda recited from memory every sermon delivered by the Buddha during his ministry.

During nearly four decades as the Buddha's personal attendant, Ānanda was at his side almost constantly and performed a range of duties, including bringing him water for washing his face and a wooden stick for cleaning his teeth, arranging his seat, washing his feet, massaging his back, fanning him, sweeping his cell, mending his robes, sleeping near him at night in case he required any assistance, accompanying him on alms rounds and on his tours of monastic residences, carrying his messages, calling monks together at assemblies, and taking care of the Buddha when he was sick and obtaining medicines for the Buddha.

Ānanda is portrayed as unstintingly faithful to his companion and teacher, as so completely devoted that he was willing to give his life for him. In one incident, Devadatta incited a wild elephant to kill the Buddha, and Ānanda threw himself in front of the charging beast. The Buddha ordered him to step aside, but Ānanda refused. The Buddha could not be harmed by the elephant, but Ānanda would have been killed, so he had to remove his attendant from the elephant's path with his supernatural powers. Afterward the Buddha recounted for other monks the numerous times in past lives when Ānanda had risked his life for him.[51]

According to some sources, Ānanda's emotional attachment to the Buddha was the main factor preventing his attainment of arhathood. He was an advanced meditator who could enter into various states of concentration, but an arhat must be free from all emotional constraints, and Ānanda's love constituted an insurmountable obstacle to his progress. Following the passing of the Buddha, Śāriputra, and Maudgalyāyana, Ānanda reportedly experienced depression, and he remarked: "My companion [Śāriputra] has passed away, and the Master has also departed. There is no friendship that equals this: mindfulness directed toward the body. The old ones now have died, the new ones do not please me much. Today I meditate all alone like a bird gone to its nest."[52]

Shortly before his entry into final nirvana, the Buddha cautioned Ānanda on the negative consequences of his emotional attachment to him and advised Ānanda to eliminate it for his own good. After the funeral ceremonies for his friend and mentor were concluded, Ānanda felt that he had only one remaining duty: to become an arhat. Kāśyapa advised him to live in a forest near the Mallas and the Śākyans in order to remove himself from the monastic assembly and its cognitive ties, but when people in the area heard that the Buddha's attendant was residing there he had to deal with a constant stream of visitors. Despite these interruptions, Ānanda successfully cultivated detachment and equanimity and managed to attain the final goal of arhathood on the evening before the convocation of the "first council."

A Semiotics of Solidarity

Indian Buddhist literature was mainly produced by monks for monks, and thus there is a pervasive concern in the literature with group cohesion. When men left their homes to join the order, they renounced a society that valued and promoted close family ties and emotional, financial, and social security support networks that operated at every stage of a person's life. Moreover, the hierarchical nature of traditional Indian society provided job security for most people, who were born into kin groups that often performed particular tasks and passed their lore on to each successive generation. At the proper age, one's parents would arrange for marriage with someone of the opposite sex who shared one's innate predispositions *(adhikāra)* and who was considered a good match in terms of interests and personality. As householders, individuals had a repertoire of expected duties and various social involvements, produced children and supported the rest of society, and had a legitimate expectation that they would be supported in turn in old age. One's children and extended family provided social security, and after death children and their descendents would perform funeral rituals to ensure a comfortable afterlife.

When a man entered the *saṃgha,* he left all of that behind to pursue nirvana, which only a tiny percentage of the community would actually attain. There were, as we have seen, various intermediate goals, such as increased equanimity, insight, calm, and various meditative states, but the texts indicate that these too remained elusive for many monastics. In order to attract new recruits and to retain those who had already joined the order, it was essential to portray the monastic lifestyle as superior in various ways to that of the larger society, as one in which a man (or woman) could find greater peace of mind, few commitments and worries, time to pursue religious goals, and comfortable companionship. Relationships between men and women are characterized as fraught with tensions, misunderstandings, conflicts, and uncertainties, but the tropes of male camaraderie developed by the monastic authors who created the *Collections* and *Monastic Discipline* describe male friendship in very different terms. In these texts, sexuality is not an issue: men engage in sexual practices with other men only as an alternative to heterosexual options, and there is no sense that the men might fall in love, develop jealousies, or experience the sorts of relationship issues common to heterosexual couples.

Male company is conceived as comparatively problem-free, and the lifestyle of Buddhist monks is described as one in which a man can travel, meditate, debate, and cohabit with his fellow monastics without the emotional entanglements and interpersonal difficulties of worldly affairs. The presentation of the monastic lifestyle and the idealized figures of monastic couples like Śāriputra and Maudgalyāyana and the Buddha and Ānanda constitute a semiotics of solidarity, in which various symbols of the preferability of the monastic lifestyle are presented. Such a lifestyle promises relief from the tensions of mundane life and a career as part of a community of fellow seekers who are closer than brothers because of their shared practices and commitment to the goals of Buddhism. Members of the order merge as a group, "like milk and water," each becoming part of a cohesive network of men whose collective aspirations and attainment of advanced meditative states make them ideal life companions.

Another aspect of this semiotic system is the negative presentation of rival groups, who are characterized as jealous of the Buddhist monastic community, as prone to infighting and animosities, and who engage in counterproductive practices, such as severe asceticism, vows of silence, prohibition of washing, and the emulation of animals, in misguided pursuit of heavenly delights. Buddhism, by contrast, presents itself as a "middle way" that avoids the ultimately unsatisfactory extremes of hedonism and self-torture and advocates practices that lead to blissful meditative states, liberation from the sufferings of repeated rebirth, and ultimately nirvana. Along the way, men are able to share the salutary companionship of exemplary comrades whose presence brings gladness to all who associate with them. Various literary characters like Śāriputra, Maudgalyāyana, and Ānanda are constructed as ideal male types. Śāriputra is wise, unstintingly humble, and gracious, a source of joy to everyone who encounters him, free from any animosities, pettiness, or annoying personal habits, who works tirelessly to promote harmony within the *saṃgha.* His doctrinal instructions are always appropriate and only second to those of the Buddha himself, while his partner Maudgalyāyana uses his extraordinary powers only to aid others. Maudgalyāyana can read the minds of his fellows but never employs this ability for personal gain or advantage over them; instead he seeks only to help them make progress on the path and does so in ways that avoid insult or injury.

Similarly, Ānanda is the ideal companion, a true friend who has no concerns for himself and is totally devoted to the Buddha and his fellow monks. The *Collections,* the *Monastic Discipline,* and various legends and accounts of the early Buddhist community have many such figures, and the clear message they present to the outside world is that the *saṃgha* is the best of all available religious orders, that its members live in peace and harmony, and that it has many exemplary monks who revel in mutually beneficial same-sex comradeship and support each other in their religious endeavors. Whether the historical figures on which these characters are based exhibited such behavior can never be known; all we have are the productions of monastic authors who sought to extol and valorize their own order and present it as an attractive lifestyle to potential recruits. The symbols of solidarity contained in their works also present for those already in the group an ideal of a perfect society that can be recreated within every monastic community.

6

The Greater Men of the Greater Vehicle

> The buddhas, like huge boa constrictors, attract beings toward their own reality with their persuasive teachings, like the boa constrictor's venomous saliva, and make them fall into the gaping mouth of their own peace.
>
> —Asaṅga, *The Ornament for Great Vehicle Discourses*

The Buddha's Body and Bodies

According to tradition, shortly after the Buddha's death five hundred arhats met in Rājagṛha to recite from memory what he had taught during his lifetime. The stated goal was to forestall the production of new texts attributed to him and to preserve his teachings intact just as he had spoken them. All had been present during many sermons, and Ānanda, who had attended the Buddha for most of his life, recounted one at a time the discourses his teacher had delivered in his presence or later repeated to him. Upāli narrated the monastic discipline, and at the end of the convocation the canon was declared closed; henceforth no new material would be accepted as the "word of the Buddha" *(buddha-vacana).*

Despite the canonizing aspirations of the participants in the first council, new texts continued to appear that contained words the authors claimed to have been spoken by the Buddha, and old texts were redacted, augmented, and altered. In addition, differing interpretations of the Buddha's teachings developed, and these led to the formation of schools and sects, some of which had their own canons. In the period immediately following the master's demise, Buddhism appears to have been a small cult centered in Magadha, the capital of the Mauryans. As the Mauryans expanded their empire and took over new territory, Buddhism also grew and moved into other areas. The major impetus for this expansion appears to have been the conversion of Aśoka, the third Mauryan emperor (ruled 272–236 BCE). After he became a Buddhist, the resources of his empire lent their force to expansion of the faith. As A. L. Basham has noted, before Aśoka's time there was little inscriptional or archeological evidence pertaining to Buddhism, but during and after his reign such evidence began to proliferate.[1] Basham contends that Buddhism was a relatively minor and localized religious movement prior to its growth under Aśoka's patronage. At their peak, the Mauryans' territory stretched from Gandhāra in the north to Mysore in the south, from Bihār to Surāṣṭra. It was the largest empire in India prior to the time of the British Raj, and with the help of royal patronage Buddhism spread widely. According to traditional histories, Aśoka sent Buddhist missions all over the subcontinent and to Sri Lanka, which led to a dramatic upsurge in Buddhist fortunes and adherents.

Lamotte contends that the Aśokan period was a time during which Buddhism flourished, but the first and second centuries CE saw a number of crises for the new religion.[2] The Mauryan empire fell within fifty years of Aśoka's death, when the brahman general Puṣyamitra Śuṅga seized power and established a new dynasty. According to some sources, the Śuṅgas persecuted Buddhists, but this was also a time in which Buddhist sculpture developed and new texts were composed. After the fall of the Śuṅgas, a period of foreign invasions ensued, with armies of Greeks, Scyths (Śaka), and Kuṣaṇas successively moving in and carving out territories in the northern areas of the subcontinent. During this age of invasion, conquest, and establishment of new dynasties, Buddhism occasionally enjoyed royal patronage; the Kuṣaṇa king Kaniṣka (born ca. 78 or 144 CE), for example, was reportedly a supporter of the *saṃgha*.

Despite the instabilities of the first few centuries CE in northern India, Buddhism continued to grow, and philosophy developed along with scholastic traditions. As the historical Buddha faded further and further into the mists of memory, his followers speculated on what sort of being he was. His legend was embellished, and it appears that some followers could not imagine that such an important figure really had a physical form composed of gross elements, that he had been born, aged, and died like ordinary men. Rather, he must have been superhuman, with knowledge and powers surpassing those of the gods. The *Points of Controversy* reports a number of debates regarding the Buddha's body and status and indicates that some schools contended that he did not really live in the world and was not like ordinary beings. He had a perfect body that was never defiled, and he had already attained full awakening before he was born.[3]

The Pāli canon presents the Buddha as a superhuman figure, but one endowed with a body composed of the four great elements, subject to birth, old age, and death, despite his great merit accumulated during past lives, his wisdom surpassing that of all other beings, and his ascension to the supreme position among creatures. For others, however, the notion that such a transcendent figure could suffer the fate of ordinary mortals was absurd; gods and demons live for millennia or even longer, and the bodies of gods are composed of nonmaterial substances and never age, and so the Buddha's physique must be at least as perfect as theirs.

Various theories about the Buddha's body were proposed. In his commentary on the *Compendium of Higher Knowledge,* Vasubandhu states that the Buddha really had two bodies: a form body *(rūpa-kāya)* and a truth body *(dharma-kāya).* The former was composed of gross elements and subject to change, but the latter was the sum total of the good qualities and wisdom he developed over countless lives and thus would not decay or change. During the Buddha's life his extraordinary physique attracted followers and prompted many to convert, but after his death a new body, comprised of his teachings and the shared memory of his exalted qualities, became the focal point of reverence.

> One who goes to the Buddha for refuge goes for refuge to arhat qualities that make him a buddha: [the qualities] principally because of which a person is called a "buddha"; [the qualities] by obtaining which he understands everything, thereby becoming a buddha. What are those qualities? Knowledge of the destruction [of the passions], etc., together with their attendants.[4]

Vasubandhu adds that one does not take refuge in the Buddha's physical body but rather in his extraordinary mental qualities. These are what constitute an awakened mind and are the reason a being is designated a buddha. The Buddha's physical body remained much the same prior to his awakening and after it; there were no significant alterations in his form or appearance. If his form body were a source of refuge, one should be able to take refuge in a buddha before he attains awakening. Vasubandhu also states that a buddha's physical body is defiled but that the unshared qualities *(aśaikṣa-dharma)* of an awakened being are not. The form body is defiled, but the truth body is pure, and this is the only true source of refuge. Similarly, the *Great Exposition Treatise* of the Everything Exists School states:

> Some say that taking refuge in the Buddha is taking refuge in the body constituted by the Thus Gone One's head, neck, stomach, back, hands, and feet. It is explained, then, that that body, born of a father and mother, is [composed of] defiled constituents and therefore is not a source of refuge. The refuge is the Buddha's fully accomplished qualities which comprise awakening, i.e., the truth body.[5]

The truth body is conceived as a buddha's participation in buddhahood. Buddhas accumulate vast stores of merit and wisdom over the course of countless lifetimes, and their practice culminates in a final existence as a fully awakened being. The qualities of buddhahood are not dependent on any individual buddha, however, and so can be said to exist prior to the moment when a particular being reaches awakening and to continue after death, since past buddhas have attained these qualities and future ones will also do so.

The Perfection of Wisdom Sūtras

Beginning around the first century CE, a new wave of texts appeared in India, claiming the status of discourses delivered by the Buddha *(sūtra)* even though he had been dead for centuries. These texts asserted that the previous teachings were given only to inferior disciples, but the new dispensation constituted a "Greater Vehicle" (Mahāyāna) to liberation, which superseded the earlier one. Rival teachings were characterized as the "Inferior Vehicle" (Hīnayāna). The earliest such texts were the Perfection of Wisdom sūtras, which, as the title implies, focused on the perfection of wisdom. This was linked to realization of emptiness *(śūnyatā)*. The early Perfection of Wisdom texts followed the bifurcation of the Buddha's body into form body and truth body, and the literary character Buddha they presented had a greatly expanded set of abilities. The Buddha of the Great Vehicle is a cosmic figure, with powers far surpassing those of gods and with an infinite lifespan. No longer bound by the laws of physics, he can place a galaxy in one of his pores without expanding it or diminishing the galaxy and the inhabitants of this galaxy do not even notice.[6] The new Buddha is effectively omnipotent, and as speculation on his enhanced powers developed, he was also credited with omniscience.[7]

The body of the Mahāyāna Buddha is nonmaterial and is not subject to aging or death. The *Heroic Meditation Career Discourse* asserts that buddhas are not really born but that they arise spontaneously as a result of their wish to benefit others. Their bodies "are not composed of the [four] great elements, and so they are not real. They are not composed of the [five] aggregates *(skandha),* sense spheres *(āyatana),* or constituents *(dhātu),* and so they are not real."[8] A number of Mahāyāna sūtras also assert that Śākyamuni attained awakening in the distant past and that his life on earth and the deeds he performed were merely a show for the benefit of his followers. The *Discourse of the Lotus of the True Doctrine* further contends that following his passing the Buddha did not really enter nirvana but appeared to do so only in order to provide a salutary lesson for his disciples.[9] If he had remained indefinitely, they would have taken him for granted and become lax in their practice, but because of his apparent demise, they concluded that since even a buddha dies they should apply themselves diligently to the pursuit of liberation.

Key aspects of the Buddha's biography are reinterpreted and new elements added. The *Skill in Means Discourse,* for example, states that the Bodhisattva did not actually enter his mother's womb. Instead, he remained in Tuṣita in a state of occultation, and the gods of that realm all thought that he had left them. In fact, he was immersed in a profound meditative state during his mother's apparent pregnancy. The text explains that a buddha is completely pure, and so he could never enter a womb, which contains various disgusting substances.[10] In this discourse, the Buddha further declares that he became awakened countless eons ago and has ceaselessly worked for the benefit of sentient beings. In his life as Śākyamuni, he only appeared to be born, leave home, practice austerities, and enact the other aspects of his traditional life story.[11] The *Heroic Meditation Career Discourse* declares that he did not die and, like all buddhas, will never enter final nirvana.[12]

The depiction shifts from Śākyamuni as an individual, and his personal biography is not as important as in earlier strata of Buddhist literature. His life on earth, during which he enacted the characteristic deeds of a buddha, was merely a show, but the real action of attaining awakening happened in the distant past. In addition, he often appears with other buddhas, which never occurs in the Pāli canon. He is still the primary character in most texts (or at least the figure who appears at the beginning and introduces the discourse), but he is both a buddha and the Buddha. When other buddhas appear, they are his equal in wisdom, compassion, and supernatural abilities; he is an instance of a type, and his uniqueness as Śākyamuni Buddha is not as pronounced as in the Pāli canon. He and other buddhas exhort audiences to devote themselves to attaining the highest state themselves. Buddhahood is no longer the exclusive preserve of a small coterie of exceptional individuals (all but one of whom are assigned to the distant past) but is the proper goal of all religious practitioners. Śākyamuni is one of an incalculable number of beings who have reached buddhahood, and his followers should aspire to equaling his attainments.

These notions represent significant departures from earlier characterizations of the Buddha's life, but the narrative is now recast in accordance with the Mahāyāna ideal of compassion, which is the driving force behind a buddha's quest for awakening. As a result of having practiced limitless salutary actions for incalculable numbers of sentient beings for unimaginable amounts of time, bodhisattvas become thoroughly habituated to working for others, and even though along the way they overcome the slightest vestiges of desire, they continue to follow the patterns they cultivated during their training.

The new discourses recognized that some Buddhists would question why they were only now hearing of these purportedly superior teachings. Some texts asserted that they were originally spoken by the Buddha during his lifetime but were taught only to advanced disciples. Following his apparent death, the Perfection of Wisdom texts were hidden in the undersea realm of the *nāgas* for safekeeping until the time for their wider dissemination arrived. The key figure in their recovery was Nāgārjuna, who traveled to the *nāga* capital and brought them back to India, where he taught them to his advanced students and wrote commentaries.

Sectarian Tropes

The early Mahāyāna texts have a distinctly polemical tone: in them the Hīnayānists are regularly denigrated as deficient in wisdom and compassion, as intent only on their own salvations and insufficiently concerned with the sufferings of others. The arhat, the ideal of the Pāli canon, is held up for censure and even ridicule. Revered elders like Śāriputra are regularly upstaged, their purported wisdom and other attainments denigrated as insignificant compared with those of the ideal figures of Mahāyāna texts, the bodhisattvas. In the *25,000 Line Perfection of Wisdom Discourse,* the Buddha declares to his Hīnayāna disciples that even if the world were filled with monks similar in worth to Śāriputra and Maudgalyāyana, their wisdom would not even approach that of a single bodhisattva who trains in the perfection of wisdom.[13] Whereas an arhat pursues liberation for him- or herself, the bodhisattva is dedicated to the liberation of all sentient beings and makes this a core part of his or her practice. An arhat may attain nirvana in as little as three human lifetimes following the point of stream entry, but a bodhisattva spends a minimum of three countless eons *(asaṃkhyeya-kalpa)* cultivating an inestimable store of merit and good qualities, all in order to benefit others.

An example of the Mahāyāna attitude toward the rival Hīnayāna is a passage in the *Discourse of the Prediction of Aśokadattā,* in which a twelve-year-old bodhisattva princess named Aśokadattā (Unrepentant Giving) refuses to pay obeisance to Hīnayāna monks when they enter her father's palace: "Your majesty, why should one who follows the path leading to supreme awakening, who is like a lion, the king of beasts, salute those who follow the Inferior Vehicle, who are like jackals?"[14] She then asserts that even a novice bodhisattva surpasses everyone on the arhat path. She changes herself into a man and then back into a woman again in order to demonstrate that the assumption that elder males possess superior wisdom is false. She asserts that she took a female form out of compassion but that in reality there is no maleness or femaleness.

The Buddha is also given a change in entourage in the new discourses. The Hīnayāna monks who accompanied him on his journeys around northern India appear in Mahāyāna texts, but they are placed in an inferior position to the bodhisattvas, who receive his main attention and with whom the Buddha shares his highest teachings. In some texts he stops talking at a certain point and orders hearers *(śrāvaka)* to leave because he is about to deliver a sermon with content unsuitable to their inferior capacities.[15]

The texts also distance him from his divine devotees, particularly Indra/Śakra and Brahmā. These two important Vedic deities played key roles in his biographies, such as when Brahmā intervened after Siddhārtha's awakening and convinced him to embark on a career of teaching. When the Bodhisattva returned to earth from the Heaven of the Thirty-Three, the gods created three staircases: he descended on the middle one, flanked by Brahmā and Śakra. Their reverence for the Blessed One is an important trope in the Pāli texts, and it is cited as the reason why Śāriputra's mother decided to convert to Buddhism.

In the Mahāyāna discourses, however, Indra's and Brahmā's positions are downgraded significantly, paralleling the changes of fortunes of the Hīnayāna arhats. This is probably a conscious response to their altered status in the larger culture. In the Vedas, Indra has more verses dedicated to him than does any other deity, and he represents the ideals of Āryan manhood. Brahmā is a revered figure associated with Vedic lore and brahmanical wisdom and is considered the creator of the universe. As Klaus Klostermaier notes, however, a "profound change" in attitude appears in Indian literature with regard to these and other Vedic gods.[16] Gavin Flood states that "from about 500 BCE through the first millennium CE, there was a growth of sectarian worship of particular deities, and Vedic sacrifice, though never dying out, gave way to devotional worship *(pūjā)*."[17] One such example of this shift is found in a passage in the *Chāndogya Upaniṣad,* in which Prajāpati becomes Indra's guru in order to teach him the true brahman wisdom *(brahma-vidyā),* which Indra thought he knew thoroughly, but now it is revealed that his understanding is merely superficial. Indra experiences a significant reduction in status: "Indra's position in the 'new salvation' is in no way better than that of any human. . . . His is only a temporary advantage. His entire realm is transitory and therefore not interesting for a seeker of immortality."[18]

Some Purāṇic texts have even more extreme notions; in the *Ancient Lore of Śiva,* for example, devotees of Śiva are told that they can make Indra and other Vedic gods their servants by reciting verses of the text: "the gods with Indra at their head await the orders of one who chants the *Ancient Lore of Śiva* day and night."[19]

The Purāṇas are mainly compositions of sectarian groups that worshipped either Śiva, Viṣṇu, or Devī. As Klostermaier notes, "The Purāṇas in their present form serve primarily the purpose to corroborate the claims of the various sects that Viṣṇu, Śiva, or Devī respectively, are the highest deity and Supreme Being."[20] He adds that in these texts the gods "become very concrete figures, with distinct personalities and definite features." The Indra of the Purāṇas is "far more stereotyped than that of the *Ṛg Veda,* far more plastic and understandable." Indra remains important as the chief of the *deva*s but is not the supreme god, nor is he even close to the deity of a particular Purāṇa in status. Rather, he is used in this literature to bolster the claims of devotees about their god or goddess, his inferior position contrasting with their exalted powers. He also has no connection with liberation, the ultimate aim of religious practice, and is portrayed as a being caught up in cyclic existence and destined to plunge into the lower destinies when his tenure as Indra has ended. After the universe is destroyed and later recreated, a new Indra will take his place.

In some Purāṇic texts, Brahmā becomes a sort of bumbling grandfather deity who has a habit of granting unwise boons to demons, thus leaving other gods to have to sort out his messes. In Mahāyāna texts, the Buddha distances himself from his former close association with Brahmā. In the *Skill in Means Discourse,* he uses Brahmā rather cavalierly in order to impress beings who are devoted to him. The Buddha reflects that "the worlds of gods and humans mostly serve Brahmā and hold Brahmā to be chief. They think, 'we have been created by Brahmā. We are born from Brahmā. The world has no maker other than Brahmā, no teacher other than Brahmā.' " Thus the Buddha decides: "I will make Brahmā come, I will wait for him. With Brahmā doing salutations, the worlds of gods and human beings that serve Brahmā will also do salutations to the Thus Gone One. The Thus Gone One will teach doctrine with Brahmā making the request, but he will not teach unrequested, lest they be uncertain as to whether to accept my doctrine." Then the Buddha uses his supernatural power to force Brahmā to appear before him, pay homage, and request that the Buddha turn the wheel of doctrine.[21]

In this changed religious environment of the development of devotional movements oriented to the superior deities Śiva, Viṣṇu, and Devī, the Buddha's previous close association with Indra and Brahmā must have appeared problematic. As Indra and Brahmā were surpassed by greater gods, Buddhists probably sensed that if the Buddha was depicted in close connection with them, he would appear to be merely a human sage; as the new and improved Buddha of Mahāyāna was constructed, a new distance was added between the Buddha and his old devotees—including Vedic gods and Hīnayānists—and the Buddha acquired new and better followers. In some Mahāyāna texts, Śiva and Viṣṇu visit him, prostrate themselves, and touch their celestial crowns to his feet, which in Indian society represents an admission that the object of reverence utterly surpasses the devotee.[22] In addition, the Buddha is shown surrounded by countless bodhisattvas who outshine both the Vedic gods and the deities of popular devotion in wisdom and power.

Why Can't Women Be Buddhas?

The Mahāyāna sūtras present a range of new masculine ideals. Most of the bodhisattvas are men, but some are women. Most Mahāyāna texts assume that buddhas must be men, and only a few advanced practitioners are cast as females. One reason for this is that the Mahāyāna texts retain the model of the major and minor physical characteristics as part of the unique persona of a buddha. These include a sheathed penis, and so presumably only a man can have this feature. This has been noted by Nancy Schuster, who states that "the 32 marks were, in Buddhist tradition, the key to visual identification of a Buddha, and were indispensable to the depiction of the Buddha in art and to the visualization of the Buddha in meditation."[23] Moreover, the body of a great man represents an Indian vision of the ideal male body, and female beauty is conceived in very different terms. Where the torso and limbs of a great man's physique are straight and have few bulges and curves, the form of ideal Indian womanhood, attested to in innumerable sculptures and paintings, is voluptuous, with huge breasts and hips, commonly depicted in a sensuous pose. From the Indian perspective, the features of a great man's body are simply inappropriate for females and would seem unnatural as aspects of a woman's form. The vast majority of Mahāyāna sūtras make some mention of the physical characteristics, and this is a probable reason why the state of buddhahood continued to be the exclusive preserve of males.

The *Discourse of the Lotus of the True Doctrine* explicitly excludes women from buddhahood. At one point in the text, the daughter of Sāgara the *nāga* king (who is not named), appears and says that she has followed Śākyamuni's career since its inception. There is no spot in the entire world as small as a mustard seed on which the Blessed One has not given up his own body for the sake of other beings. She then describes the Buddha's body: "that ethereal body, perfectly complete, subtle, radiating light in all directions, adorned with the thirty-two physical characteristics, also possessing the secondary physical characteristics, is praised by all beings." She then declares that she has aroused the mind of awakening, and Śāriputra informs her that awakening is difficult to attain, and "it may happen, sister, that a woman displays unflagging energy, performs good works for many thousands of eons, and fulfills the six perfections, but as yet there is no example of a woman having reached buddhahood." He adds that not only is it impossible for a woman to become a buddha but that no woman can even attain the rank of Brahmā, Indra, the chief guardian deity of the four quarters, a world-conquering monarch, or an irreversible bodhisattva. At that moment her resolve is rewarded, and she is transformed into a man. She then sits under a tree and attains awakening, following which she develops the major and minor physical characteristics and begins preaching the dharma.[24]

The trope of sex change runs throughout Mahāyāna sūtra literature and is portrayed as a reward for exceptionally good actions by women. There are also some transformations from men to women, but these are the result of serious misconduct that leads to immediate retribution. The best realms are commonly characterized as places in which womanhood does not even exist. In the *Discourse of the Lotus of the True Doctrine,* for example, the Buddha predicts that his hearer disciple Pūrṇa will one day become a buddha and rule over a glorious realm. Its inhabitants will come into being through apparitional birth, and no sexual intercourse will be necessary (or even possible). In this wondrous place, "no women will be there, nor fear of the places of punishment or lower states."[25] A similar description is given of the Pure Land of the buddha Amitābha (Sukhāvatī), which is perfect in every respect. One of the Pure Land's significant features is its utter lack of women, and the *Array of the Pure Land Discourse* promises that any woman who generates sincere devotion to Amitābha, coupled with disgust for the female form, will be reborn in Amitābha's realm with a glorious male body that is as hard as a diamond and endowed with the major and minor physical characteristics and the physical strength of Nārāyaṇa. This fortunate being will never again have to endure life as a female.[26]

The New Ideal Man: Vimalakīrti

The Buddha remains a central figure in Mahāyāna texts, but a number of bodhisattvas play key roles. Among the most prominent bodhisattvas are Avalokiteśvara (Lord Who Looks Down), who is said to personify the compassion of all the buddhas, and Mañjuśrī (Smooth Glory), who personifies their wisdom. Another important figure is Vimalakīrti (Stainless Reputation), the protagonist of the *Discourse Spoken by Vimalakīrti.* He is a layman but also an advanced bodhisattva, and he observes the conduct of a monk while wearing householder's clothing. He owns a house and has a wife and son but lives aloof from the world. He even has a harem but practices strict celibacy. He teaches his consorts about the pitfalls of sensuality and is characterized as "a eunuch in the midst of the harem."[27] He appears to be surrounded by servants but spends most of his time in solitude. His body also manifests the major and minor physical characteristics, but he is not yet a buddha. His form is nonphysical, and he has no need for material sustenance, but he consumes food and liquids in conformance with ordinary norms. In reality, however, he is sustained by the taste of meditative absorptions.

The lay bodhisattva, unbound by the vows of a monk, is able to enter brothels, bars, and gaming establishments, but only does so in order to teach their denizens about the evil consequences of their actions. He conducts business deals that generate profit, but he has no interest in making money and uses it only to further his conversion work. He is credited with great endurance, resolution, and physical strength, and the text extols him as a "warrior among warriors."

Distinguishing Hīnayānists and Mahāyānists is a pervasive concern of the text. It characterizes the former as overly concerned with physicality and advises them to regard the body as composed of the four great elements, as weak, perishable, transitory, unworthy of confidence, and prone to sickness and other sufferings.[28] Vimalakīrti compares the body to a ball of foam, a bubble, a mirage, a dream, an echo, or a cloud and states that it lacks self or inherent existence and so is empty. He also asserts that the body is dirty, but his description is very different from those presented in the Pāli canon, which focus on its foulness and disgusting contents. Vimalakīrti, by contrast, cautions against excessive repugnance toward the body and characterizes it as the vehicle of the religious path.[29] He also extols the Buddha's body as the perfection of physical forms. He declares that it is hard as a diamond, free from all negative qualities, and endowed with all possible positive ones. The Buddha's true form is the truth body, which is pure, supramundane, and unconditioned.[30]

A number of tropes serve to denigrate the Hīnayānists in the audience and unfavorably contrast them to the Mahāyānists. At one point in the story, huge celestial thrones are sent to Vimalakīrti's house for the comfort of his guests; the great bodhisattvas are able to expand their bodies to sit on them, but hearers cannot. This initiates a description of the qualities of bodhisattvas who have reached the irreversible levels, from which they can never backslide and which predestine them for eventual buddhahood. They can toy with space and time and engage in a vast range of activities designed to benefit sentient beings. The bodhisattvas' central goal is attainment of buddhahood because buddhas have the greatest wisdom and resources and thus are of maximum benefit to others. Vimalakīrti states that a buddha's central body is the truth body, which is born from cultivation of merit, morality, concentration, wisdom, liberation, compassion, and equanimity. He urges the assembled bodhisattvas: "the body of the Thus Gone One is born from countless good actions. It is toward such a body that you should turn your aspirations."[31]

Following an extended description of the wondrous abilities of irreversible bodhisattvas, Ānanda exclaims that he will never again consider himself the foremost of those who have attained mindfulness because these great beings are vastly superior to him. The Buddha informs him that when he gave Ānanda this designation he only meant that Ānanda was the greatest of his *Hīnayāna* disciples. Bodhisattvas are much more advanced than hearers, who "cannot even dream" of rivaling the great deeds of the bodhisattvas.[32]

This theme continues when two of the most revered hearers, Kāśyapa and Śāriputra, marvel at how much farther along the path the great bodhisattvas are than them. Kāśyapa states that the hearers are like a man born blind who cannot even conceive what the world of sighted people is like. The liberation of bodhisattvas far surpasses the hearers' own limited attainments. Kāśyapa and Śāriputra sadly admit that they have "completely degenerated faculties" because they devote their energies to personal liberation rather than to the salvation of all beings. As a result they are like a "burned and rotten seed" and are incapable of entering the Great Vehicle. Kāśyapa concludes that when Hīnayānists encounter a discourse on the dharma from the Mahāyāna point of view, they should "give forth a cry of pain that would shatter the cosmos." When bodhisattvas hear such teachings, however, they experience great exultation, like a crown prince at the moment of coronation.[33]

The denigration of arhats represents a major shift from their representation in the Pāli canon, where they are portrayed as revered figures worthy of the highest respect. In Pāli literature, great elders like Śāriputra and Maudgalyāyana have outstanding wisdom and supernatural abilities, as well as wondrous bodies that are evidence of their highly developed inner qualities, and sometimes they even deliver sermons in the Buddha's stead and he approves of their words.

In the Mahāyāna sūtras, the Buddha's abilities are significantly enhanced, and his hearer disciples suffer a corresponding diminution of status. The *Discourse Spoken by Vimalakīrti* begins with a lengthy section in which a number of these disciples are shown to be utterly deficient in their supposed areas of expertise in relation to the bodhisattvas.[34] Pūrṇa, the most proficient in perceiving past lives, is upbraided by Vimalakīrti for his inability to recognize the fact that two lay disciples he is instructing are really bodhisattvas, and so the Hīnayāna doctrines he expounds are inappropriate. Śāriputra is the main whipping boy in the sūtra and appears as a bumbling figure; he is completely overwhelmed by the wisdom and eloquence of bodhisattvas, who poke fun at him and denigrate his feeble attempts at explaining the dharma. The purpose of these tropes is clearly polemical: by negatively portraying the greatest exemplars of their rival's tradition and unfavorably contrasting them with the Mahāyāna ideal of the bodhisattva, the writers apparently intended to cast their system in a more favorable light.

This is also done directly by giving exalted epithets to bodhisattvas, many of which resonate with the highly gendered language of the Pāli texts. The bodhisattvas are extolled for their wisdom and eloquence and are also described as paragons of manliness, referred to as mighty heroes, and equated with powerful animals associated with masculinity. At the beginning of the *8,000 Line Perfection of Wisdom Discourse,* for example, the bodhisattvas in the assembly are described as "thoroughbred stallions."[35] The *Discourse of the Lotus of the True Doctrine* extols them as "lions, lords of men."[36] The *Array of the Pure Land Discourse* asserts that all the members of the assembly are "great elephants,"[37] and the *Ornament for the Great Vehicle Discourses* states that "the good, brave [bodhisattva] roams through his lives like a lion."[38] A later passage describes such a being as "intelligent, child of the Victor, Victor ground, triumphant, Victor sprout, mighty one, supreme sage, leader, greatly famous, compassionate, greatly meritorious, lord, righteous."[39]

The Buddha also receives similar epithets. In the *Discourse Spoken by Vimalakīrti,* the bodhisattva Ratnākara (Multitude of Jewels) describes him as "a bull of a man," and in the *Discourse of the Lotus of the True Doctrine,* he is referred to as "king of kings," "lion of the Śākyas," "sun of men," "chief of the world," "king of the dharma," "unsurpassed knower of the world," "unsurpassed tamer of men, master of gods and men," "ultimate man," and "father of the world."[40] The *Discourse* also extols his "manly strength."[41] Mahāyāna sūtras emphasize his supernatural abilities and wisdom surpassing that of all others, but it is important that he also be a consummate example of Indian ideals of masculinity.

Bodies and Marks

The emphasis on the body as a testament to spiritual attainment that was noted in earlier chapters continues in Mahāyāna. The *Ornament for Great Vehicle Discourses* asserts that the perfect body of a buddha is the result of his practice of morality, and it describes bodhisattvas on the tenth level *(bhūmi),* the penultimate stage before buddhahood, as "physically perfect."[42] It adds that this body affects ordinary beings who see it in profound ways and inspires spontaneous devotion: "When [beings] see the true man, from having viewed all your bodies, From a mere glimpse they develop faith; homage to you!"[43]

The commentary adds that when beings catch a glimpse of the body of a great man, endowed with the major and minor physical characteristics, they are inspired to devotion, and this is the function of his perfect body.

In the Pāli canon, there are figures who are credited with having some of the physical characteristics of a great man, but only the Buddha possesses all of them, and his are said to be clearer and more beautiful than those of others. They also surpass the physical characteristics of world-conquering monarchs. Texts that discuss these characteristics indicate that they are acquired and perfected at the very end of a bodhisattva's progress toward buddhahood and so should only appear on the most advanced practitioners. It is not surprising, then, that with the profusion of bodhisattvas in Mahāyāna texts there is a corresponding interest in the physical characteristics, because their manifestation distinguishes one who has them from others of lesser attainments. By crediting advanced bodhisattvas with bodies adorned with glorious major and minor physical characteristics, the Mahāyāna authors set them apart from even the greatest Hīnayānists, the revered figures of other religions, and the rest of humanity.

A number of Mahāyāna sūtras use this trope repeatedly, and there are innumerable references to the physical characteristics, along with graphic depictions of how they appear on the bodies of great bodhisattvas. In the *Discourse of the Lotus of the True Doctrine,* for example, one scene depicts Śākyamuni and the buddha Prabhūtaratna (Abundant Jewels) sticking out their enormous tongues, which extend to the Brahmā heaven and emit a multitude of light rays. From each tongue innumerable bodhisattvas, all endowed with the thirty-two physical characteristics, issue forth, seated on lotus thrones. Every buddha in the assembly then imitates their actions, and scores of awakened beings sitting on magnificent thrones send their tongues into the farthest reaches of the cosmos. They leave their tongues outstretched for one thousand years, all the while emitting light rays and bodhisattvas on thrones, until all at once they withdraw them with a loud sound of spitting and snapping.[44]

What are modern readers to make of this hyperbole? Why is the bizarre physiognomy of the great man presented as not only the ideal of male beauty but also proof of claims to spiritual attainment? This image of the ideal man, as far as I am aware, has no corollaries in any other culture, but it is pervasive in Indian Buddhist literature. No Buddhist author I have seen seriously questions it, and I have never seen any indication that anyone considered such a body to be odd or undesirable. The exact opposite is the case: Indian Buddhist depictions of the great man emphasize the notion that this is the very epitome of male perfection, and even when bodhisattvas or buddhas assume other shapes for didactic purposes, they always return to their true forms, generally with a mention of the sublime beauty of their physiques and the admiration of those who view them.

At the same time, there are deconstructive tendencies. In the *Cutting Diamond Perfection of Wisdom Discourse,* for example, the Buddha declares that those who saw him in his physical form did not truly see him. He asks Subhūti, "Do you think that the Thus Gone One can be seen by the possession of his physical characteristics?," and Subhūti replies, "no indeed, Blessed One, for what has been taught by the Thus Gone One as the possession of physical characteristics is truly a non-possession of no physical characteristics. Whenever there is possession of physical characteristics, there is fraud. Therefore the Thus Gone One is to be seen from no physical characteristics as physical characteristics."[45]

This passage appears to imply that it is possible to manifest the body of an awakened being without actually embodying his qualities. In Chapter 4, the story of how Māra adopted the Buddha's form and caused Upagupta to prostrate before him was discussed, and there are various other beings credited with the ability to shift shape in Indian Buddhist literature. Despite the exalted nature of buddhas and bodhisattvas, there is no source I have seen that indicates any barrier to shape shifters appearing in their forms, and so the author of this text may be sounding a cautionary note regarding the pervasive emphasis on the Buddha's physical person. A similar sentiment appears in the *25,000 Line Perfection of Wisdom Discourse,* which states that "if the thirty-two physical characteristics of a great man which the Thus Gone One possesses were existents and not nonexistent, then the Thus Gone One would not outshine the world with its gods, humans and demigods with his splendor and majesty; but he outshines it because the thirty-two physical characteristics are nonexistent and not existents."[46]

This passage applies the logic of emptiness to discourses of the physical form of the Buddha. It does not deny that he possesses the physical characteristics, nor does it deny that they are a sign of his greatness, but it indicates that they are ultimately empty of inherent existence. The body of a buddha is a product of eons of diligent practice, cultivation of morality, and a multitude of good qualities, which are manifested in his external form at the culmination of his progress toward awakening. But like all produced phenomena they are contingent and transitory, and thus people who focus on his body are directed to shift attention to his spiritual attainments, which are the real reason for his designation as a buddha. His perfect body and unique physiognomy are merely secondary phenomena.

Similarly, in the *8,000 Line Perfection of Wisdom Discourse,* the Buddha asserts that a thus gone one does not derive this appellation from the fact that he has acquired a transcendent physical form, but rather from his attainment of omniscience. Omniscience is a product of the perfection of wisdom, and a buddha's physical body is the result of his practice of skill in means over innumerable lifetimes. Omniscience forms the support of all his exalted qualities and allows him to reveal the truth body, the physical form of a buddha, and the *saṃgha* body, which continues his teachings and spreads them to others. His physical body is still important as a basis for worship, and even following his death the relics left behind after its cremation will serve as a focal point of devotion: "thus the acquisition of a distinctive physical personality is the cause of the wisdom of omniscience. Due to the firm basis of that cognition, he becomes a shrine for all beings, worthy of devotional activities, worshipped by them. After I have entered final nirvana, my relics will also be worshipped."[47]

Skill in Means

One of the core powers of bodhisattvas is the ability to adapt their teachings to the proclivities of individuals and groups. The *Discourse of the Lotus of the True Doctrine* contains the famous parable of the burning house, in which a father sees that his home is on fire, and his three young sons are playing inside, unaware of the danger. He calls to them, but they are engrossed in play and pay him no heed. Because he knows what they desire most, the father promises each his favorite type of cart. They come running at the prospect of being given the marvelous vehicles, but when they reach their father, he presents them all with the same type of cart, described as the best type. When asked whether the father can justly be accused of deceit, Avalokiteśvara exclaims to the Buddha, "no indeed Lord!," and adds that the father was concerned only with his sons' welfare and followed the most effective course of action to save them.[48]

The *Discourse Spoken by Vimalakīrti* is also concerned with this sort of skillful means and extols the abilities of bodhisattvas to devise the most effective ways to benefit beings. At one point, Vimalakīrti informs Kāśyapa that most *māras* are really bodhisattvas in disguise, who test the resolve of other bodhisattvas in various clever ways. Similarly, beggars who importune bodhisattvas for their food, clothing, or even parts of their bodies are generally also bodhisattvas working subtly to provide them with opportunities to make merit and overcome their tendencies to cling to mundane things. Vimalakīrti adds that only bodhisattvas are "capable of making such cruel demands. The power of creating difficulties for bodhisattvas does not exist in ordinary people," who "are not capable of tormenting and demanding in this way."[49] Someone who is not also a bodhisattva lacks the power to cause real difficulties to a bodhisattva, so they should view those who afflict them as compassionate fellow practitioners working for their spiritual betterment.

Vimalakīrti himself is held up as the epitome of the skillful methods of bodhisattvas. He engages in various apparently negative actions but is free from any desires, so there are no defiling consequences. He can take rebirth in hells, among animals, demigods, or other types of beings, but remains unafflicted by their distinctive passions. He "follows the way of craving but is detached from the pleasures of desire," and he can adopt any appearance he wishes without experiencing any negative aspects associated with it.[50] He "follows the way of the crippled," but still has a perfect body adorned with the major and minor physical characteristics. He and other bodhisattvas can even manifest as courtesans in order to wean men from sensual desire. The disguised bodhisattvas assume seductive female forms that incite lust but then teach their customers the dharma.[51] To further their missionary work they manifest as influential figures, such as village chiefs or prime ministers, in order to use their positions for the benefit of others.

Vimalakīrti states that immersion in the sea of passions is a key aspect of the practice of bodhisattvas and that without such activity, "it is impossible to produce the thought of omniscience."[52] When Kāśyapa hears this, he laments: "all the passions of cyclic existence are the family of the Thus Gone One," but arhats like him tragically embarked on a misguided path of personal salvation and so have rendered themselves incapable of generating the thought of awakening *(bodhi-citta)* because they have eliminated all desires. Thus they cannot commit evil acts and have no cravings. As a result they cannot develop the wish to liberate all sentient beings, and they lack the capacity to manifest great compassion *(mahākaruṇā)*.

Moreover, their strict adherence to monastic rules is ultimately a hindrance. Vimalakīrti's compassionate activities are compared to the selfish pursuit of nirvana by the hearers, who are bound by their vows. At one point in the proceedings, the bodhisattva Jagatīṃdhara (Preserver of the World) is visited by Māra disguised as Śakra, who offers Jagatīṃdhara twelve thousand female deities as his servants, but he declares that monastic regulations prevent him from accepting such a gift. Vimalakīrti steps in and informs him that the donor is really Māra, who is trying to trick him. The great lay bodhisattva then accepts the women and informs the audience that this act does not violate the norms of householders. Māra is forced to give the women to him but then demands that Vimalakīrti return them because he is unattached to possessions and supposedly has no desire for anything. Vimalakīrti readily agrees but first teaches the female deities the dharma, knowing that with the seeds of the teaching planted in their minds they will return to Māra's palace and continue their practice. They will convert many other deities and will continually undermine Māra's evil plots.[53]

Skill and Masculinity

Mahāyāna texts commonly link skill in means and masculinity. The cleverness of bodhisattvas in devising new means of conversion is a factor of their exalted level of attainment, and it is also associated with their development of perfect male bodies. The *Heroic Meditation Career Discourse* states that advanced bodhisattvas have bodies that are hard, diamondlike, real, infallible, and indestructible. They do not have stomachs or internal organs and do not produce excrement, urine, or bad odors, nor do they have any impurities. These beings appear to ingest food, but nothing actually penetrates or enters their bodies. They engage in expected activities, such as eating and excreting, but only do so out of compassion and in order to conform to worldly norms. Whatever actions they perform are motivated by pure compassion, and so even apparently morally questionable ones produce no negative karma:

> Though he appears to engage in worldly practices, he is really free from practice and transcends all practices. . . . When he appears in a forest, it is exactly as if he were in a village; when he appears among the laity, it is exactly as if he were among the religious. If he appears in white clothing, he does not have the dissipation of a layman; and if he appears as an ascetic, he does not have the arrogance of a monk.[54]

Such a bodhisattva may manifest illness for didactic purposes but is free from all bodily afflictions and never ages or suffers physical degeneration. He may seem to grow old, but all his faculties and abilities remain intact. Even his death is mere show, because he transcends all the vicissitudes of cyclic existence.[55] For such an advanced being, every aspect of his life is designed to benefit others. He may be born in the Desire Realm as a world-conquering king, surround himself with an appropriate harem and coterie of servants as well as a wife and children, and will appear to indulge in sensual pursuits, but inwardly he is always established in profound meditative concentration, and so his pure morality remains intact and unsullied by actions that would lead lesser beings to rebirth in the lower realms.[56] The text even asserts that such a bodhisattva may assume the form of a woman, hearer, or solitary realizer, but his outward appearance in no way alters the fact of his exalted status or true gender.[57]

The notion that advanced bodhisattvas can indulge in sensual activities without being affected is an important one in Mahāyāna texts. The *Bodhisattva Levels,* for example, states that great beings often use lust as a basis for providing dharma instructions:

> When a woman is alone and her mind is prey to the agony of the desire to put an end to her celibacy, the lay bodhisattva approaches her with the dharma of sexual union. He then thinks, "May she not develop a thought of unfriendliness, which would lead to demerits. May she on the contrary, under my influence, abandon unwholesome thoughts, so that the object of her desire becomes a root for good." Developing this thought of pure compassion, he resorts to the dharma of copulation, and there is no error; instead, this produces many merits.[58]

In the *Skillful Means Discourse,* the Buddha warns Ānanda not to judge such a being by ordinary standards. A bodhisattva who is capable of wallowing in the lustful mire of cyclic existence without being sullied by it is a "great hero" who cavorts with women only in order to introduce them to the three jewels (the Buddha, dharma, and *saṃgha*) and to induce them to develop the supreme thought of awakening. As long as the bodhisattva holds on to the "thought of omniscience" and engages in such actions because of a motivation to benefit others, he makes great merit and avoids negative karma.

The Buddha gives the example of a bodhisattva named Lord of the Greatly Passionate who once sat with a beautiful woman on a couch of the sort commonly used for sexual intercourse. The woman, the Buddha continues, had been his wife for the past two hundred lives. When they were together, he taught her about the dharma: "The Buddha does not praise desire; that is the domain of the foolish. Eliminate craving for sense-objects, and become the best of humanity—a buddha." Hearing these words, she experienced a sense of jubilation and faith in the Buddha, and his teaching filled her. She rose from the couch and fell to the feet of the bodhisattva and promised to forswear all sensual desires and to aspire to buddhahood. Because of the strength of her faith and resolution, she would never again be reborn as a woman, and the Buddha predicted her attainment of awakening after 9,900,000 incalculable eons.[59]

In some circumstances, situations arise that require bodhisattvas to temporarily suspend their avoidance of sexuality for the higher good of helping others still enmeshed in passion. One such story concerns Jyotis (Radiant), a brahman bodhisattva who practiced celibacy in the wilderness for 42,000 years. One day he traveled to a city where a female water carrier saw his beautiful body and threw herself at him "with a mind consumed by lust." When he asked what she wanted, she replied, "brahman, I want you!" He told her that he had no desire for sense pleasures, but she stated that she could not live without him (even though they had just met) and threatened to kill herself if he refused to have sex with her. Jyotis reflected that celibacy is a desirable state, but his compassion for the lust-obsessed woman led him to assent to her proposal: "let this woman not die, but be happy."[60]

He agreed to do whatever she wished of him and subsequently married her. They lived together for twelve years. Married life apparently cured her of her lust, and he eventually was able to extricate himself from the relationship without causing her great distress and returned to his practice of advanced meditative states. When he died he was reborn in the heaven of Brahmā. At this point in the narrative, the Buddha revealed that he was in fact Jyotis in that lifetime and that Yaśodharā was the lust-obsessed water carrier, who tried to hinder his spiritual progress then as she did in his final life. He concluded by telling Ānanda, "Son of good family, take note: something that sends other sentient beings to hell sends a bodhisattva who is skilled in means to rebirth in the world of Brahmā."[61]

Even negative contact with such an exalted being can have unanticipated future benefits. In the same text, the Buddha relates the story of the monk Priyaṃkara (Causing Pleasure) and Dakṣiṇottarā (Superior Donations). One day the monk sought alms at the house of a wealthy merchant. The merchant's daughter, Dakṣiṇottarā, "perceived the features of his handsome proportions, the sound of his voice, and his complexion with her thoughts consumed by sexual passion. With her thoughts consumed by passion, aroused by passion, obsessed by passion, burning with passion, her whole body burst into a sweat and while standing there, she died." The monk also became aroused due to the intensity of her lust for him but subsequently reflected on the nature of desire and was able to overcome these feelings. He analyzed the body from head to foot and recognized that it has nothing to warrant attraction, and he then comprehended how phenomena arise and disappear. Thus he was able to use a potentially destabilizing experience to promote spiritual advancement.[62]

The brief encounter also profoundly altered Dakṣiṇottarā's destiny. Because she felt desire for an advanced bodhisattva, this apparently counted as a form of reverence, and as a result she was born among the gods of the Heaven of the Thirty-Three. In her new divine form, s/he reflected: "After dying with my mind obsessed by lust, I transformed my woman's body to obtain a male body here. I have become fortunate beyond measure." The male divinity to whom she directed these thoughts then reflected, "if this is the reward for thoughts of lust, what would be my reward for doing prostrations and service with thoughts of faith to the bodhisattva Priyaṃkara?"[63]

The lucky god who in his previous life had been the merchant's daughter sums up his experience to the Buddha: "I caught fire with clumsy passion and could not speak a single word to him. Unable even to bestow the alms, standing there I sweated to death. At the very instant of my death, Lord, my woman's body was abandoned. I was born in paradise by transmigration and obtained this luminous body of a male."[64]

At this point Priyaṃkara makes a vow that any woman who looks at him with thoughts of desire will be turned into "the completely fearless form of a man and take the highest course of awakening."[65] A core part of his mission will be the transformation of women into men by attracting them with his beautiful body and then using his skill to effect a gender transformation. The Buddha praises this intention:

> Priyaṃkara has a continuing aspiration, that any woman who looks at him with a lustful mind will lose her female form to become a man and a truly exalted being. Ānanda, consider what good qualities this demonstrates:

> Some people generate passion and are reborn in hell, but when that passion is directed toward the heroes it results in masculinity in heaven.[66]

The Buddha approvingly adds that billions of women will become besotted with passion for Priyaṃkara and as a result will be reborn as men. This is an interesting reversal of the problems experienced by the Buddha's monastic followers in the Pāli texts discussed in the first three chapters. Those monks' beauty was a source of constant unwanted attention by women, some of whom succeeded in derailing their progress on the religious path. The single greatest threat to their training was the blandishments of lustful women, but bodhisattvas are able to rechannel this energy in positive directions, even though this runs exactly contrary to the desires of the women themselves.

Mahāyāna literature contains some examples of female bodhisattvas who use their physical charms to entice lustful men and then convince them of the futility of sensual desire, but in other stories a female form is a liability for a bodhisattva. In the *Questions of Candrottarā,* for example, the protagonist is described as surpassingly beautiful, with a body similar to a buddha's. She has golden skin, and a delightful fragrance emanates from every pore. She has attained this form as a result of diligent practice of self-restraint and generosity, and her beauty is a testament to her virtue. Unlike the bodies of buddhas and male bodhisattvas that inspire others, however, men who view her are overcome with lust, and she must use her supernatural powers to escape them. The beautiful forms of male bodhisattvas and buddhas are used to convert beings, but Candrottarā's body is a hindrance to her because the mere sight of her causes men to lose control and attempt to force themselves on her.[67]

The text makes it clear that unlike the women who view Priyaṃkara with desire and benefit from this, the men who lust after Candrottarā experience only negative results: she informs a mob of men that those who wallow in lust will be reborn in a hell realm or as animals or hungry ghosts; if they are humans, they will be one-eyed, lame, dumb, ugly, blind, or physically disabled. After levitating into the air to escape her pursuers, she tells them that she is devoid of sensual desire and that those who emulate her example reap rewards in future lives. They will be reborn as well-favored humans or gods. She reminds them that all beings transmigrate in various ways and that she has been their mother in past lives. Lust toward one's mother is unseemly, and they should recognize this. When asked by a male bodhisattva why she does not change her female form, she replies that the female form is empty, as are all phenomena, but when she receives a prediction of future buddhahood, she immediately transforms her body into a male form.[68]

In the *Heroic Meditation Career Discourse,* a bodhisattva named Māragocarānupalipta (Unstained by the Realm of Māra) uses his supernatural power to emit a great light that spotlights his marvelous body. It illuminates all of Māra's palaces and utterly eclipses him "like a block of ink." When Māra's daughters see Māragocarānupalipta's manly physique, they become profoundly aroused (Tibetan.: *chags par gyur;* Skt.: *saṃrakta*), and each propositions him for sex, promising to do whatever he wishes if he complies. He responds by creating two hundred replicas of his form and two hundred palaces in which to copulate with the women, and each believes that she alone enjoys his attentions. He fully satisfies every daughter, and they develop religious devotion. At that point he teaches them the dharma, and each generates the mind of awakening and resolves to pursue buddhahood.[69] Later in the text the Buddha proclaims that Māragocarānupalipta "disports himself with the daughters of the gods but does not experience any illicit sexual pleasure."[70] Thus he can immerse himself in aspects of cyclic existence that are the downfall of less advanced beings, but he never loses the thought of awakening, and he benefits those who would otherwise be doomed by their actions.

The *Skill in Means Discourse* indicates that such deeds serve another purpose: to forestall questions about the manhood of bodhisattvas. Men who lack desire are suspect in India, and the first several chapters provided examples of this sentiment, particularly with regard to the Buddha and his monastic followers. Moreover, men have a religiously sanctioned duty to procreate and produce sons; this repays a debt to their parents and ancestors and ensures that the lineage will continue. Those who fail to do so are viewed as deficient in an important aspect of society's expectations for males.[71]

For thousands of years, celibate ascetics have wandered around India, renouncing the settled existence of the householder. Many of India's most revered sages abandoned sexuality, often while still in the prime of life, in pursuit of religious goals, but this masculine ideal is often criticized from the perspective of the sexually active householder, who supports society through productive work and fathers male heirs who continue his lineage. This ideal, while generally regarded as inferior to that of ascetics, who pursue liberation from cyclic existence, is also valorized as an important component of any society. India has produced erotic classics like the *Kāma Sūtra* that provide information for those who are committed to sexual activity, which help them maximize sensual pleasure, one of the rewards of the household life.

Indian biographies of the Buddha stressed both elements, and stories of bodhisattvas who indulge in sensuality in their conversion work emphasize their virility and attractiveness to women, despite their primary commitment to celibacy. Because Buddhism valorizes celibacy, it must contend with critiques from the perspective of those who advocate masculine ideals of sexual performance and physical vigor, and this is one reason why its ideal figures are presented as sexually attractive and as "stallions." Where monastics must remain content to be desirable, lay bodhisattvas have the freedom to indulge in sensual activities, unhindered by vows of celibacy. Thus the *Skill in Means Discourse* asserts that when the Buddha took a wife and a retinue of courtesans, he did so not because he had any lust but because he wanted to prevent anyone from thinking that "the Bodhisattva is not really a holy man, but rather a type of natural eunuch." Such a thought would result in negative karma for the beings who denigrated him, and they would be "hapless, damaged, miserable, and deprived for a long time. To prevent doubt on the part of these sentient beings, the Bodhisattva demonstrated producing a son: Rāhula. And to do this, he acquired the Śākya maid Yaśodharā and the rest."[72]

The text further explains that the Buddha married and gathered a harem of tens of thousands of courtesans in fulfillment of commitments made in previous lives. When he made his declaration in front of the buddha Dīpaṃkara that he would one day attain buddhahood, the future Yaśodharā declared that she wished to be his wife in all of his future lifetimes. Although he felt no need for such companionship and no sensual desires, he agreed to her request.[73] During the course of his advancement toward awakening, many other women became attached to him, and they were reborn as his courtesans. More than 42,000 women eventually joined him as sexual partners in his last lifetime, and he cavorted with them all during his years in the women's quarters. But it was not really him: instead, the Buddha created physical replicas who "enjoyed, played, and took pleasure with these women," each of whom thought that she alone enjoyed sexual dalliances with the Bodhisattva. But he remained always aloof from such actions and in a state of permanent meditative absorption, unaffected by the outstanding performances of his sexual athlete doppelgängers. The Buddha concludes that despite appearances, from the time of his declaration to Dīpaṃkara he never really indulged in any sensual activities.[74]

Not all Mahāyāna texts are so sanguine about the abilities of bodhisattvas to resist the lure of sensuality. The *Discourse of the Lotus of the True Doctrine* is adamant that bodhisattvas should remain as aloof from women as possible, and its characterizations are similar to those of the Pāli texts. The Buddha instructs Mañjuśrī that bodhisattvas should not teach the dharma to females because they wish to see those women and must avoid addressing young virgins, girls, or young wives and never greet them fondly, as this might excite the women to feelings of lust. A bodhisattva should also refuse to instruct hermaphrodites and should have no interactions with such persons, nor should he even return their greetings. Whenever a bodhisattva enters a house—particularly one in which women reside—he should always keep the Thus Gone One in his thoughts, and he should avoid any passionate attachment to women. He should never display his perfect teeth to them in a smile, nor should he make potentially sexual motions with his body, and he should never engage in gossip or banter with women. He should avoid female devotees with a reputation for loose behavior and should have no dealings with vendors of pork or mutton. Moreover, "he should not frequent whores or other sensual persons, and he must avoid any exchange of civility with them. And when a sage has to preach to a woman, he should not enter into an apartment with her alone, nor should he stay to chat."[75]

The *25,000 Line Perfection of Wisdom Discourse* asserts that from the moment of the dawning of the mind of awakening, bodhisattvas are celibate, and they think, "one who is not celibate, who pursues sensual pleasures, creates an obstacle to mere rebirth in the Brahmā world; how much more to supreme awakening!"[76] Śāriputra asks the Buddha whether bodhisattvas still have parents, sons, and relatives. The Buddha responds that they do but reiterates that bodhisattvas are always celibate. He then adds that some advanced bodhisattvas might indulge in sensual behavior using skill in means, but they only do so for the benefit of others, and their minds never waver from celibacy.

A number of texts confine engagement in sensual behavior for conversion purposes to lay bodhisattvas. Asaṅga, for example, is adamant that monks should maintain their vows no matter what the circumstances and contends that when stories report that bodhisattvas immerse themselves in the sensuous aspects of cyclic existence for the benefit of others, this refers only to lay bodhisattvas.[77] The *8,000 Line Perfection of Wisdom Discourse* contains a description of how such bodhisattvas operate, and it indicates that only irreversible bodhisattvas can engage in such practices safely. It states that an irreversible bodhisattva who lives the life of a householder acquires many pleasant things but has no attachment to them. Moreover, he adheres to the tenets of Buddhist morality and "does not earn his living in an improper way, but in the right way. Neither does he incur death in a state of sin, nor does he inflict injuries on others." Such bodhisattvas are completely committed to the betterment of others and are described as "worthy men, great men, supermen, excellent men, splendid men, bulls of men, sublime men, valiant men, heroes of men, leaders of men, waterlillies of men, lotuses of men, stallions of men, elephants of men, lions of men, trainers of men."

Such great beings can resist the lure of sensual pleasures while indulging in them because they are armored with the perfection of wisdom, which enables them to recognize the emptiness of physical forms and the fleeting and ultimately unsatisfactory nature of worldly enjoyments. They are also protected by the mighty demon *(yakṣa)* Vajrapāṇi, a fearsome being who was converted to the dharma but still retains his powerful form and great strength. He follows irreversible bodhisattvas and defeats their enemies, much like a guardian angel. Due to the combination of their sublime mental equanimity and their convert demon bodyguard, no being is able to conquer them, nor are they even slightly disturbed by attacks. The Buddha concludes that a bodhisattva of this type "has faculties that are all complete, and he is not deficient in any. He possesses the organs of a virile man, not those of unmanly men. He never uses spells, mantras, herbs, magical incantations, and so forth, which are the work of women."[78]

Generosity and Self-Sacrifice

In the new dispensation of the Great Vehicle, the descriptions of the bodhisattvas' activities commonly borrow tropes of the Bodhisattva's birth stories, in which he often sacrificed parts of his body or even his life for the benefit of others. Each of these great deeds won him merit and advanced his progress toward eventual buddhahood. The *Birth Stories* recount hundreds of past lives in which the Buddha was tested in extreme ways. In a groundbreaking study of this literature, Reiko Ohnuma focuses on accounts of the Bodhisattva's sacrifice of his body for the benefit of sentient beings. In some tales, he commits suicide in order to provide food for distressed beings in danger of starving to death, but in others he gladly gives away his eyes, head, or other body parts to satisfy mere whims of undeserving supplicants. In some instances, the Bodhisattva is able to restore his lost flesh by reciting an "act of truth" that attests to his pure and utterly unselfish motivations in making the physical sacrifice. In others, he perishes but is reborn with an even better body. One interesting result of this process is that advanced bodhisattvas are often described as having bodies that not only look good but also are delicious for carnivorous beings. Suzanne Mrozik cites a passage in the *Compendium of Training* that asserts that beings fortunate enough to feast on a deceased bodhisattva's corpse ingest the merit they accumulated through their heroic practices, and this can lead to rebirth as well-favored humans or even gods. Even though they eat only in order to satisfy hunger, they inadvertently acquire great merit and become destined for nirvana. This result is attributed to the bodhisattva's past vows, which included an aspiration that those who eat his flesh will attain good rebirths and make progress on the Buddhist path.[79]

By contrast, arhats are portrayed in Mahāyāna texts as selfish and lacking in compassion because they preserve their bodies and are unwilling to perform such deeds of self-abnegation. Mahāyāna texts abound with stories of bodhisattvas who willingly cut off limbs or offer themselves up to be killed in order to benefit others, and some bodhisattvas sacrifice themselves for fairly trivial reasons in situations in which there is no apparent benefit for others. One such character is the suicidal bodhisattva Sadāprarudita (Always Weeping), whose devotion is extolled in the *8,000 Line Perfection of Wisdom Discourse*.[80] He wished to honor the great bodhisattva Dharmodgata (Exalted by Dharma), but Sadāprarudita lacked financial wherewithal and so decided to sell his body in order to purchase offerings. He walked into a town and publicly announced that he wished to auction off his body, but the text reports that Māra was aware of his intent and used his powers to prevent anyone from hearing. Sadāprarudita then reflected that "thousands of bodies of mine have been shattered, wasted, destroyed and sold again and again. I have experienced measureless pains in hells for the sake of sense pleasures, because of sense pleasures, but have never done so [to obtain] doctrines of this kind, and never for the sake of honoring such beings."

Unable to find a buyer, the devout bodhisattva wailed and cried. Then Śakra disguised himself as a corrupt brahman in order to test his resolve, transported himself to the scene, and proposed to purchase Sadāprarudita's body for use in a human sacrifice. He described in gory detail how the young bodhisattva's blood, marrow, and heart would be offered and indicated that he would be cut up while still alive, but Sadāprarudita was overjoyed at finally finding someone willing to do business. Apparently not a very good bargainer, when Śakra asked him how much he thought his body was worth, Sadāprarudita replied that he would accept any amount. Hoping to incite his purchaser to finalize the transaction, the bodhisattva then seized a knife and began stabbing himself in order to get the process of butchering underway. This caused copious amounts of blood to flow, and he followed this by attempting to break his own bones.

A merchant's daughter happened to be passing by and witnessed the scene, and instead of concluding that he was suicidally insane, she was overwhelmed by admiration. She offered to pay the money he needed to make a proper offering to Dharmodgata. Sadāprarudita then indicated that his desire to receive the dharma from the great being was based on a belief that by so doing he would acquire a better body and be of greater benefit to others: "Dharmodgata will explain the perfection of wisdom and skill in means to me. I will train in them, and as a result I will become a refuge to all beings; and after I have realized full awakening I will acquire a body of golden color, the thirty-two physical characteristics of a great man, the eighty secondary physical characteristics, the splendor of a halo the rays of which extend to infinitude," and other exalted qualities associated with buddhahood.

At this point, Śakra shed his disguise and offered Sadāprarudita a boon in recognition of his sincere devotion, but the latter replied that the only gift he wished was the supreme qualities of a buddha, which the god was unable to provide. Sadāprarudita performed an act of truth, and his body was healed, following which the merchant's daughter went to her parents' house, described her meeting with the self-harming bodhisattva, and requested that they give her large amounts of wealth in order to help him fulfill his goals. They decided that giving a significant part of their fortune to a complete stranger who had publicly mutilated himself sounded like a good idea and commented that "he must live the dharma to endure subjugation and pain in his body." They ordered servants to pile their wealth on horses, travel to where Dharmodgata was staying, and present these offerings to him.

When they arrived, however, the great bodhisattva gave only a short dharma instruction, following which he entered a meditative trance state for seven years. During this time, Sadāprarudita remained in attendance, never sitting or lying down. When he heard that Dharmodgata was about to emerge from meditation, he prepared a seat for him and wished to sprinkle the spot with water in order to prevent any dust from rising and possibly settling on his body.

Māra, however, had taken away all the water in the vicinity, hoping to thwart him, but Sadāprarudita stabbed himself several times in order to use his blood as a substitute. This so impressed the merchant's daughter and her attendants that all began emulating him, and soon the area was soaked with their blood. Śakra witnessed the scene and proclaimed this a marvelous example of true devotion to the dharma and transformed the blood into water. The story ends with praise of Sadāprarudita and his extraordinary commitment.

Such utter lack of concern for their bodies is said in a number of Mahāyāna texts to be a quality of bodhisattvas.[81] Śāntideva describes the ideal attitude thus: "I make over this body to all embodied beings to do with as they please. Let them continually beat it, and splatter it with filth. Let them play with my body; let them be derisive and amuse themselves. I have given this body to them. What point has this concern of mine?"[82] Beings with such a heroic resolve and unwavering commitment to their practice are also extolled for their toughness. The *8,000 Line Perfection of Wisdom Discourse* describes them as "the very cream of beings" and asserts that "a weakling cannot be trained in this training."[83]

Such bodhisattvas aspire to reach the highest possible level of existence. As a result of their merit, they will never be reborn in hells or as hungry ghosts or other unfortunate destinies, nor will they appear in human families of outcastes, hunters, butchers, or low-class lineages in general. They will always have perfect physiques and will never be blind, deaf, one-eyed, crippled, or hunchbacked, nor will they have withered hands or arms or suffer any physical deficiency. They will not limp or be lame, nor will they have inadvertent bodily shakes, but they will always have robust, strong limbs and torsos, good complexions, and faculties that are perfect and complete in every way.[84] Their outer forms will reflect the society's expectations for advanced religious practitioners and will indicate to all that they have performed meritorious deeds in past lives. Some irreversible bodhisattvas proclaim the connection between their past deeds and their present extraordinary physical endowments:

> Because we are fully established in the absence of self-aggrandizing conceits we have acquired golden-colored bodies, the thirty-two physical characteristics of a great man, the eighty secondary characteristics, magnificent haloes surrounding us, and we have attained the unimaginable and supreme cognition of buddhas, the supreme concentration of buddhas, the perfection of all the doctrines and qualities of buddhas.[85]

The text adds that these bodhisattvas become so powerful that nothing can hinder them; even if every being in the universe were transformed into a *māra,* they would not be able to harm such a bodhisattva.[86] It asserts that because of their exalted status gods will come to pay reverence to them, ask them questions, and encourage them to continue on the path.

They are extolled as mighty heroes in language reminiscent of that used for the Buddha in Pāli texts. Such bodhisattvas put on the "great armor" and are "real men who work for the benefit of the world."[87] They undertake the impossible task of bringing all sentient beings to liberation and devote countless lifetimes to the pursuit of buddhahood in order to be of maximum benefit to others. As a result, the text declares: "homage should be paid to those bodhisattvas who are armed with this armor. . . . A bodhisattva is armed with the great armor . . . a hero who . . . will win awakening for the sake of beings who are like space, who are like the realm of qualities [i.e., infinite]."[88]

The promise of ever greater bodies as a reward for accumulation of merit and successful meditative practice is a pervasive feature of the Mahāyāna texts. The *Discourse of the Lotus of the True Doctrine,* for example, asserts that anyone who repeats it to others will attain a perfect body adorned with thousands of wondrous physical qualities.[89] If the listener is inspired to even one moment of goodness, the speaker will always have a body with keen faculties and wisdom. His mouth will never have an unpleasant smell, and he will never be afflicted by any disease of the tongue or mouth, nor will he have any teeth that are black, yellow, or otherwise discolored, and there will be no missing teeth; both rows of teeth will be even, with no gaps between them, and the lips will be perfectly formed, as will his face. The text adds that "he will receive a very complete organ of manhood" as an added bonus.[90] The text also warns that anyone who reviles the *Discourse of the Lotus of the True Doctrine* will be punished by rebirths in vile bodies that have spots, broken teeth and gaps, and disgusting lips, with a putrid smell and stinking boils that itch all the time and produce many scabs.[91] The body is thus the focal point of both reward and punishment.

Multiple Bodies

In the Perfection of Wisdom sūtras, the Buddha's body is bifurcated into two aspects, the truth body and the form body. As buddhalogical speculation developed, new theories about the Buddha's body were posited, one of the most significant of which was the notion that he really had three bodies: (1) the truth body, (2) a complete enjoyment body *(saṃbhoga-kāya),* and (3) emanation bodies *(nirmāṇa-kāya).* The first is the accumulation of the qualities of buddhahood, the fulfillment of his training over the course of countless eons, including infinite compassion and wisdom.

The complete enjoyment body is nonmaterial and imperishable. It resides in a pure land created by a buddha by means of the vast store of merit accumulated through countless lives. It is visible and accessible only to advanced bodhisattvas, who join the buddha for pleasant discourses on the dharma. Emanation bodies are are manifested in various places for the benefit of sentient beings. Some appear as humans, but they may also be animals or other beings or even bridges and various objects that provide aid to those in need. According to the *Ornament for the Great Vehicle Discourses:*

> The varieties of the body of buddhas are the truth body, the complete enjoyment body, and emanation bodies; and the first is the ground of the other two. The body of the buddha is threefold: the nature truth body has the character of transformation of the basis. The complete enjoyment body is that by which [a buddha] causes an assembly to enjoy the dharma. Emanation bodies are emanations through which they work for the benefit of beings. In all realms, the complete enjoyment body is distinguished by its gathering of assemblies, such as [bodhisattvas,] in its buddha lands, in its names, in its bodies, in its enjoyment of the doctrine and its activities. . . . The truth body is known to be subtle and is conjoined with that [complete enjoyment body]. It is also described as the cause of their mastery of complete enjoyment, when [buddhas] manifest enjoyments at will. The truth body of all buddhas is equal because it lacks differentiations. It is subtle because it is difficult to understand. It is conjoined with the complete enjoyment body and is the cause of [a buddha's] mastery of enjoyments in displaying enjoyments at will. . . . Emanation bodies of buddhas consist of the immeasurable variety of buddha emanations. The complete enjoyment body has a nature of fulfillment of one's own aims; emanation bodies have a nature of fulfillment of the aims of others.[92]

The complete enjoyment body is the individual form of a buddha, with a particular and distinctive appearance and a personal name; this form is situated in a certain location. This is the body on which the major and minor physical characteristics are most fully manifested and reach their perfection.[93] According to Vasubandhu's *Commentary on the Compendium of the Great*

Vehicle, the main purpose of the complete enjoyment body is to bring bodhisattvas to spiritual maturity. In the *Establishment of Cognition Only,* Vasubandhu describes this form as "the wondrous body of pure merit manifested by the thus gone ones through the wisdom of sameness. It abides in a pure land, manifests great miracles, turns the wheel of doctrine, and eliminates the net of doubts for all bodhisattvas in the ten levels so that they might enjoy the pleasure of Great Vehicle doctrine."[94]

The truth body is universal and is not differentiated among buddhas. It is the basis for the other two types of bodies.[95] These may appear different in physique, but all buddhas are equal in their acquisition of wisdom and perfection of compassionate activities, and all share the distinctive and unequalled attainments of buddhahood and present the same teachings to their disciples. Emanation bodies are infinitely varied, manifested as needs arise for sentient beings, and adapted to specific circumstances and individual proclivities. Emanation bodies are created for the fulfillment of others' needs, while the complete enjoyment body is the fulfillment of the practice of a particular buddha and is the corporeal locus of his subsequent enjoyment of the state of buddhahood and his physical vehicle for sharing this with advanced bodhisattvas.

The truth body is presented as the fundamental basis of buddhahood and is the source of all good qualities and preaching of the dharma. When asked by the Buddha whether he would prefer vast stores of buddha relics or a written copy of the Perfection of Wisdom, Śakra unhesitatingly chooses the latter because it is the guide of all thus gone ones and is "the real relic/body." The Buddha approves of his response and states that the buddhas "are those who have the truth body. But, monks, you should not think that this [physical] body is my actual body. Monks, you should perceive me through the full realization of the truth body."[96] This body is produced by the perfection of wisdom, which is equated with the reality limit *(bhūta-koṭi),* a synonym for emptiness and the ultimate nature of reality *(dharmatā).*

Later in the same text, the bodhisattva Dharmodgata provides an analogy of a foolish man who mistakes a mirage for a pool of water. He asks Sadāprarudita whether the mirage comes from somewhere or goes away later, and the junior bodhisattva replies that for an illusory image there is no real coming or going. Similarly, Dharmodgata explains, those who fixate on the body of the Buddha fail to recognize his true nature and are like the man who perceives water where there is none. The Thus Gone One is not the same as his physical body because all buddhas are really the truth body, which does not arise or disappear:

> those who do not know all phenomena to be like a dream as explained by the Thus Gone One adhere to [buddhas] as though they were their nominal bodies *(nāma-kāya)* or physical bodies and imagine thus gone ones come and go. . . . But those who know all phenomena to be like a dream as they really are . . . do not imagine a going or coming of any phenomenon. . . . They know the Thus Gone One by way of his true nature. . . . Those who know the true nature of the Thus Gone One practice close to full awakening; they practice the perfection of wisdom.[97]

Śīlabhadra's *Explanation of the Buddha Level* states that the three bodies are distinguished by function and do not differ ontologically. The essential body *(svabhāvika-kāya),* equated with the truth body, is subtle, difficult to fathom, and understood only by buddhas, while the complete enjoyment body is the form in which a buddha manifests in order to share enjoyment of the dharma with advanced bodhisattvas in pure realms. Emanation bodies are coarse forms generated throughout various worlds for the benefit of beings who are spiritually immature.[98] According to Asvabhāva, the truth body can be known only through personal realization and so is inconceivable *(acintya)* and subtle. It is beyond words and concepts and is only perceived by buddhas, whose realization is nondual and nonconceptual. Ordinary beings rely on words and conceptuality, but there is no basis in thought or language for an adequate description of the truth body.

What's in a Body?

The Sanskrit term *kāya* has the primary meaning of body, and it shares the senses of the English term: it can refer to the physique of a being or to a collection of things (corpus), a substratum, or the embodiment of qualities in a person. It can also signify all of these meanings at once. The term "truth body" *(dharma-kāya)* also has multiple connotations. It can be a body in the sense of a collection of components, mainly the good qualities a buddha acquires during eons of training. In some pre-Mahāyāna texts, it refers to the corpus of the Buddha's teachings, which are the legacy he leaves behind for his followers. It effectively provides a substitute for his physical form and presence and is the guide for those who follow the Buddhist path after his passing.

It is a focal point for practice and worship, and just as disciples were able to gain merit by venerating his physical form during his life, it remains an object of reverence for later devotees.

The truth body is also a body in the sense of a substratum or basis: it is the foundation of all the excellent qualities of buddhahood and of all attainments. In addition, it denotes a buddha's knowledge of the nature of phenomena (dharma) and refers to his awakened awareness and his ability to skillfully instruct sentient beings. Thus, in the *Discourse Explaining the Thought,* the Buddha informs Mañjuśrī: "The great light of exalted wisdom and innumerable emanations appear to sentient beings from the truth body because it has been established through training and cultivating method and wisdom which observe the immeasurable realm of qualities."[99]

In the Pāli and Sanskrit *Collections* (*Nikāya* and *Āgama*), the term truth body (Pāli: *dhamma-kāya;* Skt.: *dharma-kāya*) refers to the Buddha's teachings in general, and it is stated that whoever sees the truth body sees the Buddha. Thus Buddhaghosa asserts: "Why is the Thus Gone One said to have a truth body? Because the Thus Gone One, having thought or devised in his mind the Buddha-word, which is the three baskets *(piṭaka),* aspired to words. Therefore, that body is the doctrine, because it is made of the doctrine."[100]

The Everything Exists School interpreted the term as referring to the eighteen exclusive qualities of buddhas: the ten powers, four fearlessnesses, three foundations of mindfulness, and great compassion. These are the result of merit accumulated over vast spans of time. The truth body is not mentioned in the earliest Chinese translations of the *8,000 Line Perfection of Wisdom Discourse* (*Daoxingbanruojing, Damingdujing,* and *Mohebanruochaojing*), but it appears in Kumārajīva's version (ca. fifth century). Lewis Lancaster believes that in the earliest versions there was no notion of two or three bodies, only one Buddha body, much like that of the Pāli texts.[101]

In the developed Perfection of Wisdom sūtras, there is a shift in emphasis for this term, and it comes to refer to the essence of a buddha's awakening. Where the higher doctrine *(abhidharma)* texts conceive it as the collection of exalted qualities of buddhahood, it becomes identified with the perfection of wisdom and is equated with emptiness and suchness. The connotation of this body as a collection of qualities is retained, however, but only as a secondary derivation, since these qualities result from a buddha's penetration of the perfection of wisdom and engagement in skillful activities based on this realization.

Practice and realization come together in the fulfillment of the truth body. According to the *Flower Garland Discourse,* "the truth body of the buddhas is inconceivable and has no form, no shape, and not even the shadow of images, but it can manifest itself in various forms for the many different kinds of sentient beings, allowing them to behold it in accordance with their mentalities and wishes."[102] It appears in various aspects, even as hearers or solitary realizers, and seems to have limited lifespans in most incarnations, but it never really increases or decreases. It is reflected in the minds of all sentient beings, but makes no distinctions and has no thoughts. It is conceived as an impersonal principle of reality itself, which never changes or undergoes any alteration, takes no action, and manifests in multiple forms for the benefit of sentient beings in accordance with their needs and predilections. According to the *Discourse of the Buddha Level,* "because the purified dharma realm is utterly limitless . . . activities individually establishing help and happiness for all sentient beings are utterly limitless. Yet the purified dharma realm does not come or go, does not move or shift."[103] The Buddha's wisdom is available to all sentient beings because it pervades the entire universe and is identical to the final nature of all phenomena. It is conjoined with suchness, which is the ultimate nature of all things.

Making Bodies

The notion that advanced beings are able to produce bodies magically by simply willing them into existence is mentioned three times in the Pāli *Collections* and is said to be a result of acquisition of supernatural power (Pāli: *iddhi;* Skt.: *ṛddhi*). The "Discourse on the Fruits of Asceticism" and the "Greater Discourse to Sakuladāyin" state that a meditator who concentrates with a pure mind can create a subtle body made of mind from his physical body.[104] This form has the same limbs and faculties as the original body. The process is likened to drawing a reed from a sheath, a sword emerging from a scabbard, or a snake shedding its skin. The *Path of Purification* states that a meditator wishing to produce such a body should enter the fourth meditative absorption, then revert to his or her original body and view that body as hollow.[105] The "Discourse about Poṭṭhapāda" lists the subtle body as one of three possible modes of existence: material, mind-made, and formless.[106] The mind-made body is a form in which all the greater and lesser limbs are complete and all organs are perfect. Buddhaghosa comments that this mode of existence corresponds to the Form Realm and the sixteen realms of the Brahmā gods, in which beings are reborn as a result of practice of meditative absorptions.

In Mahāyāna texts the expansion of this ability parallels the augmented powers of buddhas in other respects. Pāli texts describe the production of mind-made bodies as a process requiring intense concentration and occurring in several stages, but in Mahāyāna literature buddhas are said to produce emanation bodies spontaneously, without any conscious effort. Buddhas manifest whatever forms are needed in order to bring sentient beings to spiritual maturity. The *Ornament for Great Vehicle Discourses* compares this activity to certain celestial bells that ring spontaneously, without anyone needing to perform any actions to elicit a sound. In the same way, buddhas, "without any premeditated thought [in which they say], 'I will teach the doctrine,' and without any effort or striving on their part," produce innumerable forms in realms throughout the cosmos with "utter spontaneity."[107] This is a reflection of the compassionate nature of buddhas and requires no conscious thought on their part. It is compared to the way water quenches thirst or fire burns things because these properties are in their nature. The commentary states: "although [Buddha] does not move, does not budge, does not waver from the undefiled realm, he carries out all the activities whose characteristic is movement."[108]

In the reconception of the Buddha and his retinue in Mahāyāna texts, he becomes more an archetype and less an individual with a distinctive personality. In the Pāli canon, he is the lone buddha of his time and world, and many of his deeds are unique to him. His distinctive buddha powers were also attained by past buddhas but are not shared by any other living beings of his time. In Mahāyāna literature, he is one buddha among an innumerable host, all of whom possess the same abilities and attain the same level of realization, and who often perform as a group. Many of them are assigned names that reflect a particular ideal quality or their role in a story. The same is true of the great bodhisattvas, whose names generally reflect ideal qualities and do not sound like personal names. Those who appear once in a particular text often have appellations that reflect the part they play in a narrative, which is why they have been translated in this chapter. Many are far too long to be forms of regular address, and in many texts scores of bodhisattvas are given nominal designations that are variations on a theme or that repeat a particular quality.

The Buddha of the Pāli canon reads like a human being (though an unusual one with extraordinary abilities and a uniquely perfect body), with a distinctive (though fanciful in places) biography and individual personality. In

Mahāyāna sūtras, he retains many of the personal characteristics from earlier narratives—but he, other buddhas, and advanced bodhisattvas are also portrayed as instances of types and as symbols of valorized qualities, and they do not sound like real persons. The Buddha in Mahāyāna texts reads like the great gods of Indian imagination; details of his conventional biography are repeated but are dismissed as mere show, and the "real Buddha" is said to be a transcendent being who resides in a heavenly realm and whose wisdom, powers, and body are greater even than gods and are equaled only by those of other buddhas.

Men on Top

Despite significant shifts in doctrine and practice in Mahāyāna literature, societal discourses regarding masculinity appear to have remained fairly constant. Authors adapted them to the new dispensation, recasting the Buddha in a more exalted form but still retaining his manly qualities. His body was reconceived along the lines of Indian gods, but it still retained a human appearance and had the standard two arms and two legs, unlike some deities with multiple appendages. It was also clearly a man's body, and the major and minor physical characteristics remained the gold standard of physical perfection for Indian Buddhist writers. His spiritual accomplishments were linked with his paradigmatic masculinity.

Attainment of buddhahood—as well as the highest levels of the bodhisattva path—remained largely the preserve of men, but a number of advanced female practitioners appear in the Mahāyāna literature. There are also some new tropes applying the logic of emptiness to gender and effectively deconstructing maleness and femaleness as absolutes or as truly real, but the people in the top positions still remain men, and there is no hint of a crisis of masculinity or any serious doubts regarding the appropriateness of excluding women from buddhahood.

There is a certain logic to these notions, even though the underlying premises are false. In the Indian context, beings are thought to transmigrate from life to life, and their endowments in a given existence are the result of past actions. Men were the dominant gender in the society and held all the most powerful and prestigious social roles. Religious texts and popular literature all cast men in superior positions except when an exceptional woman bested a man in extraordinary circumstances, but most of these texts and stories served to prove the supposed rule. Since men were generally dominant, their status must have been a reward for past karma, and there was an underlying assumption that this was always true.

This is an example of what Bourdieu terms "habitus," the unexamined structures of thought that result from repeated familiarization and thus appear as natural and unremarkable, but are thoroughly socially conditioned. Indian Buddhist writers assumed the gender hierarchy of their society as well as Indian class divisions. When Buddhist texts make predictions about events in future societies or even in other worlds, they commonly place protagonists in one of the two top classes: brahmans and *kṣatriya*s. Since these are basic divisions in Indian society, it is not surprising that writers projected them onto other places and times. Their own society, the only one they knew, divided people into four classes, and so when they created imaginary future societies or speculated on the inhabitants of other worlds, they assumed that these other societies would also share the hierarchies common to Indian society.[109]

Indian literature contains a plethora of texts that present the traditional class system as an aspect of nature and as a part of the fabric of social reality for human societies. The *Five Threads (Pañcatantra),* for example, makes parallels between real and imagined hierarchies in the animal world and the classes of Indian society as part of an implicit argument that such divisions are an aspect of nature, not reflections of human invention.[110] Scores of texts in the brahmanical archive, such as the *Song of God (Bhagavad-gitā)* and *Laws of Manu (Manu-smṛti),* repeatedly warn of the chaos that would result from the mixing of castes, and this pertains both to the future fates of individuals and to society as a whole, which will collapse if hierarchy is not maintained. It is not surprising that Indian Buddhist writers assumed that men are always in a superior position to women, that brahmans and *kṣatriya*s are born at the top of the social structure as a recompense for positive deeds, or that this is a feature of all societies.

In Mahāyāna literature, the female body remains a sign of past negative actions, and women who perform extraordinary acts of merit are rewarded by a sex change, either immediately or in future lives. Men who transgress Buddhist norms might be changed into women, which represents a downgrading of their status. The conceptual trajectory of statements regarding the ultimately imaginary nature of gender are significant, however, and appear to represent a shift in attitudes among some Indian Buddhists regarding stereotypical notions of maleness and femaleness.

7

Adepts and Sorcerers

There is nothing either good or bad, but thinking makes it so.

—William Shakespeare, *Hamlet*

The mind precedes all things good and bad.

—The Buddha, *Caṇḍamahāroṣaṇa-tantra*

Buddhist Tantras

Beginning sometime around the middle of the seventh century, a new wave of texts began to appear in India, and like the Mahāyāna sūtras, they were presented as sermons delivered by the Buddha. Most of these had the term "tantra" in their titles, and some were referred to as "sūtras." They assumed the general outlines of the Mahāyāna path, and the bodhisattva remained the ideal practitioner. The goal was buddhahood, but a new set of practices was presented, and the authors of these works claimed that the tantric path to awakening is more rapid and their new techniques more powerful and effective than those found in earlier Mahāyāna texts. Tantric Buddhism produced a huge literature of primary scriptures along with commentaries that are often essential for interpreting the primary literature. Although tantric Buddhism is far too vast and complex to explore in any depth in this study, it is worth noting some aspects that relate to central themes discussed in previous chapters.

The tantras describe a plethora of meditations involving visualization and symbolism, and ritual is a core part of tantric techniques. The Buddha remains a central character, but he often describes other tantric buddhas, along with their cults and attributes, and teaches his audience how to relate to these other buddhas as objects of meditation. He also steps out of his former monastic role and urges his shocked listeners to engage in yogas involving sexual intercourse as part of their training. In the opening verses of the *Hevajra Tantra,* for example, the Buddha is said to be "residing in the vagina *(bhaga)* of the Vajrayoginī who is the essence of the body, speech, and mind of all thus gone ones,"[1] indicating that the two are in sexual embrace. His audience is scandalized to see the Buddha—who promulgated a monastic code enjoining strict celibacy and who is depicted in various texts warning his followers to avoid any involvement with sensuality—in flagrante delicto. They collectively faint and are revived by the Buddha's power.[2] He then informs them that the teachings forbidding sexual intercourse were given only to people of inferior capacities but that it is possible to use sex skillfully as part of the path.

This is an extension of the logic of emptiness: if everything is equally empty of inherent existence, there is no valid reason for rejecting some empty aspects of cyclic existence as abhorrent, forbidden, or antithetical to the path. Rather, if appropriated skillfully, anything can become an aid to the process of awakening, and tantric texts describe techniques for channeling the energy of desire for the purpose of sublimating it. Energy is energy, and it takes more effort to subdue lust than to redirect its force toward religious goals. Descriptions of tantric sexual yogas promise that adepts can use sexual intercourse as a means to access subtle levels of consciousness that normally manifest only in exceptional circumstances or as the result of a long course of training. Tantric texts assert that these techniques can clear away the coarser aspects of mind and allow the most subtle and fundamental level, the mind of clear light *(prabhāsvara-citta),* to manifest. This is the plane on which buddhas operate, and so those who use tantric techniques effectively make rapid progress.

The conception of ideal manhood shifts in significant ways in Indian Buddhist tantras. Some of the tropes discussed earlier in this study persist, including the notion of the major and minor physical characteristics as features of Śākyamuni's body. In the *Hevajra Tantra,* he proclaims: "I am the master with the thirty-two physical characteristics, the lord with the eighty secondary physical characteristics." He then adds, "I dwell in the vaginas of women in Sukhāvatī, and my name is semen *(śukra).*"[3]

Some of the buddhas he describes in this and other texts have very different physiques. A number of tantric buddhas are said to have multiple arms, legs, and heads, and some appear in fearsome aspects. Hevajra has eight faces, four legs, and sixteen arms, and he tramples four *māras* with his feet. He is a wrathful deity who wears a garland of severed heads, and his body is smeared with ashes from cremation grounds. His inner nature, however, is tranquil and blissful. His retinue includes his consort Nairātmyā and eight female buddhas.

Vajrabhairava (Terrifying Vajra) is described as possessing an outer form that combines numerous elements of things considered terrifying in medieval India. He has nine faces on multiple heads, and his main head is a ferocious buffalo with large fangs dripping blood. He has frightening wrinkles on his forehead, and his countenance resembles the raging fires that occur when the universe is destroyed. He emits a roar that causes all beings to freeze with terror and consumes human flesh while also devouring the gods Indra, Brahmā,

Vajrabhairava, image of traditional Tibetan thankas, painted by Andy Weber; reprinted by permission.

and Viṣṇu. He wears a garland of freshly severed skulls and utters wrathful mantras. He has sixteen legs and thirty-four arms. He has a distended belly and an erect penis, and he holds a freshly severed elephant skin as well as a collection of weapons and such ghastly adornments as a man impaled on a stake, intestines, an arm, a leg, and a cloth from a cemetery. His *maṇḍala* (a diagram encoding tantric doctrines and practices that is created as a basis for visualization and rituals) contains various demons and ghouls of Indian imagination as well as people impaled on spears, others being burned alive, and parts of bodies hanging from trees, and at the periphery of the *maṇḍala* are prowling dogs, jackals, and vultures. They carry bloody viscera in their mouths and utter terrible mantras.[4]

Many male tantric buddhas are associated with a female consort, but in most texts the male is the primary figure, and his female companion is a sort of adjunct and counterpoint and is not described as a primary object of practice or visualization. There are some significant female tantric buddhas, however, who are focal points of cults and who sometimes have male consorts. Examples include Tārā and Vajrayoginī. A number of tantric lineages were instituted by women adepts, some of which continue today. In addition, some gender attributes are no longer exclusive, and the *Hevajra Tantra* declares that *ḍākinī*s "have adamantine semen."[5] They bestow this on advanced yogis, and by drinking it adepts acquire supernatural power and insight.

New Ideal Men: The Adepts

The ideal of the *Hevajra Tantra* and other Indian tantric texts is the adept *(siddha),* who is characterized by supreme meditative attainments and possession of magical powers. Such a person has "passed beyond fire offerings, renunciation, and austerities and is liberated from mantra and meditation."[6] The Buddha declares: "there is nothing that one may not do, and nothing that one may not eat. There is nothing that one may not think or say, nothing that is either pleasant or unpleasant."[7] In a radical departure from the concern with social norms found in Buddhist texts discussed in previous chapters, and particularly the *Monastic Discipline,* the adept regards monastic rules as the self-imposed fetters of inferior practitioners.

The adepts are a strange assortment of antisocial and often outrageous figures, including tribal people, outcastes, beggars, criminals, expelled monks, and some upper caste members. Several of them are women. They are often depicted wearing ornaments of human bone and carrying bowls made from human skulls; they may have long, matted hair, and they wear animal skins; they defeat demons, fly through the air, pass through solid objects, and amaze audiences with displays of magic. Their acquisition of supernatural powers *(siddhi)* is a sign of their accomplishment.[8]

Adepts gather in groups at cemeteries or mountain caves, clad in animal skins or burial shrouds, feast on substances forbidden in the monastic code and considered abhorrent in brahmanical society, and fornicate in orgiastic revels. The foods they ingest include the flesh of humans, animals, cows, horses, elephants, and dogs. They also engage in sexual yogas as part of their practice. Tantric texts often contain passages that contravene conventional morality. In the *Hevajra Tantra,* for example, the Buddha exhorts his audience:

> You should kill living beings.
> You should speak lying words.
> And you should take what is not given.
> You should frequent others' wives.[9]

In a subsequent commentary, the Buddha indicates that these instructions should be understood metaphorically: "killing living beings" involves cultivating "singleness of thought"; "speaking lying words" refers to the vow to save all sentient beings; "what is not given" is a woman's bliss (in sexual yoga); and "frequenting others' wives" is meditation focused on Nairātmyā, Hevajra's consort.[10] Despite these qualifications, it appears that some practitioners took such injunctions literally, and the *Commentary on the Condensed Meaning of the Hevajra Tantra* cautions that "the rites of ritual slaying and so forth that have been described [in the tantra] are intended to frighten living beings in order to subdue them and thus establish them [on the correct path]. If one were really to kill them, one would be violating a vow of the great seal and would fall into the Avīci hell."[11]

Other descriptions of scurrilous acts, however, apparently are meant to be taken literally, including sometimes exuberant exhortations to sexual indulgence. An example of this is the Buddha's injunction to his audience in the *Secret Assembly Tantra* to engage in ritual coitus 108 times as part of a program of training.[12] Some descriptions of sexual rites are too extreme to be taken literally but still appear to contain instructions to engage in sexual relations with real consorts; an example is a passage in the *Great Violent Wrath Tantra* in which the Buddha advises the assembled (and shocked) bodhisattvas:

> In a pleasant place where there are no distractions, in secret, you should take a woman who has desire. . . . You should bring the woman near you and seat her before you. Each should gaze intently on the other, with mutual desire. . . . Then make your throbbing penis *(sphurad-vajra)* enter the opening in the center of the lotus (vagina). Give one thousand thrusts, one hundred thousand, ten million, one hundred million in her three-petalled lotus. . . . Insert your *vajra* and offer your mind with pleasure![13]

The theoretical basis of such practices is the notion that nothing is really either good or bad but that conceptuality makes it so. According to the *Great Violent Wrath Tantra,* "the mind precedes all things good and bad."[14] The *Hevajra Tantra* propounds the doctrine of the "inseparability of cyclic existence and nirvana" *(saṃsāra-nirvāṇa-abheda):* "when the truth is declared, pure and with the form of knowledge, there is not the slightest difference between cyclic existence and nirvana."[15] The Buddha tells the bodhisattva Vajragarbha, the main interlocutor of the tantra:

> In reality there is neither form nor perceiver,
> Neither sound nor hearer,
> Neither smell nor one who smells,
> Neither taste nor taster,
> Neither touch nor one who touches,
> Neither mind nor thinker.[16]

The tantra further declares that from the point of view of ultimate reality, there is no meditator nor anything on which one meditates, no deities nor mantras. Rather, reality is characterized by undifferentiated unity. The soteriological purpose of these teachings is revealed in chapter 9, where Vajragarbha is told:

> That by which the world is bound,
> By that very thing it is released from bondage.
> But the world is deluded and does not understand this truth,
> And one who does not grasp this truth cannot attain accomplishments *(siddhi).*[17]

Trainees who adhere to the literal level of Buddhist teachings and cling to rules and regulations prevent themselves from experiencing the expansive consciousness of tantric adepts, who are free from all conventional conceptual fetters and use the things that bind others to repeated rebirth as means to effect their complete liberation from all mundane realities. Passion and other afflictive emotions that lead lesser practitioners to engage in counterproductive actions with negative consequences are skillfully manipulated in tantric meditations, and adepts rechannel their energies and render them not only harmless but soteriologically beneficial. Ultimately cyclic existence and nirvana are perspectives, and so there is no real difference between them: "[all] beings are buddhas, but this is hidden by adventitious negative factors; when these are removed, beings are then actually buddhas."[18]

One who understands this insight remains unpolluted by negative emotions and can indulge in any behavior. The *Sublime Exposition Tantra* describes the life of an adept as one of ecstatic freedom: emancipated from all conventional restraints, he frequents cemeteries, cremation grounds, and other liminal places that ordinary beings avoid; eats and drinks whatever he wishes; and dances naked in a state of spiritual intoxication.[19] He views all elements of the environment indifferently, and he is able to "contemplate the unthinkable."[20] He is described as "the highest of the manifold highest class. Stainless like the sky and cool like the nature of snow, he is endowed with supreme pure colors like the hue of the radiance of the moon."[21]

Magic and Power

The ideal of the tantric adept reflects changing paradigms in Indian society. Historical evidence regarding the origins of tantric Buddhism is sketchy, but it appears that the early texts were probably composed from the middle of the seventh century to the mid-eighth century. When the Chinese pilgrim Xuanzang traveled to India from 629 to 664, he meticulously chronicled the Buddhist institutions and practices he encountered but made no mention of anything recognizably tantric. By the late seventh century, however, tantric practices had become part of the mainstream and were incorporated into the curricula of some major north Indian monastic universities. Wuxing, another Chinese pilgrim who wrote an account sometime around 680, reported seeing tantric rituals and stated that residents of these institutions were studying tantras and commentaries.[22]

As Ronald Davidson has noted, the origins of tantra lie in a historical period of conflict and social disruption.[23] Rival non-Buddhist sects of ascetics claiming supernatural powers received sponsorship from Indian rulers, and sorcerers *(vidyādhara)* were commonly employed to safeguard kingdoms, protect against enemies, and ward off the spells of the magicians of other kings. In an apparent adaptation to this environment, Buddhist tantras often contain lengthy sections on magic rites and a cornucopia of spells and enchantments, which promise the types of worldly power valued by rulers of the time. The *Hevajra Tantra,* for example, details rituals and mantras that can terrify or drive away an attacking army or destroy one's foes. There are spells that cause an enemy's head to burst and others that allow one to control young women, make rain, find things that are lost, or chase away elephants and other fearsome animals, such as tigers or wild dogs.[24]

The *Perfect Awakening of Great Radiance Tantra* describes the adept as a powerful magician whose training produces various supernatural abilities:

> When the lord of mantras has eliminated all doubts concerning the
> nature of the self
> Then he will truly become a benefactor of all beings in the world.
> He will be endowed with various wondrous abilities
> And attain the state of a magician *(mig 'phrul can).*[25]
>
> In brief, when action and birth are projected simultaneously
> The mantra adept [fulfills] the attainment that arises from mind.
> When this is accomplished, he can travel in the sky
> Just like one who has no fear of illusions.
> He will mystify with a mantra-net
> Just like a great sorcerer.[26]

Many of the tropes contained in the tantras relate to the concerns of rulers. The *Elimination of All Negative Destinies Tantra,* for example, contains lengthy descriptions of pragmatic benefits of its rituals and mantras. It promises that kings who enter its *maṇḍala* and receive its consecration will always be given protection and aid by the gods and buddhas. Their kingdoms will be blessed with good rains and abundant crops, and they will enjoy long and happy lives. Untimely death, a common worry for rulers of the time, will be prevented, and the kings' subjects will be free from diseases and plagues, famines, and foreign invasions. Their kingdoms will not suffer from destructive storms or excessive rain, and demons will be unable to harm them. The kings are assured that all their fears will be removed, that their borders will be secured, and that they will always be protected during their journeys.[27] The text further promises that anyone who has faith in the tantra and venerates it will make gods his or her slaves. During recitation of this tantra, the gods in the audience collectively declare:

> We will attend him like slaves ready to serve and to obey all his commands! We will grant every benefit, happiness, and complete accomplishment. O Blessed One, in short, we will wipe the dust of his feet with our heads. O Blessed One, we will venerate him. O Blessed One, we worship him and follow behind him.[28]

The adept uses the rituals and mantras contained in the tantras to acquire power. These texts assert that humans who follow the tantras' instructions will become mighty sorcerers who can subdue any human or demonic foes, and even gods become their servants and devotees. Some texts also indicate that adherents will gain perfect (male) bodies. The *Arising of Supreme Pleasure Tantra,* for example, states that the "first great result" of performance of good karma is birth as a man and asserts that tantric practices result in acquisition of a robust masculine physique.[29]

In other tantric texts, however, a significant shift occurs: the ideal adept need not have a perfect body because his magical power is so great that mere beauty, physical strength, and martial prowess are insignificant in comparison to the supernatural abilities acquired by tantric rituals and skillful use of mantras. The *Hevajra Tantra* asserts that "great knowledge abides in the body, free from all imaginary constructions, but although it pervades all things and exists in the body, it does not arise in the body."[30] In some tantras the image of the buddha body endowed with the major and minor physical characteristics is retained, but others characterize it as an inferior level of attainment. The *Secret Assembly Tantra* relegates the physical perfections associated with buddhas in Mahāyāna sūtras to "the stage of the lower accomplishments *(hīna-siddhi).*" Beings at this level acquire resplendent golden buddha bodies and become lords of sorcerers, but those who perfect the practices of the *Secret Assembly Tantra* utterly transcend these inferior buddhas.[31] The text further promises that practitioners who master its potent magic can destroy buddhas, even Vajradhara, the great holder of tantric lore. It contains spells that will cause his head to shatter and that can annihilate any adversary, even a buddha. It further asserts that the adept can terrify buddhas and bring them under his control. The *Wheel Binding Tantra* promises aspiring adepts that "drinking the water of bliss, the adept makes contact through practice of the non-dual yoga of non-duality; through this training all sins are eliminated. Practicing by way of contact and even sexual intercourse, one becomes liberated from all sins and acquires a purified body that is free from illness. Purified of all sins, he attains the level of a thus gone one."[32]

Indian Buddhist tantras contain numerous injunctions to adepts to acquire young and beautiful women—generally ranging in age from twelve to twenty years—and to have sex with them in order to develop supernatural powers.[33] There is no indication, however, that this attraction is based on the physical beauty of the adept, his charming personality, or his athletic or martial skills; rather, he draws women to him with magical power and gains control over them through spells and incantations. The ideal adept is a mighty sorcerer who has no need of a strong body or handsome visage to get whatever he wants. He can compel humans and gods alike to do his bidding and is completely unfettered by conventional morality. "Free from learning and ceremony and any sense of shame," the *Hevajra Tantra* declares, "the yogin wanders wherever he wills, filled with great compassion."[34] He is utterly fearless, secure in the confidence engendered by his surpassing power: "Whatever demon should appear before him, even if it is of the rank of Indra, he will have no fear, for he wanders like a lion."[35]

The Tantric Body

Tantric texts like the *Hevajra Tantra* conceive of humans in terms of a mystical physiology.[36] Within the bodies of humans there are thirty-two principal energy channels *(nāḍī),* through which subtle energies called winds *(prāṇa)* and drops *(bindu)* circulate.[37] The three main channels are (1) *lalanā,* located on the left side of the spinal column and associated with wisdom; (2) *rasanā,* situated on the right side and associated with method; and (3) *avadhūtī,* which is roughly contiguous with the spine and integrates the two main aspects of practice. A primal energy called *caṇḍālī* resides at the base of the central channel, and the tantra contains instructions for causing it to rise through a series of stages *(cakra)* located at the navel, heart, throat, and head, where the left and right channels wrap around the central channel and constrict it. This process results in increasing bliss and mastery of supernatural powers.

> Caṇḍālī ignites in the navel.
> She burns the five thus gone ones.
> She also burns Locanā and the other [female buddhas].[38]

The tantra explains that this means that when Caṇḍālī (who is both a buddha and the personification of the primal energy that one causes to rise through the *cakras*) blazes, she immolates the buddhas that represent conventional Buddhist teachings and practices, which enables the adept to move on to the more advanced instructions of the *Hevajra Tantra.* The text also turns the tables on those who cling to old orthodoxies, claiming that the orthodox are the real heretics, while only those who embrace tantric teachings are able to attain the supreme state of buddhahood.[39] A number of tantric texts go so far as to assert that the sexual yogas are ultimately essential for attainment of buddhahood: all past buddhas have engaged in them at the end of their training careers, and all future ones will also do so.

The tantras often recast elements of traditional Indian Buddhism. An example is the *Compendium of the Truth of All Buddhas,* which considers the problem that the standard biographies of Śākyamuni Buddha make no mention of him engaging in tantric ritual activities or the sexual yogas that are supposedly required for attainment of full awakening. In this text, the story is rewritten at a crucial point: Siddhārtha Gautama is sitting under the Tree of Awakening in meditation in the final stages of preparation for buddhahood, but he is interrupted by the buddhas of the ten directions, who inform him that he can complete the path only through the special practices of tantra. He recognizes that they speak the truth and that his current training regimen cannot bring him to the final attainment. He subsequently leaves behind his physical body and sends a mentally created form to a transcendent tantric realm where he is given the highest consecrations. He then performs the requisite sexual practices with a tantric consort named Tilottamā. After this he returns to earth, reenters his body, and resumes his progress toward final awakening.[40]

Tantric texts often reinterpret well-known terms and practices and give them new tantric twists. An example is the *Secret Assembly Tantra*'s description of recollection of the buddha *(buddhānusmṛti)* and recollection of the doctrine *(dharmānusmṛti),* both of which are described in the Pāli canon and in Mahāyāna texts as nonsexual devotional meditative techniques. In the *Secret Assembly Tantra,* however, the Buddha says,

> What is the meditation of recollection of the Buddha? Putting the penis *(liṅga)* in the vagina *(bhaga),* the wise man should visualize the Buddha's form and send out clouds of buddhas from his pores. What is the meditation

> of recollection of the dharma? Putting the penis in the vagina, the wise man should visualize Vajradhara and send out clouds of dharmas from his pores.[41]

Fearful and Terrible

Tantric texts that contain injunctions to engage in forbidden practices recognize that they are at variance with how traditional Buddhists understood the moral code of their religion. The *Secret Assembly Tantra* refers to such techniques as "fearful and terrible actions" but promises that adepts who are able to perform them without afflicted conceptions will quickly transcend ordinariness and attain liberation.[42] It also states that those who are deeply immersed in negative emotions have an advantage over others who abjure immoral acts and adhere to ethical codes: "Those who belong to the families of desire, anger, and obscuration are well versed in nondiscrimination, and so they attain the best accomplishments in the supreme and highest manner."[43]

Equally scandalous from the point of view of Indian social hierarchies, the *Hevajra Tantra* and other texts assert that the adept is unconcerned with caste distinctions and associates freely with people at all levels of society. No one person is closer to him than any other, he pays no homage to gods or human potentates, and he does not consider himself polluted when prostitutes or members of the lowest social classes touch him.[44] These beings also have the potential to attain buddhahood, and some of the biographies of adepts assign them to outcaste or tribal groups. The *Hevajra Tantra* asserts: "even *caṇḍāla*s and other low-caste despised people, as well as those whose minds are bent on killing, will attain accomplishment without doubt if they devote themselves to Hevajra."[45] Prostitutes and women of outcaste groups are often extolled as particularly suitable consorts for sexual yogas.

By developing a mind of utter equanimity and performing tantric techniques, one attains the state of the adept, who wanders at will, unfettered by conventions, acting as he pleases, fearless and secure in his magical abilities:

> He should give away his wealth, his wife and even his own life as offerings; abandoning those ties, he should always be a trainee of the practice. He has great strength attained by reciting magical spells *(vidyā),* and he is intent on speaking the truth. . . . [H]e should not make a distinction between purity, impurity, or purification, nor between what may or may not be drunk. Being without anger and free from conceit, he should not care about praise or

> condemnation. Adhering to the idea that everything is equal, he is always without attachment and without desire. He neither practices the fire offering *(homa)* nor worships. He neither recites [mantras] nor uses prayer beads. . . . Having a tiger skin as a garment and adorned with five seals, the yogi should imagine himself to be Heruka, who combines wisdom and method.[46]

The *Arising of Supreme Pleasure Tantra* asserts that the adept has a body that is "beautiful and pleasant to behold,"[47] but in other tantras adepts appear to be physically ordinary, and their unexceptional bodies contrast with their supernatural abilities. They engage in a range of techniques, including sexual yogas, that allow them to manipulate the subtle energies in their bodies and thus attain transcendent power and profound wisdom. David Gray notes that the purpose of this regimen is "to effect the creative re-imagination of one's body, which is to be seen no longer as filthy and incomplete, but as the perfect, divine abode of the deities."[48] A typical passage regarding such techniques in the *Secret Assembly Tantra* advises the aspiring adept:

> Having clearly understood this lucid *maṇḍala* of mind, he should offer worship intently with body, speech, and mind. Taking a sixteen-year-old girl of radiant beauty, he should decorate the *maṇḍala* with perfumes and flowers, and in the center have sex with her; when the wise one has consecrated her as Māmakī adorned with virtues, he should emit the peaceful Buddha-word adorned with the realm of space.[49]

The *Hevajra Tantra* describes a range of meditative techniques involving manipulation of subtle energies; one of the four results these practices produce is the "fruit of manly activity" *(puruṣakāra-phala).*[50] All of the tantras I have studied assume a male perspective, were written by men for men, and assumed that males would be performing their rituals. The descriptions of sexual yogas are always, as far as I am aware, addressed to males, and female consorts are not described as deriving any spiritual benefits from their participation. The Indian Buddhist tantras provide no guidelines for women who might want to engage in these yogas. Women are important and perform an essential function as consorts in tantric sexual yogas, and there are numerous injunctions prohibiting tantrikas from disparaging women, but the very presence of such admonitions demonstrates that a male audience was intended. Moreover, as Bernard Faure has argued, these injunctions assume that males are socially dominant and thus are in a position to denigrate women.[51]

It should be noted, however, that there are a number of gender-bending passages in the tantras. In the *Secret Assembly Tantra,* for example, the Buddha enters a meditative absorption and assumes the form of a woman. He then shifts back to a male physique and brings forth Moharatī, "the consort of the thus gone ones," from his body, following which he again assumes a female form.[52] In an earlier part of the same text, the buddha Mahāvairocana (the tantric aspect of Śākyamuni) enters a meditative state and causes all the other buddhas in the assembly to enter his body, speech, and mind, following which they appear as women and issue from his body. Some appear as female buddhas and later revert to their male aspects.[53] Despite these tropes, however, male buddhas remain clearly male, and their real bodies are masculine. Tropes of sex change may indicate that some tantras reject gender stereotyping, but they do not by themselves constitute evidence that their authors conceived of women as equal to men. In the *Wheel Binding Tantra,* for example, there is a spell that promises a man the ability to change his body into a female form, but this is followed by another that will transform him into a dog.[54] These physical shifts are a symbol of power gained through mastery of magic and not an attempt to undermine sexism in ancient India.

In a study of Indian and Tibetan tantra that has generated considerable controversy, Miranda Shaw suggests that much of the emphasis of this literature is on women's spirituality, and she theorizes that women adepts had considerable input in the development of tantric practices.[55] She correctly notes that some tantric lineages were instituted by women and that some adepts were female, but she ignores the fact that the overwhelming emphasis is on men and that descriptions of sexual yogas are given from the male point of view.

The tantras abound with injunctions to men to find beautiful young women to be their consorts and with often graphic descriptions of sexual practices in which they insert their *vajras* into their partners' lotuses, but I have not seen any corresponding instructions for women adepts in Indian Buddhist tantric texts. Both partners are promised sexual ecstasy, but only the one performing the insertion appears to gain supernatural abilities, advanced meditative states, or liberation. The female consort does not attain any soteriological benefits in any text I have studied, and her role is as facilitator in her partner's religious progress. I have not encountered any evidence of a corresponding women's spirituality in any Indian Buddhist tantric text.

Ronald Davidson reaches a similar conclusion in his study of the origins of Buddhist tantra in medieval India and asserts that far from being, as Shaw contends, a period of enhanced religious opportunities for women, the era saw a significant decline in their sanctioned spiritual involvement; he describes "a dramatic deterioration of support for and involvement of women in Buddhist activities at any and every level, whether in the monastery, in the lay community, or in the newly evolving siddha systems."[56] Shaw argues that because women were involved in tantric practices they must have had considerable input into the development of tantric systems, but that the fact that they are seldom mentioned is an example of "androcentric bias." It is possible that women were more prominent in tantric circles than is generally thought, but their absence from the tantric literature cannot alone be taken as evidence.

Gender and Sex

The ability to change gender is a common attribute of tantric buddhas and adepts. In a passage of the *Hevajra Tantra,* Nairātmyā assumes Hevajra's male form: "her breasts disappear, and his *vajra* is manifest with a bell (testicles) on each side, where the lotus had been." She is described as completely at ease in male aspect, while he shifts into female anatomy and copulates with his/her consort. The adept should transcend attachment to gender and be comfortable in any form. Completely unbound by any fixed identity, he can appear as an animal, god, or inanimate objects and regards all such appearances as temporary: "from this the perfection of the great seal would result for the yogi of such manifest power."[57] Behind these tropes is the notion that buddhas eliminate the coarser levels of consciousness, which contain the negative afflictive tendencies that cause lesser beings to engage in harmful acts that result in negative karma, continued rebirth, and suffering. Buddhas fully manifest the mind of clear light and are free from defiling mental states. This subtle consciousness transcends all distinctions, including those of gender, race, and class: "The nature of mind, groundless and baseless, is neither male nor female, nor neuter. It has no signs, nor is it classified in families. It is colorless and shapeless. It does not abide, nor is it anything at all. This exalted wisdom of the sphere of reality is the cause of all seals of skillful means."[58]

Despite the presence of discourses that undermine gender stereotypes and stories of sex changes, some social aspects of sexual behavior remain unchallenged. In tantric texts, men are generally the initiators of sexual activities, and women respond to them. Moreover, certain types of actions are specific to men and women: women may be sexually provocative and seductive, but men never engage in this sort of behavior. When men become stimulated by women, it is in response to their displays of stereotypical feminine behavior: flaunting their secondary sexual characteristics, engaging in coy or seductive actions, or propositioning men for sex.

Even fearsome *ḍākinīs* employ coquettish wiles in order to attract adepts. The *Sublime Exposition Tantra* has a number of passages that sound like ritualized courtship in which *ḍākinīs* or other women the adept wishes to utilize as tantric consorts make stylized gestures, to which he responds in certain prescribed ways. It asserts that "if he engages in conversation with one of these women, she will certainly be attracted to him."[59] It further advises him to insert his big toe into soil, and she will respond by drawing a diagram. If he scratches his head, she will glance at him from the corner of her eyes. He next places his finger on her cheek, chin, or nose, and again she gives him a sidelong look. As the courtship continues, "she looks at him in a passionate way and knits both of her brows. She mutters forcefully, cries, or becomes angry for no reason."[60] In descriptions of how an adept should attract women to him, it is assumed that the man will initiate the process, and each stage is guided by his actions. The women respond to the adept, and ultimately his magical power breaks down any resistance and secures their acquiescence.[61]

Tantric men are sorcerers who use mantras and rituals or displays of manly feats to attract women. One such instance occurs in a graphic scene in the *Secret Essence Tantra,* in which Mahāvairocana manifests a wrathful aspect and defeats a host of demons and deities: "Then the transcendent lord . . . assumed a form with nine heads, eighteen arms, and eight legs, and then with a fearsome voice he grew exceedingly wrathful in accordance with the skillful means that instructs through aggression." He uttered a terrible mantra that eviscerated a host of demons and gods including Maheśvara, and tore out their entrails, severed their limbs, ate their flesh, and wore their bones as ornaments. Seeing their men eviscerated, torn limb from limb and cannibalized, and their body parts displayed as trophies by the rampant buddha, the female deities became sexually aroused: "They expanded and contracted their lotus-maṇḍalas (vaginas) and then, just as iron joins with a magnet, the great demoness Manurākṣasī and others . . . embraced the body of the transcendent lord." He then uttered the mantric syllable *hūṃ,* which caused the lotus-maṇḍalas of the female deities to contract strongly, following which they engaged in sexual intercourse.[62]

The purpose of such tropes appears to be to establish the notion that the true adept is unfettered by conventional beliefs and practices, utterly free in his thoughts and actions, and able to employ any means in pursuit of his own religious goals and those of others. This freedom gives him unparalleled power and mastery over the world and its inhabitants: "in the supreme accomplishment of all sacraments *(samaya),* meditating on the *vajra* body, you will become a sorcerer *(vidyādhara)* among the great sacraments.[63] In invisibility and so forth you alone will illumine the thousand worlds, you will steal from all the buddhas and enjoy the women of the gods."[64]

Rejection of the assumed hierarchies and social identities of ancient India extends to societal conceptions. The *Secret Assembly Tantra* states that people whose natures are prone to passion, hatred, and delusion can attain freedom from dualistic thought by means of the tantra's meditative techniques and thus can "attain ultimate accomplishment." Even members of despised castes who perform the lowliest tasks, people who enjoy violence and murder, and great sinners can become adepts. The only exception is those who revile their teachers. Reverence for the guru is essential, but the tantras commonly state that beings who engage in the greatest evils can still become adepts and attain liberation from cyclic existence:

> Those who destroy life and delight in lying, those who covet others' possessions and are attached to sensual desires, those who eat excrement and drink urine, all these are worthy of the practice. The trainee who desires his mother, sister, and daughter attains extensive accomplishment, the dharma nature of the supreme Great Vehicle. Even fornicating with the mother of the Lord Buddha he is not defiled; rather, that wise one, free from dualistic thought, attains the buddha-nature.[65]

Such beings utterly transcend social conventions and are unconcerned with the expectations of others. They are enjoined to eat feces and drink urine in order to overcome any lingering notions of some substances as repugnant and others as pure.[66] Bodily wastes, which are viewed as polluting in traditional Indian society, are empty of inherent existence. Babies who have not been socialized often consume their feces with no apparent distaste, but as they grow up learn to view human waste as foul. The adept reverses the process of acculturation and regards all aspects of cyclic existence with complete equanimity, no longer attached to any preconceived judgments. The *Secret Assembly Tantra* advises aspiring adepts to consume meat and to visualize it as the flesh of humans, cows, elephants, horses, and dogs and adds that the buddhas and bodhisattvas approve of such practices. One who can engage in the tantra's socially condemned techniques free from any sense of shame or self-consciousness will become "a lord of the Desire Realm of high rank, and he will become beautiful, powerful, exalted, radiant, delightful to behold. Without rituals of arousing, by his glance alone he conquers the whole world. This is the ultimate awakening, the secret of all buddhas, and the true secret of mantra, transcending body, speech, and mind."[67]

Imagined Bodies

Tantric texts commonly use visualizations as a core aspect of the path. In these yogas, one imagines oneself to be a buddha, with the body, speech, and mind of a fully awakened being and as enjoying the total liberation from all aspects of cyclic existence that characterizes the state of one who has attained the highest level of the path. The first part of such visualizations is the "generation stage" *(utpatti-krama),* in which the meditator imagines a fully formed buddha in front of him, embodying all the qualities of buddhahood, including infinite wisdom and compassion, and practicing skillful means for the benefit of all sentient beings. The meditator generates a "subtle body" *(mayā-deha)* comprised of subtle energies. This is the basis for his future arising as a buddha, who will be endowed with a form composed of such energies, which will be nonmaterial and enduring.

The next phase of this yoga, the "completion stage" *(niṣpanna-krama),* involves bringing the subtle energies (winds) that course throughout the body into the central channel and causing them to move upward through the *cakra*s. The winds are the "mounts" *(aśva)* of minds and are mentally manipulated by the meditator. As the winds rise through the central channel, the meditator experiences feelings of immutable bliss, invites the visualized buddha to enter him, and imagines that he is transformed in the buddha's image. Ideally this process should involve the wisdom consciousness realizing emptiness, producing a mental image of the buddha (i.e., the meditator first has a direct realization of emptiness and then generates the image of a buddha while still in this frame of mind); recognizing the emptiness of both the buddha and the meditator's own body, speech, and mind, the meditator merges with the buddha, perceiving himself as transformed into the object of his visualization.

Some completion stage practices involve sexual yogas with a partner, who can be either real or imagined. According to tantric theory, at the moment of orgasm coarser levels of consciousness drop away and a subtle mind manifests. Sexual yogas make use of this natural occurrence by manipulating winds and employing visualizations of oneself and one's partner as male and female buddhas whose sexual embrace symbolizes the actualization of compassion and wisdom in the completion of buddhahood. The bliss of orgasm is associated with the innate great bliss that is fully known by buddhas.

Some lineages of Tibetan Buddhism contend that one may attain buddhahood merely by visualizing a consort in the act of sexual union, but others—including Tsong Khapa and the Gelukpa tradition generally—maintain that one must employ an actual partner (referred to as an "action seal"; Tibetan: *las kyi phyag rgya;* Skt.: *karma-mudrā*) in the final stages of practice.[68] The bliss of union—which is conjoined with the wisdom consciousness realizing emptiness—approximates the mental state of buddhas, who perceive all appearances as manifestations of luminosity and emptiness and who are untroubled by the vicissitudes of phenomenal reality. Sexual yogas often involve retention of semen by male practitioners. In such contexts, the semen is referred to as "mind of awakening" *(bodhicitta),* and the movement of winds through the central channel is equated with generation of the aspiration to become a buddha.

Some tantric texts maintain that seminal retention is equivalent to celibacy. The *Monastic Discipline,* as we saw previously, prohibits sexual penetration of any orifice as far as the width of a sesame seed for monks and nuns, but the *Wheel Binding Tantra,* for example (chapter 26), asserts that celibacy is maintained as long as semen is either not emitted or drawn back through a reverse hydraulic process.

According to tantric theory, sexual yogas are appropriate and effective only for advanced practitioners, who have ideally directly realized emptiness—or for those who have at least acquired significant control over energies within the subtle body. Such practice also requires initiation under a qualified tantric master and a long period of preliminary training. Trainees who have not received the requisite initiations or instructions will receive no soteriological benefit by imitating the actions of adepts and will inevitably harm themselves and others. Among contemporary Tibetan Buddhists, actual practice of these techniques appears to be quite rare, despite the assertion by some masters that they are necessary for final attainment of buddhahood. Moreover, many tantric practitioners are monks or nuns who have taken vows of monastic celibacy, and so sexual congress would be a violation of those vows that would result in negative karma.

Tantric Physiology: Literal or Figurative?

Adepts are presented in tantric texts as possessing the normal number and configuration of limbs and other body parts, but many tantric buddhas are described as having assorted permutations of human physiology (and a few buddhas, including Vajrabhairava, have features of animals). Some have multiple heads, arms, and legs; some have distended bellies, skin of various colors, and fangs or other protuberances; and they hold a range of weapons and symbolic accoutrements. Many are fearsome in appearance and engage in acts of extreme violence or have sex with multiple partners, who are aroused by their power and acts of aggression. Such behaviors are described as skillful means designed to effect transformations in the recipients of their actions and the soteriological messages they encode.

Chapter 14 of the *Sublime Exposition Tantra* contains a graphic description of the tantric buddha Heruka, whose appearance is compared to the great conflagration that destroys the universe at the end of a cosmic cycle. He treads on Bhairava and Kālarātrī,[69] and he bares his sharp and frightening teeth. He has three eyes, which inspire fear in those who see him, and his "supreme body" has blue skin, which is adorned with a garland of skulls that have been blessed by buddhas, and on top of his head is a double *vajra* with a half moon. He has six faces manifesting various attitudes, including valor, revulsion, passion, mirth, and anger, and he makes constant licking motions with his tongue. He is in sexual embrace with his consort Vārāhī, whose knees are wrapped around his waist. His faces are blue, yellow, red, green, and white, and he emits terrifying mantras. He compresses his consort's breasts and holds a horrifying garment made from human flesh and dripping blood. His hands grasp various tantric implements, including a *ḍamaru* drum, a chopper, a hook, and a skull cup.[70]

Adepts are taught to imagine their bodies being transformed into those of the tantric buddhas, but it is not clear in any text I have seen how far this is taken in practice. The impossible physiology of many of these buddhas would make movement difficult, and a number of questions regarding functionality are never addressed, as far as I am aware. For example, how would one move with eight or sixteen legs in close proximity at the lower part of the body? In statues and paintings, multilegged buddhas are often portrayed standing upright with the upper body erect, balancing on two, four, eight, or more legs, but do they have separate hip flexors for each limb? Are there individual sets of hip joints and corresponding skeletal and muscular structures? Multiple legs in close proximity at the lower part of an upright body would probably get in each other's way, and the gait of such a being would be tottering and ungainly. Running would probably be impossible, and a shuffling or shambling stride would presumably be necessary.

How should one visualize the multiple arms of the buddha that is the template of imaginary transformation? Do all of these arms have rotator cuffs? Are there individual shoulders along the sides of the back? Images of multiple-armed buddhas depict them with recognizably human arms—with fingers, wrists, forearms, biceps, and triceps—but it is not clear whether all these arms function as one or are capable of independent movement. Do they work like the multiple appendages of centipedes, or do they operate independently, like the tentacles of an octopus? What is their actual range of motion, and to what extent is the movement of a particular arm limited by the close proximity of other limbs? No tantric text I have studied provides any practical instructions to meditators regarding how they should imagine the actual functioning of their visualized buddha bodies and their components, and representations of tantric buddhas are generally posed in a static posture that does not suggest movement.

These forms are imaginary creations, products of consciousness perceived as permutations of the subtle body, which is composed of subtle energies. Like holograms, they are able to assume physical configurations that evolution has never produced, forms that encode ideals of tantric theory and practice that would be ungainly if they were composed of coarse matter. These include the system of reversals of conventional Buddhist notions and norms that pervades tantric texts and rituals. In the early chapters we saw how the physical form of the Buddha proclaimed his supreme spiritual attainments and testified to his buddhahood. His beauty and serene countenance, coupled with his superhuman strength and dignified bearing, convinced skeptics of the veracity of his claims to have attained the highest level of the religious path, and they formed a core component of his ministry.

The bodies of demonic-looking tantric buddhas proclaim their attainments in a different way: they appear as fearsome creatures, bedecked with garlands of skulls, often wearing bloody skin as a garment, holding frightening weapons, spouting flames, and trampling gods and other creatures under their feet. They should be imagined as profoundly terrifying, but this is tempered by the notion that their inner nature is serene and identical in all relevant respects with more benign-looking buddhas. This truth is recognized only by advanced practitioners, however, and lesser beings perceive merely the outward horrific forms. The Buddha of the Pāli canon and Mahāyāna sūtras had a physique that was attractive to all who viewed it. His followers were drawn to him by the way his body proclaimed his inner virtues, but the fearsome buddhas of the tantras are recognized in their true natures only by a small coterie of adepts who know the code and can see beyond appearances. This seems to be an aspect of the claim made in many tantras that they are advanced teachings, appropriate only for the most elite practitioners.

Avalokiteśvara with one thousand arms in the Potala, Lhasa. Photograph by John Powers.

Initiation and Training

Beginning with the early adept cults, tantric initiation involves gaining membership in a community. One's identity as a tantric practitioner is closely connected to the initiations one has received and the liturgies of visualization *(sādhana)* one performs. Those who take tantric vows join the Vajra Vehicle (Vajrayāna) tradition, but one's immediate community includes those who belong to a particular lineage, who have received empowerments *(abhiṣeka)* from the same guru, and who regularly perform the same liturgies of visualization. Within a particular lineage, feelings of belonging may vary considerably, however, and some people take initiations as a form of blessing but do not intend to engage in regular subsequent practice of *sādhanas*. More committed practitioners are urged to perceive members of the lineage as their "*vajra* brothers and sisters" and to rely on them as a support group.

While Vajrayāna in India may have originated with antisocial cults that lived at the margins of society and openly rejected its norms, within a short time it was incorporated into the curriculum of north Indian monastic universities like Nālandā and Vikramaśīla. From at least the eighth century, tantric initiations and rituals were part of the routine of these institutions, and scholar monks engaged in study and commentary on tantric texts. As tantra became part of the monastic mainstream, there was a growing tendency to interpret the more extreme passages in tantras metaphorically, and this has continued in Tibet, where Vajrayāna is regarded by all four Buddhist orders as the supreme path and where it is an integral part of the society.

The tantras were the last major production of Buddhist canonical texts in India, and they continued to be promulgated until around the twelfth century. Soon after that, Buddhism experienced a rapid decline in fortunes and adherents, in connection with Muslim invasions in the northern parts of the subcontinent. These invasions targeted the bastions and important figures of rival faiths, and the major Buddhist institutions were directly in the way of the invading armies. Nālandā and Vikramaśīla were sacked and destroyed, along with many smaller establishments. The marauding Muslim armies dealt Indian Buddhism a deathblow from which it never recovered, but it continued to flourish in neighboring countries and today is experiencing a resurgence in other parts of the world.

8

Conclusion: Oversights and Insights

> The form of representation cannot be divorced from the purpose and the requirements of the society in which the given language gains currency.
>
> —E. H. Gombrich

When I first began reading Indian Buddhist literature, I generally overlooked the tropes highlighted in this book as examples of odd Indian imaginings and mythologies. Indian Buddhist notions of gender and the body were so foreign to contemporary understandings that I simply had no interpretive grid within which to situate them and so paid little attention. There was no pattern for me, and these esoteric discourses of maleness and femaleness, sex and physiology, appeared as disconnected bits of culturally specific superstition and as irrelevant to the philosophical and moral insights that seemed to me at the time to be the most interesting features of Indian Buddhist literature. Most of the notions they presented were easily dismissed as simply wrong from the point of view of modern science and contemporary perspectives on gender and social roles, and so it seemed defensible to mentally consign them to the garbage heap of history, to borrow a phrase.

As my interest in cultural history has developed, however, things that I overlooked previously come back to my attention and require that I take notice of them. When I first began exploring some of the literature on Western notions of masculinity and the body, images of previously unnoticed Indian tropes leapt into my mind and began to arrange themselves into settled categories, and then sections of a book, and finally chapters. The more I read and thought, the more the book came together in my head and demanded that I write it. As I acceded to the imperative, an analytical perspective based on the work of Michel Foucault, Thomas Laqueur, and R. W. Connell provided the interpretive element of the study, which was supplemented by insights from a number of other theorists.

One of the initial difficulties I faced was in learning how to read the trope of the body of the "great man," endowed with the thirty-two major physical characteristics and the eighty minor characteristics. Having spent a lifetime observing various body types and most of a professional career in historical studies, I am reasonably certain that no human being has actually developed such a physique. Whatever the Buddha looked like, he probably did not have a fist-sized cranial bump, a sheathed penis, arms reaching down to his knees, and a three-foot-long tuft of hair in the middle of his forehead, among other physical abnormalities. Why, then, did his followers assign such a bizarre physiognomy to him, and why did the image have such staying power? Why was it adopted and expanded by the authors of the Mahāyāna sūtras and scholastic treatises? And why did it play a very minor role in conceptions of the body in other countries in which Buddhism became established? The major and minor characteristics are a particular obsession of Indian writers but are seldom highlighted by non-Indian Buddhists when discussing the Buddha. What appeared to ancient Indians as the very epitome of masculine perfection has not resonated with Buddhists in other countries, and these characteristics are rarely even mentioned by contemporary Buddhists, particularly in the West.

One probable reason for the importance of these tropes in India is that Buddhism developed in a religious environment in which physical beauty was closely linked with spiritual accomplishment. A beautiful body was seen as a reflection of inner qualities that could not be verified by the senses. Fools and charlatans can make themselves appear wise by mouthing words of wisdom, but they cannot fake the body of a great man. Indian Buddhist texts report that some other advanced masters had a few of the physical characteristics, and universal monarchs have all of them, but in the Buddha they are said to be uniquely perfected and more visible than in any other person of his time. Thus do these traits serve to set him apart from all humans and gods and provide his followers with a powerful trope to use in arguing for the superiority of their tradition in what appears to have been a hotly contested religious marketplace.

It needs to be remembered that the Buddhist texts we have examined in this study and the earliest iconic Buddha images were produced long after the Buddha died, and so his physiognomy was no longer available for inspection to verify that it indeed was marked by the signs of a great man. The literary character "Buddha," constructed by his followers and then recast in successive waves of new scriptures and theorized by scholastic monks and buddhalogians, could be whatever the creators wished, because the historical personage had long ago passed on. They did not, of course, enjoy carte blanche; they needed to conform to social expectations and thus presented a figure that resonated with ideals of male beauty and religious mastery. Indian religious and secular literature often assigns unusual physical characteristics to extraordinary individuals, and the mythologies of gods commonly ascribe to them physical markings as signs of superiority. The Buddha needed to compete not only with human sages propounding rival systems but with the cults of the plethora of Indian divinities, and so it is not surprising that the constructors of his legend imagined his body as the locus of not merely a handful of distinguishing characteristics but as displaying them in all of its parts.

Clever tailoring can disguise a range of physical defects; makeup and other such artifices can hide blemishes and add color and detail where none exist; but the stories in which the Buddha bares his perfect body for inspection by his audiences are meant to convey the naked truth of his unique spiritual attainments. Only an extraordinary being can have any of the physical characteristics of a great man, and during his lifetime the Buddha alone had all of them perfected to the highest degree. Any later claimant to his position would have to be able similarly to display these attributes on his physique, and no amount of makeup (and probably not even modern plastic surgery) can create convincing facsimiles on bodies that lack them.[1]

Similarly, the bodies of his monastic followers were advertisements for the superiority of Buddhism to its rivals. Portraying monks as young, athletic, physically beautiful, and profoundly attractive to women served to distinguish them from other groups, who are routinely characterized as comprised of mainly old, infirm men who further emaciate and degrade their bodies through unproductive ascetic practices. The image of healthy, robust, clean Buddhist monks with dignified comportment is clearly designed to conform to Indian cultural ideals. The tropes of masculinity developed in Buddhist texts are part of a larger program of representing the community as worthy of alms and as the best choice for men considering a full-time religious vocation. As we have seen in this study, such tropes are found in a wide variety of texts composed over the course of centuries, and so they clearly had staying power. In this study I have focused mainly on works that were widely circulated and influential, supplementing them with citations from more obscure parts of Indian Buddhist literature to demonstrate how widespread these discourses were. Examples could be multiplied many times over, and the notes for this study contain numerous variations on the core themes of masculinity, sex, and the body that were not discussed.

The depiction of women is an aspect of these discourses. Masculinity is defined in India, as in all societies, in contrast and opposition to femininity. Thomas Laqueur has convincingly argued that in Western societies from at least the time of the Greeks until well into the eighteenth century, medical experts were convinced that there is only one sex and that female genitalia are inverted opposites of male equipment, but no such discursive dynamic existed in India. Buddhist literature on men and women, as well as classical medical texts, clearly differentiate the two sexes. Secondary sexual characteristics are highlighted, and men and women are viewed as utterly distinct (although as we have seen it is considered possible for a person to change sex in exceptional circumstances). Indian authors—as well as sculptors and painters who incorporated the images of masculinity and femininity highlighted in this study into their depictions of male and female figures—not only emphasized the apparent differences in physiognomy but also exaggerated them, and in the case of the characteristics of the great man and other tropes created additional imagined distinctions. The ideal Indian female body, with its impossibly large breasts and hips, in artistic representations almost always posed in a sexually suggestive manner, stands in contrast to the slim and ascetic-looking images of the Buddha produced by Indian artists, which generally depict him with rounded features and limbs and devoid of sexual overtones.

Men and women have different sets of genitalia, a fact that can be empirically verified, but gender is discursively produced, using anatomy as its basis. As Laqueur notes, "the reproductive organs are but one sign among many of the body's place in a cosmic and cultural order that transcends biology."[2] Each society develops its own notions of gender-specific traits and behaviors and then acculturates its citizens to them. The process is largely unconscious, and thus its operations are subtle and often impossible to detect for those who reproduce them on a daily basis. The body is lived and experienced differently in different societies, and one of the tasks of historians is to uncover and analyze the perceptions of members of a given culture regarding how they viewed themselves and their bodies in relation to others and the world they inhabited. Gender distinctions, produced through a sort of unconscious consensus and diffused throughout a society, become self-regulating because there is no central organization that either dictates their nature and parameters or that meets in secret to ensure that these distinctions are enforced. Rather, even people who are oppressed by the discourses of a particular body regime participate in its perpetuation, as Foucault noted, and are generally unaware of its contingent and culturally specific nature.

Gender exists in historically situated systems of knowledge and power. In Joan Scott's view, gender includes both biology and society; it is "a constitutive element of social relationships based on perceived differences between the sexes . . . a primary way of signifying relationships of power."[3] Wherever there are gender distinctions, there are also operations of power, and even though there is no central committee of patriarchs who meet to outline the coming year's program of oppression, there are groups that benefit from a particular gender regime. As feminists have noted, men in general hold power over women as a result of these discourses, but some men benefit more than others. Status and class are also factors in power equations, and Buddhist texts demonstrate a pervasive concern with social class and how it is perceived while also critiquing aspects of the caste system of the day. The Buddha's *kṣatriya* birth and royal status are highlighted in Indian Buddhist texts, and he praises a number of monks for being true brahmans—that is, they are portrayed as exemplars of the idealized qualities of saintliness, religious practice, and self-restraint that are connected with an important Indian ideal of masculinity. This exists alongside the paradigm of the warrior and ruler *kṣatriya,* whose virile, athletic physique is conjoined with a disciplined intellect capable of diplomacy as well as military strategy. The Buddha embodies both ideals at the same time; the religious brahman motif is juxtaposed with the more physical *kṣatriya* paradigm. The Buddha is able to balance the two effortlessly and is portrayed both as a religious leader who wins the admiration of skeptical brahmans with his dharma discourses and perfect body and as a virile, mighty warrior whose perfect form is the envy of other men and an object of sexual attraction for women. This resonates with Mary Douglas's view that bodies reflect the ideals and beauty concepts of the societies that create them. There is no universal standard of beauty, and the growing corpus of studies of how different cultures construct and reify their physical ideals demonstrates this. According to Douglas, "the human body is always created in an image of a society and . . . there can be no natural way of considering the body that does not involve at the same time a social dimension."[4]

This much has been well established by the work of Foucault, Laqueur, and Douglas, among others, but it does not change the fact that people in all societies have the same genital equipment at birth and undergo similar changes at puberty unless some extenuating circumstance intervenes. With the exceptions of hermaphrodites or people born with defective organs, men share certain anatomical characteristics across times and cultures, and women share another set of physical attributes. Much of the human body is similar for both genders, and gender distinctions may not be easily perceived by other species, but there is more to sex than simply what society dictates. Most people follow a similar developmental trajectory from birth through puberty to full adulthood, and each gender performs some distinctive biological functions. Discourses relating to masculinity and femininity are generated on this basis and then reified into an association with nature, and these distinctions function as true for those who live and perceive within a particular regime.

There is no way to know what actual influence the discourses studied in this book had on the people of Buddhist India. People read books and relate to art works from a variety of perspectives, and these may vary from time to time and in accordance with changing religious imperatives. Did Indian Buddhist men who observed the representation of the major physical characteristics of a great man in Buddha images aspire to a body like his? Did women who read or heard the Pāli *Collections* dream of one day being born with a prominent lump on top of their heads or a penis covered by a sheath? It is unlikely that this was a common reaction, but in some of the texts examined in this book certain characters do make such cognitive connections. Whether this was a widespread occurrence among Indians who read or heard these texts is a matter of conjecture. The Pāli texts reserve the status of buddhahood for a single person in a given age, and so most devout Buddhists would probably have aimed for a better rebirth or perhaps future attainment of arhathood and would never have imagined themselves as candidates for the body of a great man.

One of the significant shifts in Mahāyāna, however, is the expansion of opportunity, at least on a theoretical level. With the development of the bodhisattva ideal, Mahāyānists were told that they should aspire to become buddhas for the benefit of other sentient beings, and one result of the fulfillment of their commitment in practice would be eventual embodiment in a form approximating that of the Buddha, endowed with the physical characteristics of a great man. The final apotheosis would be a fully actualized buddha body, distinct from all others and associated with a particular personality and individual career, but fully embodying the highest ideals of Buddhism, both physically and mentally.

During the period from the time of the Buddha until Buddhism's eventual demise on the subcontinent, the religion spread into other areas of Asia, where it continued to flourish and expand in later centuries. The images of masculinity we have examined in this study generally failed to resonate with Buddhists in other countries, and so the Buddha was modified to fit different cultural norms. In China, for example, apocryphal sūtras were composed in which the Buddha was portrayed as advocating Confucian ideals of filial piety and views about women.[5] In Southeast Asia, texts were written that claimed that the Buddha had visited Sri Lanka and other surrounding countries, thus creating a fictional geographical link between those places and the founder of the tradition. In the modern West, the Buddha is often portrayed as an early advocate of the scientific method or as a rational and empirical philosopher who taught an effective form of psychotherapy ideally designed to reduce the stresses of modern life. Philip Almond notes that when eighteenth-century British scholars recounted the life of the Buddha, he was presented as "an ideal Victorian gentleman."[6] The cranial bump and sheathed penis have no place on the body of this Buddha, and he has little in common with the sexual stallion and mighty warrior of Indian imaginings. Just as each society creates its own notions of ideal men and women, so Buddhists create buddhas in their own respective images.

Appendixes

Notes

Bibliography

Index

APPENDIX I

The Major and Minor Physical Characteristics of a Great Man

The following charts list common traits presented in a variety of sources. Details vary between texts, but most of these are commonly found in the literature discussing the body of the great man. The Pāli terms for the major physical characteristics are mainly drawn from the "Discourse on the Physical Characteristics" and supplemented by material from commentarial literature.[1] The main sources for the Sanskrit equivalents are the *Great Glossary,*[2] the *Ornament for Clear Realizations,*[3] and Lamotte's listing in his translation of the *Compendium of the Great Vehicle.*[4] The *Great Glossary* is the main source for the Sanskrit terms for the secondary physical characteristics. The *Commentary on the Questions of King Milinda* also has a list, but because it differs in many respects from the Sanskrit list these have not been included.[5]

The Thirty-Two Major Physical Characteristics of a Great Man

English	*Pāli*	*Sanskrit*
1. flat feet	suppatiṭṭhita-pāda	supratiṣṭhita-pāda
2. palms and soles are marked with thousand-spoked wheels	heṭṭhā-pāda-talesu cakkāni jātāni	cakrāṅkita-hasta-pāda
3. projecting heels	āyata-paṇhi	āyata-pāda-pārṣṇi

(continued)

The Thirty-Two Major Physical Characteristics of a Great Man *(continued)*

English	*Pāli*	*Sanskrit*
4. long fingers and toes	dīgh-aṅgulī	dīrghāṅgulī
5. soft and tender hands and feet	mudu-taluṇa-hattha-pāda	mṛdu-taruṇa-hasta-pāda
6. webbed fingers and toes	jāla-hattha-pāda	jāla-hasta-pāda Mv jālāvanaddha-hasta-pāda
7. hidden ankles	ussaṅka-pāda	utsaṅga-pāda
8. legs like an antelope's	eṇi-jaṅghā	eṇi-jaṅghā
9. can touch his knees in a standing posture with either hand without bending	thitako va anonamanto ubhohi pāṇi-talehi jannukāni parimasati parimajati	sthitānavanata-pralamba-bāhutā
10. penis covered by a sheath	kosohita-vattha-guhya	kośahita-vastra Mv kośopagata-vasti-guhya
11. golden-colored skin	suvaṇṇa-vaṇṇa-cchavi	suvarṇa-cchavi
12. skin so smooth and delicate that no dust settles on it	sukhama-cchavi	sūkṣma-cchavi
13. one hair for each pore, curled to the right	ekeka-lomā	ekaika-roma-pradakṣiṇā-varta
14. each hair turns upward and curls to the right	uddhagga-loma	ūrdhvāṃgu-roma Mv ūrdhvaga-roma
15. body grows straight like Brahmā	brahmujju-gatta	
Mv: compact thighs		Mv suvarti-toru
16. body has seven protuberances	sattussada	saptotsada
17. torso like a lion	sīha-pubbaddha-kāya	siṃha-pūrvārdha-kāya
18. no indentation between the shoulders	cit-antaraṃsa	cit-āntarāṃsa
19. physical proportions like a banyan tree	nigrodha-parimaṇḍala	nyagrodha-parimaṇḍala
20. bust is equally rounded	sammavatta-kkhanda	susaṃvṛta-skandha
21. supremely acute sense of taste	rasagghas-aggi	rasa-rasāgratā
22. jaw like a lion's	sīha-hanu	siṃha-hanu
23. forty teeth	cattārīsa-danta	catvāriṃśati-danta

The Thirty-Two Major Physical Characteristics of a Great Man *(continued)*

English	*Pāli*	*Sanskrit*
24. even teeth	sama-danta	sama-danta
25. teeth close together, no gaps	avivara-danta	avirala-danta
26. white and lustrous teeth	susukka-dāṭha	suśukla-danta
27. long and slender tongue	pahūta-jihvā	prabhūta-tanu-jihva
28. divine voice like a karavīka (Skt.: kalaviṅka) bird or Brahmā	karavīka-bhāṇi brahma-ssara	kalaviṅka-svara brahma-svara
29. blue-black eyes	abhinīla-netta	abhinīla-netra
30. eyelashes like a cow's	gopakhuma	gopakṣmā-netra
31. tuft of hair between the eyebrows	uṇṇā	ūrṇā
32. prominent lump on top of the cranium	unhīsa	uṣṇīsa[a]

a. The *Mahāvyutpatti* also lists an even forehead *(sama-lalāṭa)*, #3. Lamotte cites this as an even and broad forehead *(sama-vipula-lalāṭa)*, *Mahāyāna-saṃgraha*, p. 55.

The Eighty Minor Physical Characteristics

English	*Sanskrit*
1. copper-colored fingernails	tāmra-nakha
2. smooth fingernails	snigdha-nakha
3. prominent fingernails	tuṅga-nakha
4. rounded fingers	vṛttāṅguli
5. tapering even fingers	anupūrva-citrāṅguli
6. well-developed fingers	citrāṅguli
7. concealed veins	nigūḍha-śira
8. unknotted veins	nirgranthi-śira
9. concealed ankles	nigūḍha-gulpha
10. even feet	sama-pāda
11. gait of a lion	siṃha-vikrānta-gāmi
12. gait of an elephant	nāga-vikrānta-gāmi
13. gait of a swan	haṃsa-vikrānta-gāmi
14. gait of a bull	vṛṣabha-vikrānta-gāmi
15. gait that sways to the right	pradakṣiṇāvarta-gāmi
16. steady gait	avakra-gāmi

(continued)

The Eighty Minor Physical Characteristics *(continued)*

English	*Sanskrit*
17. pleasing gait	cāru-gāmi
18. rounded limbs	vṛtta-gātra
19. smooth limbs	mṛdu-gātra
20. regular limbs	anupūrva-gātra
21. pure limbs	śuci-gātra
22. slender limbs	mṛṣṭa-gātra
23. flawless limbs	viśuddha-gātra
24. perfect male sex organ	paripūrṇa-puruṣa-vyañjana
25. body with broad and graceful limbs	suvibhaktāṅga-pratyaṅga
26. even pace	sama-krama
27. youthful limbs	sukumāra-gātra
28. unmarred limbs	adīna-gātra
29. unimpaired limbs	unnata-gātra
30. well-shaped limbs	susaṃhata-gātra
31. well-built, perfect kneecaps	pṛthu-cāru-jāṇu-maṇḍala
32. clear and pure sight	vitimira-viśuddhāloka
33. rounded belly	vṛtta-kukṣi
34. well-shaped belly	mṛṣṭa-kukṣi
35. regularly shaped belly	abhugna-kukṣi
36. slim abdomen	kṣāmodara
37. deep navel	gaṃbhīra-nābhi
38. navel coiled clockwise	pradakṣināvara-nābhi
39. agreeable in all respects	samanta-prāsādika
40. pure conduct	śuci-samācāra
41. limbs free from freckles and black spots	vyapagata-tilaka-kālaka-gātra
42. hands are delicate like cotton	tūla-sadṛśa-sukumāra-pāṇi
43. fine hand lines	anupūrva-pāṇi-lekha
44. deep hand lines	gambhīra-pāṇi-lekha
45. long hand lines	āyata-pāṇi-lekha
46. face not too long	mātyāyata-vadana
47. mouth like a bimba fruit	Mv: bimboṣṭha bimba-pratibimba-darśana-vadana
48. pliable tongue	mṛdu-jihvā
49. slender tongue	tanu-jihvā
50. red tongue	rakta-jihvā
51. voice like a roaring elephant or thundering clouds	gaja-garjita-jīmūta-ghoṣa

The Eighty Minor Physical Characteristics *(continued)*

English	*Sanskrit*
52. articulate, melodious voice	noccavacana-śabda Mv madhura-caru-mañju-svara
53. rounded canine teeth	vṛtta-daṃṣṭrā
54. sharp canine teeth	tīkṣṇa-daṃṣṭrā
55. regular canine teeth	anupūrva-daṃṣṭrā
56. even canine teeth	sama-daṃṣṭrā
57. white canine teeth	śukla-daṃṣṭrā
58. prominent nose	tuṅga-nāsa
59. well-shaped nose	suci-nāsa
60. clear eyes	viśuddha-netra
61. large eyes	viśāla-netra
62. thick eyelashes	citra-pakṣma
63. white and dark parts of eyes beautifully contrast like the petals of a white and dark lotus	sitāsita-kamala-śakala-nayana
64. long eyebrows	āyata-bhrū
65. glossy eyebrows	ślakṣṇa-bhrū
66. even eyebrows	sama-roma-bhrū
67. smooth eyebrows	snigdha-bhrū
68. large and long ears	pīnāyata-karṇa
69. identical ears	sama-karṇa
70. unimpaired hearing	anupahata-karṇendriya
71. well-formed forehead	supariṇata-lalāṭa
72. broad forehead	pṛthu-lalāta
73. well-developed head	suparipūrṇottamāṅga
74. hair the color of a black bee's	bhramara-sadṛśa-keśa or asita-keśa
75. thick hair	cita-keśa
76. glossy hair	ślakṣṇa-keśa
77. undisheveled, untousled hair	asaṃlulita-asaṃluḍita-keśa
78. soft hair	aparuṣa-keśa
79. fragrant hair	surabhi-keśa
80. palms and soles marked with śrīvatsa, svastika, madyāvarta, and lalita symbols	śrīvatsa-svastika-nandyāvarta-lalita-lakṣito-pāṇi-pāda

Sources: List from *Dīgha-nikāya,* vol. III., pp. 144–5; *Mahāvyutpatti.* pp. 22–23.

APPENDIX 2

Epithets of the Buddha

Indic texts contain a plethora of epithets relating to the Buddha. Some extol his mental qualities, and others relate to the Buddha's paradigmatic masculinity. An entire chapter of the *Extensive Sport* is devoted to such epithets, and there are numerous other examples in Pāli and Sanskrit texts. This appendix contains a sampling of such terms drawn from the texts used in this study.

Spiritual Attainments

English	*Pāli*	*Sanskrit*
accomplished in knowledge and conduct		vidyācaraṇa-sampanna
arhat	arahat	arhat
awakened one	buddha	buddha
blessed one	bhagavat	bhagavan
fully awakened one	samma-sambuddha	samyak-sambuddha
great seer		mahārṣi
knower of worlds		loka-vid
light maker		prabhakara
teacher of gods and humans		śāstā deva-manuṣyānām
thus gone one	tathāgata	tathāgata
unsurpassed knower of worlds		lokavid-anuttara
well gone one	sugata	sugata

Images of Masculinity

English	*Pāli*	*Sanskrit*
best of men	narottama	narottama
best of men		nara-śreṣṭha
bull of a man	narāsabha	narārṣabha
bull of a man	purisa-usabha	puruṣārṣabha
charioteer of men to be tamed	purisa-damma-sārathi	puruṣa-damya-sārathi
chief of men		puruṣaṃgava
chief of the world		loka-nātha
crusher of your enemies		tvamari-pramardana
elephant of a man		puruṣa-nāga
endowed with strength		balavān
father of the world		loka-pitā
god among men	nara-deva	nara-deva
god of gods		deva-deva
great man	mahāpurisa	mahāpuruṣa
hero man	nara-vīra	nara-vīra
hero of men		puruṣa-śūra
highest man		parama-puruṣa
highest man		agra-puruṣa
highest man		puruṣardhīra
king of dharma	dhamma-rāja	dharma-rāja
king of kings		rājātirāja
king of kings	rājābhirāja	rājābhirāja
king of kings		narendra-rājñā
lion	sīha	siṃha
lord of bipeds		dvipadendra
lord of men	narenda	narendra
lion, lord of men		narendra-siṃha
lion of the Śākyas		śākya-siṃha
lion roaring in the forest		siṃho nadate vane
lord of the earth		bhūmi-pāla
lotus of men		puruṣa-puṇḍarīka
manly		puruṣaka
manly	narassika	narasaka
manly		pauṃsya
man-lion	nara-sīha	nara-siṃha
man-lion	purisa- sīha	puruṣa-siṃha
manliness	purisa-kāra	puruṣa-kāra
manliness		puruṣatva

Images of Masculinity *(continued)*

English	*Pāli*	*Sanskrit*
manly strength	purisa-parakkama	
manly strength	purisa-thāma	
master of Māra		māreśvara
monument of men		cetiyaṃ narāṇāṃ
nāga	nāga	nāga
stallion of a man	purisājañña	puruṣājāneya
superior to all gods		sarva-devottama
supreme god		atideva
sun of men		narāditya
thoroughbred stallion	ājānīya	ājāneya
true man	sappurisa	sat-puruṣa
ultimate man	purisottama	puruṣottama
unsurpassed charioteer for men to be trained		anuttaraḥ puruṣa damya-sārathi
unsurpassed tamer of men, master of gods and men		puruṣa-damyasādhi śāstā devānāṃ ca manuṣyāṇāṃ ca
true man	sappurisa	sat-puruṣa
virile	purisa-bhava	puruṣa-bhava

Notes

1. The Ultimate Man

1. See, for example, Rita Gross, *Buddhism after Patriarchy: A Feminist History, Analysis, and Reconstruction of Buddhism* (Albany: State University of New York Press, 1993), pp. 23–25, who states that although Buddhism traditionally is "androcentric and patriarchal," it also contains "quasi-feminist" elements that recognize "women's equality and dignity" and their religious potential; and Karma Lekshe Tsomo, *Sakyadhītā: Daughters of the Buddha* (Ithaca, NY: Snow Lion Publications, 1998), p. 22: "In theory, there are no limitations set on women's spiritual potential. The Buddha made no gender distinctions when discussing the goal of human perfection."

2. As we will see, however, lust is only one of a variety of motivations behind women's sexual advances toward monks, though it is clearly the most prominent one. Some use their sexual wiles in an attempt to entice former husbands back to the home life so that they can have financial support and help in rearing their children. Others seem to enjoy the challenge of attracting an unwilling partner; and in some stories, the women who proposition monks appear to have ambiguous or mixed motivations.

3. Leonard Zwilling, "Homosexuality as Seen in Indian Buddhist Texts," in *Buddhism, Sexuality, and Gender,* ed. José Ignacio Cabezón (Albany: State University of New York Press, 1992), pp. 203–214; and José Ignacio Cabezón, "Homosexuality and Buddhism," in *Homosexuality and World Religions,* ed. Arlene Swidler (Valley Forge, PA: Trinity Press International, 1993), pp. 81–101. Bernard Faure's *The Red Thread:*

Buddhist Approaches to Sexuality (Princeton, NJ: Princeton University Press, 1998) should also be mentioned in this context. Faure focuses on Buddhist views of male sexuality, but his primary concern is East Asia, and most of the sources he cites are from China and Japan.

4. The focus on the Buddha as an ascetic meditation master and philosopher is not only found among Western interpreters. See, for example, Ven. Weragoda Sarada Maha Thero, *The Greatest Man Who Ever Lived: The Supreme Buddha* (Singapore: Singapore Buddhist Meditation Center, 1998); and Walpola Rahula, *What the Buddha Taught* (New York: Grove Press, 1974).

5. The Pāli canon is the scriptural collection of the Theravāda tradition, which is dominant in Southeast Asia. It is written in an Indic language called Pāli and divided into "three baskets" (*tipiṭaka;* Sanskrit [Skt.] *tripiṭaka*): (1) discourses (*sutta;* Skt. *sūtra*), (2) monastic discipline (*vinaya*), and (3) higher doctrine (*abhidhamma;* Skt. *abhidharma*). It was probably compiled around the end of the first century CE. Most of the texts used in the first three chapters of this study are drawn from this collection and from commentaries in Pāli and Sanskrit scholastic texts. A useful chronology of Pāli canonical and para-canonical works is provided by Steven Collins in *Nirvana and Other Buddhist Felicities: Utopias of the Pali Imaginaire* (Cambridge: Cambridge University Press, 1998), pp. xvii–xix.

6. The mid-nineteenth-century "muscular Christianity" movement was an attempt to create an alternative discourse, which emphasized stories of Christian heroes and linked devotion with exercise and robust health, but this is not part of the theology of any current major Christian denomination, and it is now of interest mainly to historians.

7. *Majjhima-nikāya,* ed. Robert Chalmers (London: Pali Text Society, 1960), II.166–167.

8. *Dīgha-nikāya,* ed. J. E. Carpenter (London: Pali Text Society, 1960), I.123.

9. See, for example, Mark 8:27–30 and Matthew 16:13–20. Leo Steinberg quotes a passage from the *Summa Theologiae* (III, Quarto 37, art. 1) of Thomas Aquinas, which provides seven reasons for why Jesus allowed himself to be circumcised. The first was "to show the reality of his human flesh against the Manichee who taught that he had a body which was merely appearance; against Apollinarius who said that the body of Christ was consubstantial with his divinity; and against Valentinus who taught that Christ brought his body from heaven": Leo Steinberg, *The Sexuality of Christ in Renaissance Art and in Modern Oblivion,* 2nd ed. (Chicago: University of Chicago Press, 1996), p. 56. Steinberg also cites a passage from St. Bernard that contains a similar sentiment: "Man, carnal, animal, and sensual, could not know, love, or imitate anything that was not both proportionate and similar to himself. So, in order to raise man out of this state, the Word was made flesh; that He might be known and loved and imitated by man who was flesh." From *Breviloquium,* IV, 3, pp. 144–145, quoted in Steinberg, *Sexuality of Christ,* p. 121.

10. Nicephorus the Patriarch, *Antirrhetic II.* Quoted in *Fragments for a History of the Human Body,* ed. Michel Feher, trans. Anna Canogne (New York: Urzone, 1989), 1:158.

11. Steinberg, *Sexuality of Christ,* pp. 12–13.

12. *Matsaranandāvadāna,* verse 66, in *Five Buddhist Legends in the Campū Style: From a Collection Named Avadānasāra-samuccaya,* ed. Ratna Handurukande (Bonn: Indica et Tibetica Verlag, 1984), p. 108. The Avadānas are legends regarding the Buddha and his followers, most of which are generally believed to have been composed prior to the arising of Mahāyāna, that is, before the first century CE. For discussions of this literature, see Sharmistha Sharma, *Buddhist Avadānas: Socio-Political Economic and Cultural Study* (Delhi: Eastern Book Linkers, 1985); and Edward Thomas, "Avadāna and Apadāna," *Indian Historical Quarterly* 9 (1933): 31–36.

13. *Saṃyutta-nikāya,* ed. Leon Feer (London: Pali Text Society, 1960), I.94. In a later passage, he describes a person "moving from light to light": he or she is born to a wealthy *kṣatriya* or brahman family, is "handsome, attractive, graceful, possessing supreme beauty of complexion," and easily gets the necessities of life: food, water, clothing, and so forth. (I.94–95). In another discourse of this collection, the Buddha tells Nandaka that a disciple who has confidence in the Buddha, the doctrine (*dharma*), and the monastic community (*saṃgha*) will have a long life span and will be "endowed with beauty"; see "Connected Discourse on Stream Entry," in *Saṃyutta-nikāya,* ed. Leon Feer, V.390.

14. In keeping with the fact that this is a study of gender categories, gender-specific pronouns are carefully chosen. When discussing Pāli literature—which holds out no possibility of a woman becoming a buddha—exclusively male pronouns are used in relation to the state of buddhahood. Female buddhas do appear in some tantric texts (though they are far outnumbered by males), but even in tantra, where female figures play more important roles, most female buddhas are subordinate to their male consorts, and only a few—such as Tārā and Vajrayoginī—function on their own as primary focal points of cults. As an example of the Pāli canon's stance on women's religious potentialities, in the "Discourse on the Many Types of Elements," in *Majjhima-nikāya,* ed. Robert Chalmers (London: Pali Text Society, 1960), III.66–67, the Buddha instructs Ānanda on what is possible and impossible: it is impossible for a woman to be a fully awakened one, a buddha; only men can accomplish this; a woman cannot be a universal monarch (*cakravartin*); a woman cannot occupy the position of the god Sakka (Skt. *Śakra,* who rules over a heavenly realm), Māra, or Brahmā. The same list of limitations is found in the *Abhidharmakośa,* ed. Dwarikadas Shastri (Varanasi: Bauddha Bharati, 1981), p. 1085.

15. For example, in the *Theragāthā* (*Paramattha-dīpanī Theragāthā-Aṭṭhakathā: The Commentary of Dhammapālācariya,* ed. F. L. Woodward; London: Pali Text Society, 1952, II.109), Vimala is described as having a body "pure as a dewdrop on a lotus leaf" and similar to that of the Bodhisattva (future Buddha) in his last birth because of

his past practice of virtuous conduct, meditation, and so forth. This text contains anecdotes about and verses by Buddhist monks who lived during the Buddha's time from the *Verses of the Elder Monks,* along with a commentary attributed to Dhammapāla, who probably wrote it sometime during the middle of the sixth century.

16. Buddhaghosa, *Visuddhimagga,* ed. Caroline Rhys Davids (London: Pali Text Society, 1975), p. 211; see also *Samantapāsādikā,* ed. J. Takakusu and M. Nagai (London: Pali Text Society, 1968), I.124.

17. N. P. Chakravarti, "Appendix: Notes on the Painted and Inscribed Inscriptions of Cave XXI–XXVI," in *Ajaṇṭā: The Colour and Monochrome Reproductions of the Ajaṇṭā Frescoes Based on Photography,* ed. Ghulam Yazdani (London: Oxford University Press, 1930–1955) 3:112. Work on the caves of Ajaṇṭā probably began before 250 CE but was abandoned until 450, when Mahāyāna-oriented monks settled there and resumed construction. The complex was finally abandoned in the seventh century and only rediscovered in the nineteenth century by British army officers. This inscription obviously dates from the Mahāyāna period. For a non-Buddhist version of the idea that one's present situation is the result of past activities and that past karmas are proclaimed by one's present state, see the *Bṛhat saṃhitā* of Varāha Mihira, ed. H. Kern (Calcutta: Baptist Mission Press, Bibliotheca Indica Series, 1865), pp. 348ff., which indicates that one's actions are largely preordained by one's lot at birth.

18. Roy Porter, *Flesh in the Age of Reason* (London: Allen Lane, 2002), p. 246. See also Reiko Ohnuma, *Head, Eyes, Flesh, and Blood: Giving away the Body in Indian Buddhist Literature* (New York: Columbia University Press, 2007), pp. 224–225, which notes the linkage between physical beauty and moral excellence in the *Jātakas:* "this is a world in which *physical features are always indicative of moral status,* and *moral attainments must be reflected by their corresponding physical effects.*"

19. See Reiko Ohnuma, *Head, Eyes, Flesh, and Blood,* p. 225, which makes a similar point.

20. These literary productions are also closely linked with images of the Buddha created by artists over the centuries, the earliest of which appeared centuries after his death, when the legend of the Buddha was already well established. Both texts and images depict a character that is an artifact of a particular time and culture and that served as the basis for later elaborations and permutations. The focus of this section is on the Buddha figure created by his followers in ancient India; there are, of course, other Buddhas, such as those venerated in Southeast Asia, Tibet, and China, all of whom share a common ancestry with the Indian Buddha.

21. Michael Radich makes a similar point: "It is rarely or never an adequate conception of the religious goal of Buddhism to imagine its realization as a purely gnostic, cognitive or 'spiritual' matter. Rather, this religious goal must logically entail some somatic dimension . . . inasmuch as it always entails the radical transcendence of all suffering and therefore all the species of finitude, conditionality, and limitation that give rise to suffering"; see The "Somatics of Liberation: Ideas about Embodiment in Bud-

dhism from its Origins to the Fifth Century CE" (PhD diss., Harvard University, 2007), pp. 17–18.

22. See, for example, R. W. Connell, *Masculinities,* 2nd ed. (Crows Nest, New South Wales, Australia: Allen & Unwin, 2005), pp. 84, 226.

23. Ibid., p. 44.

24. See Michel Foucault, *Discipline and Punish: The Birth of the Prison,* trans. Alan Sheridan (London: Penguin Books, 1991), p. 128.

25. Connell, *Masculinities,* p. xviii.

26. See Mary Douglas, *Natural Symbols: Explorations in Cosmology* (New York: Vintage Books, 1973), pp. 137–139.

27. Pierre Bourdieu, *The Logic of Practice,* trans. Richard Nice (Cambridge: Polity Press, 1990), p. 73.

28. *Dīgha-nikāya,* III.144–145. A complete list, along with Pāli and Sanskrit equivalents, is given in Appendix 1.

29. The gait of a lion is also valued in Indian medical literature. The *Sāmudrika Śāstra,* for example, considers it to be the ideal gait for a human male; see *Agniveśa's Caraka Saṃhitā,* ed. Ram Karan Sharma and Vaidya Bhagwan Dash (Varanasi: Chowkhamba Sanskrit Series Office, 1999), II.467. The *Caraka Saṃhitā* is generally thought to have been compiled between 400 and 200 BCE.

30. The eighty minor physical characteristics are not found in the *Nikāya*s or the *Vinaya.* They first appear in the legends of early Buddhist figures (*Avadāna*). They are also mentioned in the Chinese translation of the *Discourse of the Great Final Release* (*Mahāparinirvāṇa-sūtra*) of the *Dīrghāgama* (T1, 12b) and the *Aśoka Discourse* (*Aśoka-sūtra*) of the *Samyuktāgama* (T2, 166c). In Pāli literature, the list is found in the *Commentary on the Questions of King Milinda* (*Milindapañha-ṭīkā*: Padmanabh S. Jaini, ed.; London: Pali Text Society, 1961, pp. 17–18) and the *Commentary on the Ornament for the Conquerors* (*Jinālaṃkāra-ṭīkā* by Buddhadatta; Rangoon: Sudhammavati Pitaka Press, 1940, p. 198). Buddhadatta (ca. 5th century) is said to have been a contemporary of Buddhaghosa, and tradition holds that the two met in Sri Lanka. The text mentions the *Visuddhimagga,* so Buddhadatta was apparently aware of Buddhaghosa's work. In some Mahāyāna texts, the concept of the Buddha's physical characteristics is even further expanded: the *Avataṃsaka-sūtra* devotes two chapters to the Buddha's physical characteristics, and he is said to have "an ocean of physical characteristics" (in Buddhabhadra's Chinese translation, chapter 29 is entitled "The Ocean of Physical Characteristics," and chapter 30 is "The Merit of Light of the Buddha's Minor Physical Characteristics"; T9, 601a–606c). Étienne Lamotte gives a bibliography of both groups of physical characteristics in Buddhist literature in his translation of the *Compendium of the Great Vehicle* [*La Somme du Grand Véhicule d'Asaṅga* (*Mahāyānasaṃgraha*)] (Louvain-la-Neuve: Institut Orientaliste, 1973), pp. 54*–58*.

31. Buddhaghosa, *Sumaṅgala-vilāsinī* (a commentary on the *Dīgha-nikāya*), ed. T. W. Rhys Davids, J. E. Carpenter, and W. Stede (London: Pali Text Society, 1886–1932),

II.446. He goes on to say that even in old age the Buddha's fingers are as soft as those of a newborn baby.

32. Ibid., II.447.

33. Ibid., II.449. This is apparently a positive attribute for men according to Indian medical literature. Caraka, for example, states that the ideal male physique includes a chest that is wide and plump and an inconspicuous spine and collar bone; see *The Caraka Saṃhitā* (Jamnagar: Shree Gulabkunverba Ayurvedic Society, 1949), III.1172.

34. *Saṃyutta-nikāya,* V.158.

35. *Aṅguttara-nikāya,* ed. Richard Morris (London: Pali Text Society, 1961), III.223.

36. *Abhidharmakośa-bhāṣya,* ed. Prahlad Pradhan (Patna: K. P. Jayaswal Research Institute, 1967), p. 266.

37. *Sumaṅgala-vilāsinī,* II.448: *yena kammena yaṃ nibbattaṃ.* Similarly, the "Lakkhaṇa-sutta" (*Dīgha-nikāya* III.144–145) states that the Buddha perfected his various physical attributes by performance of "various mighty deeds, generosity, discipline, abstinence, [as well as] honoring his parents, ascetics, and brahmans." The *Abhisamayālaṃkāra* (chapter 8, verses 13–17), ed. Eugene Obermiller and Th. Stcherbatsky (Osnabrück: Biblio Verlag, 1970), pp. 35–36, lists the thirty-two characteristics, and verses 18–30 describe the karmic factors that led to each of them. Peter Harvey provides a useful chart that lists each characteristic and the action(s) that produced it in *Encyclopedia of Buddhism,* ed. Damien Keown and Charles Prebish (London: Routledge, 2007), pp. 100–101. Eugene Burnouf discusses them in Appendix VIII to his *Le Lotus de la bonne loi* (Paris: Maisonneuve, 1925), 2:553–647.

38. Guang Xing, *The Concept of the Buddha: Its Evolution from Early Buddhism to the Trikāya Theory* (London: Routledge Curzon, 2005), p. 27. According to the *Abhidharmakośa* (Pradhan ed., p. 266), each characteristic is produced by cultivation of one hundred merits. A number of texts indicate that the characteristics are acquired sequentially, and so when a bodhisattva perfects the karmas that will produce a certain characteristic, it becomes manifest on his body in the next reincarnation; see *Pañcaviṃśati-sāhasrikā-prajñā-pāramitā-sūtra,* ed. Nalinaksha Dutt (London: Luzac, 1934), p. 69. The *Abhidharmakośa* (p. 265) states that once a bodhisattva begins to cultivate these characteristics, he is "predestined" and will henceforth always be born in good realms, will have all organs intact, will remember past lives, will be a male, and will never be nonsexual *(saṇḍha)* or otherwise physically deficient.

39. The *Mahāvibhāṣā* (ca. 3rd century CE) states: "How long does it take to complete the maturation of the physical characteristics? Answer: It usually takes one hundred great eons *(mahākalpa),* but Śākyamuni Bodhisattva took only ninety-one due to his industrious work" (T 27.890b). This training began only after he had already undergone three countless eons *(asaṃkhyeya-kalpa)* of training, and his main goal during this phase of his maturation was development of the physical characteristics.

40. This idea is also found in the *Karuṇāpuṇḍarīka-sūtra,* where King Ambara gives away his genitals and flesh because he hopes to receive a sheathed penis and

golden skin. See *Karuṇāpuṇḍarīka,* ed. Isshi Yamada (London: School of Oriental and African Studies, 1968), 2:380.

41. *Mahāvastu,* ed. E. Senart (Paris: l'Imprimerie Nationale, 1977), II.305. The *Mahāvastu* is a large and composite work comprising materials from a range of sources and periods. It is generally believed by scholars that some portions date from the second century BCE. J. J. Jones, who translated the text into English, thinks that it was not completed until around the third or fourth century CE. See *The Mahāvastu* (London: Pali Text Society, 1973), 1:xi.

42. Several Indian sources indicate that a dangling penis is regarded as aesthetically unpleasing, and this is probably one reason why the ideal man is endowed with one that is hidden. In the *Abhidharmakośa,* for example, Vasubandhu notes that the Vaibhāṣikas contend that the male organ is physically ugly, but he responds by pointing out that the Buddha's sheathed penis is beautiful (Pradhan ed., p. 59).

43. *Sumaṅgala-vilāsinī* (3 vols.), ed. T. W. Rhys Davids, J. E. Carpenter, and W. Stede (London: Pali Text Society, 1886–1932), II.447. The *Citralakṣaṇa* of Nagnajit, a treatise on art and iconography, describes the measurements of the body parts of a universal monarch *(cakravartin),* who is said to have the thirty-two physical characteristics, but of a slightly inferior quality: "like an elephant king, he keeps his sexual organs withdrawn as if in a cavity"; see *An Early Document of Indian Art: Citralakṣaṇa of Nagnajit,* trans. A. Dallapicolla and B. N. Goswamy (New Delhi: Manohar, 1976), p. 102. The *Citralakṣaṇa* states than when artists fashion an image of a universal monarch, the penis should be made as long as six digits and should be two digits in diameter. The scrotum should be six digits long, and "the testicles should not hang too much and both should be shown evenly round." Interestingly, there is no description of a buddha's private parts. According to the *Mahāvibhāṣā* (T27.889a), a universal monarch also has the thirty-two physical characteristics, but a buddha's are superior in six ways: being magnificent, distinctive, complete, in the proper place, in accordance with superior wisdom, and in accordance with the destruction of the afflictions.

44. *Gaṇḍavyūha-sūtra,* ed. D. T. Suzuki and H. Izumi (Tokyo: Society for the Publication of the Sacred Books of the World, 1959), p. 400.

45. Alexander Soper, "Aspects of Light Symbolism in Gandhāran Sculpture," *Artibus Asiae,* 12, no. 4 (1949): 325. The text he discusses is a Mahāyāna work originally written in Sanskrit but now only extant in Chinese (觀仏三昧海經, T643, which was translated into Chinese by Buddhabhadra around 412 CE). The title is sometimes reconstructed as *Buddhānusmṛti-samādhi-sūtra* or *Buddhānusmṛti-samādhi-sāpara-sūtra.* It contains an interesting passage in which the Buddha leaves an image or reflection (sometimes translated as a shadow) of himself in a cave so that later followers can see what he looked like. This is discussed by Marylin Rhie in *Early Buddhist Art in China and Central Asia* (Leiden: E. J. Brill, 1999), 2:118.

46. *Lalitavistara,* ed. P. L. Vaidya (Darbhanga: Mithila Institute, 1958), p. 310. The date of this text is uncertain. Some scholars place its origins as early as 300 BCE,

but others believe that the text as we know it today probably came together around the beginning of the first century CE. Hearers and solitary realizers are two types of Buddhist practitioners who work to attain nirvana and are mainly intent on their own liberation.

47. *Sumaṅgala-vilāsinī,* II.450. Buddhaghosa describes the Buddha's tongue as *"pahūta,"* implying that it has maximum flexibility.

48. *Arthaviniścaya-sūtra and Its Commentary,* ed. N. H. Samatani (Patna: K. P. Jayaswal Research Institute, 1971), p. 297.

49. *The Caraka Saṃhitā,* III.1172. Caraka also lists as desirable qualities a voice that is mighty and deep, large jaws, a chest that is wide and plump, and an inconspicuous spine and collar bone, all of which are also listed among the thirty-two physical characteristics or eighty secondary physical characteristics.

50. *Atthasālinī (Dhammasaṅgaṇī Commentary,* ed. Edward Müller; London: Pali Text Society, 1979), p. 15. This is an interesting notion, and it may reflect a tacit acknowledgment on Buddhaghosa's part that no ordinary man could possibly have spoken all of the discourses, *vinaya* passages, and *abhidharma* texts attributed to the Buddha while also spending long periods in meditative retreat, walking from place to place, begging for food in alms rounds, and so forth. Rather than admitting that some of the Buddha's discourses may have been constructed by others, Buddhaghosa provides an explanation for how one person could have taught so much in a human lifetime.

51. *Jivhā,* the Pāli word for tongue, is a feminine noun.

52. "Brahmāyu-sutta," "Division on Brahmans" *(Brāhmaṇa-vagga), Majjhima-nikāya,* II.136.

53. Donald Lopez discusses some of these controversies in his article, "Buddha," in *Critical Terms for the Study of Buddhism* (Chicago: University of Chicago Press, 2005), pp. 13–36.

54. For a discussion of this idea, see Hubert Durt, "Note sur l'origine de l'Anavalokitamūdatā," *Indogaku Bukkyōgaku Kenkyū* 16, no. 1 (December 1967): 450–443. He mentions (pp. 446–445) several sources asserting that no one could fly over the Buddha's head or look down on him from above and that it was impossible to clearly view the top of his head.[Pub note: in Japanese journals, the page numbers are reversed.]

55. *Lalitavistara,* p. 88.

56. *Sumaṅgala-vilāsinī,* II.452.

57. Alex Wayman, "Contributions Regarding the Thirty-Two Characteristics of the Great Person," *Sino-Indian Studies* 4, (1957): 250, n.88.

58. *Sumaṅgala-vilāsinī,* II.451.

59. In a study of early Buddhist art, Susan and John Huntington note that Indian Buddha images generally have only a few of the physical characteristics, most commonly the *uṣṇīṣa, ūrṇā,* webbed fingers, and *cakras*. Images of buddhas (not just Śākyamuni) also have elongated earlobes, suggesting their former lives of pleasure when they wore

heavy earrings. See Susan L. Huntington and John C. Huntington, *Leaves from the Bodhi Tree: The Art of Pāla India (11th–12th Centuries) and Its International Legacy* (Dayton, OH: Dayton Art Institute, 1990), p. 103. They suggest that there are two reasons why only a few appear: the physical characteristics that are used are representative of the rest, and those characteristics depicted are the ones most suited to plastic art. It is difficult to imagine, for example, how a statue could portray the Buddha's exquisite sense of taste, and a tongue that covers his face would probably be distracting and not particularly appealing.

60. *Sumaṅgala-vilāsinī,* II.435.

61. *Agniveśa's Caraka Saṃhitā,* II, chap. VII.16, p. 263. Caraka also states that the ideal masculine type is characterized by organs that are smooth and pleasing in appearance, by large quantities of semen, and by strong sexual desire. The ideal male's body is firm, compact, and durable, and he does not feel hunger, thirst, or heat as intensely as other men. He has firm and compact joints, a face that is clear and looks happy, a soft complexion, and great strength. Most of these features are attributed to the Buddha in Indic texts.

62. The "Brahmāyu-sutta" contains an extended discussion that meticulously describes his physical mannerisms.

63. *Sumaṅgala-vilāsinī,* II.448.

64. For example, Dhammapāla's (ca. sixth century) *Udāna-aṭṭhakathā,* ed. Peter Masefield (London: Pali Text Society, 1995), p. 887. This is a common feature of descriptions of the Buddha. Hubert Durt cites Xuanzang's report of a tradition that the Buddha was over six feet tall. Once an arrogant brahman tried to measure the Buddha's height with a six-foot pole, but the latter kept growing taller ("Note sur l'origine de l'Anavalokitamūdatā," p. 445).

65. See, for example, the "Sela-sutta" of the *Majjhima-nikāya,* II.106–107.

66. T. W. Rhys Davids, *Dialogues of the Buddha, Part I* (London: Pali Text Society, 1889), p. 110. The thirty-two physical characteristics of a great man are mentioned in many discourses of the Pāli canon and in a number of other texts, including the following: "Mahāpadāna-sutta," *Dīgha-nikāya,* II.17–19; "Lakkhaṇa-sutta," *Dīgha-nikāya,* III.143–144; "Brahmāyu-sutta," *Majjhima-nikāya,* II.136–137, *Mahāvastu,* I.226, 2.29; Asaṅga's *Bodhisattva-bhūmi,* ed. Wogihara Unrai (Tokyo: Sankibo Buddhist Bookstore, 1971), pp. 259–260; the *Abhisamayālaṃkāra,* pp. 35–36); the *Aṣṭasahāsrikā-prajñāpāramitā-sūtra,* ed. P. L. Vaidya (Darbhanga: Mithila Institute, 1960), pp. 537–538; and the *Ratnagotra-vibhāga,* ed. E. H. Johnston (Patna: Bihar Research Society, 1950), pp. 94–95. Max Muller has made a list of the physical characteristics from various sources in his edition of the *Dharma-saṃgraha:* Max Muller and K. Kasawara, eds., *The Dharmasaṃgraha, An Ancient Collection of Buddhist Technical Terms* (Oxford: Clarendon Press, 1885), p. 1. He lists a total of thirty-seven major characteristics found in a range of texts. Thirty-two is the standard number, but the *Gaṇḍavyūha-sūtra* lists only twenty-eight; see *Gaṇḍavyūha-sūtra,* p. 399.

67. Rhys Davids, *Dialogues of the Buddha, Part I,* p. 110.

68. Hajime Nakamura, *Gotama Buddha,* vol. 11: *Nakamura Hajime Senshū* (Tokyo: Shunjusha, 1969), p. 513. All of the sources Nakamura cites are Buddhist works. He discusses the physical characteristics in footnotes 76–80. These refer to pp. 512–513, where he discusses the Buddha's physical features. My thanks to Carol Hayes for translating the relevant portions.

69. Sten Konow, *The Two First Chapters of the Daśasāhasrikā Prajñāpāramitā* (Oslo: Norske Videnskaps-Akademie, 1941, vol. 1), p. 78. Austine Waddell also relates this concept to Viṣṇu-Nārāyaṇa in "Buddha's Diadem or Uṣṇīṣa," *Ostasiatische Zeitschrift* 3 (1914): 131ff., but the association is tenuous. In the *Lalitavistara,* Buddha is said to be endowed with the thirty-two marks and the strength of Nārāyaṇa, but there is no indication that Nārāyaṇa possesses the thirty-two physical characteristics; see *Lalitavistara,* ed. S. Leffman (Halle: Verlag der Buchhandlung des Waisenhauses, 1902), p. 110. In the *Abhidharmakośa* (p. 413), Vasubandhu declares that the Buddha's body is as powerful as Nārāyaṇa's, a notion that is found in other Buddhist texts. Viṣṇu-Nārāyaṇa is referred to as a "great man," among other epithets, in the *Mahābhārata,* but he is not described as having the thirty-two physical characteristics of the Buddha.

70. *Atharvaveda Saṃhitā,* ed. R. Roth and W. D. Whitney (Bonn: F. Dummler, 1966), VIII.115.1.

71. *Śathapatha Brāhmaṇa,* trans. J. Eggeling (Sacred Books of the East; Delhi: Motilal Banarsidass, 1963) (5 vols.), vol. 4, p. 81.

72. *Atharvaveda Saṃhitā,* I.18.

73. *Viṣṇu Purāṇa,* ed. and trans. H. H. Wilson (Delhi: Nag Publishers, 1980), II:751. All of these occur among descriptions of the Buddha's major or minor physical characteristics. The *śrīvatsa* is a symbol associated with Viṣṇu, of whom Kṛṣṇa is said to be an incarnation. It is curious that it also appears among the secondary physical characteristics of the Buddha. It should also be noted that while both Kṛṣṇa and Rāma are credited with having beautiful complexions, one of the thirty-two physical characteristics of the Buddha is golden-colored skin, while both Kṛṣṇa and Rāma are said to have dark complexions.

74. *The Rāmāyaṇa of Vālmīki: An Epic of Ancient India,* trans. Robert P. Goldman (Princeton, NJ: Princeton University Press, 1984), vol. 1.1, pp. 121–126. A similar description is presented in vol. 2.2, pp. 82–84. See also vol. 5, ch. 33, pp. 201–202, where Rāma is said to have eyes like lotus petals; to equal the sun in splendor and the earth in forbearance; and to have a smooth complexion, a perfectly proportioned body, four pronounced canine teeth, and prominent lips, jaw, and nose. The four pronounced canine teeth and prominent jaw and nose are also attributed to the Buddha in some texts.

75. *Rāmāyaṇa,* trans. Goldman, vol. 2.3, p. 85, verses 11–12. The Buddha is also said in a number of sources to have a gait like a bull elephant in rut, an interesting im-

age for an ascetic teacher who practiced total celibacy and enjoined his disciples to practice it as well.

76. *Bhāgavata-purāṇaṃ Śrīmadbhāgavata cūrṇi kā ṭīkā,* ed. Pāṇḍeya Rāmateja Śāstrī (Kāśī: Paṇḍita Pustakālaya, 1960), I.26–28. My thanks to McComas Taylor for alerting me to this passage.

77. Chapter 69 of Varāha Mihira's (born ca. 505 CE) *Bṛhat saṃhitā*, an astrology manual, describes five types of "great man" and says that they are born when the planets from Mars to Saturn are in the ascendancy and are in their houses. His list of physical characteristics has some commonalities with the Buddhist lists, such as flat feet and one hair to each pore, but most are different. In chapter 68, Mihira links physiology to birth: men who will be kings have dry feet and soft soles, toes close together, and no sinews showing beneath the skin; those born with crooked feet with sinews showing will be poor; those with soles the color of burnt clay will murder brahmans; and those with yellow soles will have sex with prohibited women. See *The Bṛhat saṃhitā of Varāha Mihira,* ed. H. Kern (Calcutta: Baptist Mission Press, Bibliotheca Indica Series, 1865), pp. 348ff.

78. Buddhaghosa, *Papañcasūdanī* (a commentary on the *Majjhima-nikāya*), ed. J. H. Woods, D. Kosambi, and I. B. Horner (London: Pali Text Society, 1922–1938), II.761. Some Jain texts assert that Mahāvīra possessed several of the major physical characteristics, including the *uṣṇīṣa, ūrṇā,* physical proportions like those of a banyan tree *(nigrodha-parimaṇḍala),* a bust that is equally rounded with even neck and shoulders *(sammavatta-kkhanda),* and a lack of indentation between the shoulders *(cit-antaraṃsa)*; and statues of Mahāvīra commonly have long arms.

79. When I presented my research to the Australasian Association of Buddhist Studies monthly symposium in May 2007, Mark Allon pointed out that it could be the case that this was a part of brahmanical oral lore at the time of the Buddha but that it was never written down and so is now lost. This fits with the way it is presented in Buddhist texts, which always associate it with brahmans, but if it is indeed lost there is no way to verify the hypothesis.

80. Margaret M. Lock and Nancy Scheper-Hughes, "The Mindful Body: A Prolegomenon to Future Work in Medical Anthropology," *Medical Anthropology Quarterly* 1 (1987): 7.

81. Suzanne Mrozik, *Virtuous Bodies: The Physical Dimensions of Morality in Buddhist Ethics* (New York: Oxford University Press, 2007), p. 5.

82. Connell, *Masculinities,* p. 77.

83. Michel Foucault, *The Will to Knowledge: History of Sexuality I,* trans. Robert Hurley (London: Penguin Books, 1990), p. 95.

84. Pierre Bourdieu, *In Other Words: Essays toward a Reflexive Sociology,* trans. Matthew Adamson (Stanford, CA: Stanford University Press, 1990), p. 22.

85. The Sanskrit and Pāli term is *bodhi,* which is often translated as "enlightenment," but this brings with it significant conceptual baggage, and so I prefer to render it

as "awakening," which is the literal meaning of the Indic word. It implies that the Buddha has woken up from the sleep of ignorance, in which ordinary beings spend their lives.

86. See, for example, *Mahāvastu,* I.167–168 and II.15–17, which describe how hosts of gods came to view the Buddha while he was in his mother's womb and indicate that he enjoyed the attention. He is said to have been encased in a transparent crystal casket during the pregnancy, allowing his mother and other beings to observe his behavior at any time. It also prevented his perfect body being soiled by the foul substances of the womb.

87. *Theragāthā* (*Paramattha-dīpanī Theragāthā-Aṭṭhakathā,* II.147): *attānaṇ dassetuṇ obhāsaṇ vissajjento.* See also "Connected Discourse on the Aggregates," *Saṃyutta-nikāya,* III.120, for a similar account. Similarly, *Theragāthā* II.16 describes how Vasabha saw his physique and was "won over by the majesty of the Buddha." The most extensive description of the Buddha's body, comportment, and physical habits that I have found is in the "Brahmāyu-sutta," *Majjhima-nikāya,* II.136–137. Like Vakkali, Brahmāyu is also said to have joined the order after seeing the Buddha's body and similarly became obsessed by his physical presence. Brahmāyu "followed the Blessed One for seven months like a shadow, never leaving him," and during this time chronicled the various aspects of his comportment and physical habits for the benefit of his brahman teacher Uttara, who told him that "the thirty-two physical characteristics of the great man have been handed down in our hymns."

88. See *Lalitavistara,* pp. 11–19.

89. Ibid., 19.

90. Ibid., 18. *Lalitavistara* (p. 53) expands on this description and adds that Māyā "was not subject to female coquetry, deceit, or envy, or to the natural feminine passions." She was also highly moral, unlike most women. Even more remarkably in a society that assumed women to be constantly driven by raging sexual passion, she "never had any thought of desire for any man," nor could any man develop desire for her, despite her great beauty, because of her association with the Buddha. Thus she was physically stunning but sexless in the eyes of others. More details regarding her exemplary attributes and those of his family are given in *Lalitavistara,* pp. 18–19.

91. The major physical characteristics are mentioned in numerous places in the Pāli suttas, always in connection with brahmans who are said to be well versed in the Vedas and the lore of the great man, including "Brahmāyu-sutta," *Majjhima-nikāya,* II.133–146; "Sela-sutta," *Majjhima-nikāya,* 92 (on p. 146 Robert Chalmers indicates that this is identical to the "Sela-sutta" of the *Sutta-nipāta,* ed. Dines Andersen and Helmer Smith [London: Pali Text Society, 1990], pp. 104–112); "Ambaṭṭha-sutta," *Dīgha-nikāya,* I.107; "Mahāpadāna-sutta," *Dīgha-nikāya,* II.17; "Lakkhaṇa-sutta," *Dīgha-nikāya,* III.142–149; "Assalāyana-sutta," *Majjhima-nikāya,* II.148; and "Saṅgārava-sutta," *Majjhima-nikāya,* II.207–208.

92. Harold Garfinkel, ed., *Studies in Ethnomethodology* (Englewood Cliffs, NJ: Prentice-Hall, 1967), pp. 116–185; and Erving Goffman, "The Arrangement between the Sexes," *Theory and Society* 4 (1977): 301–331.

2. A Manly Monk

1. In "Dating the Buddha: A Red Herring Revealed," in *The Dating of the Historical Buddha,* Part 2, ed. Heinz Bechert (Göttingen: Vandendoeck & Ruprecht, 1992), pp. 239–259, Richard Gombrich gives some good evidence for 404 BCE as the year of the Buddha's death, but several articles in the same three-volume collection from the most important symposium on this issue in recent years point out that this chronology is at variance with the traditional dates of the early Buddhist councils and the reign of the Mauryan emperor Aśoka. Gombrich's proposed date implies a rather short (about sixty-year) period between the first two Buddhist councils, which conflicts with accounts in early histories that assert a one hundred-year gap between them. Following this chronology, Hajime Nakamura posits the date of the Buddha's death as 383 BCE; see "Glimpse into the Problem of the Date of the Buddha," in *The Dating of the Historical Buddha,* ed. Bechert Part 1 (Göttingen: Vandendoeck & Ruprecht, 1991), pp. 296–299. Other articles in the collection posit dates as late as 368 BCE. My thanks to Charles Prebish for his clarification of the issues in this controversy. In his article, "Cooking the Buddhist Books: The Implications of the New Dating of the Buddha for the History of Early Buddhism," *Journal of Buddhist Ethics* 15 (2008): 1–21, Prebish analyzes various hypotheses regarding the Buddha's dates with reference to the reign of Aśoka, the early Buddhist councils, and the rise of Buddhist sectarianism.

2. See, for example, Walpola Rahula, *What the Buddha Taught,* p. 1.

3. *Saṃyutta-nikāya* II.212 describes the Buddha's various meditative attainments and his magical powers: "To whatever extent I wish, I wield the various kinds of magical power: having been one, I become many; having been many, I become one; I appear and vanish; I go unhindered through a wall, through a rampart, through a mountain as though going through space; I dive in and out of the earth as though it were water; I walk on water without sinking as though it were earth; seated cross-legged, I travel in space like a bird; with my hand I touch and stroke the moon and sun so powerful and mighty; I exercise mastery with the body as far as the Brahmā World." A similar description of his supernatural powers is presented in *Saṃyutta-nikāya* V.264–265. The *Abhidharmakośa* (pp. 425–426) also credits the Buddha with the power of three types of physical displacement *(gati),* and claims that the Buddha has a unique power of rapid displacement, in which he can travel to other worlds as quickly as he thinks of it (referred to as "displacement by mind": *manojava*).

4. See Appendix 2 for a listing of epithets of the Buddha along with Sanskrit and Pāli equivalents. Several colleagues who have read draft versions of this study or attended conference presentations in which I discussed aspects of my research have pointed out that the Sanskrit term *puruṣa,* which is part of many of these epithets, does not necessarily mean "man" but can be the more generic "person." This is true, but the contexts in which it is used in discourses highlighted in this study clearly indicate that the authors assumed a masculine referent. Ancient India was a male-dominated

and patriarchal society, and the men who composed the texts examined in this study would not have entertained the notion that the "ultimate man" could be a woman. The marks of a "great man" *(mahāpuruṣa)* include a sheathed penis, which obviously marks this figure as male, as does the attribute of a perfectly formed set of male genitalia, one of the eighty secondary physical characteristics. The range of epithets that incorporate the term *puruṣa* provides further evidence for this. In the Indian cultural context, "bull of a person," "best of persons," "lion of a person," and so forth would sound even more nonsensical than they do in contemporary English. The language of these discourses is profoundly gendered, and their authors would not have conceived of women as bulls, stallions, lions, rutting elephants, and so forth. When the Buddha is described as "manly" *(puruṣaka),* "personable" obviously will not do as a translation. With few exceptions, traditional hierarchies were assumed in Buddhist discourses of gender, and there is little point in trying to rewrite them from the perspective of contemporary sensibilities, particularly if we wish to understand their cultural context.

5. Wendy Doniger, *Women, Androgynes, and Other Mythical Beasts* (Chicago: University of Chicago Press, 1980), p. 239.

6. "Khanda-saṃyutta," *Saṃyutta-nikāya,* III.84–85.

7. The *brahma-vihāras* are advanced meditative states. See Damien Keown, *Dictionary of Buddhism* (Oxford: Oxford University Press, 2003), p. 41.

8. The four "means of gathering" *(saṃgraha-vastu)* are methods used by teachers to attract students: (1) giving *(dāna),* which involves giving away teachings of doctrine and material goods; (2) speaking pleasantly *(priya-vādita),* which attracts students to one's teachings of doctrine through interesting words; (3) beneficial activities *(artha-caryā),* actions that accord with what trainees want; and (4) concordant function *(samanarthatā),* which involves making one's actions accord with one's words.

9. See Keown, *Dictionary of Buddhism,* p. 221.

10. Ibid., p. 38.

11. The three doors of deliverance are emptiness, wishlessness, and signlessness.

12. See Keown, *Dictionary of Buddhism,* p. 38.

13. *Lalitavistara,* p. 8.

14. *Itivuttaka,* ed. Ernst Windisch (London: Pali Text Society, 1975), p. 15.

15. "Mahāsudassana-sutta," *Dīgha-nikāya,* II.186199. The Buddha reveals that he was this king in a past life.

16. *Lalitavistara,* pp. 175–176.

17. See *Mahāvastu,* II.3, which says that it would be improper for a buddha's mother ever to engage in sexual activity.

18. Ibid., I.144.

19. *Lalitavistara,* p. 29; *Mahāvastu,* I.145. *Mahāvastu,* I.147, asserts: "In that conception . . . in which the mothers of bodhisattvas conceive a bodhisattva for his last existence, those best of women live a pure, completely perfect and chaste life. For these supreme women no passion for any man arises, not even for their husbands."

20. *Lalitavistara,* p. 51, reports that when the Buddha appeared in the womb he was not a shapeless embryo but a fully formed human with all the major and minor physical characteristics of a great man.

21. *Mahāvastu,* II.16. The belief that male fetuses are lodged in the right side is a common notion in Indian medical literature. The *Abhidharmakośa* (p. 127) states that a male embryo remains in the right side of the womb, crouching with his head forward. A female embryo will be on the left side with her vagina forward because she believes she is having sexual intercourse (apparently a male fetus also believes this). Caraka also indicates that male fetuses reside in the right side of the womb and females in the left: *The Caraka Saṃhitā,* III.1013.

22. *Lalitavistara,* p. 48.

23. *Abhidharmakośa,* p. 120.

24. *Mahāvastu,* I.148, asserts that all bodhisattvas emerge from their mothers' right sides, but without piercing them, and that the birth happens quickly, without extended labor. A similar trope is found in the *Viṣṇu Purāṇa* (II. 520), which recounts the story of a queen who gave birth from her right side. The child was said to be exceptional (not surprisingly), and the gods came and took care of him, as in stories of the Buddha's birth.

25. *Majjhima-nikāya,* III.121. *Dīgha-nikāya* II.13 contains a similar description.

26. *Mahāvastu,* II.18.

27. *Lalitavistara,* p. 134.

28. Ibid., p. 63.

29. *Sutta-nipāta,* pp. 131–132. The *Lalitavistara* (p. 74) also states that Asita examined the Buddha and saw that his body had all the major and minor physical characteristics of a great man: "it surpassed the body of Śakra, Brahmā, and the Guardians of the World." His body was more brilliant than a hundred thousand suns, and all his limbs were beautiful.

30. *Buddhacarita,* ed. E. H. Johnston (*Aśvaghoṣa's Buddhacarita, or Acts of the Buddha;* Delhi: Motilal Banarsidass, 1984), p. 6. Aśvaghoṣa probably flourished during the second century CE. His probable dates are around 111–151.

31. Michael Radich, "The Somatics of Liberation," p. 73.

32. *Lalitavistara,* pp. 84–85. This excuse is unique among all that I have heard offered by children trying to avoid going to church.

33. Ibid., p. 84.

34. *Buddhacarita,* p. 16.

35. The harem is described in *Majjhima-nikāya,* I.504–505.

36. *Lalitavistara,* p. 133. This is an interesting notion, since it and other texts that describe this period of his life depict him as a sexual stallion, who constantly engaged in carnal intercourse with multitudes of women. If one compares these accounts with his later emphasis on sexual abstinence and eradication of desire, it is difficult to see how such sexual indulgence resonates with the dharma. Perhaps it is an exceptionally subtle "skillful means."

37. David M. Halperin, "How to Do the History of Male Homosexuality," *GLQ: A Journal of Gay and Lesbian Studies* 6 (2000): 93.

38. *Lalitavistara,* p. 100. His daughter is referred to here as Gopā, but most sources give Siddhārtha's wife's name as Yaśodharā. In the *Mahāvastu,* her father's name is given as Mahānāma, and her name as Yaśodharā. A similar concern about Siddhārtha's manliness is expressed in *Mahāvastu,* II.73.

39. *Mahāvastu,* II.73–74. The inclusion of argument in this list is interesting because it indicates that a king must be able to convince and persuade and that physical strength and martial skills are not enough.

40. *Mahāvastu,* II.75.

41. *Lalitavistara,* p. 107.

42. *Mahāvastu,* II.76.

43. *Mūlasarvāstivāda-vinaya,* T 24.1450.111–112; see also T 1442, ch. 18, p. 720c.12–13. For a discussion of the relation between this Vinaya and the Pāli one, see Gregory Schopen, "On Avoiding Ghosts and Social Censure: Monastic Funerals in the *Mūlasarvāstivāda-vinaya,*" *Bones, Stones, and Buddhist Monks: Collected Papers on the Archaeology, Epigraphy, and Texts of Monastic Buddhism in India* (Honolulu: University of Hawai'i Press, 1997), pp. 204–237.

44. *Mahāvastu,* II.147.

45. Ibid.

46. *Buddhacarita,* p. 34. According to G. P. Malasekera, this Udāyin is a different personage from the one discussed in Chapter 3. He was the son of a brahman in Kapilavastu who later joined the order and became an arhat. He once spoke some spontaneous verses comparing the Buddha to a mighty elephant, and on one occasion was publicly rebuked by the Buddha for derogatory remarks to Ānanda; see *Dictionary of Pāli Proper Names* (Delhi: Munishram Manoharlal Publishers, 1998), pp. 375–376.

47. *Buddhacarita,* pp. 34–35.

48. Ibid., p. 37.

49. An influential statement of this idea can be found in chapter 6 of the *Laws of Manu*; see Georg Bühler, trans., *The Laws of Manu* (New York: Dover Publications, 1969), pp. 205–214).

50. *Buddhacarita,* p. 38.

51. Ibid., p. 21.

52. *Mūlasarvāstivāda-vinaya,* I.120. This passage is discussed in John Strong, "A Family Quest: The Buddha, Yaśodharā, and Rāhula in the *Mūlasarvāstivāda Vinaya,*" in *Sacred Biography in the Buddhist Traditions of South and Southeast Asia,* ed. Juliane Schober (Honolulu: University of Hawai'i Press, 1997), p. 115. Strong comments that in contrast to canonical biographies in which Siddhārtha leaves the palace after becoming thoroughly disgusted with worldly life, "this presents a rather different picture of the Bodhisattva at this crucial moment. Instead of turning away . . . from sexuality and abandoning the family life, the Bodhisattva here, in his last act as a prince, affirms

the householder's state and fulfills his sexual duty by engendering a son." Strong cites a subsequent passage in which the Bodhisattva, following his impregnation of his wife, has five dreams and a "reed" (which appears to be a euphemism for his penis) emerges from his "navel" and reaches up to the sky.

53. Charles Archaimbault reports a legend from Laos in which an evil disciple attempted to besmirch the Buddha's reputation by implying that his practice of celibacy was unnatural and probably an attempt to hide his impotence. Some of his followers became confused and doubted the Buddha's manliness, and in response he asked: "Do you really question my virility? Do you actually think my virtues are a reflection of impotence?" He then went to a secluded place and returned with cupped hands full of semen. He said: "Here is proof of my manhood!" and then went to the Mekong River and washed his hands. The potency of his semen was so great that a fish goddess who happened to be passing by became pregnant, and she later gave birth to the great arhat Upagupta; see Archaimbault, *La course de pirogues au Laos* (Ascona: Artibus Asiae Publishers, 1972), p. 55. John Strong also cites several noncanonical legends in which the Buddha's seminal discharge inadvertently resulted in Upagupta's conception; see *The Legend and Cult of Upagupta* (Delhi: Motilal Banarsidass, 1994), p. 220.

54. *Mahāvastu,* II.159.

55. "Canda-kinnara-jātaka" (*Jātaka* 485): *The Jātaka Together with Its Commentary,* ed. V. Fausboll (London: Pali Text Society, 1963), vol. IV, pp. 282–283.

56. His recounting of this story appears in *Mahāvastu,* II.166–175. In the following sections, he describes several other occasions when he abandoned her.

57. *Buddhacarita,* p. 54.

58. Ibid., p. 62.

59. These details are mentioned in the *Buddhacarita,* p. 65.

60. Ibid., pp. 68–69.

61. Ibid., p. 69.

62. Ibid., pp. 81–82.

63. Ibid., pp. 86–87.

64. Ibid., p. 108.

65. Ibid., p. 108.

66. Ibid., p. 113.

67. *Lalitavistara,* p. 177.

68. Ibid., p. 177.

69. Ibid., p. 174.

70. "Mahāsīhanāda-sutta," *Majjhima-nikāya,* I.78. This section contains a lengthy description of his ascetic practices.

71. The *Buddhacarita,* p. 141, however, asserts that his body remained beautiful during the period of austerities and that he gained great psychic power as he lost physical strength.

72. *Lalitavistara,* p. 184.

73. *Majjhima-nikāya,* I.81. The details of his practice of fasting are described in the "Mahāsaccaka-sutta," *Majjhima-nikāya,* I.243.

74. *Lalitavistara,* p. 199. Maheśvara is an epithet of the god Śiva.

75. The Desire Realm (Kāma-dhātu) is one of the three spheres within cyclic existence and the one in which humans abide. Its main feature is desire, which drives the actions of its inhabitants. The other two realms are the Form Realm and Formless Realm, which are inhabited by various types of gods.

76. *Buddhacarita,* p. 150.

77. *Lalitavistara,* p. 232.

78. Ibid., p. 233. They roughly correspond in reverse to the thirty-two good qualities attributed to Siddhārtha's mother, Māyā.

79. "Māra-saṃyutta," *Saṃyutta-nikāya,* I.124–125.

80. *Saṃyutta-nikāya,* I.126.

81. The *Lalitavistara,* p. 236, provides an interesting excursus depicting the desireless ascetic describing in graphic detail to these beautiful women how revolting their bodies are.

82. *Mahāvastu,* III.285–286.

83. *Lalitavistara,* p. 218.

84. Ibid., pp. 242–243. The taunts cover several pages of text. The *Great Matter* (II.270) also contains a similar trash-talking episode, in which Siddhārtha roars at Māra fourteen times and says: "Now evil Māra, I will strike you down. As a strong wrestler a weak one, so will I strike you down, evil one. As a strong bull a weak one, so will I crush you, evil one. As an elephant a weakened antelope, so will I strike you down, evil one. As a strong wind a frail tree, so will I strike you down, evil one . . . as the universal king Pṛthu vanquished the regional kings, so will I vanquish you, evil one. As a fine stallion terrifies a whole herd of horses, so will I terrify you, evil one. As a lion, king of beasts, tears apart all lesser animals, so will I tear apart your snare of ignorance." He then vows to "bind, terrify, conquer, and overcome" Māra.

85. "Sakka-saṃyutta," *Saṃyutta-nikāya,* I.235.

86. *Buddhacarita,* p. 161.

87. *Lalitavistara,* p. 297. See also *Majjhima-nikāya,* I.247.

88. *Lalitavistara,* p. 297.

89. Ibid., p. 297.

90. "Mahāssapura-sutta," *Majjhima-nikāya,* p. 273.

91. *Mahāvastu,* III.114–116.

92. *Buddhacarita,* p .47.

93. *Mahāvastu,* III.257.

94. Ibid., III.261.

95. Donald K. Swearer, trans, "Bimbā's Lament," in *Buddhism in Practice,* ed. Donald Lopez Jr. (Princeton, NJ: Princeton University Press, 1995), pp. 550–551.

96. *Vinaya Piṭakaṃ,* ed. Hermann Oldenberg (London: Pali Text Society, 1969), III.23.

97. The Buddha's stomach problems are mentioned in a number of places, including *Theragāthā* (*Paramattha-dīpanī Theragāthā-aṭṭakathā,* pp. 56–57). After his last meal, he experienced severe abdominal distress, bloody diarrhea, and sharp pains.

98. "Pubbakamma-piloti," in *The Apadāna of the Khuddaka Nikāya,* ed. Mary E. Lilley (London: Pali Text Society, 1925), pp. 299–301. The other episodes in past lives and their karmic effects on this final life are as follows: (5) he slandered an innocent solitary realizer in a former life, and so he was accused by Sundarī of sexually molesting her; (6) he jealously slandered a monk with six supernatural powers in a previous life and so was slandered by a woman named Ciñcamānavikā in this life; (7) he wrongly accused the sage Isigana of being unchaste when he was a brahman with five hundred disciples, and so the Buddha and his five hundred disciples were falsely slandered when Sundarī was murdered by a rival ascetic group that wished to tarnish the *saṃgha*'s reputation (reported in the *Udāna,* pp. 44–45); (8) in a past life, he cursed the disciples of the Buddha Vipaśyin, saying, "these bald-headed recluses should be offered horse barley"; as retribution in this life, he had to eat horse barley for three months; (9) as a brahman named Jotipāla in a past life, he reviled the buddha Kāśyapa, saying, "bald-headed recluses, awakening is difficult to attain," and for this he had to perform six years of austerities in his present life; and (10) in a past life, hatred led him to knock over a solitary realizer's bowl, and this was why he returned in this life with an empty bowl from a brahman village. These are mentioned in the *Milindapañha,* and Lamotte discusses them in his translation of the *Vimalakīrti-nirdeśa-sūtra* (*The Teaching of Vimalakīrti*), trans. Sara Boin-Webb (London: Pali Text Society, 1976), pp. 294–298. Lamotte relates these episodes to conflicting notions about the Buddha's body. Issues relating to how a Buddha can have residual bad karma are discussed by Jonathan Walters in his article, "The Buddha's Bad Karma: A Problem in the History of Theravāda Buddhism," *Numen,* vol. XXXVII, fasc. 1, 1990, pp. 70–95.

99. *Mahāvastu,* I.167–170.

100. *Lalitavistara,* p. 147.

101. The "Sekha-sutta" of the *Majjhima-nikāya* (I.354) states that when some people from Kapilavastu came to see the Buddha, he had back pain and was too distracted to preach, so he asked Ānanda to give a sermon on the higher training in his stead. At other times he asked Maudgalyāyana ("Saḷāyatana-saṃyutta," *Saṃyutta-nikāya,* IV.183–4) and Śāriputra ("Sangīti-sutta," *Dīgha-nikāya,* III.209; *Aṅguttara-nikāya,* V.122, 125) to preach in his stead for the same reason.

102. *Saṃyutta-nikāya,* V.153; a similar description is found in *Dīgha-nikāya,* II.99.

103. During the "first council," Ānanda was reportedly rebuked for several faults with regard to his service of the Buddha. One was his failure to recognize that the

Buddha was providing Ānanda with an opportunity to ask him to remain in the world. Another was Ānanda's leading role in persuading the Buddha to institute an order of nuns, which the Buddha declared would shorten the duration of the "true dharma" by five hundred years. He was also chastised for allowing some women to view the Buddha's naked body, including his sheathed penis, after he died. Ānanda defended this last action by declaring that he did so in the hope that the sight of the perfect man would make the viewers ashamed of their inferior bodies, which would lead them to plant virtuous roots, enabling them to be reborn as men.

104. "Devatā-saṃyutta," *Saṃyutta-nikāya,* I.27.

105. Buddhaghosa comments that monks who enjoy sensual pleasures lay down on their left sides and ghosts lie on their backs. "The lion, the king of beasts, lies down on its right side." He goes on to say that the lion sleeps without fear, wakes up and takes stock of its surroundings, then lets out a roar of mastery. See *The Buddha's Last Days: Buddhaghosa's Commentary on the Mahāparinibbāna-sutta,* trans. Yang-Gyu An (London: Pali Text Society, 2003), p. 137.

106. *Saṃyutta-nikāya,* I.28.

107. "Indriya-saṃyutta," *Saṃyutta-nikāya,* V.217.

108. Ernst Waldschmidt, ed., *Das Mahāparinirvāṇasūtra* (Berlin: Akademie-Verlag 1950–1951), pp. 392–394.

109. "Mahāparinibbāna-sutta," *Dīgha-nikāya,* II.143–144.

110. *Great Disciples of the Buddha: Their Lives, Their Works, Their Legacy,* trans. Nyanaponika Thera and Hellmuth Hecker (Boston: Wisdom Publications, 1997), p. 109, reports that Mahākāśyapa had seven of the thirty-two physical characteristics of a great man, but no references are provided, and I have not found any corroboration of this in Pāli or Sanskrit texts. Étienne Lamotte cites various sources that attribute thirty of the physical characteristics to Nanda and Devadatta. A brahman named Bāvari is said to possess three, and Mahākāśyapa's ex-wife is said to have one (golden skin), but Lamotte makes no specific mention of Mahākāśyapa in this connection; see *Traité de la grande vertu de sagesse* (Louvain: Institut Orientaliste, 1949), pp. 285–287. Lamotte also cites a Chinese text in which it is claimed that among the Śākyas of the Buddha's time some had three, ten, or thirty of the physical characteristics.

111. Susan L. Huntington, "Early Buddhist Art and the Theory of Aniconism," *Art Journal* 49 (1990): 401–408.

112. T 51.860b.18–23. *The Travels of Fa hsien,* trans. H. A. Giles (Cambridge: Cambridge University Press, 1923), pp. 30–31. In the *Aṭṭhasālinī* (*The Aṭṭhasālinī, Buddhaghosa's Commentary on the Dhammasaṅgaṇī,* ed. Edward Müller [London: Pali Text Society, 1979], p. 16), Buddhaghosa says that when the Buddha was in Tuṣita he created some emanational buddhas *(nirmāṇa-buddha)* that were exact replicas of himself. Humans could not distinguish them from the real Buddha in terms of body, voice, words, and the rays of light that issued from their forms; only the highest gods could tell them apart.

113. I am assuming that legends of the Buddha and his physical appearance probably began to develop and circulate during his lifetime and then were embellished and altered in subsequent centuries and that artists first began to create Buddha images several centuries after his passing, but it is probable that the actual situation was more complex than this scenario suggests. Early artists probably inherited stories and descriptions of the Buddha, and some of these are probably reflected in the texts we now have from this period, but the Buddhist canon was developing, new works were being added and earlier ones redacted by scholars, and a commentarial literature was being composed. Artistic representations may well have played a role in this process, and it is conceivable that some of the descriptions found in the canon as we know it today were inspired by Buddha figures created by artisans of this period. There could well have been a reflexive process in which (mainly oral) textual traditions dictated aspects of artistic works and images influenced buddhalogical speculations.

114. S. L. Huntington and J. C. Huntington, *Leaves from the Bodhi Tree,* p. 259. In the Pāla period, artistic depictions of the Buddha's hair were standardized into rows of small curls all forming clockwise spirals.

115. Ibid., p. 123.

116. Ibid., p. 104. This event occurred at Bodh Gaya, and the Huntingtons note that "the site of Bodh Gaya and the Vajrāsana Buddha became dynastic symbols of the Pāla reign."

117. Ibid., p. 137.

118. Jean-Luc Marion, *God without Being,* trans. Thomas Carlson (Chicago: University of Chicago Press, 1991), p. 12.

119. Ibid.

120. Ibid., pp. 13–14.

121. Ibid., p. 17.

122. Ibid., p. 18.

123. It should be noted that Buddhist texts use the term "brahman" in different senses, and the slippage between contexts can sometimes be confusing. Sometimes it refers to people born into the brahman class *(varṇa),* but in many instances the Buddha states that he reserves the term for people who have the ideal qualities of a brahman, including saintliness, contemplativeness, and so forth. He often distinguishes between brahmans who arrogantly think themselves superior to others merely because of an accident of birth that led to their occupying a high social position and others who embody Indian religious ideals. When used in the latter sense, a brahman need not be someone born into a brahman family. In this sense, there is a distinction between the social institution of brahmanhood and the ideals associated with brahman status, and the Buddha often uses this to imply that many of those who claim to be brahmans and pride themselves on their superiority fail to live up to the ideal and so are not "true brahmans." It is clear in Indian texts that not all people born into brahman families pursued religious careers. Some brahmans removed themselves from society and

pursued liberation or other religious goals, while others served as village priests and performed sacrifices (including blood sacrifices that are condemned by Buddhists) for a living, and many brahmans supported themselves in a variety of other ways.

124. He is generally referred to as Sakka (Skt. Śakra) in Pāli *suttas* and seldom as Indra, the name most often used in the Vedas. The probable reason for this is that Sakka is an epithet, and so using it sounded more familiar than "Indra," which connotes sovereignty. Thus the Buddha calls him by a name that sounds like a form of address used by a friend or a teacher in a superior position, that avoids the implicit status attribution of "Your Majesty" or "Lord."

125. *The Hymns of the Rig-Veda in the Samhita and Pada Texts,* ed. F. Max Müller (Varanasi: Chowkhamba Sanskrit Series, 1965), 1.80.15.

126. Ibid., 7.30.1.

127. Ibid., 8.66.9ab.

128. Ibid., 10.29.7ab.

3. Sex and the Single Monk

1. *Vinaya Piṭakaṃ,* III.38–39.

2. The passage asserts that she "sat down on his male organ."

3. *Vinaya Piṭakaṃ,* III.36–37. The Buddha explains that five things make a penis ready to ejaculate—sexual passion, excretion, urination, winds, and itching bites from vermin—and he asserts that it is impossible that this monk's ejaculation could have been caused by sensual desire.

4. Ibid., III.37. The passage declares that he "agreed to enter [her], agreed to having entered, agreed to remain, and agreed to withdraw [his penis]."

5. Ibid.

6. Ibid.

7. Ibid., III.39.

8. Ibid., III.38.

9. Ibid., III.111.

10. Ibid., III.8–9. The same notion is found in *Saṃyutta-nikāya,* I.223–224, and *Majjhima-nikāya,* I.444–445. The *Vinaya* passage adds that the Buddha recognized that eventually there would be a need for such rules. He stated that there were some buddhas in the past who neglected to promulgate a code of conduct, and as a result their dispensations did not last long after their deaths. The key factor, he asserted, is institution of a regular recitation of the rules *(prātimokṣa)* in a communal setting.

11. *Shan-Chien-P'i-P'o-Sha: A Chinese Version by Saṅghabhadra of Samanta-pāsādikā,* trans. P. V. Bapat and A. Hirakawa (Poona: Bhandarkar Oriental Research Institute, 1970) p. 139.

12. *Vinaya Piṭakaṃ,* III.15–18.

13. Ibid., III.20–21.

14. I assume from the context and the Buddha's words that Sudinna was expelled, even though the text does not explicitly state this. He is said to have committed "an offence involving defeat" and so was no longer in communion with the order, which would seem to entail that he could not continue as a member.

15. *Shan-Chien-P'i-P'o-Sha,* p. 156.

16. Ibid., p. 163.

17. The Pāli term is *odantika,* literally meaning "final ablution"; the connotation is that it is a bath one takes after having sex. The terms used in this section are apparently meant to indicate that when people have sex they experience a sense of shame and feel soiled, and so they engage in such acts in hiding and then wash themselves afterward.

18. *Vinaya Piṭakaṃ,* III.29.

19. *Shan-Chien-P'i-P'o-Sha,* pp. 197–198.

20. *Vinaya Piṭakaṃ,* III.28.

21. Buddhaghosa comments that this is because the three orifices have flesh that is easily stimulated, leading to sexual pleasure. He adds that sexual deviants have only two erogenous zones but does not explain why this is the case (*Shan-Chien-P'i-P'o-Sha,* p. 198). In her translation of the *Vinaya,* I. B. Horner avoids spelling out the three orifices (rectum, vagina, and mouth). Throughout this section, which contains a number of sexually explicit passages, she either omits material or uses sanitized language. In the introduction, she states: "because of the outspokenness and crudeness which it contains . . . [it] appears unsuitable for incorporation in a translation designed principally for Western readers" (III.197). Despite apparently being scandalized by some of the language, she helpfully provides a complete version of the Pāli text in the notes.

22. *Vinaya Piṭakaṃ,* III.28–29. Buddhaghosa elaborates on this unlikely scenario, in which a monk's enemies, seeking to entice him to break his vows, bring a woman to his residence, force him to the floor, pin down his limbs, and then insert his organ into her rectum, vagina, or mouth. If he resists throughout the ordeal, he is blameless, but if he ejaculates or enjoys it in any way he is guilty of an offense (*Shan-Chien-P'i-P'o-Sha,* p. 198).

23. *Vinaya Piṭakaṃ,* III.36.

24. The text states that she proposed that he should "stroke" or "rub" *(ghaṭṭeti)* inside her and withdraw before ejaculation or stroke outside and ejaculate inside, apparently thinking that these permutations vary sufficiently from the standard act of copulation to fall outside the stated rules.

25. *Vinaya Piṭakaṃ,* III.37.

26. Ibid. In a similar but bizarre story, a monk reportedly fell in love with a woman who died before he could tell her how he felt. He later gathered her bones and fornicated with them. This was declared to be a lesser offense of wrongdoing (*Vinaya Piṭakaṃ,* III.37). Sex with the living is always more problematic than necrophilia in the estimation of the compilers of the *Vinaya. Vinaya Piṭakaṃ,* III.37–38, contains

stories of monks who had sex with a female *nāga,* a female *yakṣa,* a female ghost, and a sexual deviant; all were expelled from the order, while monks who committed acts of necrophilia performed expiation and were reinstated.

27. Foucault, *The Will to Knowledge,* p. 24.

28. Serinity Young, *Courtesans and Tantric Consorts: Sexualities in Buddhist Narrative, Iconography, and Ritual* (New York: Routledge, 2004), p. 5.

29. *Itivuttaka,* p. 114.

30. "Eka-nipāta," *Aṅguttara-nikāya,* I.1–2. In another sermon in the same collection, the Buddha returns to the same theme: "Monks, women ensnare the minds of men: whether walking, standing still, sitting, or lying down, whether laughing, talking, singing, or crying, whether sick or even dying, women ensnare the minds of men" (*Aṅguttara-nikāya,* III.68).

31. See Thomas Laqueur, "Orgasm, Generation, and the Politics of Reproductive Biology," in *The Making of the Modern Body: Sexuality and Society in the Nineteenth Century,* eds. Catherine Gallagher and Thomas Laqueur (Berkeley: University of California Press, 1987), p. 4. Laqueur argues that in the classical West the heat of men was considered a sign of their greater perfection, but in India the exact opposite is the case. Coolness is better, and men have it in greater abundance than women.

32. See Wendy Doniger and Sudhir Kakar, trans, *Vatsyayana Kamasutra* (Oxford: Oxford University Press, 2003), p. 33.

33. *Atthasālinī (Dhammasaṅgaṇī Commentary,* ed. Edward Müller; London: Pali Text Society, 1979), p. 70. In *Visuddhimagga,* ed. Caroline Rhys Davids (London: Pali Text Society, 1975), p. 211, Buddhaghosa compares women to demons *(yakṣa).* Demons disguise their true form so they can devour victims, and women adorn themselves with clothes and makeup to hide physical defects and ensnare men.

34. Patrick Olivelle, trans., *Saṃnyāsa Upaniṣads* (New York: Oxford University Press, 1992), p. 213.

35. *Majjhima-nikāya,* I.426.

36. Wendy Doniger, *Asceticism and Eroticism in the Mythology of Śiva* (Delhi: Oxford University Press, 1975), p. 55.

37. *Ṛg Veda,* 1.179.4.

38. *Theragāthā-aṭṭhakathā,* I.141.

39. *Vinaya Piṭakaṃ,* III.35. When he reported the incident to the Buddha, Sundara was asked whether he had assented; when he indicated that he had not, he was absolved of wrongdoing.

40. *Ṛṣipañcaka-jātaka,* in *Five Buddhist Legends in the Campū Style,* p. 16.

41. *Dīgha-nikāya,* II.141.

42. *Vinaya Piṭakaṃ,* IV.132–133.

43. "Satipaṭṭhāna-saṃyutta," *Saṃyutta-nikāya,* V.170. The *Buddhacarita* presents a similar notion, stating that it would be better for a man to venture into the neighborhood of an enemy with a drawn sword or a poisonous snake than to go near a

woman if he does not have mindfulness and wisdom. Aśvaghoṣa adds that women entice men "whether sitting or lying down, whether walking or standing, even when portrayed in pictures." They are "pre-eminent in power" and "conceal their real nature" (*Buddhacarita,* part 2, p. 65).

44. David White notes that semen is called *saumya* (lunar) and is linked with the moon. The association of the moon with semen also relates to the sun: semen and the moon are cold, while the sun (associated with women) is hot, and the two are antithetical to each other. When the moon gets close to the sun his essence is dissipated; similarly, female uterine fluid is related with heat and semen with coolness, and so females are said to dissipate men with the heat of their lust. See White, *The Alchemical Body: Siddha Traditions in Medieval India* (Chicago: University of Chicago Press, 1996), p. 25.

45. See *Taittirīya Saṃhitā with the Commentary of Mādhava,* ed. Rajendralal Misra (Calcutta: Bibliotheca Indica, 1860), 2.3.5.1–3; *Maitrāyaṇī Saṃhitā (Die Saṃhitā der Maitrāyaṇīya-Śākhā),* ed. Leopold von Schroeder (Wiesbaden: Franz Steiner Verlag, 1972), 21.7; and *Kāṭhaka Saṃhitā,* ed. Leopold von Schroeder (Wiesbaden: Steiner Verlag, 1970–1972), 11.3. The myth has its origins in *Ṛg Veda* 10.85.2, in which Candra is replenished by taking more *rasa.* Humans can achieve the same result through elixir therapy *(rasāyana).*

46. *The Caraka Saṃhitā,* III.9866.

47. *Agniveśa's Caraka Saṃhitā,* vol. III, p. 9871, states that semen melts like ghee during sexual intercourse and moves from its natural residence in bodily tissues into the seminal vesicle.

48. *Mahābhārata,* 12.207.21; quoted in Doniger, *Women, Androgynes, and Other Mythical Beasts,* p. 49. The *Mahābhārata* adds that a man who restrains his desires develops seed that is rich like butter. The *Caraka Saṃhitā,* III.1381, asserts that just as sugar pervades the whole cane, so semen pervades the whole body; it is "a formative principle in all bodies in the universe."

49. *Caraka Saṃhitā,* 1.25.39; quoted in Doniger, *Women, Androgynes, and Other Mythical Beasts,* p. 45.

50. *Agniveśa's Caraka Saṃhitā,* vol. V, ch. XXX.191, p. 176.

51. Ibid., vol. V, ch. XXX.134, p. 164. He also says that semen can become polluted due to excessive physical exercise, by inserting one's penis into orifices other than the vagina, from sex with women who are not passionate, and from old age, worry, grief, injury by sharp instruments, burning, and other factors, such as black magic. He also warns that fasting and aversion toward women can lead to impotence.

52. Doniger, *Women, Androgynes, and Other Mythical Beasts,* p. 44.

53. Peter Brown, *The Body and Society: Men, Women and Sexual Renunciation in Early Christianity* (New York: Columbia University Press, 1988), p. 19.

54. Joseph S. Alter, *The Wrestler's Body: Identity and Ideology in North India* (Berkeley: University of California Press, 1992), p. 129.

55. Alter, *The Wrestler's Body,* p. 130.

56. *Yoga-tattva,* cited by Mircea Eliade, *Yoga: Immortality and Freedom* (London: Routledge & Kegan Paul, 1958), p. 129.

57. See Kenneth Zysk, *Asceticism and Healing in Ancient India: Medicine in the Buddhist Monastery* (New York: Oxford University Press, 1991), p. 4. Dominik Wujastyk agrees with the thrust of this hypothesis in *The Roots of Āyurveda: Selections from Sanskrit Medieval Writings* (New Delhi: Penguin Books, 1998), p. 2.

58. Monier Monier-Williams, *A Sanskrit-English Dictionary* (Delhi: Motilal Banarsidass, 1979), p. 580.

59. Yaśomitra's list includes castrated men *(lūṇa-paṇḍaka)* in the place of *oppakamika-paṇḍaka.* Asaṅga provides a list of five types that are mostly the same: (1) sexual deviant by birth *(jāti-paṇḍaka),* (2) envious sexual deviant *(īrṣyā-paṇḍaka),* (3) sexual deviant for a fortnight *(pakṣa-paṇḍaka),* (4) moistened sexual deviant *(āsecanaka-paṇḍaka),* and (5) sexual deviant through effort *(āpata-paṇḍaka).* Asaṅga states that *paṇḍaka*s can take on the discipline of a lay disciple but cannot be given lay disciple status because it is not suitable for them to associate with the monastic community. See *Abhidharma-samuccaya,* ed. Nathmal Tatia (Patna: K. P. Jayaswal Research Institute, 1975), p. 68.

60. Wendy Doniger states that the word *napuṃsaka* designates eunuchs, impotent men, and androgynes; see *Women, Androgynes, and Other Mythical Beasts,* p. 308.

61. Zwilling, "Homosexuality as Seen in Indian Buddhist Texts," p. 204.

62. Monier-Williams, *A Sanskrit-English Dictionary,* p. 170.

63. *Samantapāsādikā,* V.1015–1017.

64. *Abhidharmakośa,* pp. 226–227. In another section (pp. 38–39), Vasubandhu asserts that eunuchs and bisexual beings are alien to (1) the dharmas of defilement, lack of discipline, and moral transgression, having cut off the roots of good; and (2) the dharmas of purification, discipline, acquisition of the fruits of training, and detachment.

65. *Samantapāsādikā,* V.1042.

66. Quoted in Gary Taylor, *Castration: An Abbreviated History of Western Manhood* (New York: Routledge, 2000), p. 144.

67. *Abhidharmakośa,* p. 260. Caraka states that when a man is born without testes it is the result of in utero damage and blames this on the mother. He also links sexual pathologies to use of abnormal sexual positions by parents (*The Caraka Saṃhitā,* III.1012).

68. *The Caraka Saṃhitā,* III.1001.

69. Ibid., III.1061. See also Ronald B. Inden and Ralph Nicholas, *Kinship in Bengali Culture* (Chicago: University of Chicago Press, 1976), pp. 54–55. *The Suśruta Saṃhitā* states that if there are equal amounts of semen and blood, the child will be a eunuch (3.3.5).

70. *Vinaya Piṭakaṃ,* I.85: *etha maṃ āyasmanto dūsethā.*

71. In Indian literature, these are the sort of people who commonly commit lewd deeds. The *Kāmasūtra,* for example (*Kāmasūtra of Vātsyāyana,* S. C. Upadhyaya,

trans.; Bombay, 1963, 2.9.35), states that "low persons, such as slaves and elephant drivers" are the sort of people who engage in deviant sexual practices.

72. *Vinaya Piṭakaṃ,* I.85–86.

73. Every discussion of these beings I have seen in Indian literature presents them in uniformly negative terms, but Janet Gyatso cites a Tibetan medical text in which they are said to be an ideal type for Buddhist practice because their sexual energies are evenly balanced between male and female. See Gyatso, "One Plus One Makes Three: Buddhist Gender, Monasticism, and the Law of the Non-Excluded Middle," *History of Religions* 43, no. 2 (2003): 89–115.

74. Stephan Beyer, *The Buddhist Experience* (Encino, CA: Dickenson, 1974), p. 85. Beyer states that he believes this text probably was composed in Central Asia around the seventh century, but he adds that its attitudes reflect Indian notions. The text also lists four reasons for rebirth as a hermaphrodite, described as "the lowest possible state among men": "1. uncleanness where there should be reverence and respect; 2. lust for the bodies of other men; 3. the practice of lustful things upon his own body; and 4. the exposure and sale of himself in the guise of a woman to other men."

75. Zwilling, "Homosexuality as Seen in Indian Buddhist Texts," p. 205.

76. *Kṣudrakavastu,* Sde dge *tha,* pp. 39a.6–b.5; quoted by Gregory Schopen, *Buddhist Monks and Business Matters: Still More Papers on Monastic Buddhism in India* (Honolulu: University of Hawai'i Press, 2004), p. 26. Another monk, "tormented by dissatisfaction," cut off his own penis in order to eradicate his lustful desires, but the Buddha admonished him, saying, "monks, that stupid man cut off one thing, but another should have been cut off [i.e., his desire]" (*Vinaya Piṭakaṃ,* II.110).

77. *Vinaya Piṭakaṃ,* II.110.

78. Debates regarding celibacy have raged within Christian churches down to the present day. Although many of the early church fathers valorized celibacy and considered it to be a way to attain saintliness, other theologians have condemned the practice. Luther, for instance, viewed clerical celibacy as unnatural, and Calvin spoke against the "tyranny" and "cruelty" of a practice that would "strangle millions of souls by the cruel cords of a wicked and diabolical law." He viewed it as desexualization, a practice that turns men into women, "making a female creature out of a male." Luther also stated that such clerics "unman themselves" (quoted by Gary Taylor in *Castration,* p. 78).

79. G. Taylor, *Castration,* p. 193.

80. "Sabbāsava-sutta," *Majjhima-nikāya,* I.11.

81. G. Taylor, *Castration,* p. 79.

82. *Vinaya Piṭakaṃ,* I.89. Buddhaghosa, however, believes that only *napuṃsaka-paṇḍakas*, *pakkha-paṇḍakas*, and *oppakkamika-paṇḍakas* are excluded (*Samantapāsādikā,* p. 1016). The *Vinaya* also prohibits recitation of the *prātimokṣa* in the presence of sexual deviants or hermaphrodites as well as other distasteful people, such as seducers of nuns, schismatics, or a person who has killed his or her mother, father, or an arhat (*Vinaya Piṭakaṃ,* I.134).

83. *Vinaya Piṭakaṃ,* I.90–91. *Vinaya Piṭakaṃ,* I.93, adds still more classes of people who cannot be ordained: people with eczema, leprosy, consumption, and epilepsy.

84. Quoted by Olivelle, *Saṃnyāsa Upaniṣads,* p. 174. He cites a similar passage on p. 242 from the *Bṛhat Saṃnyāsa Upaniṣad.*

85. *Vinaya Piṭakaṃ,* I.93. People seeking ordination are also asked whether they are free (i.e., not slaves) or in the armed services and whether they have parental consent. For full ordination, a man must also be at least twenty years old and have a preceptor who has agreed to provide religious instruction. *Vinaya Piṭakaṃ,* II.270–271, contains a list of prerequisites for women seeking ordination, all of which relate to their physical appearance, health, and how they would be perceived by others as representatives of the *saṃgha.* The regulations forbid ordination of women who do not look like women, are sexually deficient, have stagnant blood, dress like men, and whose bodies ooze too much or are deformed, as well as those who are female sexual deviants, are "man-like women," have indistinct sexuality, or are female hermaphrodites. The passage indicates that women should be questioned about these things before they are given ordination.

86. *Vinaya Piṭakaṃ,* I.34.

87. *Samantapāsādikā,* I.254.

88. *Vinaya Piṭakaṃ,* III.110–112.

89. A seminal discussion of Western notions about masturbation is Thomas Laqueur's *Solitary Sex: A Cultural History of Masturbation* (New York: Zone Books, 2003). Roy Porter and Lesley Hall discuss the notion that masturbation leads to physical degeneration in *The Facts of Life: The Creation of Sexual Knowledge in Britain, 1650–1950* (New Haven, CT: Yale University Press, 1995), pp. 28–30 and 91–105.

90. There are also a number of accounts of auto-eroticism among Buddhist nuns and rules prohibiting such behavior. One such nun, described as a former concubine of a king (*Vinaya Piṭakaṃ,* IV.261), fashioned a dildo for herself. One day she forgot to hide it, and a "modest" nun reported her. The Buddha declared that making a device to stimulate the genitals is an offense. On another occasion, he agreed with his stepmother, Prajāpatī, that women's genitals emit an offensive smell and that nuns should be allowed to insert a cloth into them while bathing, but in order to ensure that this not lead to sensuality he stated that their fingers should not penetrate beyond two finger joints (*Vinaya Piṭakaṃ,* IV.262).

91. *Saṃyutta-nikāya,* V.420.

92. *Dīgha-nikāya,* I.7.

93. *A Path of Righteousness: Dhammapada,* ed. David J. Kalupahana (Lanham, MD: University Press of America, 1986), verse 361, p. 105.

94. This is apparently a different Udāyin from the one encountered in Chapter 2, who was a priest's son and reportedly encouraged the Bodhisattva to indulge in sensual pleasures. G. P. Malasekera reports that this Udāyin was an elder *(thera)* who had a cruel streak and killed some crows, following which he cut off their heads. He was

also reportedly rather corpulent, but still well liked by women. See Malasekera, *Dictionary of Pāli Proper Names* (Delhi: Munishram Manoharlal Publishers, 1998), p. 276.

95. *Vinaya Piṭakaṃ,* III.119–121.

96. Ibid., III.127–128.

97. Ibid., III.128.

98. Ibid., III.131–132.

99. The commentary on this term (Ibid., III.187) states that "comfortable" means that it is convenient for sexual activities.

100. *Vinaya Piṭakaṃ,* IV.68, reports another incident in which Udāyin met privately with his former wife, and the Buddha declared that it is an offense for monks and nuns to sit together in private. But he added that it is permissible if the monk stands while the nun sits, or if he sits but thinks of something other than sex, or if he is insane.

101. Ibid., III.205–206.

102. Ibid., IV.20–21.

103. Foucault, *The Will to Knowledge,* p. 96.

104. Ibid.

105. Brown, *The Body and Society,* p. 39.

106. Connell, *Masculinities,* p. 214.

107. Foucault, *The Will to Knowledge,* p. 21.

108. *Vinaya Piṭakaṃ,* III.24.

109. Ibid., IV.459.

110. Ibid., IV.259–260. *Vinaya Piṭakaṃ,* I.293, reports a variation of this story, in which a group of nuns bathed naked with some prostitutes. The prostitutes made fun of them: "Why are you celibate when you are young? Surely you should be enjoying the pleasures of the senses! When you are old, then become celibate; thus you will experience both extremes." The nuns became ashamed when they were ridiculed, and a monk who witnessed the scene declared: "nakedness of women is impure, it is abhorrent, it is objectionable." He suggested that nuns use bathing cloths when washing, which was later adopted as a norm. The *Vinaya* also prohibits various sorts of hair-related affectations, such as long hair, beards, moustaches, goatees, or shaped chest hair (*Vinaya Piṭakaṃ,* I.133–134).

111. Ibid., I.304.

112. The Buddha rejects the practice of nakedness in several other places. In *Vinaya Piṭakaṃ,* I.90, for example, a monk who owns no clothes is ordained, and he is unable to obtain robes and goes begging in the nude. People who see him declare that Buddhist monks are just like ascetics of other sects, and the Buddha responds by issuing a rule forbidding monks from being naked in public.

113. Ibid., IV.15–16. In a variation on the nakedness theme, *Vinaya Piṭakaṃ,* II.121, describes a group of monks who greeted naked people, caused others who were naked to greet them, and gave things to naked men and accepted things in return. They also

ate food while naked. The Buddha mandated that monks should always be fully clothed and that they must wear three robes when in public.

114. Ibid., II.222.

115. Ibid., II.137.

116. Ibid., II.140.

117. Halperin, "How to Do the History of Male Homosexuality," p. 96.

118. José Ignacio Cabezón, "Homosexuality and Buddhism," in *Homosexuality and World Religions,* ed. Arlene Swidler (Valley Forge, PA: Trinity Press International, 1993), p. 82.

119. *Samantapāsādikā,* II.261.

120. *Vinaya Piṭakaṃ,* I.79–80.

121. Foucault, *The Will to Knowledge,* p. 39.

122. Yaśodhara's commentary on the *Kāmasūtra,* for example, uses the expression "third nature" (*tṛtīyā prakṛti,* or neuter gender) to designate people who are neither male nor female, including hermaphrodites; see *Kāmasūtra of Vātsyāyana,* p. 186.

123. Beyer, *The Buddhist Experience,* pp. 52–53.

124. *Shan-Chien-P'i-P'o-Sha,* p. 169. The *Vinaya Piṭakaṃ,* I.61, has another story of a monk who had sex with a female monkey.

125. *Vinaya Piṭakaṃ,* I.33–34.

126. Ibid., I.190.

127. *Samantapāsādikā,* I.259.

128. *Shan-Chien-P'i-P'o-Sha,* p. 196.

129. Janet Gyatso, "Sex," in *Critical Terms for the Study of Buddhism,* ed. Donald S. Lopez Jr. (Chicago: University of Chicago Press, 2005), pp. 271–272.

130. Sukumar Dutt, *Buddhist Monks and Monasteries of India* (Delhi: Motilal Banarsidass, 1989), p. 76. He adds that when one examines these accounts closely, "their invented character becomes transparent."

131. Foucault, *The Will to Knowledge,* p. 23.

132. *Udāna,* pp. 21–33. Nanda's story is recounted in detail by Aśvaghoṣa in *Handsome Nanda (Saundara-nanda),* which has been edited and translated by E. H. Johnston as *The Saundarananda, or Nanda the Fair* (Kyoto: Rinsen Books, 1971).

133. *Theragāthā-aṭṭhakathā,* II.14.

134. *Udāna,* pp. 5–6.

135. *Theragāthā-aṭṭhakathā,* I.52–53. A similar account is given of the arhat Puṇṇamāsa in *Theragāthā-aṭṭhakathā* I.38–39.

136. "Devatā-saṃyutta," *Saṃyutta-nikāya,* I.9.

137. Ibid., I.9. In a variation on this theme, "Māra-saṃyutta," *Saṃyutta-nikāya,* I.117, reports that Māra once appeared to the monks in the guise of a brahman, "with large matted hairknot, clad in an antelope hide, old, crooked like a roof bracket, holding a staff of *udambara* wood," all of which represent Vedic authority. He repeated the exhortation quoted in text, and the monks gave the same reply as Samiddhi.

138. *Visuddhimagga,* p. 270.

139. *Theragāthā-aṭṭhakathā,* I.99.

140. *Udāna,* pp. 39–40.

141. *Theragāthā-aṭṭhakathā,* II.263–264.

142. "Opamma-saṃyutta," *Saṃyutta-nikāya,* II.268–272. The Buddha concludes by urging monks to use wooden pillows in order to keep the evil one at bay.

143. *Theragāthā-aṭṭhakathā,* I.178.

144. *Theragāthā-aṭṭhakathā,* II.104–105. A similar description of Maudgalyāyana states that he "tears apart the army of death . . . knocks down the army of death as an elephant knocks down a reed hut" (*Theragāthā-aṭṭhakathā,* III.106). A later passage states that "these numerous famous gods, with supernormal powers, 10,000 gods with Brahmā at their head, stand with cupped hands revering Maudgalyāyana. Homage to you, thoroughbred stallion of a man, homage to you, best of men!" (*Theragāthā-aṭṭhakathā,* III.108).

145. Ibid., I.107.

146. A number of others, like Piṇḍola, are described as learned brahmans with a deep knowledge of the Vedas who became dissatisfied with the lore they studied and joined the order. Piṇḍola is described as "chief among the lion-roarers" (Ibid., II.4–5).

147. Ibid., I.89–90. *Vinaya Piṭakaṃ,* I.178–179, has a similar description of a merchant's son named Soṇa Koḷivisa, who "was delicately nurtured" and had downy hair on the soles of his feet. *Theragāthā-aṭṭhakathā,* II.275, states that he was generous to a solitary realizer in a previous life and was born with a body like gold, with fine golden hair on the soles of his feet and palms. He was raised in luxury, and so the monks he approached for ordination feared that he lacked the requisite toughness of a world renouncer, but he reportedly persevered and became an exemplary ascetic.

148. *Theragāthā-aṭṭhakathā,* II.36.

149. *Itivuttaka,* pp. 75–76.

150. *Theragāthā-aṭṭhakathā,* II.255–256.

151. Ibid., II.272–273.

152. *Sutta-nipāta,* ed. Dines Andersen and Helmer Smith (London: Pali Text Society, 1990), p. 12. A later section contains a similar sentiment: "The monk who abhors the world will seek out a lonely lodging under trees, in mountain caves; for him who delights in these various lodgings, what dangers are there? The monk does not tremble in his quiet dwelling. How many dangers are there in the world to be overcome by a monk living in solitary dwellings and going toward the region of immortality?" (*Sutta-nipāta,* p. 186).

153. *Theragāthā-aṭṭhakathā,* I.80.

154. "Devatā-saṃyutta," *Saṃyutta-nikāya,* I.5.

155. *Udāna,* pp. 18–20.

156. *Theragāthā-aṭṭhakathā,* I.238.

157. "Bakkula-sutta," *Majjhima-nikāya,* III.126–128.

158. *Visuddhimagga,* pp. 20–21.

159. *Theragāthā-aṭṭhakathā,* II.193–200. A similar story is told of Bāgasamāla, who saw a beautiful woman dancing while he was seeking alms. He too saw that she was like a death snare spread out to trap him, and realizing the danger, he developed profound disgust for the world and also became an arhat. The story of Candana also repeats this theme; in this instance Candana's former wife attempted unsuccessfully to seduce him (*Theragāthā-aṭṭhakathā,* II.126).

160. "Kukkuravatika-sutta," *Majjhima-nikāya,* I.387–392.

161. *Abhidharmakośa,* pp. 282–283. *Abhidharmakośa,* p. 136, describes people of other orders who are attached to rules and rituals or take vows to act like a bull or a dog. It also describes the Nirgranthas, who adopt vows of nudity; brahmans who always carry a staff or wear antelope hides; and Paśupātas with matted hair and bodies smeared with ashes. On p. 241 Vasubandhu asserts that in the *gosava* sacrifice, a brahman will drink water like a cow, graze in grass, and "have sex with his mother, his sister, or a woman of his clan; he must copulate with them wherever he finds them. In this manner this bull [believes that] he will conquer the world."

162. "Dhamma-cetiya-sutta," *Majjhima-nikāya,* II.121–122.

163. Ibid., II.121–122.

164. *Saṃyutta-nikāya,* I.78.

165. Patrick Olivelle notes that world renouncers shaved the tops of their heads and their faces, but not their armpits or crotches (*Saṃnyāsa Upaniṣads,* p. 124).

166. Walter O. Kaelber, *Tapta Mārga: Asceticism and Initiation in Vedic India* (Albany: State University of New York Press, 1989), p. 20.

167. "Brahmajāla-sutta," *Dīgha-nikāya,* I.1–46, describes a range of views and practices attributed to other orders and compares them unfavorably with the Buddha's doctrine.

168. *Visuddhimagga,* p. 507.

169. *Sutta-nipāta,* p. 67, verse 381.

170. *Udāna,* pp. 43–44.

171. Lock and Scheper-Hughes, "The Mindful Body," p. 31.

172. *Saṃyutta-nikāya,* II.269.

173. *Visuddhimagga,* pp. 26–27.

174. Foucault, *The Will to Knowledge,* p. 125.

175. Ibid.

176. Connell, *Masculinities,* p. 43.

4. The Problem with Bodies

1. See Ohnuma, *Head, Eyes, Flesh, and Blood,* pp. 217–218, for a discussion of this paradox. On p. 220 she notes: "the same body that the bodhisattva denigrates as foul and impure . . . is treated by others . . . as sacred and physically beautiful." She adds that even the corpse of an advanced bodhisattva is described as beautiful.

2. *Visuddhimagga,* pp. 128–129.

3. "Māgandiya-sutta," *Majjhima-nikāya,* I.510.

4. *Sutta-nipāta,* p. 34.

5. *Theragāthā-aṭṭhakathā,* II.242–243.

6. *Dhammapada,* p. 88, verse 124.

7. "Mahāsaccaka-sutta," *Majjhima-nikāya,* I.237–247.

8. Ibid., I.233–234.

9. There are a number of such classifications in Indian Buddhist texts. One extensive classification can be seen in *Pañcaviṃśati-sāhasrikā-prajñā-pāramitā-sūtra,* pp. 19–20.

10. "Mahārāhulovāda-sutta," *Majjhima-nikāya,* I.424.

11. *Abhidharmakośa,* pp. 337–338.

12. Ibid., pp. 338–339.

13. The image is much like a hunter with a baited trap. Lustful women know that Buddhist monks like to meditate on corpses, and so they lurk nearby waiting for an unsuspecting monk to approach in preparation for performing this meditation.

14. *Visuddhimagga,* pp. 180–188; *Atthasālinī,* pp. 197–200.

15. *Theragāthā-aṭṭhakathā,* II.133–136.

16. *Visuddhimagga,* pp. 194–196; *Atthasālinī,* p. 200.

17. *Vinaya Piṭakaṃ,* III.68–70. The same story is found in the "Ānāpāna-saṃyutta," *Saṃyutta-nikāya,* V.320–322.

18. See *Visuddhimagga,* p. 184.

19. Ibid., p. 198.

20. Ibid., pp. 212–213.

21. Ibid., p. 213.

22. This story is found in John Strong, *The Legend and Cult of Upagupta* (Princeton, NJ: Princeton University Press, 1992), p. 105.

23. "Sevitabbāsevitabba-sutta," *Majjhima-nikāya,* III.46–48. A similar passage is found in *Dīgha-nikāya,* II.281–282.

24. "Vedanā-saṃyutta," *Saṃyutta-nikāya,* IV.211–213. *Majjhima-nikāya,* I.181, and *Dīgha-nikāya,* I.70–71, contain similar passages.

25. *Saṃyutta-nikāya,* IV.211–212. See also *Saṃyutta-nikāya,* V.151–152.

26. "Kāyagatāsati-sutta," *Majjhima-nikāya,* III.89.

27. "Satipaṭṭhāna-sutta," *Majjhima-nikāya,* I.57.

28. The four great elements *(mahābhūta)* are an important concept in Indian philosophy and medical literature. They are the basic components of all material things, and their various combinations account for the diversity of phenomena in the universe. According to Vasubandhu (*Abhidharmakośa,* p. 8), the great elements are so called because "they bear their own unique characteristics, as well as those derived from secondary matter. They are called 'great' because they are the point of support for all derived matter. Or it is because they assemble on a large scale in the mass of the earth, water, fire, and air, where their modes of activity are manifested together."

29. "Mahāsatipaṭṭhāna-sutta," *Dīgha-nikāya,* II.295.

30. *Dīgha-nikāya,* II.290–294. *Dīgha-nikāya,* II.94–95, contains a similar passage.

31. *Majjhima-nikāya,* III.99.

32. *Abhidharmakośa,* p. 342.

33. *Visuddhimagga,* p. 306.

34. "Nidāna-saṃyutta," *Saṃyutta-nikāya,* II.82–83.

35. *Majjhima-nikāya,* I.186.

36. Ibid., I.185.

37. "Mahārāhulovāda-sutta," *Majjhima-nikāya,* I.421–422.

38. "Sāmaññaphala-sutta," *Dīgha-nikāya,* I.77.

39. *Dhammapada,* p. 81, v. 41.

40. *Atthasālinī,* pp. 322–323.

41. Zysk, *Asceticism and Healing in Ancient India,* p. 4.

42. Dominik Wujastyk, *The Roots of Āyurveda: Selections from Sanskrit Medieval Writings* (New Delhi: Penguin Books, 1998), p. 40.

43. Ibid., p. 2.

44. *Agniveśa's Caraka Saṃhitā,* vol. II, p. 354; *The Caraka Saṃhitā,* vol. III, p. 1001. This notion was also found in early Western medical texts. See Thomas Laqueur, *Making Sex: Body and Gender from the Greeks to Freud* (Cambridge, MA: Harvard University Press, 1990), pp. 39–40, for a discussion of Hippocrates' ideas on the subject.

45. *Agniveśa's Caraka Saṃhitā,* vol. II, p. 351.

46. Ibid., vol. II, p. 351.

47. *The Caraka Saṃhitā,* vol. III, p. 1012.

48. Ibid., vol. III, p. 1011.

49. Ibid., vol. III, p. 1061.

50. *Agniveśa's Caraka Saṃhitā,* vol. II, p. 356. These are described in the *Suśruta Śārira,* 2.38–40. According to Ben Barker-Benfield, Western medical thought up to the late nineteenth century also associated fetal abnormalities and physical deficiencies with weak sperm, which was said to result from poor diet, lack of exercise, or excessive shedding of semen; see Barker-Benfield, "The Spermatic Economy: A Nineteenth Century View of Sexuality," *Feminist Studies* 1, no. 1 (1972): 50.

51. *Shan-Chien-P'i-P'o-Sha,* p. 158.

52. *Agniveśa's Caraka Saṃhitā,* vol. II, p. 467.

53. This is a common notion in Indian literature. White foods such as rice or barley are believed to produce better quality sperm. The *Viṣṇu Purāṇa* (II.566), for example, contains a story of a man who desired a son and prepared a dish of rice, barley, pulse, butter, and milk for himself in order to increase the potency of his sperm, hoping to "give birth to a prince of martial prowess," but his wife inadvertently ate the dish, and so he chastised her and started the process again.

54. *The Caraka Saṃhitā,* vol. III, p. 1013.

55. *Agniveśa's Caraka Saṃhitā,* vol. II, p. 467.

56. *The Caraka Saṃhitā,* vol. III, p. 1121.

57. This was also a common notion in Enlightenment medical discourses in Europe. See Porter and Hall, *The Facts of Life,* pp. 87–88.

58. *The Caraka Saṃhitā,* vol. III, p. 1013.

59. Ibid., vol. I, p. 14.4–7. See also Wujastyk, *The Roots of Āyurveda,* pp. 155ff., which contains a passage from Suśruta that describes the process of refinement.

60. *The Caraka Saṃhitā,* vol. III, p. 1381.

61. Doniger, *Women, Androgynes, and Other Mythical Beasts,* p. 20.

62. The fact that women regularly lose menstrual blood during their monthly periods is one of the reasons why they are considered congenitally weaker than men in Indian medical literature. Men who practice self-control can retain their semen and thus acquire power, but women helplessly shed their vital energies.

63. *Shan-Chien-P'i-P'o-Sha,* p. 158. On p. 356, semen is distinguished by color. Buddhaghosa lists ten kinds: blue, yellow, red, white, wood-colored, skin-colored, oil-colored, milk-colored, butter-colored, and ghee-colored. He adds that if "even the amount that can satisfy a fly" is intentionally emitted by a monk, this constitutes an offense.

64. *The Caraka Saṃhitā,* vol. III, pp. 1359ff.

65. Ibid., vol. III, p. 1362. On p. 1011 he states that men who wish to replenish their semen should ingest substances that are white in color, oily, and cooling, all of which are associated with semen both in popular literature and in medical lore in India. He suggests that rice, barley, milk, and ghee are good choices.

66. Ibid., vol. III, p. 1369.

67. Ibid., vol. III, p. 1364.

68. Ibid., vol. III, p. 1388. There appears to be some contradiction here with the notion that men should guard their semen and emit as little as possible. Perhaps the imperative to produce sons overrides such concerns. It also appears that the concoction produces such large quantities of semen that the man will have plentiful reserves.

69. Ibid., vol. III, p. 1355.

70. *The Bṛhat saṃhitā of Varāha Mihira,* trans. N. C. Iyer (Delhi: Sri Satguru Publications, 1987), chap. 69. In his extensive classification of penis types, Varāha Mihira states that if the penis leans to the left, a man will be poor; if it is crooked, he will have no sons and be poor; if it points down to the ground, he will be poor; if it is covered with muscles, he will have few sons; if the tip is large, he will live in comfort; if the tip is soft, he will have urinary diseases; if the tip cannot be seen, he will be a king; if the penis is long, he will be poor; if it is straight and round or small with sinews, he will be rich. Men with one testicle will die by drowning. If the testicles are of differing shapes, a man will have a strong desire for sexual intercourse; if they are both the same shape, he will be a king; if they hang down, he will live for one hundred years. If the tip is red, he will be rich; if it is white or of dull color, he will be poor; if he makes a strong noise when urinating, he will have a comfortable life; but if his urination is silent, he will be poor.

71. *Kāmasūtra,* ed. Devadatta Shastri, 2.1.4–6; see also Zysk, *Conjugal Love in India,* pp. 71–73.

72. In *Making Sex: Body and Gender from the Greeks to Freud,* Laqueur discusses this idea at length.

73. Wujastyk, *The Roots of Āyurveda,* pp. 5–6. This notion is also found in the *Kāma Sūtra,* 2.1.16–18.

74. Wujastyk, *The Roots of Āyurveda,* pp. 5–6.

75. Kaelber, *Tapta Mārga,* p. 40.

76. The notion that conception can occur by drinking semen is also mentioned by Wendy Doniger in *Asceticism and Eroticism in the Mythology of Śiva,* p. 277. She refers to the female equivalent of semen as *rati.*

77. *Shan-Chien-P'i-P'o-Sha,* p. 158.

78. A similar dynamic operated in Western medical thinking until well into the nineteenth century. According to Ben Barker-Benfield, sperm and blood were closely associated, and sperm was considered to be a distillation of food and associated with a man's vital energy. Just as in classical India, loss of sperm was believed to result in reduction of physical vitality and could lead to various pathologies and early death ("The Spermatic Economy," pp. 45–74).

79. *Bṛhadāraṇyaka Upaniṣad,* 6.4.19.

80. Ibid., 6.4.4–5.

81. Mrozik, *Virtuous Bodies,* p. 31.

82. *Atthasālinī,* p. 321.

83. Ibid., pp. 321–322. See also *Samantapāsādikā,* III.1078–1079.

84. *Visuddhimagga,* p. 447.

85. *Atthasālinī,* p. 322. See also Sumaṅgala's *Abhidhammata-vibhāvinī,* ed. Hammalawa Saddhatissa (London: Pali Text Society, 1989), p. 151, in which he argues that femininity and masculinity pervade all parts of women's and men's bodies, respectively. He states that the sexual organs are the central defining characteristic of each gender and that the external signs of gender (such as shape of hands, smile, tendency to play with baskets, and so forth) are outward manifestations.

86. Roy Porter traces the origins of these discourses in chapter 13, "Flesh and Form," of his classic study *Flesh in the Age of Reason,* pp. 227–243.

87. "Cūḷasaccaka-sutta," *Majjhima-nikāya,* I.232. A similar idea is found in *Avadāna-śataka,* 31, in which the monks of Jetavana are described as suffering from gastrointestinal distress. The Buddha remarks that he is never plagued by illness because due to past practice of good deeds, particularly from giving away all or parts of his body to others, he is "endowed with a stomach whose digestion is regular, by means of which everything I eat, drink, chew, and enjoy is digested with perfect ease"; see J. S. Speyer, ed., *Avadānaçataka: A Century of Edifying Tales Belonging to the Hīnayāna* (The Hague: Mouton, 1958), 1:172. Reiko Ohnuma remarks: "Thus, the gift of the body does not merely lead one to spiritual enlightenment; it also improves digestion!" (*Head, Eyes, Flesh, and Blood,* p. 225).

88. Doniger, *Women, Androgynes, and Other Mythical Beasts,* p. 311. The theme of sex change in Buddhism is explored by Diana Paul in *Women in Buddhism* (Berkeley: Asian Humanities Press, 1979), esp. chap. five, "The Bodhisattvas with Sexual Transformation," pp. 166–216; and by Nancy Schuster, "Changing the Female Body: Wise Women and the Bodhisattva Career in Some *Mahāratnakūṭa Sūtras,*" in *Buddhism: Critical Concepts in Religious Studies,* ed. Paul Williams (London: Routledge, 2005), pp. 329–367. Schuster makes the important point that although there are ample sources for misogyny in Buddhism, there are also counterdiscourses: "there are many Mahāyāna scriptures which insist that only the ignorant make distinctions between the religious aspirations and intellectual and spiritual capacities of men and women" (p. 340). She asserts that this is the consistent position of the *Mahāratnakūṭa* collection of texts.

89. Reported in Doniger, *Asceticism and Eroticism in the Mythology of Śiva,* p. 58.

90. *Viṣṇu Purāṇa,* vol. II, p. 503.

91. *Mahābhārata,* 13.12.1–49.

92. *Paṭisambhidā-magga,* ed. Arnold C. Taylor (London: Pali Text Society, 1979), XXII.23, p. 210. This ability is specifically credited to Abhibhū, a disciple of the buddha Sikhin, but such transformations are relatively common in stories of Buddhist adepts like Maudgalyāyana.

93. *Visuddhimagga,* pp. 378–379.

94. *Theragāthā-aṭṭhakathā,* II.182–183.

95. *Vimalakīrti-nirdeśa-sūtra ('Phags pa dri ma med par grags pas bstan pa'i mdo),* sDe dge edition, beginning on p. 369.3.

96. Ibid., p. 423.3.

97. Ibid., p. 423.5.

98. Ibid., p. 426.7.

99. Ibid., p. 427.5–6.

100. Ibid., p. 427.6. In his translation of the text, Étienne Lamotte provides several other examples of sex changes from Buddhist literature; see *The Teaching of Vimalakīrti,* trans. Sara Boin-Webb (London: Pali Text Society, 1976), p. 169, n.37. Nancy Schuster translates some interesting passages relating to female sex change from Chinese versions of several Indian Mahāyāna sūtras in "Changing the Female Body," pp. 337–340. This story is also discussed by Alan Cole in *Text as Father: Paternal Seductions in Early Mahāyāna Buddhist Literature* (Berkeley: University of California Press, 2005), pp. 283–287.

101. *Abhidharmakośa,* p. 232.

102. Soreyya's story is recounted in the *Dhammapada Commentary* (*Dhammapada-aṭṭhakathā*), ed. H.C. Norman (London: Pali Text Society, 1970), vol. I.1, pp. 325–332.

103. *Shan-Chien-P'i-P'o-Sha,* p. 211.

104. *Aṣṭasāhasrikā-prajñā-pāramitā-sūtra,* pp. 180–181.

105. "Sakkapañha-sutta," *Dīgha-nikāya,* II.271.

106. *Madhyamāgama,* T 26, chap. 33, p. 634b.5–10. The same story, with a bit less detail, is found in the *Dīrghāgama,* T 1, chap. 10, p. 63a.34.

107. *Śūraṃgama-samādhi-sūtra ('Phags pa dPa' bar 'gro ba'i ting nge 'dsin kyi mdo)* [Peking ed.], ed. Daisetz T. Suzuki (Tokyo: Tibetan Tripitaka Research Institute, 1958), vol. 32, pp. 300b.7–301a.2.

108. This is attained in the fourth level of the path of preparation *(prayoga-mārga),* the second of the five paths to liberation.

109. *Abhidharmakośa,* pp. 246–247.

5. The Company of Men

1. "Magga-saṃyutta," *Saṃyutta-nikāya,* V.2.

2. *Vinaya Piṭakaṃ,* I.301–302. Gregory Schopen provides a slightly different account from a Gilgit manuscript in *Buddhist Monks and Business Matters: Still More Papers on Monastic Buddhism in India* (Honolulu: University of Hawai'i Press, 2004), p. 8.

3. Mohan Wijayaratna, *Buddhist Monastic Life according to the Texts of the Theravāda Tradition,* trans. Steven Collins (Cambridge: Cambridge University Press, 1990), p. 117.

4. *Vinaya Piṭakaṃ,* II.290–292. This is also declared by the Buddha shortly before his passing in the "Mahāparinibbāna-sutta," *Dīgha-nikāya,* II.154. Two examples of Channa's bad behavior are given in *Vinaya Piṭakaṃ,* III.176–177 and II.24–25.

5. *Theragāthā-aṭṭhakathā,* II.97.

6. *Vinaya Piṭakaṃ,* I.45.

7. Ibid., I.60–61.

8. Ibid., I.20–21.

9. Wijayaratna, *Buddhist Monastic Life,* p. 19.

10. Charles Prebish, *Buddhist Monastic Discipline: The Sanskrit Prātimokṣa Sūtras of the Mahāsaṃghikas and the Mūlasarvāstivādins* (University Park: Pennsylvania State University Press, 1975), pp. 8–9. Sukumar Dutt thinks that this period lasted only fifty years; see *Buddha and Five after Centuries;* London: Luval, 1957, p. 23.

11. *Vinaya Piṭakaṃ,* I.152.

12. See Olivelle, *Saṃnyāsa Upaniṣads,* p. 115. Brahmanical *saṃnyāsins* were supposed to remain in a fixed residence *(dhruvaśīla)* during this period.

13. *Vinaya Piṭakaṃ,* I.159.

14. Ibid., I.149.

15. "Cūlagosiṅga-sutta," *Majjhima-nikāya,* I.206–207.

16. "Gaṇaka-moggallāna-sutta," *Majjhima-nikāya,* III.1. See also *Saṃyutta-nikāya,* V.269–270.

17. *Vihāras* were typical in the north, *guhās* in the south.

18. *Vinaya Piṭakaṃ,* III.172, 175.

19. *Visuddhimagga,* p. 16.

20. Cited by Dutt, *Buddhist Monks and Monasteries in India,* p. 67.

21. According to Dutt (*Buddhist Monks and Monasteries of India,* p. 66), the original *pātimokkha* mentioned in the "Mahāpadāna-sutta" (*Dīgha-nikāya,* II.49) was not a list of offenses against the monastic code but rather a chanted recital by the assembled monks that constituted a confession of faith. It was done not every fortnight but every six years. Dutt cites verses from the *Dhammapada* as an example of this early formula: "Patience is the highest kind of asceticism. Nibbāna is said by the buddhas to be the highest goal. One who is a monk never harms others, and one who injures others is not an ascetic. The injunction of the buddhas is: avoid all sins, accumulate all good qualities, purify your own mind." This formula is found only once in the entire Pāli canon, in the "Mahāpadāna-sutta," which states that it is an ancient practice.

22. "Gopaka-moggallāna-sutta," *Majjhima-nikāya,* III.7–10.

23. "Mahāparinibbāna-sutta," *Dīgha-nikāya,* II.76–77.

24. *Dīgha-nikāya,* II.80–81.

25. *Dhammapada,* p. 93, v. 194.

26. *Vinaya Piṭakaṃ,* III.21, IV.91, 120, 182, 299.

27. Ibid., I.351.

28. *Aṅguttara-nikāya,* V.104–106.

29. *Vinaya Piṭakaṃ,* I.351–352.

30. Wijayaratna, *Buddhist Monastic Life,* p. 9.

31. "Mahāpadāna sutta," *Dīgha-nikāya,* II.5: *sāvakayugaṃ aggaṃ bhaddayugaṃ.* The "Satipaṭṭhāna-saṃyutta," *Saṃyutta-nikāya,* V.164–165, declares that every buddha in the past has had a similar pair of chief disciples.

32. In the *Jātakas*, the Bodhisattva and Maudgalyāyana are said to have lived together in thirty-one former lives. In thirty of these, Śāriputra and Maudgalyāyana also lived together. When the Bodhisattva was Śakra, king of the gods, Śāriputra was the moon good and Maudgalyāyana was the sun god (*Jātaka* 450). When they had lives as animals, they were generally not equals, and Śāriputra was commonly in the superior position. When they were humans, they were roughly equal in most cases: in *Jātaka* 525, for example, Śāriputra was a prince and Maudgalyāyana was a royal minister; in *Jātaka* 545 Śāriputra was king of *nāgas* and Maudgalyāyana was the king of their main enemies, the *supaṇṇas*. The only time Maudgalyāyana appears in the *Jātakas* without Śāriputra is when he is born as Śakra (*Jātaka* 78).

33. *Mahāvastu,* I.13–14 and III.58–59.

34. Ibid., III.58–59.

35. Ibid., III.59.

36. In Pāli texts this character is generally referred to as Assaji.

37. *Mahāvastu,* III.60.

38. *Vinaya Piṭakaṃ,* I.39–40. This was apparently a standard greeting among ascetics when they encountered each other, and the *Vinaya-piṭakaṃ* reports that while he was on the road to Sarnath following his awakening, the Buddha was addressed in the same words by an ascetic.

39. *Mahāvastu,* III.60–64. *Vinaya Piṭakaṃ,* I.41–43, has a similar account.

40. *Aṅguttara-nikāya,* II.131.

41. "Saccavibhaṅga-sutta," *Majjhima-nikāya,* III.248.

42. This incident is reported in the "Brahma-saṃyutta," *Saṃyutta-nikāya,* I.150–152; *Sutta-nipāta,* pp. 123–124; and *Mahāvagga,* section 10.

43. "Anaṅgaṇa-sutta," *Majjhima-nikāya,* I.24–32.

44. "Satipaṭṭhāna-saṃyutta," *Saṃyutta-nikāya,* V.162.

45. *Theragāthā-aṭṭhakathā,* III.119–120.

46. "Satipaṭṭhāna-saṃyutta," *Saṃyutta-nikāya,* V.162.

47. Maudgalyāna's death is reported in two main sources, the *Dhammapada Commentary* on verses 137–140 and the *Jātaka Commentary* on *Jātaka* 523. My account mainly follows that found in Eugene Watson Burlingame, trans., *Buddhist Legends: Translated from the Original Pali Text of the Dhammapada Commentary* (London: Pali Text Society, 1969), pp. 304–308. The *Dhammapada Commentary* states that the naked ascetics had hoped to profit from Maudgalyāna's death by receiving the offerings that the great elder had caused to be given to the Buddhist order, but King Ajātaśatru heard of the murder and sent spies to catch the culprits. The murdering thugs were caught boasting of their evil deed in a bar and were executed, and during interrogation they informed the spies that the naked ascetics had hired them. The king had them all captured, placed in a pit filled with straw, and burned alive.

48. Thera and Hecker, trans., *Great Disciples of the Buddha,* p. 58. Thera and Hecker cite the *Commentary* on the "Ukkacelā-sutta" of the *Saṃyutta-nikāya.*

49. "Ukkacelā-sutta," *Saṃyutta-nikāya,* V.163–164.

50. Thera and Hecker, trans., *Great Disciples of the Buddha,* p. 140.

51. This story is recounted in the preamble to the *Cullahaṃsa-jātaka* (*Jātaka* 533), p. 333.

52. *Theragāthā-aṭṭhakathā,* III.120.

6. The Greater Men of the Greater Vehicle

1. A. L. Basham, "Aśoka and Buddhism: A Reexamination," *Journal of the International Association of Buddhist Studies* 5 (1982): 140.

2. Étienne Lamotte, *History of Indian Buddhism,* trans. Sara Boin-Webb (Louvain-la-Neuve: Institut Orientaliste, 1988), p. 351.

3. *Kathāvatthu,* ed. Arnold C. Taylor (London: Pali Text Society, 1979), pp. 559–560. In her introduction to the English translation, Caroline Rhys Davids contends that this text was composed around 246 BCE and is a record of the controversies of the second Buddhist council held in Patna. See *Points of Controversy or Subjects of Discourse,* trans. Shwe Zan Aung and C. A. F. Rhys Davids (London: Pali Text Society, 1969), p. xxxi.

4. *Abhidharmakośa,* p. 245.

5. *Mahāvibhāṣā-śāstra:* Louis de la Vallée Poussin, "Documents d'Abhidharma 2. La Doctrine des Refuges," *Mélanges Chinois et Bouddhiques,* 1, 1931–1932, p. 75. This text was probably composed around the third century CE.

6. See, for example, *Śūraṃgama-samādhi-sūtra ('Phags pa dPa' bar 'gro ba'i ting nge 'dsin kyi mdo),* Peking ed. vol. 32, p. 82.3.4.

7. Lewis Lancaster, "The Oldest Mahāyāna Sūtra: Its Significance for the Study of Buddhist Development," *The Eastern Buddhist* 8, no. 1 (1975): 30–41.

8. *Śūraṃgama-samādhi-sūtra,* pp. 73.4.8–5.2.

9. *Saddharma-puṇḍarīka-sūtra,* ed. Hendrik Kern and Bunyiu Nanjio (Osnabrück: Biblio Verlag, 1970, Biblioteca Buddhica X), pp. 316–317.

10. *Upāyakauśalya-sūtra ('Phags pa Thabs la mkhas pa'i mdo),* sDe dge ed., mDo sde vol. *za,* p. 593.4.

11. See also the *Śūraṃgama-samādhi-sūtra,* pp. 72.2.8–3.2, which states that advanced bodhisattvas acquire the ability to manifest in any form they choose and can even appear as a hearer or solitary realizer, but that they remain committed to the Great Vehicle. They can also assume the physical form of a buddha and display the events of a buddha's life for the upliftment of others.

12. *Śūraṃgama-samādhi-sūtra,* p. 83.2.2–3.

13. *Pañcaviṃśati-sāhasrikā-prajñā-pāramitā-sūtra,* p. 39.

14. *Aśokadattā-vyākaraṇa-sūtra ('Phags pa Mya ngam med kyis byin pa lung bstan pa'i mdo),* sDe dge, dKon brtsegs, vol. *ca,* p. 456.2–3.

15. This term is used in Mahāyāna texts to refer to the Buddha's Hīnayāna disciples who listened to his teachings and practiced in accordance with them. The other main type of Hīnayāna disciple is the solitary realizer *(pratyeka-buddha).*

16. Klaus Klostermaier, *Hinduism: A Short History* (Oxford: Oneworld Publications, 2000), p. 56.

17. Gavin Flood, *Introduction to Hinduism* (Cambridge: Cambridge University Press, 1996), p. 103.

18. Klostermaier, *Hinduism,* p. 56.

19. *Śivapurāṇa (Śrīśivamahāpurāṇam),* ed. Nag Sharan Singh (Delhi: Nag Publishers, 1986), 1.2.32: *etac chivapurāṇaṃ hi gāyate yo 'harniśam ājñāṃ tasya pratīkṣeran devā indrapurogamāḥ.* My thanks to McComas Taylor for providing this reference.

20. Klostermaier, *Hinduism,* p. 62.

21. *Upāyakauśalya-sūtra,* pp. 806.4–807.2.

22. See, for example, *Saddharma-puṇḍarīka-sūtra,* p. 55.

23. Nancy Schuster, "Changing the Female Body," p. 332.

24. *Saddharma-puṇḍarīka-sūtra,* pp. 263–266.

25. Ibid., pp. 205–206.

26. *Sukhāvatī-vyūha-sūtra,* ed. F. Max Müller and Bunyiu Nanjio (Amsterdam: Oriental Press, 1972), p. 19, v. 34.

27. *Vimalakīrti-nirdeśa-sūtra ('Phags pa Dri ma med par grags pas bstan pa'i mdo),* p. 366.4. The description of Vimalakīrti begins on p. 364.2.

28. Ibid., p. 367.3.

29. Ibid., p. 368.1–3.

30. Ibid., p. 383.5–6.

31. Ibid., p. 369.1.

32. Ibid., p. 457.4–5.

33. Ibid., p. 415.5–7.

34. This begins on *Vimalakīrti-nirdeśa-sūtra,* p. 369.3.

35. *Aṣṭasāhasrikā-prajñā-pāramitā-sūtra,* p. 1. The same description can be found in *Pañcaviṃśati-sāhasrikā-prajñā-pāramitā-sūtra,* p. 14.

36. *Saddharma-puṇḍarīka-sūtra,* p. 9.

37. *Sukhāvatī-vhūha-sūtra,* p. 2.

38. *Mahāyāna-sūtrālaṃkāra,* p. 29, v. 10.

39. Ibid., p. 166, verses 73–74.

40. *Saddharma-puṇḍarīka-sūtra,* p. 24: *narendra-rājñā;* 28: *śākya-siṃha;* 34: *narāditya;* 46: *loka-nātha;* 58: *dharma-rāja;* 65: *lokavid-anuttara;* 65: *puruṣa-damyasādhi śāstā devānāṃ ca manuṣyāṇāṃ ca;* 16: *puruṣottama;* 77: *loka-pitā.*

41. Ibid., p. 130.

42. *Mahāyāna-sūtrālaṃkāra,* pp. 97 and 171.

43. Ibid., p. 177, v. 50.

44. *Saddharma-puṇḍarīka-sūtra,* p. 387.

45. *Vajracchedikā-prajñā-pāramitā-sūtra,* ed. Edward Conze (Rome: Is.M.E.O., 1974), p. 30. The same idea is expressed again on p. 38: "Those who saw me by my form, those who followed me by my voice, have been engaged in wrong practice. Those beings will not see me. From the dharma buddhas are seen. Indeed the guides are the truth bodies. But the real nature of things *(dharmatā)* cannot be discriminated, and so must not be discriminated."

46. *Pañcaviṃśati-sāhasrikā-prajñā-pāramitā-sūtra,* p. 234.

47. *Aṣṭasāhasrikā-prajñā-pāramitā-sūtra,* p. 21.

48. *Saddharma-puṇḍarīka-sūtra,* pp. 72–76.

49. *Vimalakīrti-nirdeśa-sūtra,* p. 416.3–6.

50. Ibid., p. 429.5–6.

51. Ibid., p. 435.6–7.

52. Ibid., p. 432.4.

53. Ibid., pp. 389.5–393.4.

54. *Śūraṃgama-samādhi-sūtra,* p. 77.3.2–4.

55. Ibid., p. 77.2.1–2.

56. Ibid., p. 76.4.1–5.

57. Ibid., p. 81.4.6–7.

58. Asaṅga, "Śīla-paṭala," *Bodhisattva-bhūmi,* ed. Nalinaksha Dutt (Patna: K. P. Jayaswal Research Institute, 1978), p. 194.

59. *Upāyakauśalya-sūtra,* pp. 574.7–576.2.

60. Ibid., p. 577.1–6.

61. Ibid., p. 578.2.

62. Ibid., pp. 581.2–582.4.

63. Ibid., p. 583.4.

64. Ibid., p. 584.6–7.

65. Ibid., p. 585.5.

66. Ibid., p. 586.5–7.

67. Śāntideva, *Śikṣā-samuccaya,* ed. Cecil Bendall (Osnabrück: Biblio Verlag, 1970), pp. 79–82.

68. See Paul, *Women in Buddhism,* pp. 195–197.

69. *Śūraṃgama-samādhi-sūtra,* pp. 86.1.3–86.2.1.

70. Ibid., p. 88.4.5.

71. The same attitude is also found in contemporary India, and men who do not perform actions and attitudes expected of them commonly have to contend with questions about their manhood. During my first fieldwork trip there, an Indian man, on being informed by my wife that we had been married for two years but had no children, asked her, "Is your husband then not a lusty man?" and indicated that he was willing to offer himself as a substitute who could get the job done. This encounter was repeated on several other occasions in various permutations.

72. *Upāyakauśalya-sūtra,* pp. 597.7–598.2.

73. Ibid., p. 598.1.

74. Ibid., p. 598.4.

75. *Saddharma-puṇḍarīka-sūtra,* p. 280.

76. *Pañcaviṃśati-sāhasrikā-prajñā-pāramitā-sūtra,* p. 36.

77. "Śīla-paṭala," *Bodhisattva-bhūmi,* p. 108.

78. *Aṣṭasāhasrikā-prajñā-pāramitā-sūtra,* p. 166.

79. Mrozik, *Virtuous Bodies,* pp. 40–41. See also Ohnuma, *Head, Eyes, Flesh, and Blood,* p. 227, which quotes a passage from the *Śikṣā-samuccaya* in which Śāntideva asserts that when an advanced bodhisattva dies, carnivorous beings that eat his or her flesh "are reborn in a happy destiny, among the gods in heaven." She also notes that the flesh of advanced practitioners is particularly tasty, and so beings are attracted to it: "The moral power of the bodhisattva is thus inseparable from the wonderful taste of his flesh, and spiritual salvation is indistinguishable from the physical satiety one experiences after eating a good meal" (p. 228). The beneficial effect of consuming a bodhisattva's flesh is a recurring theme in Mahāyāna sūtras. Paul Demiéville cites a number of texts that assert that beings accumulate merit from the mere physical presence of bodhisattvas. He gives a number of examples of bodhisattvas' vows to the effect that beings will benefit from seeing, smelling, or eating bodhisattvas and that their flesh will cure illnesses and eliminate defilements. See Mark Tatz, trans., *Buddhism and Healing: Demiéville's Article "Byo" from Hōbōgirin* (Lanham, MD: University Press of America, 1985), pp. 44–50.

80. Ohnuma, *Head, Eyes, Flesh, and Blood,* pp. 244–251.

81. See, for example, the *Saddharma-puṇḍarīka-sūtra* (p. 11), which praises beings who give their bodies and other things that are dear to them to the Buddhist monastic order: "Some give their children and wives; others their own flesh; or offer, when asked, their hands and feet, striving to gain supreme awakening. Some give their heads, others their eyes, others their own beloved bodies, and after cheerfully bestowing their gifts they aspire to the knowledge of the thus gone ones."

82. Śāntideva, *Bodhicaryāvatāra,* ed. Vidhushekhara Bhattacharya (Calcutta: Asiatic Society, 1960), p. 33.

83. *Aṣṭasāhasrikā-prajñā-pāramitā-sūtra,* p. 210.

84. Ibid., p. 211.

85. Ibid., p. 243.

86. Ibid., p. 221.

87. Ibid., pp. 216–217: *satpuruṣā lokārthakarā.*

88. Ibid., pp. 97–98.

89. *Saddharma-puṇḍarīka-sūtra,* p. 354.

90. Ibid., p. 350: *paripūrṇa-puruṣa-vyañjana.*

91. Ibid., pp. 482–483.

92. *Mahāyāna-sūtrālaṃkāra,* pp. 47–48.

93. The *Abhisamayālaṃkāra,* p. 35 (8.12), ascribes the thirty-two major physical characteristics to complete enjoyment bodies.

94. *Vijñapti-mātratā-siddhi,* T 31.57c–58a.

95. *Mahāyāna-sūtrālaṃkāra,* p. 47.

96. *Aṣṭasāhasrikā-prajñā-pāramitā-sūtra,* p. 48.

97. Ibid., pp. 253–254.

98. Śīlabhadra, *Budhabhūmi-vyākhyāna: The Budhabhūmi-sūtra and the Budhabhūmi-vyākhyāna,* ed. Kyoo Nishio (Tokyo: Kokusho Kankokai, 1982), p. 125.

99. *Wisdom of Buddha: The Saṃdhinirmocana-sūtra,* trans. John Powers (Berkeley: Dharma Publishing, 1995), p. 305.

100. *Sumaṅgala-vilāsinī,* III.865.

101. Lancaster, "The Oldest Mahāyāna Sūtra," p. 36.

102. *Avataṃsaka-sūtra,* T 10.37c.

103. *Buddha-bhūmi-sūtra,* ed. Nishio, p. 6.

104. "Sāmmañña-phala-sutta," *Dīgha-nikāya,* I.76–78; and "Mahāsakuladāyi-sutta," *Majjhima-nikāya,* II.17–18.

105. *Visuddhimagga,* p. 406.

106. "Poṭṭhapāda-sutta," *Dīgha-nikāya,* I.195–202.

107. *Mahāyāna-sūtrālaṃkāra,* p. 40, verses 18–19.

108. Ibid., p. 40.

109. Ancient Indians knew of the existence of other societies and places, but their depictions tend to reflect their societal prejudices, and even travel accounts commonly contain fanciful material, much like the travelogues of Marco Polo and Xuanzang.

The lore regarding these others was generally uncomplimentary, and foreigners were often depicted as engaging in immoral practices and as having societal norms that were inferior to those of India. Thus Vasubandhu, for example, asserts that Persians commonly have sex with their mothers, sisters, and other forbidden women (*Abhidharmakośa,* p. 241).

110. See McComas Taylor, *The Fall of the Indigo Jackal: The Discourse of Division and Pūrṇabhadra's Pañcatantra* (Albany: State University of New York Press, 2007), which shows how these tropes were used to present socially constructed hierarchies as a fundamental aspect of reality and which examines how the tropes are reflected throughout the brahmanical archive.

7. Adepts and Sorcerers

1. David Snellgrove, ed., *The Hevajra Tantra: A Critical Study* (Oxford: Oxford University Press, 1980), pt. 2, p. 2. This is a common opening trope for tantras of the Yoginī class, such as the *Secret Assembly Tantra (Guhya-samāja-tantra),* the *Secret Essence Tantra (Guhya-garbha-tantra),* the *Great Violent Wrath Tantra (Caṇḍamahāroṣaṇa-tantra),* and the *Sublime Exposition Tantra (Abhidhānottara-tantra),* but some, including the *Wheel Binding Tantra (Cakrasaṃvara-tantra),* do not use this opening scene. A similar trope is found at the beginning of the *Secret Assembly Tantra:* "Thus have I heard: once the Blessed One was dwelling in the vaginas of the women who are the essence of the adamantine body, speech, and mind of all thus gone ones"; see *Guhyasamāja Tantra or Tathāgataguhyaka,* ed. S. Bagchi (Darbhanga: Mithila Institute, 1965), p. 1. Yoginī class tantras contain extreme teachings and practices and are deliberately shocking to traditional Buddhists. Tantras of other classes are more in accord with the Mahāyāna mainstream; see John Powers, *Introduction to Tibetan Buddhism,* 2nd ed. (Ithaca, NY: Snow Lion Publications, 2007), pp. 279–293, for a discussion of the classes of tantras.

2. This is a recurring trope in Indian Buddhist tantras. The Buddha appears in sexual embrace, enjoins his audience to follow his example, and further exhorts his followers to indulge in a range of actions prohibited in the *Monastic Discipline* and other sources that valorize monasticism. When they hear these teachings, his followers collectively faint, and then he revives them. Another example of this trope is found in the *Secret Assembly Tantra,* p. 16, where advanced bodhisattvas are overcome with fear and faint when they hear the tantra's teachings. On p. 31, even buddhas "tremble and faint" because of the unfamiliar pronouncements. On p. 66, the buddhas again faint, and the tantra promises that its magical spells are so powerful that "with the use of all mantras even the hosts of buddhas themselves will be driven out according to this rite."

3. *Hevajra Tantra,* p. 50.

4. See *The Vajrabhairava Tantras,* ed. and trans. Bulcsu Siklós (Tring: Institute of Buddhist Studies, 1996), pp. 38–59.

5. *Hevajra Tantra,* p. 60: *śukraṃ bhaved vajraṃ. Ḍākinīs* are ambiguous and liminal figures in tantric literature. They are sometimes portrayed as buddhas or as custodians of tantric lore and in other contexts are demonic, flesh-eating female demons that haunt cremation grounds and other fearsome places. They possess great power that can be accessed by sufficiently resolute adepts. These portrayals are not exclusive, and there is considerable overlap. As noted earlier, it is assumed in Indian medical literature that women have a semen equivalent, and so the statement that *ḍākinīs* have semen may refer to female rather than male semen. Given the pervasiveness of gender-bending images in the tantras, however, I read this as an instance of a female figure being attributed with a characteristic that is generally the exclusive preserve of males. David Gray discusses various portrayals of these and other female figures in tantric and nontantric literature in *The Cakrasamvara Tantra (The Discourse of Śrī Heruka) (Śrīherukābhidhāna): A Study and Annotated Translation* (New York: American Institute of Buddhist Studies, 2007), pp. 77–93. Another useful study is Martin Kalff's PhD dissertation, "Selected Chapters from the *Abhidhānottara-tantra:* The Union of Female and Male Deities (Columbia University, 1979), which has extensive discussions of various female figures associated with tantric practice.

6. *Hevajra Tantra,* p. 20.

7. Ibid., p. 24.

8. The most influential grouping of Buddhist *siddhas* is found in Abhayadatta's (ca. twelfth century) hagiography, *Lives of the Eighty-Four Adepts (Caturśīti-siddha-pravṛtti).* Many of the *siddhas* are also known through compositions of prose and poetry, particularly inspired verse compositions *(dohā).*

9. *Hevajra Tantra,* p. 56. The *Guhya-samāja-tantra* (p. 94) contains a similar injunction: "this is the secret law proclaimed by all the buddhas: kill living beings, speak false words, take what is not given, and frequent women. One should exhort all beings with this *vajra* way, for this is the eternal sacred law of all buddhas." On p. 105, the same text asserts: "In various forms you should have sex with all the women who dwell in the three worlds. . . . This is the most wonderful sacred law."

10. *Hevajra Tantra,* p. 56.

11. *Hevajra-piṇḍārtha-ṭīkā* Tibetan: *Kye'i rdo rje bsdus pa'i don gyi rgya cher 'grel pa*), Narthang ed., p. 15.86b, 5–6; cited by Snellgrove, *The Hevajra Tantra,* pt. 1, p. 86, n.1. A similar notion is found in the *Guhya-garbha-tantra:* "The primordial uncreated real nature appears as a magical apparition in the manner of an optical illusion. Although all rites of sexual union and liberation have been performed, they have not [really] been performed, even to the extent of an atomic particle." See Gyurme Dorje, "The *Guhyagarbhatantra* and Its XIVth Century Commentary *Phyogs-bcu mun-sel*" (PhD diss., University of London, 1987), vol. 1, part 1, p. 226, v. 14. This appears to indicate that in meditation one visualizes various sorts of actions prohibited in the Buddhist moral code as a way of transcending attachment to rules and regulations, but one only does so mentally and continues to observe standard ethical behavior. Passages

from the *Guhya-garbha-tantra* cited in this study are translated from the Tibetan text Gyurme Dorje provides in part 1, volume 1.

12. *Guhya-garbha-tantra,* p. 94.

13. *Caṇḍamahāroṣaṇa-tantra: The Caṇḍamahāroṣaṇa Tantra: A Critical Edition and English Translation, Chapters I–VIII,* ed. Christopher S. George (New Haven, CT: American Oriental Society, 1974), pp. 20–28. The text goes on to describe in graphic detail a range of physical positions that should be employed to produce maximum pleasure.

14. Ibid., p. 32.

15. *Hevajra Tantra,* p. 38. On p. 66, it asserts: "Cyclic existence is thus, and so is nirvana; there is no nirvana other than cyclic existence, we say. . . . The wise one continues in cyclic existence, but this cyclic existence is recognized as nirvana."

16. Ibid., p. 14.

17. Ibid., p. 34.

18. Ibid., p. 70.

19. *Abhidhānottara-tantra* (Tibetan: *mNgon par brjod pa'i rgyud bla ma*), sDe dge rGyud 'bum, vol. *ka* (New York: Tibetan Buddhist Resource Center, n.d.), W22084–0962, pp. 597.6–598.1.

20. Ibid., p. 584.6: *bsam du med pa'i sgom pa.*

21. Ibid., p. 611.2–3.

22. Wuxing indicates that the introduction of tantric Buddhism into the curriculum of the north Indian monastic universities was a recent phenomenon: "recently the mantra method has come to be venerated throughout the land"; see *Zhenyan zongjiao shi,* T 2396, vol. 75, p. 431a.

23. Ronald Davidson, *Indian Esoteric Buddhism: A Social History of the Tantric Movement* (New York: Columbia University Press, 2002), pp. 25–70.

24. *Hevajra Tantra,* pp. 8–10.

25. *Mahāvairocana-abhisaṃbodhi-tantra: Mahāvairocana-abhisaṃbodhi-vikurvitādhiṣṭhāna-vaipulya-sūtrendra-rāja-nāma-dharma-paryāya;* Tibetan: *rNam par snang mdzad chen po mngon par rdzogs par byang chub pa rnam par sprul pa byin gyis rlab pa shin tu rgyas pa mdo sde'i dbang po'i rgyal po shes bya ba'i chos kyi rnam grangs:* Sde dge edition, vol. *tha* (New York: Tibetan Buddhist Resource Center, n.d.), W22084–0971, p. 374.6–7.

26. Ibid., p. 418.3–5.

27. *Sarvadurgati-pariśodhana-tantra: The Sarvadurgatipariśodhana Tantra: Elimination of All Evil Destinies,* ed. Tadeusz Skorupski (Delhi: Motilal Banarsidass, 1983), pp. 198–202. Similarly, the *Cakrasaṃvara-tantra* promises that adepts who master its mantras and rituals will attain sovereign power over human rulers and gods and will be able to draw beautiful women to them for sex: "one may definitely summon the king or queen with one's mind. Gods, demigods, and men will instantly be brought under one's power. Through one's ferocity, one may slay them with a mere word. The adept controls, defeats, and suppresses with just a word. With a word he may

immobilize rivers, chariots, war machines, the ocean, elephants, horses, and similarly clouds, people, or even birds. With a word he brings about everything, whatever he desires with his mind. The application of attraction is the means of seducing all women"; *Tantra-rāja-śrīlaghusaṃvara-nāma;* Tibetan: *rGyud kyi rgyal po dpal bde mchog nyung ngu,* sDe dge bKa' 'gyur, rGyud 'bum vol. *ka* (New York: Tibetan Buddhist Resource Center, n.d.), W22084–0962, p. 483.5–7.

28. *Sarvadurgati-pariśodhana-tantra,* pp. 226–228.

29. *Saṃvarodaya-tantra: The Saṃvarodaya Tantra: Selected Chapters,* ed. Shinichi Tsuda (Tokyo: Hokuseido Press, 1974), p. 74.

30. *Hevajra Tantra,* p. 2.

31. *Guhya-samāja-tantra,* p. 100.

32. *Cakrasaṃvara-tantra,* chap. 27, pp. 463.7–464.2.

33. For example, Kambala's commentary on the *Cakrasaṃvara-tantra* advises aspiring adepts to have sex with women of varying ages for the sake of specific attainments: "First, excite the lotus of an eleven-year-old for the sake of alchemy *(bcud kyi len, rasāyana).* Second, have sex with a twelve-year-old for the sake of the commitments. Third, first meditate on mantra for the sake of magical power with a menstruating sixteen-year-old. Fourth, you will be able to travel in the sky by having sex with a twenty-year-old, who is the nature of wisdom. Fifthly, for the sake of consecration, [have sex with] a twenty-five-year-old. These practices are prescribed in accordance with the sequential purification of the five wisdoms, the mirror-like [wisdom] and so forth"; *Sādhana-nidāna-śrīcakrasaṃvara-nāma-pañjikā* Tibetan: *dPal 'khor lo sdom pa'i dka' 'grel sgrub pa'i thabs kyi gleng gzhi:* sDe dge bsTan 'gyur, rGyud vol. *ba* (New York: Tibetan Buddhist Resource Center, n.d.), W23703–1332, pp. 10.6–11.1. Similarly, in a later section Kambala describes a sexual yoga that combines ritual, coitus, and visualization: "By the power of the great seal one will effortlessly attain complete, unsurpassed awakening. One will purify clear light and wisdom and will thus always be regarded as a yogi. By engaging in this meditation, if one stabilizes the jewel-like mind one receives blessings and is consecrated in the awakening of a buddha. Take a sixteen-year-old and decorate her with all adornments. After you have located a woman with a beautiful face and large eyes, you should practice the consort ritual with her. You should also practice the secret observance [involving various sorts of sexual activities] in four periods through the great ritual. You should have no doubt that after six months everything will be attained" (p. 85.4–7). I owe this reference to David Gray, *The Cakrasamvara-tantra,* pp. 108 and 120. My translation follows the Tibetan text and differs slightly from his.

34. *Hevajra Tantra,* p. 20.

35. Ibid., p. 20.

36. This physiology is primarily associated with the Yoginī tantras, and Tibetan doxographers generally consider it to be exclusive to the highest yoga tantra *(anuttara-yoga-tantra)* class.

37. *Hevajra Tantra,* p. 4.

38. Ibid., p. 6.

39. Ibid., p. 50: "Those things by which men of violent actions are bound others turn into skillful methods and through them gain release from the bonds of existence. By passion the world is bound, by passion too it is released, but heretical Buddhists do not know the practice of reversals."

40. *Sarva-tathāgata-tattva-saṃgraha,* ed. Yamada Isshi (New Delhi: Śata-piṭaka Series, 1981), p. 531.

41. *Guhya-samāja-tantra,* p. 22.

42. The *Caṇḍamahāroṣaṇa-tantra* (p. 32) contains a similar sentiment: "The same terrible action that leads people to hell undoubtedly leads them to liberation when it is conjoined with skillful method."

43. *Guhya-samāja-tantra,* p. 15.

44. *Hevajra Tantra,* p. 58.

45. Ibid., p. 72.

46. *Saṃvarodaya-tantra,* pp. 134–135.

47. Ibid., p. 125.

48. Gray, *The Cakrasamvara Tantra,* p. 61.

49. *Guhya-samāja-tantra,* p. 14. In a further rejection of conventional norms of religious practice and worship, the text goes on to advise adepts to present feces, urine, semen, and blood to the buddhas as offerings and states that "the buddhas and bodhisattvas of great renown are pleased" by such things.

50. *Hevajra Tantra,* p. 68.

51. Bernard Faure, *The Power of Denial: Buddhism, Purity, and Gender* (Princeton, NJ: Princeton University Press, 2003), p. 124: "far from extolling wisdom and women as a superficial reading would suggest, this imagery presupposes and reinforces the inferiority of women."

52. *Guhya-samāja-tantra,* p. 5.

53. Ibid., p. 2.

54. *Cakrasaṃvara-tantra,* chap. 47, p. 487.

55. Miranda Shaw, *Passionate Enlightenment: Women in Tantric Buddhism* (Princeton, NJ: Princeton University Press, 1994), pp. 35–40, 195–205. On pp. 36–37, she asserts: "since these texts were not created by men in isolation from women, they do not express exclusively male views. These views grew out of communal exploration and practice and proceed from the insights of *both women and men.* Indeed, many of the insights contained in tantric writings can only find their source in practices done by women and men together. The texts openly present tantra as a religious path on which the lives of women and men are closely intertwined. I contend that the extensive descriptions of the interactions and shared practices of women and men are in themselves sufficient evidence that the *yoginī-tantras* are the products of circles consisting of both women and men. Therefore, I include women among the creators of the *tantras* and conclude that the texts reflect the views and interests of women as well as those of men."

56. Davidson, *Indian Esoteric Buddhism,* p. 91. David Gray also discusses Shaw's theories at length in *The Cakrasamvara Tantra,* pp. 93–103, and echoes Davidson's conclusions. On p. 94, Gray states that the portrayals of women in tantric texts range "from positive to hostile" and express the male perspective.

57. *Hevajra Tantra,* p. 48.

58. *Guhya-garbha-tantra,* pp. 199–200. The *Mahāvairocana-abhisaṃbodhi-tantra* (p. 308.1–4) contains a similar notion: "The mind . . . is not blue, nor yellow, nor red, nor white, nor purple, nor transparent, nor short, nor long, nor round, nor square, nor bright, nor dark, nor male, nor female, nor neuter."

59. *Abhidhānottara-tantra,* p. 657.3.

60. Ibid., p. 657.3–5. The same sequence of courtship practices and a similar description of how an adept attracts women are found in chapter 16 of the *Cakrasaṃvara-tantra.*

61. The opening part of this chapter of the *Abhidhānottara-tantra* (beginning on p. 656.3) describes in detail the sorts of clothing preferred by certain types of women who might become one's tantric consorts, along with a range of stereotypically female behaviors, such as laughing and singing, sexually enticing gestures, and various physical postures women assume when relating to men. Many of these women are said to "become angry for no reason" (see in particular 657.6). This text is unusual in that some of the women are described as ugly, misshapen, hairy, or smelly, some have bad teeth, and others have various physical deformities. In most tantric texts, ideal consorts are described as young and very attractive. See pp. 657–658 for examples of ugly consorts.

62. *Guhya-garbha-tantra,* pp. 240–241.

63. As we have seen, the term *vajra* often refers to the penis in tantric texts, but it can also signify a five-pointed scepter that is one of the core symbols of tantric Buddhism, which is often referred to as the "Vajra Vehicle" (Vajrayāna). In some texts, the *vajra* is also a diamond or an adamantine substance, and in others a thunderbolt. In some contexts, discourses play on these various connotations.

64. *Guhya-samāja-tantra,* p. 45.

65. Ibid., p. 15.

66. See, for example, *Caṇḍamahāroṣaṇa-tantra,* pp. 28–29.

67. *Guhya-samāja-tantra,* pp. 19–20.

68. See Powers, *Introduction to Tibetan Buddhism,* pp. 481–496.

69. Bhairava is a form of Śiva, and Monier-Williams identifies Kālarātrī as a manifestation of Durgā; see *A Sanskrit-English Dictionary,* p. 278, col. 3.

70. *Abhidhānottara-tantra,* pp. 574.1–576.2. The rest of the chapter is devoted to detailed descriptions of the female deities in his retinue.

8. Conclusion

1. The *Mūlasarvāstivāda Vinaya* contains a story that the Buddha's cousin Devadatta once tried to convince King Ajātaśatru to use his power to remove the Buddha

from his position as head of the order and to replace him with Devadatta. On the face of it, this seems like an improbable scenario because Devadatta is portrayed in a highly negative way in Indian Buddhist literature, but although the king refused the request, he did not do so because of Devadatta's conduct but rather because of his physical appearance. Devadatta did not have the body of a buddha, and so he could not function as one. Ajātaśatru pointed out that he did not have golden skin like the Buddha. Hoping to correct this deficiency, Devadatta convinced a goldsmith to gilt him, but all he achieved was intense pain. In another version, Ajātaśatru notes that Devadatta lacked a wheel pattern on his palms and soles, and so the latter commissioned a blacksmith to brand him. The resulting marks were unsightly, however, and failed to match the beauty of a Buddha's *cakras*. True virtue, as marked by physical endowments, cannot be faked. See Raneiro Gnoli, ed., *The Gilgit Manuscript of the Saṅghabedavastu: Being the 17th and Last Section of the Vinaya of the Mūlasarvaāstivādin, Part 2* (Rome: Instituto Italiano Per il Medio ed Estremo Oriente, 1978), pp. 163–164.

2. Laqueur, *Making Sex*, p. 25.

3. Joan Scott, "Gender: A Useful Category of Historical Analysis," *American Historical Review* 91 (1986): 1065, 1067.

4. Douglas, *Natural Symbols: Explorations in Cosmology*, p. 70.

5. One particularly egregious example of gender discourse in China is the apocryphal *Blood Bowl Sūtra (Xuepen jing)*, which portrays women in a highly negative light and condemns them to hell for the supposed sin of monthly menstruation. For a discussion of this text, see Alan Cole, *Mothers and Sons in Chinese Buddhism* (Stanford, CA: Stanford University Press, 1998).

6. Philip Almond, *The British Discovery of Buddhism* (Cambridge: Cambridge University Press, 1988), p. 79.

Appendix 1: The Major and Minor Physical Characteristics of a Great Man

1. "Lakkhaṇa-sutta," *Dīgha-nikāya*, III.142–145, and its commentary, the *Sumaṅgala-vilāsinī*, II.445–452, III.918–940.

2. *Mahāvyutpatti* [abbreviated Mv]: *Hon'yaku myōgi taishū*, ed. Sakaki Ryōzaburō (Tokyo: Suzuki Gakujutsu Zaidan), 1965 (2 vols.).

3. *Abhisamayālaṃkāra*, VIII.vv.13–20.

4. Étienne Lamotte, *La Somme du Grand Véhicule d'Asaṅga (Mahāyānasaṃgraha)* (Louvain-la-Neuve: Institute Orientaliste, 1973), Tome II, pp. 54*–58*.

5. *Milinda-ṭīkā*, ed. Jaini, pp. 17–18.

Bibliography

Texts in Asian Languages

Abhidhammata-vibhāvinī of Sumaṅgala. *The Abhidhammatthasaṃgraha of Bhandantācariya Anuruddha and the Abhidhammatthavibhāvinī-ṭīkā of Bhandantācariya Sumaṅgalasāmi.* Hammalawa Saddhatissa, ed. London: Pali Text Society, 1989.

Abhidhānottara-tantra (Tib. *mNgon par brjod pa'i rgyud bla ma*). sDe dge rGyud 'bum, vol. *ka.* New York: Tibetan Buddhist Resource Center, n.d., W22084-0962, pp. 495–740.

Abhidharmakośa of Vasubandhu. *Abhidharmakośa and Bhāṣya*. Dwarikadas Shastri, ed. Varanasi: Bauddha Bharati, 1981.

Abhidharmakośa of Vasubandhu. *Abhidharmakośa-bhāṣya*. Prahlad Pradhan, ed. Patna: K. P. Jayaswal Research Institute, 1967.

Abhidharmasamuccaya of Asaṅga. *Abhidharmasamuccayabhāṣyam.* Nathmal Tatia, ed. Patna: K. P. Jayaswal Research Institute, 1976.

Abhisamayālaṃkāra (traditionally attributed to Maitreya). *Prajñāpāramitā-upadeśa-śāstra, the work of Maitreya.* Eugene Obermiller and Th. Stcherbatsky, eds. Osnabrück: Biblio Verlag, 1970.

Aṅguttara Nikāya. R. Morris, ed. 6 vols. London: Pali Text Society, 1885–1910.

Apadāna. The Apadāna of the Khuddaka Nikāya. Mary E. Lilley, ed. London: Pali Text Society, 1925.

Arthaviniścaya-sūtra. Arthaviniścaya-sūtra and Its Commentary. N. H. Samatani, ed. Patna: K. P. Jayaswal Research Institute, 1971.

Aśokadattā-vyākaraṇa-sūtra ('Phags pa Mya ngam med kyis byin pa lung bstan pa'i mdo). sDe dge edition: bKa' 'gyur sDe dge'i par ma, vol. *ca.* New York: Tibetan Buddhist Resource Center, n.d., W22084–0928, pp. 450–480.

Aṣṭasāhasrikā-prajñāpāramitā-sūtra. P. L. Vaidya, ed. Darbhanga: Mithila Institute, 1960.

Atharvaveda Saṃhitā. R. Roth and W. D. Whitney, eds. Bonn: F. Dummler, 1966.

Atthasālinī of Buddhaghosa. *The Atthasālinī, Buddhaghosa's Commentary on the Dhammasaṅgaṇī.* Edward Müller, ed. London: Pali Text Society, 1979.

Avataṃsaka-sūtra. Taishō shinshū daizōkyō. Takakusu Junjiro and Watanabe Kaigyoku, eds. Tokyo: Daizōkyōka, 1924–1934, vol. 9 (T9).

Bhāgavata-purāṇa. Śrīmadbhāgavata cūrṇi kā ṭīkā. Pāṇḍeya Rāmateja Śāstrī, ed. Kāśī: Paṇḍita Pustakālaya, 1960.

Bodhicaryāvatāra of Śāntideva. Vidhushekhara Bhattacharya, ed. Calcutta: Asiatic Society, 1960.

Bodhisattva-bhūmi of Asaṅga. *Bodhisattvabhūmi: Fifteenth Section of Asaṅgapada's Yogācārabhūmi.* Nalinaksha Dutt, ed. Patna: K. P. Jayaswal Research Institute, 1978.

Bodhisattva-bhūmi of Asaṅga. *Bodhisattvabhūmi: A Statement of the Whole Course of the Bodhisattva. Being the Fifteenth Section of the Yogācārabhūmi.* Wogihara Unrai, ed. Tokyo: Sankibo Buddhist Bookstore, 1971.

Budhabhūmi-vyākhyāna of Śīlabhadra. *The Budhabhūmi-sūtra and the Budhabhūmi-vyākhyāna.* Kyoo Nishio, ed. Tokyo: Kokusho Kankokai, 1982.

Buddhacarita of Aśvaghoṣa. *Aśvaghoṣa's Buddhacarita, or Acts of the Buddha.* E. H. Johnston, ed. Delhi: Motilal Banarsidass, 1984.

Cakrasaṃvara-tantra. Tantra-rāja-śrīlaghusaṃvara-nāma (Tib. *rGyud kyi rgyal po dpal bde mchog nyung ngu*). sDe dge rGyud 'bum vol. *ka.* New York: Tibetan Buddhist Resource Center, n.d., bKa' 'gyur W22084–0962, pp. 427–493.

Caṇḍamahāroṣaṇa-tantra. The Caṇḍamahāroṣaṇa Tantra: A Critical Edition and English Translation, Chapters I–VIII. Christopher S. George, ed. New Haven, CT: American Oriental Society, 1974.

Caraka Saṃhitā. Kaviraj Kunjalal Bhishagratna, ed. Varanasi: Chowkhamba Sanskrit Series Office, 1977.

Caraka Saṃhitā. Agniveśa's Caraka Saṃhitā. Ram Karan Sharma and Vaidya Bhagwan Dash, eds. Varanasi: Chowkhamba Sanskrit Series Office, 1999.

Dhammapada. A Path of Righteousness: Dhammapada. David J. Kalupahana, ed. Lanham, MD: University Press of America, 1986.

Dhammapada-aṭṭhakathā. H.C. Norman, ed. London: Pali Text Society, 1970.

Dharma-saṃgraha. Dharmasaṃgraha, An Ancient Collection of Buddhist Technical Terms. F. Max Müller and K. Kasawara, eds. Oxford: Clarendon Press, 1885.

Dīgha Nikāya. T. W. Rhys Davids and J. E. Carpenter, eds. 3 vols. London: Pali Text Society, 1889, 1903, 1910.

Dīrghāgama. Taishō shinshū daizōkyō. Takakusu Junjiro and Watanabe Kaigyoku, eds. Tokyo: Daizōkyōka, 1924–1934, vol. 1 (T1).

Gaṇḍavyūha-sūtra. D. T. Suzuki and H. Izumi, eds. Tokyo: Society for the Publication of the Sacred Books of the World, 1959.

Guhya-garbha-tantra. *The Guhyagarbhatantra and Its XIVth Century Commentary Phyogs-bcu mun-sel*. Gyurme Dorje. PhD diss., University of London, 1987 (5 vols.).

Guhya-samāja-tantra. *Guhyasamāja Tantra or Tathāgataguhyaka*. S. Bagchi, ed. Darbhanga: Mithila Institute, 1965.

Hevajra Tantra. *The Hevajra Tantra: A Critical Study*. David Snellgrove, ed. 2 vols. Oxford: Oxford University Press, 1980.

Itivuttaka. Ernst Windisch, ed. London: Pali Text Society, 1975.

Jātaka. *Jātaka together with Its Commentary*. V. Fausboll, ed. London: Pali Text Society, 1963.

Jinālaṅkāra of Buddharakkhita. James Gray, ed. London: Pali Text Society, 1981.

Jinālaṅkāra-ṭīkā of Buddhadatta. Rangoon: Sudhammavati Pitaka Press, 1940.

Kāma-sūtra. *Kāmasūtra of Vātsyāyana*. S. C. Upadhyaya, trans. Bombay: Taraporevala's Treasure House of Books, 1963.

Kāṭhaka Saṃhitā. Leopold von Schroeder, ed. Wiesbaden: Steiner Verlag, 1970–1972.

Kathāvatthu. Arnold C. Taylor, ed. London: Pali Text Society, 1979. English translation: *Points of Controversy or Subjects of Discourse*. Shwe Zan Aung and C. A. F. Rhys Davids, trans. London: Pali Text Society, 1969.

Lalitavistara. P. L. Vaidya, ed. Darbhanga: Mithila Institute, 1958.

Madhyamāgama. Taishō shinshū daizōkyō. Takakusu Junjiro and Watanabe Kaigyoku, eds. Tokyo: Daizōkyōka, 1924–1934, vol. 26 (T26).

Madhyānta-vibhāga-bhāṣya of Vasubandhu. Gadjin Nagao, ed. Tokyo: Suzuki Research Foundation, 1964.

Mahāparinirvāṇa-sūtra. *Das Mahāparinirvāṇasūtra*. Ernst Waldschmidt, ed. Berlin: Akademie-Verlag, 1950–1951.

Mahāvairocana-abhisaṃbodhi-tantra. *Mahāvairocana-abhisaṃbodhi-vikurvitādhiṣṭhāna-vaipulya-sūtrendra-rāja-nāma-dharma-paryāya* (Tib. *rNam par snang mdzad chen po mngon par rdzogs par byang chub pa rnam par sprul pa byin gyis rlab pa shin tu rgyas pa mdo sde'i dbang po'i rgyal po shes bya ba'i chos kyi rnam grangs*). Sde dge edition, vol. *tha*. New York: Tibetan Buddhist Resource Center, n.d., W22084–0971, pp. 306–421.

Mahāvastu. *Mahāvastu-avadāna*. E. Senart, ed. Paris: l'Imprimerie Nationale, 1977.

Mahāvibhāṣā. Taishō shinshū daizōkyō. Takakusu Junjiro and Watanabe Kaigyoku, eds. Tokyo: Daizōkyōka, 1924–1934, vol. 27 (T27).

Mahāvyutpatti (Hon'yaku myōgi taishū). Sakaki Ryōzaburō, ed. 2 vols. Tokyo: Suzuki Gajujutsu Zaidan, 1965.

Mahāyāna-sūtrālaṃkāra of Asaṅga. *Mahāyānasūtrālaṃkāraḥ.* S. Bagchi, ed. Darbhanga: Mithila Institute, 1970.

Maitrāyaṇī Saṃhitā. Die Saṃhitā der Maitrāyaṇīya-Śākhā. Leopold von Schroeder, ed. Wiesbaden: Franz Steiner Verlag, 1972.

Majjhima Nikāya. V. Trenckner and Robert Chalmers, eds. 3 vols. London: Pali Text Society, 1960.

Matsaranandāvadāna. Five Buddhist Legends in the Campū Style: From a Collection Named Avadānasārasamuccaya. Ratna Handurukande, ed. Bonn: Indica et Tibetica Verlag, 1984.

Milinda-ṭīkā. Padmanabh S. Jaini, ed. London: Pali Text Society, 1961.

Mūlasarvāstivāda-vinaya. Taishō shinshū daizōkyō. Takakusu Junjiro and Watanabe Kaigyoku, eds. Tokyo: Daizōkyōka, 1924–1934, vol. 24 (T24).

Pañcaviṃśati-sāhasrikā-prajñā-pāramitā-sūtra. Nalinaksha Dutt, ed. London: Luzac, 1934.

Papañcasūdanī of Buddhaghosa. J. H. Woods, D. Kosambi, and I. B. Horner, eds. 5 vols. London: Pāli Text Society, 1922–1938.

Paramattha-dīpanī of Dhammapāla. *Paramattha-dīpanī Theragāthā-Aṭṭhakathā: The Commentary of Dhammapālācariya.* F. L. Woodward, ed. London: Pali Text Society, 1952.

Paramatthajotikā. Sutta-Nipāta Commentary: Being Paramatthajotikā. Helmer Smith, ed. London: Pali Text Society, 1966.

Paṭisambhidā-magga. Arnold C. Taylor, ed. London: Pali Text Society, 1979.

Ratnagotravibhāga Mahāyānottaratantra-śāstra of Asaṅga. *The Uttaratantra of Maitreya: Containing Introduction, E. H. Johnston's Sanskrit Text, and E. Obermiller's English Translation.* Patna: Bihar Research Society, 1950.

Ṛg Veda. The Hymns of the Rig-Veda in the Samhita and Pada Texts. F. Max Müller, ed. Varanasi: Chowkhamba Sanskrit Series, 1965.

Saddharma-puṇḍarīka-sūtra. Saddharmapuṇḍarīka. Hendrik Kern and Bunyiu Nanjio, eds. Osnabrück: Biblio Verlag, 1970 (Biblioteca Buddhica X).

Sādhana-nidāna-śrīcakrasaṃvara-nāma-pañjikā of Kambala (Tib. *dPal 'khor lo sdom pa'i dka' 'grel sgrub pa'i thabs kyi gleng gzhi*). sDe dge bsTan 'gyur, rGyud vol. *ba.* New York: Tibetan Buddhist Resource Center, n.d., W23703–1332, pp. 1–158.

Samantapāsādikā of Buddhaghosa. J. Takakusu and M. Nagai, eds. 5 vols. London: Pali Text Society, 1968.

Saṃvarodaya-tantra. The Saṃvarodaya Tantra: Selected Chapters. Shinichi Tsuda, ed. Tokyo: Hokuseido Press, 1974.

Samyuktāgama. Taishō shinshū daizōkyō. Takakusu Junjiro and Watanabe Kaigyoku, eds. Tokyo: Daizōkyōka, 1924–1934, vol. 2 (T2).

Samyutta Nikāya. Léon Feer, ed. 6 vols. London: Pali Text Society, 1960.

Sarvadurgati-pariśodhana-tantra. The Sarvadurgatipariśodhana Tantra: Elimination of All Evil Destinies. Tadeusz Skorupski, ed. Delhi: Motilal Banarsidass, 1983.

Sarva-tathāgata-tattva-saṃgraha. Yamada Isshi, ed. New Delhi: Śata-piṭaka series, 1981.

Śathapatha Brāhmaṇa. J. Eggeling, trans. (Sacred Books of the East, vol. 43). 5 vols. Delhi: Motilal Banarsidass, 1963.

Śiva-purāṇa. Śrīśivamahāpurāṇam. Nag Sharan Singh, ed. Delhi: Nag Publishers, 1986.

Sukhāvatī-vhūha-sūtra. F. Max Müller and Bunyiu Nanjio, eds. Amsterdam: Oriental Press, 1972.

Sumaṅgalavilāsinī of Buddhaghosa. T. W. Rhys Davids, J. E. Carpenter, and W. Stede, eds. 3 vols. London: Pāli Text Society, 1886–1932.

Śūraṃgama-samādhi-sūtra ('Phags pa dPa' bar 'gro ba'i ting nge 'dsin kyi mdo). Peking ed.: Daisetz T. Suzuki, ed. Tokyo: Tibetan Tripitaka Research Institute, 1958. vol. 32, pp. 70.1.4–98.1.7 (376a.4–343b.7).

Śūraṃgama-samādhi-sūtra ('Phags pa dPa' bar 'gro ba'i ting nge 'dsin kyi mdo). sDe Dge edition, mDo sde, vol. *da:* bKa' 'gyur sDe dge'i par ma. New York: Tibetan Buddhist Resource Center, n.d., W22084–0940, pp. 508–633.

Suśruta Saṃhitā. Ram Karan Sharma and Vaidya Bhagwan Dash, eds. Varanasi: Chowkhamba Sanskrit Series Office, 1998.

Sutta-nipāta. Dines Andersen and Helmer Smith, eds. London: Pali Text Society, 1990.

T: Taishō shinshū daizōkyō. 100 vols. Takakusu Junjiro and Watanabe Kaigyoku, eds. Tokyo: Daizōkyōka, 1924–1934.

Taittirīya-saṃhitā. Taittirīya *Saṃhitā with the Commentary of Mādhava.* Rajendralal Misra, ed. Calcutta: Biblioteca Indica, 1860.

Theragāthā. Hermann Oldenberg and Richard Pischel, eds. London: Pali Text Society, 1966.

Udāna. Paul Steinthal, ed. London: Pali Text Society, 1948.

Udāna-aṭṭhakathā of Dhammapāla. Peter Masefield, ed. London: Pali Text Society, 1995.

Upāyakauśalya-sūtra ('Phags pa Thabs la mkhas pa'i mdo). sDe dge edition, mDo sde vol. *za:* bKa' 'gyur sDe dge'i par ma. New York: Tibetan Buddhist Resource Center, n.d., W22084–0951, pp. 568–620.

Vajrabhairava-tantra. The Vajrabhairava Tantras. Bulcsu Siklós, ed. and trans. Tring: Institute of Buddhist Studies, 1996.

Vajracchedikā-prajñā-pāramitā-sūtra. Edward Conze, ed. Rome: Is.M.E.O., 1974.

Vijñapti-mātratā-siddhi of Xuanzang. Taishō shinshū daizōkyō. Takakusu Junjiro and Watanabe Kaigyoku, eds. Tokyo: Daizōkyōka, 1924–1934, vol. 31 (T31). French translation: Louis de la Vallée Poussin. *Vijñapti-mātratā-siddhi: La Siddhi de Hiuan-tsang.* 2 vols. Paris: Paul Geuthner, 1928.

Vimalakīrti-nirdeśa-sūtra ('Phags pa dri ma med par grags pas bstan pa'i mdo). sDe dge edition, mDo sde, vol. *ma:* bKa' 'gyur sDe dge'i par ma. New York: Tibetan Buddhist Resource Center, n.d., W22084–0945, pp. 349–480.

Vinaya Piṭakaṃ. Hermann Oldenberg, ed. London: Pali Text Society, 1969. English translation: I. B. Horner, *The Book of the Discipline.* 6 vols. London: Pali Text Society, 1951.

Vinaya-sūtra. Vinayasūtra and Auto Commentary on the Same. P. V. Bapat and V. V. Gokhale, eds. Patna: Prasad Jayaswal Research Institute, 1982.

Viṣṇu Purāṇa. H. H. Wilson, ed. Delhi: Nag Publishers, 1980.

Visuddhimagga of Buddhaghosa. C. A. F. Rhys Davids, ed. London: Pali Text Society, 1975.

Zhenyan zongjiao shi of Wuxing. Taishō shinshū daizōkyō. Takakusu Junjiro and Watanabe Kaigyoku, eds. Tokyo: Daizōkyōka, 1924–1934, vol. 75 (T2396).

Texts in Western Languages

Almond, Philip. *The British Discovery of Buddhism.* Cambridge: Cambridge University Press, 1988.

Alter, Joseph S. *The Wrestler's Body: Identity and Ideology in North India.* Berkeley: University of California Press, 1992.

An, Yang-gyu, trans. *The Buddha's Last Days: Buddhaghosa's Commentary on the Mahāparinibbāna-sutta.* London: Pali Text Society, 2003.

Archimbault, Charles. *La course de pirogues au Laos.* Ascona: Artibus Asiae Publishers, 1972.

Babu, D. Sridhara. "Reflections on Andra Buddhist Sculptures and Buddha Biography." In *Buddhist Iconography,* pp. 97–101. Delhi: Tibet House, 1989.

Bapat, P. V., and Akira Hirakawa. *Shan-Chien-P'i-P'o-Sha: A Chinese Version by Saṅghabhadra of Samantapāsādikā.* Poona: Bhandarkar Oriental Research Institute, 1970.

Bareau, André. "The Place of the Buddha Gautama in the Buddhist Religion during the Reign of Aśoka." In *Buddhist Studies in Honour of Walpola Rahula,* ed. S. Balasooriya, pp. 1–9. London: Fraser, 1980.

———. *Recherches sur la biographie du Bouddha dans les Sūtrapiṭaka et les Vinayapiṭaka anciens.* 2 vols. Paris: École Française d'Extrême-Orient, 1963, 1977.

———. "The Superhuman Personality of the Buddha and Its Symbolism in the *Mahāparinirvāṇasūtra* of the Dharmaguptaka." In *Myth and Symbols: Studies in Honor of Mircea Eliade,* ed. Joseph Kitagawa and Charles Long, pp. 9–22. Chicago: University of Chicago Press, 1969.

Barker-Benfield, Ben. "The Spermatic Economy: A Nineteenth Century View of Sexuality." *Feminist Studies* 1, no. 1 (Summer 1972): 45–74.

Basham, A. L. "Aśoka and Buddhism: A Reexamination." *Journal of the International Association of Buddhist Studies* 5 (1982): 131–143.

Bechert, Heinz, ed. *The Dating of the Historical Buddha, Part 2.* Göttingen: Vandendoeck & Ruprecht, 1992.

Beyer, Stephan. *The Buddhist Experience: Sources and Interpretations.* Encino, CA: Dickenson, 1974.

Bhattacharya, Benoytosh. *The Indian Buddhist Iconography.* Calcutta: Firma K. L. Mukhopadhyay, 1958.

Bond, George D. *The Word of the Buddha: The Tipiṭaka and Its Interpretation in Theravāda Buddhism.* Colombo: Gunasena, 1982.

Bourdieu, Pierre. *In Other Words: Essays toward a Reflexive Sociology.* Trans. Matthew Adamson. Stanford, CA: Stanford University Press, 1990.

Brod, Harry, and Michael Kaufman, eds. *Theorizing Masculinities.* Thousand Oaks, CA: Sage Publications, 1994.

Bronkhorst, Johannes. *The Two Sources of Indian Asceticism.* Bern: Peter Lang, 1993.

Brown, Peter. *The Body and Society: Men, Women and Sexual Renunciation in Early Christianity.* New York: Columbia University Press, 1988.

Bühler, Georg, trans. *The Laws of Manu.* New York: Dover Publications, 1969.

Burlingame, Eugene Watson, trans. *Buddhist Legends: Translated from the Original Pāli Text of the Dhammapada Commentary.* London: Pali Text Society, 1969.

Burnouf, Eugene. *Le Lotus de la bonne loi.* Paris: Maisonneuve, 1925.

Butler, Judith. *Gender Trouble: Feminism and the Subversion of Identity.* New York: Routledge, 1990.

Bynum, Caroline Walker, Stevan Harrell, and Paula Richman, eds. *Gender and Religion: On the Complexity of Symbols.* Boston: Beacon Press, 1986.

Cabezón, José Ignacio. "Homosexuality and Buddhism." In *Homosexuality and World Religions,* ed. Arlene Swidler, pp. 81–101. Valley Forge, PA: Trinity Press International, 1993.

Chandra, Lokesh. *Buddhist Iconography: Compact Edition.* New Delhi: International Academy of Indian Culture and Aditya Prakashan, 1991, 1999.

Cole, Alan. *Mothers and Sons in Chinese Buddhism.* Stanford, CA: Stanford University Press, 1998.

———. *Text as Father: Paternal Seductions in Early Mahāyāna Buddhist Literature.* Berkeley: University of California Press, 2005.

Collins, Steven. *Nirvana and Other Buddhist Felicities: Utopias of the Pali Imaginaire.* Cambridge: Cambridge University Press, 1998.

———. *Selfless Persons: Imagery and Thought in Theravāda Buddhism.* Cambridge: Cambridge University Press, 1982.

Connell, R. W. *Masculinities.* Crows Nest, New South Wales, Australia: Allen & Unwin, 2005.

Corwell, Andrea, and Nancy Lindisfarne. *Dislocating Masculinity: Comparative Ethnographies.* London: Routledge, 1994.

Cowell, E. B., and R. A. Neil. *The Divyāvadāna, A Collection of Early Buddhist Legends.* Delhi: Indological Book House, 1987.

Crary, Jonathan, and Sanford Kwinter, eds. *Incorporations.* New York: Urzone, 1992.

Dallapicolla, Anna L., and B. N. Goswamy, trans. *An Early Document of Indian Art: The Citralakṣaṇa of Nagnajit.* New Delhi: Manohar, 1976.

Davidson, Ronald M. *Indian Esoteric Buddhism: A Social History of the Tantric Movement.* New York: Columbia University Press, 2002.

Dayal, Har. *The Bodhisattva Doctrine in Buddhist Sanskrit Literature.* London: Routledge & Kegan Paul, 1932.

Deheja, Vidya. *Discourse in Early Buddhist Art: Visual Narratives of India.* New Delhi: Munishram Manoharlal Publishers, 1997.

———. *Representing the Body: Gender Issues in Indian Art.* New Delhi: Kali for Women, 1997.

Demiéville, Paul. *Buddhism and Healing: Demiéville's Article "Byo" from Hōbōgirin.* Trans. Mark Tatz. Lanham, MD: University Press of America, 1985.

Deshpande, S. H. *Physical Education in Ancient India.* Delhi: Bharatiya Vidya Prakashan, 1992.

Doniger, Wendy. *Asceticism and Eroticism in the Mythology of Śiva.* Delhi: Oxford University Press, 1975.

———. *Women, Androgynes, and Other Mythical Beasts.* Chicago: University of Chicago Press, 1980.

Doniger, Wendy, and Sudhir Kakar, trans. *Vatsyayana Kamasutra.* Oxford: Oxford University Press, 2003.

Dundas, Paul. "Food and Freedom." *Religion* 15 (1985): 161–198.

Durt, Hubert. "Note sur l'origine de l'Anavalokitamūdatā." *Indogaku Bukkyōgaku Kenkyū* 16, no. 1 (1967): 450–443; reprinted in *Samadhi: cahiers d'études bouddhiques* 6 (1972): 23–30.

Dutt, Sukumar. *Buddha and Five after Centuries.* London: Luval, 1957.

———. *Buddhist Monks and Monasteries of India.* Delhi: Motilal Banarsidass, 1989.

Eckel, Malcolm David. "The Power of the Buddha's Absence: On the Foundations of Mahāyāna Ritual." *Journal of Ritual Studies* 4, no. 2 (1990): 61–95.

Eliade, Mircea. *Yoga: Immortality and Freedom.* London: Routledge & Kegan Paul, 1958.

Endo, Toshiichi. *Buddha in Theravāda Buddhism: A Study of the Concept of Buddha in the Pāli Commentaries.* Colombo: Buddhist Culture Center, 2002.

Faure, Bernard. *The Power of Denial: Buddhism, Purity, and Gender.* Princeton, NJ: Princeton University Press, 2003.

———. *The Red Thread: Buddhist Approaches to Sexuality.* Princeton, NJ: Princeton University Press, 1998.

Feher, Michel, ed. *Fragments for a History of the Human Body, Part 1.* New York: Urzone, 1989.

Filliozat, Jean. *The Classical Doctrine of Indian Medicine: Its Origins and Its Greek Parallels.* Delhi: Munshiram Manoharlal, 1964.

———. "Continence and Sexuality in Buddhism and in the Discipline of Yoga." In *Religion, Philosophy, Yoga,* pp. 327–339. Delhi: Motilal Banarsidass, 1991.

Forth, Christopher E. *The Dreyfus Affair and the Crisis of French Manhood.* Baltimore: Johns Hopkins University Press, 2004.

Foucault, Michel. *The Will to Knowledge: The History of Sexuality Volume I.* Trans. Robert Hurley. London: Penguin Books, 1976.

Foucher, A. *The Beginnings of Buddhist Art.* Trans. L. A. Thomas and F. W. Thomas. New Delhi: Asian Educational Services, 1994.

———. *On the Iconography of the Buddha's Nativity: Memoirs of the Archaeological Survey of India, no. 46.* Trans. H. Hargreaves. New Delhi: Archaeological Survey of India, 1999.

Gallagher, Catherine, and Thomas Laqueur, eds. *The Making of the Modern Body: Sexuality and Society in the Nineteenth Century.* Berkeley: University of California Press, 1987.

Garfinkel, Harold. "Passing and the Managed Achievement of Sex Status in an Intersexed Person." In *Studies in Ethnomethodology.* ed. Harold Garfinkel, pp. 116–185. Englewood Cliffs, NJ: Prentice-Hall, 1967.

Geertz, Clifford. "Religion as a Cultural System." In *The Interpretation of Cultures,* pp. 87–125. New York: Basic Books, 1973.

Giles, H. A., trans. *The Travels of Fa hsien.* Cambridge: Cambridge University Press, 1923.

Goffman, Erving. "The Arrangement between the Sexes." *Theory and Society* 4 (1977): 301–331.

Goldman, Robert P., trans. *The Rāmāyaṇa of Vālmīki: An Epic of Ancient India.* Princeton, NJ: Princeton University Press, 1984.

Gombrich, Richard F. "Dating the Buddha: A Red Herring Revealed." In *The Dating of the Historical Buddha,* part 2, ed. Heinz Bechert, pp. 239–259. Göttingen: Vandendoeck & Ruprecht, 1992.

———. "The Significance of Former Buddhas in the Theravādin Tradition." In *Buddhist Studies in Honour of Walpola Rahula,* ed. S. Balasooriya, pp. 62–72. London: Fraser, 1980.

Gomez, Luis. "Mahāsāṃghika." In *The Encyclopedia of Religion,* vol. 9, ed. Mircea Eliade, pp. 120–122. New York: Macmillan, 1987.

———. "Sarvāstivāda." In *The Encyclopedia of Religion,* vol. 13, ed. Mircea Eliade, pp. 75–80. New York: Macmillan, 1987.

Gramsci, Antonio. *Selections from the Prison Notebooks.* Eds. Q. Hoare & G. N. Smith. New York: International Publishers, 1971.

Gray, David B. *The Cakrasamvara Tantra (The Discourse of Śrī Heruka) (Śrīherukābhidhāna): A Study and Annotated Translation.* New York: American Institute of Buddhist Studies, 2007.

———. "Mandala of the Self: Embodiment, Practice, and Identity Construction in the Cakrasamvara Tradition." *Journal of Religious History* 30 (2006): 294–310.

Griffiths, Paul J. *On Being Buddha: The Classical Doctrine of Buddhahood.* Albany: State University of New York Press, 1994.

Gross, Rita. *Buddhism after Patriarchy: A Feminist History, Analysis, and Reconstruction of Buddhism.* Albany: State University of New York Press, 1993.

Gyatso, Janet. "Sex." In *Critical Terms for the Study of Buddhism,* ed. Donald S. Lopez Jr., pp. 271–290. Chicago: University of Chicago Press, 2005.

Habito, Ruben. "The Development of the Buddha-body Theory." *Shūkyō Kenkyū* 1.2–3, no. 237 (1978): 1–22.

Halperin, David M. "How to Do the History of Male Homosexuality." *GLQ: A Journal of Gay and Lesbian Studies* 6 (2000): pp. 87–124.

Hamilton, Sue. "From the Buddha to Buddhaghosa: Changing Attitudes toward the Human Body in Theravāda Buddhism." In *Religious Reflections on the Human Body,* ed. Jane Marie Law, pp. 46–63. Bloomington: Indiana University Press, 1995.

Harrison, Paul. "Is the Dharma-kāya the Real Phantom Body of the Buddha?" *Journal of the International Association of Buddhist Studies* 15 (1992): 44–94.

———. "Searching for the Origin of Mahāyāna: What Are We Looking for?" *The Eastern Buddhist* 18 (1995): 48–69.

———. "Some Reflections on the Personality of the Buddha." *Otani Gakuho* 74, no. 4 (1995): 1–29.

———. "Who Gets to Ride in the Great Vehicle? Self Image and Identity among the Followers of the Early Mahāyāna." *Journal of the International Association of Buddhist Studies* 10 (1987): 67–89.

Herdt, Gilbert, ed. *Third Sex/Third Gender: Beyond Sexual Dimorphism in Culture and History.* New York: Zone Books, 1994.

Hirakawa, Akira. *A Study of the Vinayapiṭaka.* Tokyo: Sankibo Busshorin, 1960.

Holt, John C. *Discipline: The Canonical Buddhism of the Vinayapiṭaka.* Columbia, MO: South Asia Books, 1983.

Huntington, John C. "The Origin of the Buddha's Image, Early Image Traditions and the Concept of Buddhadarśanapuṇya." In *Studies in Buddhist Art of South Asia,* ed. A. K. Narain, pp. 23–58. New Delhi: Kanak Publications, 1985.

Huntington, Susan L. *The Art of Ancient India.* New York: Weatherhill, 1985.

———. "Early Buddhist Art and the Theory of Aniconism." *Art Journal* 49 (1990): 401–408.

Huntington, Susan L., and John C. Huntington. *Leaves from the Bodhi Tree: The Art of Pāla India (11th–12th Centuries) and Its International Legacy.* Dayton, OH: Dayton Art Institute, 1990.

Inden, Ronald B., and Ralph Nicholas. *Kinship in Bengali Culture.* Chicago: University of Chicago Press, 1976.

Jaini, H. S. "Buddha's Prolongation of Life." *Bulletin of the School of Oriental and African Studies* 21 (1958): 546–552.

Johnson, Sally, and Ulrike Hanna Meinhof, eds. *Language and Masculinity.* Oxford: Blackwell Publishers, 1997.

Jones, Colin, and Roy Porter. *Reassessing Foucault: Power, Medicine, and the Body.* London: Routledge, 1994.

Kaelber, Walter O. *Tapta Mārga: Asceticism and Initiation in Vedic India.* Albany: State University of New York Press, 1989.

Kalff, Martin M. "Selected Chapters from the Abhidhānottara-tantra: The Union of Female and Male Deities." PhD diss., Columbia University, 1979.

Kant, Immanuel. *Lectures on Philosophical Theology.* Allen W. Wood and Gertrude M. Clark, trans. Ithaca, NY: Cornell University Press, 1978.

Karetzky, Patricia Eichenbaum. *The Life of the Buddha: Ancient Scriptural and Pictorial Traditions.* Lanham, MD: University Press of America, 1992.

Katz, Nathan. *Buddhist Images of Human Perfection.* New Delhi: Motilal Banarsidass, 1982.

Keown, Damien. *Dictionary of Buddhism.* Oxford: Oxford University Press, 2003.

Keown, Damien, and Charles S. Prebish, eds. *Encyclopedia of Buddhism.* London: Routledge, 2007.

Keyes, Charles F. "Ambiguous Gender: Male Initiation in a Northern Thai Buddhist Society." In *Gender and Religion,* ed. C. W. Bynum et al., pp. 66–96. Boston: Beacon Press, 1986.

Kimmel, Michael S., Jeff Hearn, and R. W. Connell. *Handbook on Studies on Men and Masculinities.* Thousand Oaks, CA: Sage Publications, 2005.

Kinnard, Jacob N. *Imaging Wisdom: Seeing and Knowing in the Art of Indian Buddhism.* Richmond: Curzon, 1999.

Konow, Sten. *The Two First Chapters of the Daśasāhasrikā Prajñāpāramitā.* Oslo: Norske Videnskaps-Akademie, 1941, #1.

La Vallée Poussin, Louis de. "Documents d'Abhidharma 2. La Doctrine des Refuges." *Mélanges Chinois et Bouddhiques,* 1, 1931–1932, pp. 65–109.

———. "Studies in Buddhist Dogma: The Three Bodies of the Buddha (Trikāya)." *Journal of the Royal Asiatic Society of Great Britain and Ireland* (1906):27 943–947.

Lamotte, Étienne. *History of Indian Buddhism: From the Origins to the Śaka Era.* Trans. Sara Boin-Webb. Louvain-la-Neuve: Université Catholique de Louvain, Institut Orientaliste, 1988.

———, trans. *Abhidharma-samuccaya: The Compendium of the Higher Teaching (Philosophy).* Trans. Sara Boin-Webb. Fremont, CA: Asian Humanities Press, 2001.

———. *La Somme du Grand Véhicule d'Asaṅga (Mahāyānasaṃgraha).* 2 vols. Louvain-la-Neuve: Institut Orientaliste, 1973.

Lancaster, Lewis. "The Oldest Mahāyāna Sūtra: Its Significance for the Study of Buddhist Development." *The Eastern Buddhist* (new series) 8 (1975): 30–41.

Lang, Karen. "Lord Death's Snare: Gender-Related Imagery in the *Theragāthā* and the *Therīgāthā.*" *Journal of Feminist Studies in Religion* 2 (1986): 59–75.

———. "Shaven Heads and Loose Hair: Buddhist Attitudes toward Hair and Sexuality." In *Off with Her Head: The Denial of Women's Identity in Myth, Religion, and Culture,* ed. Howard Eilberg Schwartz and Wendy Doniger, pp. 31–52. Berkeley: University of California Press, 1995.

Laqueur, Thomas. *Making Sex: Body and Gender from the Greeks to Freud.* Cambridge, MA: Harvard University Press, 1990.

———. *Solitary Sex: A Cultural History of Masturbation.* New York: Zone Books, 2003.

Liebert, Gösta. *Iconographic Dictionary of the Hindu Religions, Buddhism-Hinduism-Jainism.* Leiden: E. J. Brill, 1976.

Lock, Margaret M., and Nancy Scheper-Hughes. "The Mindful Body: A Prolegomenon to Future Work in Medical Anthropology." *Medical Anthropology Quarterly* 1 (1987): 6–41.

Lopez, Donald S., Jr. "Buddha." In *Critical Terms for the Study of Buddhism* ed. Donald S. Lopez Jr., pp. 13–36. Chicago: University of Chicago Press, 2005.

Louie, Kam. *Theorising Chinese Masculinity: Society and Gender in China.* Cambridge: Cambridge University Press, 2002.

Luders, H. *A List of Brahmi Inscriptions from the Earliest Times to about* AD *400 with the Exception of those of Aśoka.* Calcutta: Archaeological Survey of India, 1912.

———. *Corpus Inscriptionum Indicarum,* vol. II, part II: *Bharhut Inscriptions.* Calcutta: Archaeological Survey of India, 1963.

Mac an Ghaill, Mairtin. *Understanding Masculinities: Social Relations and Cultural Arenas.* Buckingham & Philadelphia: Open University Press, 1996.

MacQueen, Graham. "Inspired Speech in Early Mahāyāna Buddhism I." *Religion* 11 (1981): 303–319.

———. "Inspired Speech in Early Mahāyāna Buddhism II." *Religion* 12 (1982): 49–65.

Maha Thero, Ven. Weragoda Sarada. *The Greatest Man Who Ever Lived: The Supreme Buddha.* Singapore: Singapore Buddhist Meditation Centre. 1998.

Makransky, John. *Buddhahood Embodied: Sources of Controversy in India and Tibet.* New York: State University of New York Press, 1997.

Malasekera, G. P. *Dictionary of Pāli Proper Names.* 2 vols. Delhi: Munishram Manoharlal Publishers, 1998.

Malamoud, Charles. "Indian Speculations about the Sex of the Sacrifice." In *Fragments for a History of the Body, Part One,* ed. Michel Feher, pp. 74–103. New York: Urzone, 1989.

Marion, Jean-Luc. *God without Being.* Trans. Thomas Carlson. Chicago: University of Chicago Press, 1991.

McArthur, Meher. *Reading Buddhist Art: An Illustrated Guide to Buddhist Signs and Symbols.* London: Thames & Hudson, 2004.

Meulenbeld, G. Jan, and Dominik Wujastyk, eds. *Studies on Indian Medical History.* Groningen: Egbert Forsten, 1987.

Meyer, Johann Jakob. *Sexual Life in Ancient India.* Delhi: Motilal Banarsidass, 1989.

Miller, Barbara Stoler, ed. *The Powers of Art Patronage in Indian Culture.* Delhi: Oxford University Press, 1992.

Mitra, Debala. *Buddhist Monuments.* Calcutta: Sahitya Samsad, 1971.

Mrozik, Suzanne. *Virtuous Bodies: The Physical Dimensions of Morality in Buddhist Ethics.* New York: Oxford University Press, 2007.

Nagao, Gadjin. "The Life of the Buddha: An Interpretation." *The Eastern Buddhist* 20, no. 2 (1987): 1–31.

———. "On the Theory of the Buddha-body (Buddhakāya)." *The Eastern Buddhist* 6, no. 1 (1973): 25–53.

Naik, A. V. "Inscriptions of the Deccan: An Epigraphical Survey (circa 300 BC–1300 AD)." *Bulletin of the Deccan College Research Institute* 11 (1948): 3–4.

Nakamura, Hajime. *Gotama Buddha.* Los Angeles and Tokyo: Buddhist Books International, 1987. Japanese edition: *Nakamura Hajime Senshū,* vol. 11. Tokyo: Shunjusha, 1969.

Ñāṇamoli, Bhikkhu. *The Life of the Buddha, According to the Pāli Canon.* Sri Lanka: Kandy Buddhist Publication Society, 1972.

Nanda, Serena. *Neither Man nor Woman: The Hijras of India.* Belmont, CA: Wadsworth, 1990.

Narain, A. K. *Studies in Buddhist Art of South Asia.* New Delhi: Kanak Publications, 1985.

Nattier, Jan. *A Few Good Men: The Bodhisattva Path according to the Inquiry of Ugra (Ugraparipṛcchā).* Honolulu: University of Hawai'i Press, 2003.

Nyanponika, Thera, and Hellmuth Hecker. *Great Disciples of the Buddha: Their Lives, Their Works, Their Legacy.* Boston: Wisdom Publications, 1997.

Ohnuma, Reiko. *Head, Eyes, Flesh, and Blood: Giving away the Body in Indian Buddhist Literature.* New York: Columbia University Press, 2007.

Olivelle, Patrick. *Saṃnyāsa Upaniṣads.* New York: Oxford University Press, 1992.

Paul, Diana. *Women and Buddhism: Images of the Feminine in the Mahāyāna Tradition.* Berkeley: University of California Press, 1985.

Perera, L. P. N. *Sexuality in Ancient India: A Study Based on the Pali Vinayapitaka.* Kelaniya: University of Kelaniya, 1993.

Phillips, Kim M., and Barry Reay, eds. *Sexualities in History: A Reader.* New York: Routledge, 2002.

Porter, Roy. *Flesh in the Age of Reason.* New York: Norton, 2004.

Porter, Roy, and Lesley Hall, eds. *The Facts of Life: The Creation of Sexual Knowledge in Britain, 1650–1950.* New Haven, CT: Yale University Press, 1995.

Porter, Roy, and Mikulas Teich, eds. *Sexual Knowledge, Sexual Science: The History of Attitudes to Sexuality.* Cambridge: Cambridge University Press, 1994.

Powers, John. *Introduction to Tibetan Buddhism.* 2nd ed.. Ithaca, NY: Snow Lion Publications, 2007.

Prebish, Charles S. *Buddhist Monastic Discipline: The Sanskrit Prātimokṣa Sūtras of the Mahāsaṃghikas and the Mūlasarvāstivādins.* University Park: Pennsylvania State University Press, 1975.

———. "Cooking the Buddhist Books: The Implications of the New Dating of the Buddha for the History of Early Indian Buddhism." *Journal of Buddhist Ethics* 15 (2008): 1–21.

———. "The Prātimokṣa Puzzle: Fact versus Fallacy." *Journal of the American Oriental Society* 94, no. 2 (1974): 168–176.

Radich, Michael. "The Somatics of Liberation: Ideas about Embodiment in Buddhism from Its Origins to the Fifth Century CE." PhD diss., Harvard University, 2007.

Rahula, Walpola. *What the Buddha Taught.* New York: Grove Press, 1974.

Ray, Reginald. *Buddhist Saints in India: A Study in Buddhist Values and Orientations.* New York: Oxford University Press, 1994.

Reynolds, Frank. "The Several Bodies of the Buddha: Reflections on the Neglected Aspects of Theravāda Tradition." *History of Religions* 16 (1977): 374–389.

Rhie, Marylin. *Early Buddhist Art in China and Central Asia.* Leiden: E. J. Brill, 1999.

Rosenfield, John M. *The Dynastic Arts of the Kushans.* New Delhi: Munishram Manoharlal Publishers, 1993.

Rowell, Teresina. "The Background and Early Use of the Buddha-Kṣetra Concept." *The Eastern Buddhist* 6 (1932–1935): 199–246; 7 (1936–1939): 131–145.

Rowland, Benjamin. *The Evolution of the Buddha Image.* New York: Asia House, 1963.

Schlingloff, Dieter. *Studies in the Ajanta Painting: Identifications and Interpretations.* Delhi: Ajanta Publications, 1987.

Schopen, Gregory. *Bones, Stones, and Buddhist Monks: Collected Papers on the Archaeology, Epigraphy, and Texts of Monastic Buddhism in India.* Honolulu: University of Hawai'i Press, 1997.

———. *Buddhist Monks and Business Matters: Still More Papers on Monastic Buddhism in India.* Honolulu: University of Hawai'i Press, 2004.

———. "The Phrase *'sa pṛthivīpradeśaś caityabhūto bhavet'* in the *Vajracchedikā:* Notes on the Cult of the Book in Mahāyāna." *Indo-Iranian Journal* 17 (1975): 147–181.

Scott, Joan. "Gender: A Useful Category of Historical Analysis." *American Historical Review* 91 (1986): 1053–1075.

Schuster, Nancy. "Changing the Female Body: Wise Women and the Bodhisattva Career in Some *Mahāratnakūṭasūtras.*" *Journal of the International Association of Buddhist Studies* 4 (1981): 24–69; reprinted in *Buddhism: Critical Concepts in Religious Studies,* ed. Paul Williams, pp. 329–367. London: Routledge, 2005.

Senart, E. C. M. *Essai sur la Légende du Buddha.* Paris: Imprimerie nationale, 1882.

Sharma, Sharmistha. *Buddhist Avadānas: Socio-Political Economic and Cultural Study.* Delhi: Eastern Book Linkers, 1985.

Shaw, Miranda. *Passionate Enlightenment: Women in Tantric Buddhism.* Princeton, NJ: Princeton University Press, 1994.

Silk, Jonathan. "The Fruits of Paradox: On the Religious Architecture of the Buddha's Life Story." *Journal of the American Academy of Religion* 71 (2003): 863–881.

Snellgrove, David L. "Śākyamuni's Final Nirvāṇa." *Bulletin of the School of Oriental and African Studies* 36 (1973): 399–341.

———. "In Search of the Historical Buddha." *South Asian Review* 7 (1973): 151–157.

Soper, Alexander. "Aspects of Light Symbolism in Gandhāran Sculpture." *Artibus Asiae* 12 (1949): 252–283.

Stablein, William. "Medical Soteriology of Karma in the Buddhist Tantric Traditions." In *Karma and Rebirth in Classical Indian Traditions,* ed. Wendy Doniger, pp. 193–216. Berkeley: University of California Press, 1980.

Steinberg, Leo. *The Sexuality of Christ in Renaissance Art and in the Modern Oblivion.* New York: Pantheon Books, 1983.

Strong, John. "A Family Quest: The Buddha, Yaśodharā, and Rāhula in the *Mūlasarvāstivāda Vinaya.*" In *Sacred Biography in the Buddhist Traditions of South and Southeast Asia,* ed. Juliane Schober, pp. 113–128. Honolulu: University of Hawai'i Press, 1997.

———. *The Legend and Cult of Upagupta.* Princeton, NJ: Princeton University Press, 1992.

Swearer, Donald K., trans. "Bimbā's Lament." In *Buddhism in Practice,* ed. Donald Lopez Jr., pp. 541–552. Princeton, NJ: Princeton University Press, 1995.

Taylor, Gary. *Castration: An Abbreviated History of Western Manhood.* New York: Routledge, 2000.

Taylor, McComas. *The Fall of the Indigo Jackal: The Discourse of Division and Pūrṇabhadra's Pañcatantra.* Albany: State University of New York Press, 2007.

Thomas, Edward. "Avadāna and Apadāna." *Indian Historical Quarterly* 9 (1933): 31–36.

Tsomo, Karma Lekshe. *Sakyadhītā: Daughters of the Buddha.* Ithaca, NY: Snow Lion Publications, 1998.

Waddell, Austine. "Buddha's Diadem or Uṣṇīṣa." *Ostasiatische Zeitschrift* 3 (1914): 131–168.

Waldschmidt, Ernst. "The *Varṇaśatam:* An Eulogy of One Hundred Epithets of Lord Buddha Spoken by the Gṛhapati Upāli(n)." *Nachrichten der Akademie der Wissenschaften, Philologisch-historische Klasse.* Göttingen: Akademie der Wissenschaften, 1979, pp. 3–19.

Walters, Jonathan. "The Buddha's Bad Karma: A Problem in the History of Theravāda Buddhism." *Numen* 37, fasc. 1 (1990): 70–95.

Wayman, Alex. "Contributions Regarding the Thirty-Two Characteristics of the Great Person." *Sino-Indian Studies* 4, no. 3–4 (1957): 243–260.

Weiss, Michell G. "*Caraka Saṃhitā* on the Doctrine of Karma." In *Karma and Rebirth in Classical Indian Traditions,* ed. Wendy Doniger, pp. 90–115. Berkeley: University of California Press, 1980.

Whitaker, Jarrod Leigh. "Drinking Status, Wearing Duty: Magic, Power, and Warrior Ethics in Ancient India." PhD diss., University of Texas at Austin, 2005.

White, David Gordon. *The Alchemical Body: Siddha Traditions in Medieval India.* Chicago: University of Chicago Press, 1996.

Wijayaratna, Mohan. *Buddhist Monastic Life according to the Texts of the Theravāda Tradition.* Trans. Steven Collins. Cambridge: Cambridge University Press, 1990.

Willemen, Charles, Bart Dessein, and Collette Cox. *Sarvāstivāda Buddhist Scholasticism.* Leiden: E. J. Brill, 1998.

Williams, Paul. *Mahāyāna Buddhism: The Doctrinal Foundations.* London: Routledge, 1989.

———. "Some Mahāyāna Buddhist Perspectives on the Body." In *Religion and the Body,* ed. Sarah Coakley, pp. 205–230. Cambridge: Cambridge University Press, 1997.

Wilshire, Martin G. *Ascetic Figures before and in Early Buddhism: The Emergence of Gautama as the Buddha.* Berlin and New York: Mouton de Gruyter, 1990.

Wilson, Liz. *Charming Cadavers: Horrific Configurations of the Feminine in Indian Buddhist Hagiographic Literature.* Chicago: University of Chicago Press, 1996.

Wimalaratana, Bellanwila. *Concept of Great Man (Mahāpurisa) in Buddhist Literature and Iconography.* Singapore: Buddhist Research Society, n.d.

Wujastyk, Dominik. *The Roots of Āyurveda: Selections from Sanskrit Medieval Writings.* New Delhi: Penguin Books, 1998.

Xing, Guang. *The Concept of the Buddha: Its Evolution from Early Buddhism to the Trikāya Theory.* London: Routledge, 2005.

Young, Serinity. *Courtesans and Tantric Consorts: Sexualities in Buddhist Narrative, Iconography, and Ritual.* New York: Routledge, 2004.

Zwilling, Leonard. "Homosexuality as Seen in Indian Buddhist Texts." In *Buddhism, Sexuality, and Gender,* ed. José Cabezón, pp. 203–214. Albany: State University of New York Press, 1992.

Zysk, Kenneth. *Asceticism and Healing in Ancient India: Medicine in the Buddhist Monastery.* New York: Oxford University Press, 1991.

———. *Conjugal Love in India: Ratiśātra and Ratiramaṇa.* Leiden: E. J. Brill, 2002.

Index

Harvard University Press is a member of Green Press Initiative (greenpressinitiative.org), a nonprofit organization working to help publishers and printers increase their use of recycled paper and decrease their use of fiber derived from endangered forests. This book was printed on 100% recycled paper containing 50% post-consumer waste and processed chlorine free.